翻译讲堂

Stevenson's Essays
A Translation and
Appreciation

斯蒂文森散文
翻译与赏析

〔美〕叶子南 编著

商务印书馆
The Commercial Press

图书在版编目（CIP）数据

斯蒂文森散文翻译与赏析：英汉对照 /（美）叶子南编著 . —北京：商务印书馆，2024
（翻译讲堂）
ISBN 978-7-100-23294-4

Ⅰ.①斯⋯　Ⅱ.①叶⋯　Ⅲ.①罗伯特·斯蒂文森—散文—文学翻译—英、汉②罗伯特·斯蒂文森—散文—文学欣赏—英、汉　Ⅳ.① I561.076 ② H315.9

中国国家版本馆 CIP 数据核字（2024）第 035285 号

权利保留，侵权必究。

翻译讲堂
斯蒂文森散文翻译与赏析
〔美〕叶子南　编著

商 务 印 书 馆 出 版
（北京王府井大街36号　邮政编码100710）
商 务 印 书 馆 发 行
北京市十月印刷有限公司印刷
ISBN 978 - 7 - 100 - 23294 - 4

2024年6月第1版	开本 880×1230　1/32
2024年6月北京第1次印刷	印张 13⅝
定价：68.00 元		

致　谢

本书翻译写作过程中，美国马里兰大学荣休教授、斯蒂文森研究专家 Robert-Louis Abrahamson 博士为我提供了不少帮助和材料，并给予我精神支持；文稿完成后，我的同事明德大学蒙特雷国际研究学院的蔡力坚教授阅读了全部译文，并提出了宝贵建议；还有不少同事、朋友和学生在本书翻译过程中也给予了我很多帮助和鼓励，这里恕不一一列出。在本书编辑出版过程中，商务印书馆的责任编辑许晓娟女士认真负责，付出了很多心血。笔者衷心感谢上述诸多同仁和朋友，没有他们的帮助，本书是很难以目前这个面貌与读者见面的。书中谬误，文责自负。

译者的话

在我的床头放着一本油印的《英国散文选读》。这是四十年前我在杭州大学时的散文教材，其中一篇就是斯蒂文森的散文《黄金国》，字里行间是忆平工整的课堂笔录，记下了任课教授鲍屡平先生的细致讲解。那是我第一次接触斯蒂文森的作品。

罗伯特·路易斯·斯蒂文森在中国广为人知，但这个声名源自他的小说。他的《金银岛》《绑架》《化身博士》有众多中国读者，以至于我们说起他时就冠以小说家的名称。但是斯蒂文森的成就绝不仅限于小说。他在儿童文学、游记、散文、诗歌等方面也成就卓著。特别是他的散文，虽不如查尔斯·兰姆、威廉·哈兹里特的有名，但也堪称是19世纪的散文精品。可惜在中国，他散文方面的成就并未得到很好的介绍。偶尔能在一些英美散文集中看到几篇他的散文作品，但较为集中的译介几乎没有，特别是他的一些散文名篇，至今没有看到靠得住的译文，甚至根本没有译文，如他的《微尘与幻影》《圣诞说教》《倔老头与年轻人》《狗性》等在当时有一定影响的散文精品，中国读者至今仍无缘赏读。因此，我决定来翻译介绍几篇斯蒂文森的散文作品。

我选择了英汉对照加注释附导读的呈现形式，因为我觉得本书选择的文章大多没有故事情节，是思想精神的大餐，属于阳春白雪的作品，读者群可能不会像小说那么大，也许有很大一部分读者都能直接阅读英文。可是这些散文的原文很难理解，并不是一般有些英文基础的人可以顺利读下去的，语言、社会、文化、历史、宗教等诸多方面都有数不尽的障碍，所以对照加注释的方法，有助于读者充分欣赏他的散文。当然，这种对照加注释的形式也是我驾轻就熟的。过去二十多年来，我在《中国翻译》上就是用这种形式向广大英语学习者介绍如何学习翻译的。

斯蒂文森英年早逝。这就像在石火光一般短暂人生中，释放出巨大的能量，散发出耀眼的光芒。他在《三重甲》结束时说，"在人生激情四射的那一刻，他站在生命的巅峰上，一跃便到了另一世界"，而斯蒂文森也正是在他创作快要达到巅峰时，突然离开人世的。在四十四岁短暂的一生中，他奉献给读者那么多杰出的作品，他是在和时间竞赛！特别令我们肃然起敬的是，斯蒂文森是拖着病体完成这些作品的。疾病和斯蒂文森一生形影不离，正是在与病魔的拼搏中，他写出了一首首儿歌，一个个故事，一篇篇美文。不像有些文化人那样无病呻吟，斯蒂文森是有病也不呻吟。眼下人们喜欢谈"正能量"，你只要去读读斯蒂文森的散文，看看他的《三重甲》《微尘与幻影》，就能在文中发现积极向上的慧语哲言俯拾皆是。对于时下沉醉于卿卿我我的年轻人来说，这些文字若流入了他们的心田，就能成为精神的激励，把他们从百无聊赖中唤醒，抖擞起精神，踏上有意义的人生之路。

斯蒂文森年轻时是个叛逆者。他出身基督教家庭，父亲用宗教严格管束他的行为，因此他对宗教起了叛逆之心，这些在他的散文里可见一斑。但是斯蒂文森却堪称是个回头浪子。在生命的最后几年，斯蒂文森已慢慢回归到了他早年背叛的宗教。不过在斯蒂文森眼里，上帝不是教条，而是风雨人生中的依靠，正是在艰难苦恨的斗争中，人才铸就了对上帝的信仰。因此他回归的不是世俗的宗教，而是一种宗教精神。也许心底里，耶稣基督从来就没有真正离开过他。

翻译斯蒂文森的散文，是一次精神之旅。译者随作者一起见危难而不惧，看透人世间的微尘幻影，带着自身的缺陷，追求高尚的目标；也和作者一道摆脱老年的平庸，重拾少年的壮志，却又对弱者无限同情；也与作者一起饱受书香熏陶，带着一颗永不疲倦的心走向黄金之国，满怀期待地自我放逐到海角天涯。在作者，这个海角是南太平洋的孤岛；在译者，这个天涯就是大洋彼岸的加利福尼亚。

2020年1月24日星期五

目录

El Dorado ·· 2
黄金国 ·· 3
Aes Triplex (1) ·· 24
三重甲（一）·· 25
Aes Triplex (2) ·· 48
三重甲（二）·· 49
Aes Triplex (3) ·· 66
三重甲（三）·· 67
Pulvis et Umbra (1) ·· 86
微尘与幻影（一）·· 87
Pulvis et Umbra (2) ······································· 112
微尘与幻影（二）··· 113
A Christmas Sermon (1) ···································· 138
圣诞说教（一）··· 139
A Christmas Sermon (2) ···································· 164
圣诞说教（二）··· 165
Crabbed Age and Youth (1) ································· 182
倔老头与年轻人（一）······································· 183
Crabbed Age and Youth (2) ································· 208
倔老头与年轻人（二）······································· 209

Crabbed Age and Youth (3)	226
倔老头与年轻人（三）	227
The Character of Dogs (1)	242
狗性（一）	243
The Character of Dogs (2)	266
狗性（二）	267
The Character of Dogs (3)	286
狗性（三）	287
Books Which Have Influenced Me (1)	304
那些影响了我的书（一）	305
Books Which Have Influenced Me (2)	328
那些影响了我的书（二）	329
Davos in Winter	348
冬季达沃斯	349
Despised Races	370
被鄙视的种族	371
An Island Landfall	394
又见陆地	395
译后记	423

对于朝前看的人,眼前永远有新的地平线。

——《黄金国》

El Dorado

It seems as if a great deal were attainable in a world where there are so many marriages and decisive battles[1], and where we all, at certain hours of the day, and with great gusto and despatch, stow a portion of victuals finally and irretrievably into the bag which contains us[2]. And it would seem also, on a hasty view, that the attainment of as much as possible was the one goal of man's contentious life. And yet, as regards the spirit, this is but a semblance[3]. We live in an ascending scale when we live happily, one thing leading to another in an endless series. There is always a new horizon for onward-looking men, and although we dwell on a small planet, immersed in petty business and not enduring beyond a brief period of years, we are so constituted that our hopes are inaccessible, like stars, and the term of hoping is prolonged until the term of life[4]. To be truly happy is a question of how we begin and not of how we end, of what we want and not of what we have. An aspiration is a joy forever[5], a possession as solid as a landed estate, a fortune which we can never exhaust and which gives us year by year a revenue of pleasurable activity[6]. To have many of these is to be spiritually rich.

Life is only a very dull and ill-directed theatre unless we have some interests in the piece; and to those who have neither art nor science, the world is a mere arrangement of colours, or a rough footway where they may very well break their shins. It is in virtue of his own desires

黄金国

人在世上好像真可大有作为，因为世间有那么多联姻婚嫁、决战厮杀，因为我们每日都按时急匆匆、乐滋滋地将食物一去不返地放入自己的皮囊。而且乍一看，在这你争我斗的人生里，唯一的目标仿佛真是获取利益，多多益善。可是从精神层面看人生，此种观点却只触及表相。正因为不停地追求进取，人才感到幸福，一件事完成后，另一件随之而来，如此永无止境。对于朝前看的人，眼前永远有新的地平线。虽然我们生活在一个小小的星球上，为尘世的琐事日夜奔忙，加之生命又极其短暂，可是造化使我们永难企及希望，恰如天上的繁星，无法摘取；希望和生命似同枝连理，希望会延伸至生命的尽头。真正的幸福是启程时的欣喜，而非抵达处的欢乐；真正的幸福源于想有而没有的渴望，而非一切到手的满足。渴望是一种永恒的喜悦，一笔如地产般稳固的财产，一份取之不尽的财富，正因我们热望满怀，才能年复一年参与令人欣喜的世事。一个人如有很多渴望，就是精神的富豪。

人生只是一出枯燥的戏文，编导得又十分拙劣，要想让人生不乏味，我们就得对这出戏文兴致勃勃。一个人若无艺术爱好，又缺

and curiosities that any man continues to exist with even patience, that he is charmed by the look of things and people, and that he wakens every morning with a renewed appetite for work and pleasure. Desire and curiosity are the two eyes through which he sees the world in the most enchanted colours: it is they that make women beautiful or fossils interesting: and the man may squander his estate and come to beggary, but if he keeps these two amulets he is still rich in the possibilities of pleasure[7]. Suppose he could take one meal so compact and comprehensive that he should never hunger anymore; suppose him, at a glance, to take in all the features of the world and allay the desire for knowledge; suppose him to do the like in any province of experience — would not that man be in a poor way for amusement ever after?[8]

One who goes touring on foot with a single volume in his knapsack reads with circumspection, pausing often to reflect, and often laying the book down to contemplate the landscape or the prints in the inn parlour[9]; for he fears to come to an end of his entertainment, and be left companionless on the last stages of his journey. A young fellow recently finished the works of Thomas Carlyle[10], winding up, if we remember aright, with the ten note-books upon Frederick the Great[11]. "What!" cried the young fellow, in consternation, "is there no more Carlyle? Am I left to the daily papers?" A more celebrated instance is that of Alexander[12], who wept bitterly because he had no more worlds to subdue. And when Gibbon had finished the DECLINE AND FALL[13], he had only a few moments of joy; and it was with a "sober melancholy" that he parted from his labours.

Happily we all shoot at the moon with ineffectual arrows[14]; our hopes are set on inaccessible El Dorado; we come to an end of nothing

科学头脑，世界便只是五颜六色的组合，或可比为崎岖的旅程，让人历尽坎坷。但正因有了欲望和好奇，人才能永远耐心地活下去，才能见物而喜，遇人而乐，才能在晨起时重新激起想工作、要欢乐的冲动。欲望和好奇是两只眼睛，人通过它们观看世界，世界于是也色彩纷呈。正因有了欲望和好奇，女人才能美得倾国倾城，岩石竟会让人兴趣盎然。人可倾家荡产，沦为乞丐，可只要有这两样财宝，他就仍可能有无限的欢乐。假如一个人可以饱食一餐，便不再饥肠辘辘，看上一眼就饱览大千，消解求知的欲望，假如万事皆能这样一劳永逸，是否那人便再难有乐趣兴致可言？

一个人徒步旅行，行囊中仅一册书，他有意细读慢品，时而止步沉思，时而放下书本，去看周遭的景物或客栈墙上的名画，生怕走到兴致的尽头，在旅途的最后一程无书陪伴。一位年轻人最近读完了托马斯·卡莱尔的作品，若我记得没错，他读毕《腓特烈大帝》时的笔记已有十本。这位年轻人惊异地哀叹："怎么？再没有卡莱尔了？难道我只能每天去读报纸？"名人也一样，亚历山大因再无天下可征服，居然失声痛哭；吉本写完《罗马帝国衰亡史》后快乐的心绪仅续片刻，封笔脱稿那一瞬间心中尽是"清冷的悲哀"。

我们弯弓射月，纵然徒劳，却射得乐此不疲；我们将希望设在那无法企及的"黄金国"；于是此生前行的路就永无止境。兴致与希望恰如芥菜收种不断，循环不息。你也许认为，孩子降生，麻烦

here below[15]. Interests are only plucked up to sow themselves again, like mustard[16]. You would think, when the child was born, there would be an end to trouble; and yet it is only the beginning of fresh anxieties; and when you have seen it through its teething and its education, and at last its marriage, alas! it is only to have new fears, new quivering sensibilities[17], with every day; and the health of your children's children grows as touching a concern as that of your own. Again, when you have married your wife, you would think you were got upon a hilltop, and might begin to go downward by an easy slope. But you have only ended courting to begin marriage. Falling in love and winning love are often difficult tasks to overbearing and rebellious spirits[18]; but to keep in love is also a business of some importance, to which both man and wife must bring kindness and goodwill. The true love story commences at the altar[19], when there lies before the married pair a most beautiful contest of wisdom and generosity, and a life-long struggle towards an unattainable ideal. Unattainable? Ay, surely unattainable, from the very fact that they are two instead of one.

"Of making books there is no end,[20]" complained the Preacher; and did not perceive how highly he was praising letters as an occupation. There is no end, indeed, to making books or experiments, or to travel, or to gathering wealth. Problem gives rise to problem. We may study for ever, and we are never as learned as we would. We have never made a statue worthy of our dreams. And when we have discovered a continent, or crossed a chain of mountains, it is only to find another ocean or another plain upon the further side. In the infinite universe there is room for our swiftest diligence and to spare[21]. It is not like the works of Carlyle, which can be read to an end. Even in a corner of it, in a private park, or in the

就此结束。但新的焦虑却刚刚开始；孩子要成长，要念书，最后还要结婚，哪一步不牵动你的心？每日都有新的惶恐，都有新的焦虑不安，孙辈的健康让你担心，不亚于你担心自己的健康。你和妻子步入婚姻殿堂，本以为那是人生巅峰，从峰上下来的路定能走得轻松。但那只是结束了恋爱，开始了婚姻。坠入爱河、赢得芳心对于高傲自大的人并非易事，可要让爱情常驻也是要事一桩，为此夫妻彼此都要相敬如宾。真正的爱情始于圣坛，一路上夫妻两人做一场绝妙的竞争，看谁更智慧，看谁更大度，他们一生都在朝不可企及的目标奋进。不可企及？没错，是不可企及，因为夫妻毕竟是两人而非一体。

"著书之事，永无止境。"传道者不无抱怨地说，没有意识到他把文字生涯看得那么高尚。确实著书没有止境，试验、游历、聚财也没有止境。一个问题引出另一个问题。我们尽可以读书不倦，但仍不能饱学如愿。我们竖起的雕像，总比不上梦中那座更令人向往。我们发现了一个大陆，跨越了一片峻岭，却看见横在眼前的是又一块大陆，又一片汪洋。在这个无穷的宇宙中，最勤勉的人也大有进步的空间。这不同于卡莱尔的著作可以读完。即便是在宇宙的一隅，在幽幽的庭园里，独立的村落旁，仍可见时序更迭气候万千，就算一生漫步其间，新事仍可层出不穷，我们仍会惊喜不断。

neighbourhood of a single hamlet, the weather and the seasons keep so deftly changing that although we walk there for a lifetime there will be always something new to startle and delight us.

There is only one wish realisable on the earth; only one thing that can be perfectly attained: Death. And from a variety of circumstances[22] we have no one to tell us whether it be worth attaining.

A strange picture we make on our way to our chimaeras[23], ceaselessly marching, grudging ourselves the time for rest; indefatigable, adventurous pioneers. It is true that we shall never reach the goal; it is even more than probable that there is no such place; and if we lived for centuries and were endowed with the powers of a god[24], we should find ourselves not much nearer what we wanted at the end. O toiling hands of mortals![25] O unwearied feet, travelling ye know not whither! Soon, soon, it seems to you, you must come forth on some conspicuous hilltop, and but a little way further, against the setting sun, descry the spires of El Dorado[26]. Little do ye know your own blessedness; for to travel hopefully is a better thing than to arrive, and the true success is to labour[27].

地球上只有一个愿望可以实现，那个能圆满实现的愿望便是死亡。死亡的例子众多各异，但却无人告诉我们死亡是否为一值得实现的理想。

我们向那子虚乌有的理想挺进，一路上绘一幅非比寻常的自画像，画中的探索者不停地前行，吝啬得不愿歇息，不屈不挠，勇往直前。不错，我们永远不会达到目标，甚至可能根本就没有那个目标。假若人寿数百年，还赋有神力无边，我们仍会发现，期盼中的终点和现在一样遥远。啊，凡人劳苦的双手！不倦的双腿，却不知道旅途走向何方！你似乎感到，马上就要登临峰顶一览四野，但衬着夕阳，在不远处，你却又见黄金国里楼宇的尖顶。你不知道自己是何其多福，因为满怀希望向前远比抵达目标更美好，而真正的成功恰在于辛劳。

注　释

1. 这个 many marriages and decisive battles 源自斯蒂文森写的散文集《童女与少年》(*Virginibus Puerisque*)，其中在说到婚姻时有这样的句子 "(marriage) is a field of battle, and not a bed of roses"，是作者对 19 世纪英国婚姻状况的看法，也折射出当时社会中金钱地位渗透在婚姻决策中的现实。

2. 这个 a portion of victuals finally and irretrievably into the bag which contains us 是在说食物入口，其中的 bag 大可指人体，小可指胃，都说得通。在这里作者表述的方法似乎有一定意义，比如 stow 有积累存放的意思，finally and irretrievably 有一去无回的意思，都多少有些讽刺夸张的味道，在某种程度上成为作者写作的特征。因此，翻译的时候，仅仅说把食物吃下去，尽管是原文说的意思，却略显不足，最好也反映一点原文的写作特色，保留一点夸张的口气，如"因为我们每日都按时急匆匆、乐滋滋地将食物一去不返地放入自己的皮囊"。

3. 此处的 a semblance 表示外表或表象的意思。换句话说，作者在说，把获取作为人生的唯一目标是表面的、肤浅的、不深刻的。

4. 这个 term (of life) 表示 the duration of a person's life 或者说 the end of one's life，所以这句的大意就是，希望的长短和生命的长短是一致的，也就是说，只要生命在希望就在。

5. 这句 "An aspiration is a joy forever" 借用了济慈的名句 "A thing of beauty is a joy forever" (Keats, *Endymion*, I, 1)。由于是名句，翻译的时候就要考虑到这层互文的关系，也就是说，是否需要

借助济慈名句的名译法，让中译文也能使读者联想到济慈的名句？但是这句译文繁多各异，很难找到一个有代表性的译文，加之本译文的读者也可能并非纯文学爱好者，译者即便有意复制一个文学典故供读者赏识，读者却可能无心甚至无鉴赏能力，所以不去追踪著名译文也罢，就根据意思翻译出来基本达到要求："渴望是一种永恒的喜悦"。

6. 这一长句以及接下来的一句都用经济生活用语表达，landed estate、fortune、revenue、rich 都和经济有关，作者是在用最易懂的语言来阐述一个精神的议题。翻译的时候估计译者都能顺其自然地用经济相关的词，如地产、财产、财富、富豪等。刻意避免反而不好。

7. 这个 rich in the possibilities of pleasure 有人翻译成"就仍然有无尽的欢乐"，应该说这个译文是正确的。但是为了使译文更接近原文，仍有微调的空间，比如上述译文就没有将 possibilities 的意思包括进去，原文仅说"有欢乐的可能"（有很多可能让你欢乐的事物），并没有说"有欢乐"。应该说在这类译文中这个细节并不会造成很大的问题，因为作者其实强调的重点就是只要有这两样东西，你就有欢乐，但文字的表述确实有这个 possibilities。若是在非文学文本中，特别是在一些正规文本的翻译中，这个 possibilities 就更应注意，但这里该词分量较轻。不过参考译文还是译成"他就仍<u>可能</u>有无限的欢乐"，把原文的可数名词换成了助动词，保留了 possibilities 的语义。

8. 这三个 suppose 构成了写作上的排比，可以说有一定的"气势"，翻译时是否需要见细不察，整体把握，还是求文字准确，锱铢必较？如原文的 so compact and comprehensive 在现在的译文中就消失了，其实放进去也未必不可以，如"吃上精美丰盛的一餐"；再比如 in any province of experience 是否更需要按照原文来行文，如"在生活经历中的任何方面"？在所有这些地方，译者其实都面临选择，而各种因素都会影响译者的决策。在本文中，我都采取了放弃细节对应的策略，旨在总体效果的呈现，而非细节处的精准对应，如："假如一个人可以饱食一餐，便不再饥肠辘辘，看上一眼就饱览大千，消解求知的欲望，假如万事皆能这样一劳永逸，是否那人便再难有乐趣兴致可言？"这个问题我们在导读中再细说。

9. 有学者认为，这句实际是在回忆前一天傍晚散步的情景，依据是 "Autumn Effect"（1875）中下面这句："As I sat reading in the great arm-chair, I kept looking round with the tail of my eye at the quaint, bright picture that was about me, and could not help some pleasure and a certain childish pride in forming part of it."。此处的 the prints 似指墙上的画作或图案。

10. 托马斯·卡莱尔（Thomas Carlyle, 1795—1881）是 19 世纪苏格兰著名哲学家、评论家、讽刺作家、历史学家，其主要著作包括《法国革命》《论英雄》《过去与现在》等。

11. 腓特烈大帝（Frederick the Great）是普鲁士国王。在 18 世纪普鲁士崛起的过程中，腓特烈大帝起到关键作用。

12. 此处的 Alexander 是指亚历山大大帝（Alexander the Great，公元前 356 年—前 323 年），即亚历山大三世、马其顿帝国国王、亚历山大帝国皇帝，生于古马其顿王国首都佩拉，世界古代史上著名的军事家和政治家，欧洲历史上最伟大的四大军事统帅（亚历山大大帝、汉尼拔、恺撒大帝、拿破仑）之首。他曾师从古希腊著名学者亚里士多德，以其雄才大略，先后统一希腊全境，进而横扫中东地区，占领埃及全境，荡平波斯帝国，率大军开到印度河流域，征服全境约500万平方公里。

13. 爱德华·吉本（Edward Gibbon, 1737 — 1794）是英国著名历史学家，其最重要的著作就是他的史学名著《罗马帝国衰亡史》(The History of the Decline and Fall of the Roman Empire)，这部一共有六册之多的史书出版于1776年到1788年之间。吉本一般被认为是欧洲启蒙时代史学的代表人物。

14. 此处 shoot at the moon 中的 the moon 就是指不容易的事，可能是远大的目标，也可能是一项具体的艰难任务，不同的读者会有不同的解读，而 shoot 就是为达到目标采取的行动；而 ineffectual arrows 中的 arrows 就是指为达到目标而用的手段，ineffectual 是指行动的结果，就是未成功。

15. 这里的 here below 是指在这个世界上、在地球上，below 是相对于 heaven 而言的。这句就是说，在这个尘世上没有东西是最终的结果（There is no final thing for us in this world）。

16. 此处的大意是希望、兴趣等欲望会不断产生出来（Hopes breed hopes, and interests breed interests）。作者用了一个比喻，把这种循环催生的过程比喻成播种收割芥菜。我们种下芥菜，收割起来，但是菜籽却永远不会一粒不剩地收起来，总会有些芥菜籽落在了地里，于是新的芥菜便又生出来了。mustard 这个词是《圣经》中常用的，在《马太福音》《马可福音》《路加福音》中均有出现，如 "It is like a grain of mustard seed, which a man took, and cast into his garden; and it grew, and waxed a great tree; and the fowls of the air lodged in the branches of it."（Luke 13: 19）翻译的时候，译者可以考虑保留 mustard 一词，因为这并不是一个中文读者完全不可以理解的比喻。有的学生将这个词换成了"野草"（恰如野草），基本意思是一样的，但就失去了《圣经》的典故。这个典故当然也比较牵强，分量不重，所以译者可以自己掂量决定。参考译文选择了保留 mustard 这个词。

17. 这里的 new quivering sensibilities 和前面的 new fears 是差不多的意思，都表示人的心情恐惧不安，大意和 sensitiveness 或者 over-sensitiveness 接近。翻译选词时不必过于拘谨，大意出来就差不多。其中的 quivering 基本就是 shaking 的意思，即表达人在焦虑紧张等情况下会轻微颤抖的意思，未必需要按字面复现在译文中，整个短语译成"焦虑不安"或"悸动不安"基本到位。

18. 在 to overbearing and rebellious spirits 这个短语中的 spirits，表面看是"精神"的意思，但这里实际指的是人，即有这种桀骜不驯性格的人。这可以根据上下文看出来，词典中也可查到，如牛津词典中就有当人解释的词条（he was a leading spirit in the conference）。

19. 这个 at the altar 是指基督教教堂中的圣坛，很多仪式都是在教堂的圣坛前举行的，这里指的是婚礼的圣坛。

20. "著书之事，永无止境"（著书多，没有穷尽）本句出自《圣经》："Of making many books there is no end."（Ecclesiastes 12: 12）斯蒂文森的引文中缺了一个 many。

21. 这个 and to spare 其实是个习惯表达法，表示有足够的东西，绰绰有余（with something extra or left over），有时 to spare 前面还会放一个名词，比如 and money to spare，有时则是和 enough 连用（enough and to spare）。本句中就是在说人们有很多可改进的空间，表达程度而已，翻译时不必过于在意。这个用法其实也有《圣经》的背景，如"How many hired servants

of my father's have bread *enough and to spare*" (Luke 15: 17)。

22. 这句的基本意思就是，那么多死了的人都没有回来告诉我们他们的经历，没有回来告诉我们到底死亡是否值得努力争取。这里 from a variety of circumstances 可以解释为 because of a variety of circumstances we have not one to tell us…。类似的句子有 From the evidence they heard, the jury had to convict. (= Because of the evidence they heard, the jury had to convict.)。

23. 这里 strange picture 指的是我们自己的写照（a picture we make out of ourselves），因为下面描述的就是我们不屈不挠奋斗的画面（ceaselessly marching, grudging ourselves the time for rest…）。这句中的 chimaeras 是指希腊神话中由三种动物合起来的怪兽，是不存在的动物，在这里比喻不真实的、没有根据的超奇想象，也就是指我们没有根据的理想，我们的目标，即 El Dorado。

24. 此处的两件事都是假设的，不是真实的，因为人不可能活几百年，人也没有神一般的能力，所以这里动词的过去时态是表达与事实相反的事件。

25. O toiling hands of mortals 这句出自索福克罗斯的悲剧（Sophocles, *The Tragedies of Sophocles*, 1859, p.292），但原句接下来是"O luckless races of men, to whom destiny is untoward"，而我们这里接下来那句"O unwearied feet, travelling ye know not whither"仅在斯蒂文森这篇中出现，疑为作者之语。要注意的是，这几句文体上像《圣经》类古旧的文字。杭州大学已故教授鲍屡平先生就认为其颇像圣经体："The last few sentences are quite biblical. They are written in the style of the Bible."（在鲍老师课堂上所做笔记）。翻译时是否也要和原文一样显出和前面文字的差异，会是译者考虑的一个问题。如果仅仅是传达语义，似可不突

出这点差异，因为中文读者中大多数人并不熟悉圣经文体，加之目前现代版《圣经》颇为流行，古雅语言的特色已不复存在。但如果从文学角度看，这几句还是具有所谓的"前景化"特征，翻译时同样反映出这种"前景化"也说得过去。本译文未将前景因素考虑进去。

26. 这个长句中有几个地方需要点评。首先 come forth 一般是 come out of 的意思。鉴于此处是比喻人在追求理想的目标，在没有达到目标前的状态就应该是 out of 后面的状态，也就是离开那里，达到顶峰，但翻译时不用明言。另外 conspicuous 一词表示 clearly visible，此处这样解释也符合语境。但也有人认为，从该语义出发，还可引申出更符合语境的意思：with extensive views。本译文就采用了这个解释。至于 descry 一词，就是 catch sight of 的意思。其实 descry the spires of El Dorado 的意思就是 see El Dorado，若仅求达意，翻译成"又看见了黄金国"就可以了。但是为表达原文写作的特点，还是保留为好。这个 spires 其实处理起来也很棘手，因为我们不知道到底是什么样的 spires。首先想到的是教堂的尖顶，但富人的城堡也有尖顶，其他建筑未必就没有，所以这里选用了比较中性的"楼宇的尖顶"。关于题目的讨论详见导读。

27. 最后一句广为引用，是点睛之笔，有人认为这句可释义为 "True success in life is in activity not accomplishment"，labour 一词是活动（activity）的意思。斯蒂文森这个"为动而动"的主题在稍后写的 *Travels with a Donkey*（1879）中再一次出现："For my part, I travel not to go anywhere, but to go. I travel for travel's sake. The great affair is to move"。另外，本译文中 labour 仍然采用更接近单词本义的译法，没有做过多的引申。

导 读

岂能止步黄金国

这篇散文写于1878年春季，同年发表于英国的《伦敦》杂志（*The London*，11 May，1878）。这本刊物与众不同，它虽是英国杂志，却在法国更出名，与其说出版是为读者，还不如说是为作者。那年四、五月间，斯蒂文森完成了这篇散文，寄给了正在编辑《伦敦》杂志的著名诗人威廉·欧内斯特·亨利（William Ernest Henley）。收到稿件后，亨利在回信中连声道谢，觉得真是好文一篇，但也感到十分可惜，因为亨利认为，这样一篇佳作本该有50万读者，可惜他编辑的这本《伦敦》是小众刊物，无法让这篇散文广为传诵。同年5月11日"El Dorado"一文在《伦敦》上刊出，据说斯蒂文森得稿费16英镑。

该文发表后深得好评，文中有些句子已成经典，如"To travel hopefully is a better thing than to arrive"就脍炙人口。本文后来收入作者在1881年出版的著名散文集《童女与少年》（*Virginibus Puerisque*），但首次发表应为1878年，因为据说第一次发表时并未署名。他去世后，这篇散文也被收入各种文集，如 *World's Best Essays*, 10 vols. (St Louis, 1900) 和 *The Lost Art of Conversation: Selected Essays* (New York, 1910)。

文章题目 El Dorado 原指一个子虚乌有的传说，在西班牙文中这个词指 golden one，随着时间的变化，先由指人变成指城市，再指王国或帝国，也就是指一个具体的地方，特别是指西班牙征服者在南美各地探索寻觅但从来没有发现的地方。后来这个词引申出隐喻含义，专指永远无法达到或并不存在的目标，本文中的 El Dorado 就是指百般努力都达不到的目标。

至于本文题目的翻译，有很大灵活度。十多年前我把本文中的前面一两段译成中文发表于《中国翻译》的"自学之友"专栏，当时结合文中的意思，用了"望不尽的地平线"这个和 El Dorado 文字毫无关系的题目。但是今天呈现在这里的是斯蒂文森这篇散文的全貌，就不宜采用类似"望不尽的地平线"这样解释性的题目了。关于题目翻译，我的一般建议是：若即若离。有的场合固然需要完全贴近原文（如严肃的政论文），有的场合也许应该完全离开原文（如有些影视作品），但大多数情况下，最好还是能让人见到译文题目就可追溯到原文。我们常看到有的影视作品题目的译文很优美，但就是想不到原文是什么。问题的另一个极端是，完全按照原文，结果有时很拘谨，毫无灵气。若即若离的好处就是能让读者追溯到原文。比如苏兹贝格（Arthur Hays Sulzberger）那本回忆录 *Seven Continents and Forty Years* 的译文就是"若即若离"的典范:《七大洲风云四十年》。译文仅加了一个"风云"，便可读性陡增，原文的"影子"全都在译文里了。总之，题目的翻译没有定论，译者得根据语境灵活处理。比如这里我还是把它翻译成一个地方，因为文章结束时这个 El Dorado 是作为地点出现的，所以译成"黄金国"，接近西班牙语原文的意思，这也是字典中最常用的译法（陆谷孙主编的《英汉大词典》译成"黄金国"或"黄金城"）。若取其隐喻含义，翻译成"不可企及的目标"，就不很符合文章结束处的语境了。当然也有看法不同的，认为翻译成"黄金国"或"黄金城"不便读者理解，还不如翻译成"理想国"好。更有些人喜欢寻找文化对应词，将 El Dorado 翻译成"香格里拉"。虽然"香格里拉"也有理想之地的意思，但是和原文在文化上颇多差异，不是一个很合适的译法。

读者阅读完这篇不长的散文，定会感到鼓舞。用现在年轻人的话说，该文是满满的正能量。确实，你仿佛看到一位精神饱满的人不畏艰苦，百折不挠，英勇地走在人生的路上。文中鼓舞人的警句俯拾皆是，比如：

○ 对于朝前看的人，眼前永远有新的地平线。
○ 真正的幸福是启程时的欣喜，而非抵达处的欢乐；真正的幸福源于想有而没有的渴望，而非一切到手的满足。
○ 一个人如有很多渴望，就是精神的富豪。
○ 满怀希望向前远比抵达目标更美好。
○ 正因有了欲望和好奇，人才能永远耐心地活下去，才能见物而喜，遇人而乐，才能在晨起时重新激起想工作、要欢乐的冲动。

这样的乐观态度是来自哪里呢？我们不妨看看文章写作时的斯蒂文森。阅读他的年谱，我们发现当时斯蒂文森年仅28岁。同时我们也知道这位作家除作品有名外，还有一事同样非常"有名"，那就是跟随他短短一生的疾病。他从小就体弱多病，经常咳血，过去一般都认为他从小就患有肺结核病，但从来没有确切的诊断。不过后来有些研究认为斯蒂文森的病并非肺结核，而是支气管扩张，和遗传有关。这样一个疾病缠身的人，疲惫地奔跑于世界各地，却仍然有着文中那种无法抑制的热情，确实让我们刮目相看。也许，这满满的正能量也有爱情的助力。就在本文写作前两年，斯蒂文森在巴黎第一次和范妮·奥斯本相遇，这位来自加州的女子后来成为了斯蒂文森的妻子，一直到他去世都在他身边。我们不得不说，在这篇积极向上的散文里，很难排除对爱情的期盼：他和范妮在巴黎开启爱情也可称为"启程时的欣喜";他对范妮的欲望和好奇,横扫了疾病给他带来的阴霾,"使他能耐心地活下去,才能见物而喜,遇人而乐";而他期盼的婚姻也许是眼前"新的地平线"。但是这样理解本文的动力还是太狭隘。斯蒂文森的这种正能量几乎洋溢在他很多篇散文里。他那充满哲理的《微尘与幻影》和《三重甲》就是最好的佐证,说明作者积极向上的动力源泉并不仅局限于爱情。一个人并不健康,却有着非常健康的心灵,这是非常值得人们敬仰的。

　　那么这样一篇散文,翻译时应该用怎样的策略呢?没错,这确实是一篇地地道道的文学作品。若要按文学类翻译的一般原则看,难免要关注一些语言的特征,因为文学是语言的艺术。但是文学也并非千篇一律,有些可以精细雕琢,有些却不宜过细处理,见细不察也未尝不可。利奇(Geoffrey Leech)就把小说分为两类(Class 1 和 Class 2),认为第一类小说不以语言取胜,但第二类小说则常在语言结构里包含特殊意义。我们这篇不是小说,但道理是一样的。有的散文不以语言取胜,但有的就可能要仔细挖掘语言结构等处的细节,寻找原作者借语言形式潜藏的含义。我们读斯蒂文森这篇散文,当然应不时注意到原文语言的特征,看看有没有结构等细节处的艺术元素需要反映在译文中。但是我们读着读着就被作者的文章所感动。斯蒂文森的正能量影响了读者,他积极向上的生活态度也感染了译者,于是译者就觉得自己得让译文也像原文一样感染中文的读者,不能只求细节处的精准。你看这句:Suppose he could take one meal so compact and comprehensive that he should never hunger anymore; suppose him, at a glance, to take in all the features of the world and allay the desire for knowledge; suppose him to do the like in any province of experience—would not that man be in a poor way for amusement ever after?（见注释 8）译者首先想到的就是 compact 和 comprehensive 这两个词。这是实实在在的两个实义词！不是两个介词或连接词那类虚词。但翻译时放进去总觉得句子较长。换个场合，如在实用的政经文本中，译者也许会毫不犹豫地保留在译文里，或在一些求传播效果的文本中，译者也许会毫不犹豫地抛弃它们。但是在这样的文学作品中，译者就会相对谨慎些，随便删掉有实际意义的词，毕竟不是翻译这类文本时应该推荐的。不过在经过一番掂量后，我还是在译文中放弃了这两个词，译成"假如一个人可以饱食一餐，便不再饥肠辘辘……"。原因是，若加上 compact 和 comprehensive 的意思，那么与后面文字的协调就会受到影响，汉语这整句话的行文就得重起炉灶，而目前选中的行文结构，与前面和后面的整个行文是一气呵成的。这样决定的前提当然是这两个词的分量比较轻，拿掉并不影响文句的意思，因此才敢见细不察。不过你若细看，译文中那"饱"（食）字却也不声不响地把 compact 和 comprehensive 的意思给肩负起来了。

　　再比如"It is in virtue of his own desires and curiosities that any man continues to exist with even patience, that he is charmed by the look of things and people"这句。译者是否可以沿用原文的结构翻译，比如翻译成"但正因有了欲望和好奇，人才能永远耐心地活下去，才能见到事物和人物而着迷"，或"被事和人的外表所迷倒"，或"被事和人所迷倒"。这几种译法在细节上和原文是更贴近的。但是，这是文学语言吗？这样的文字能感动读者吗？我翻译斯蒂文森的《微尘与幻影》时，有的段落让我热泪盈眶，要是那段让我流泪的文字在汉语里都是"被事和人的外表所迷倒"这样的文句，你觉得你的读者也能像你一样热泪盈眶吗？不行，我必须跳出那个原文的牢笼，所以在取其形还是求其意的抉择中，我选择了文句的大意,而没有斤斤计较于原文的结构和细节:"但正因有了欲望和好奇,人才能永远耐心地活下去,才能见物而喜,遇人而乐"。我当然损失了一些东西,比如:"喜""乐"与原文的 charm 并非无缝对接;"见物"和 the look 多少有点联系,可"遇人"和 the look 没有直接联系。只是上述几个不足之处,仍然无法让我回过头来拥抱"被……迷倒"那样的译文。我觉得这些丢失的东西在这个文本中都是"小物件",大件物品我一个都没丢。权衡一下整体效果上的"得",这点"失"还是值得的。

  散文翻译要求译者能被散文感动,一个心灵游离在散文外的译者是很难把握好原文的精髓的。译者必须入境,跟原作者一起心潮起伏,和原作者一起笑语欢声,也和原作者一起热泪盈眶,他郁闷时你苦恼,他畅快处你淋漓,这样你才能因感动而入境。你若心灵已深入文章,文章绝不会亏待你,好词好句往往会不期而至、水到渠成。

放手去做的人是有精神的,而只要去做,即便出师未捷,精神仍可长存。

——《三重甲》

Aes Triplex (1)

The changes wrought by death are in themselves so sharp and final,[1] and so terrible and melancholy in their consequences, that the thing stands alone in man's experience, and has no parallel upon earth. It outdoes all other accidents because it is the last of them. Sometimes it leaps suddenly upon its victims, like a Thug;[2] sometimes it lays a regular siege and creeps upon their citadel during a score of years. And when the business is done, there is sore havoc made in other people's lives, and a pin knocked out by which many subsidiary friendships hung together.[3] There are empty chairs, solitary walks, and single beds at night. Again in taking away our friends, death does not take them away utterly, but leaves behind a mocking, tragical, and soon intolerable residue, which must be hurriedly concealed. Hence a whole chapter of sights and customs striking to the mind, from the pyramids of Egypt to the gibbets and dule trees of mediaeval Europe.[4] The poorest persons have a bit of pageant going towards the tomb; memorial stones are set up over the least memorable; and, in order to preserve some show of respect for what remains of our old loves and friendships, we must accompany it with much grimly ludicrous ceremonial, and the hired undertaker parades before the door. All this, and much more of the same sort, accompanied by the eloquence of poets, has gone a great way to put humanity in error;[5] nay, in many philosophies the error has been embodied and laid down with every circumstance of logic;[6] although in real

三重甲（一）

死亡造成的变化本身是剧烈、终极的，其后果可怖可悲，在人的经历中独一无二，没有什么意外事件可以与之相比。死亡超越所有人生中其他的意外，因为死亡之后再无意外。有时它如强盗，令人猝不及防；有时它似围城，经年反复，慢中求胜。当死亡的目的一得逞，它就在别人的生活中留下伤痛苦难，由死者维系的友情圈也随之而散。相继而来的是空空的座椅，孤寂的散步，长夜的独眠。死亡带走了我们的朋友，却带得不彻底，留下的残余将人嘲弄、令人悲痛，以至人们无法忍受，不得不将它们急忙掩藏。于是，人们弄出了一整套令人惊心难忘的场景与习俗，从埃及的金字塔，到中世纪欧洲的绞刑架、处死树不一而足。最穷困的人多少也有一队人马为他送葬，最不值得纪念的人也有纪念碑立在坟旁，而为展示旧爱老友在我们心中存留的敬意，我们还得献上一套荒唐可笑的仪式，请来送葬的队伍到门前大显排场。所有这些，还有更多类似的荒唐之举，再加上文人的滔滔赞语，手段无以复加，把人类推向谬误之高峰；更有甚者，在很多哲学里，这种谬误竟被包装得甚合逻辑颇有道理；好在真实生活中，由于生活匆忙，人们也没有

life the bustle and swiftness, in leaving people little time to think, have not left them time enough to go dangerously wrong in practice.

As a matter of fact, although few things are spoken of with more fearful whisperings[7] than this prospect of death, few have less influence on conduct under healthy circumstances. We have all heard of cities in South America built upon the side of fiery mountains, and how, even in this tremendous neighbourhood, the inhabitants are not a jot more impressed[8] by the solemnity of mortal conditions than if they were delving[9] gardens in the greenest corner of England. There are serenades and suppers and much gallantry[10] among the myrtles overhead; and meanwhile the foundation shudders underfoot, the bowels of the mountain growl, and at any moment living ruin may leap sky-high into the moonlight, and tumble man and his merry-making in the dust.[11] In the eyes of very young people, and very dull old ones, there is something indescribably reckless and desperate in such a picture. It seems not credible that respectable married people, with umbrellas, should find appetite for a bit of supper within quite a long distance of a fiery mountain;[12] ordinary life begins to smell of high-handed debauch when it is carried on so close to a catastrophe; and even cheese and salad, it seems, could hardly be relished in such circumstances without something like a defiance of the Creator. It should be a place for nobody but hermits dwelling in prayer and maceration, or mere born-devils drowning care in a perpetual carouse.[13]

And yet, when one comes to think upon it calmly, the situation of these South American citizens forms only a very pale figure[14] for the state of ordinary mankind. This world itself, travelling blindly and swiftly in overcrowded space, among a million other worlds travelling blindly and

闲工夫去思考这些大道理，因此在实践中人们就没有足够时间铸成大错。

实际上，虽然没有什么事件能像死亡那样把人吓得语低声弱、谈之色变，但也很少有什么事件像死亡那样对健康人的行为少有影响。我们都听说过南美火山旁的城镇，即便在这样可怕的地方，居民也不会被死亡的严峻威胁而惊扰，也能像英国远郊绿野上的菜农一样过悠闲的生活。头顶上是桃金娘树丛中的小夜曲、晚餐、奢华场面；脚底下大地颤抖，山体内咆哮怒吼，每一刻流动的岩浆都可能冲向月光满溢的天空，将人和他作乐寻欢的场面颠覆埋葬。在非常年轻的人或迟钝的老年人眼里，这样一幅景象尽显出人的不计后果、轻率鲁莽。很难想象，手拿阳伞未雨绸缪的尊贵夫妇，远望着火山竟还有用餐的胃口；在离灾难这么近的地方竟能正常生活，怎能不让人闻到一丝任性狂欢的味道；在那样的场合本该连奶酪和色拉都无心品尝，人们居然能酒宴寻常，怎能不让人觉得这些人有那么点无视造物主？谁都不适合在这种地方生活，除非那人是潜心祈祷、虔修禁食的修士，或是以酒度日、无视危险的天生恶魔。

然而，你静下心来一想，对照普通人的境遇，这些南美人所面临的险境就微不足道了。这个地球本身，盲目匆忙地在拥挤的太空运行，而四周百万星球也盲目匆忙地与之擦肩而过，无端而来的一击，就能把这地球像爆竹一样给炸裂了。在病理学家的眼里，这个

swiftly in contrary directions, may very well come by a knock[15] that would set it into explosion like a penny squib. And what, pathologically looked at,[16] is the human body with all its organs, but a mere bagful of petards? The least of these is as dangerous to the whole economy[17] as the ship's powder-magazine to the ship; and with every breath we breathe, and every meal we eat, we are putting one or more of them in peril. If we clung as devotedly as some philosophers pretend we do to the abstract idea of life,[18] or were half as frightened as they make out we are, for[19] the subversive accident that ends it all, the trumpets might sound[20] by the hour and no one would follow them into battle—the blue-peter might fly at the truck,[21] but who would climb into a sea-going ship? Think (if these philosophers were right) with what a preparation of spirit we should affront the daily peril of the dinner-table: a deadlier spot than any battlefield in history, where the far greater proportion of our ancestors have miserably left their bones![22] What woman would ever be lured into marriage, so much more dangerous than the wildest sea[23]? And what would it be to grow old? For, after a certain distance, every step we take in life we find the ice growing thinner below our feet, and all around us and behind us we see our contemporaries going through. By the time a man gets well into the seventies, his continued existence is a mere miracle; and when he lays his old bones in bed for the night, there is an overwhelming probability that he will never see the day. Do the old men mind it, as a matter of fact? Why, no. They were never merrier; they have their grog at night, and tell the raciest stories; they hear of the death of people about their own age, or even younger, not as if it was a grisly warning, but with a simple childlike pleasure at having outlived someone else; and when a draught might puff them out like a

满是器官的人体危如累卵，无异于装满爆竹的囊袋。它们中间最微不足道的一个器官就能危及整个机体，恰如船上的炸药库能危及整艘航船。我们一口一口呼吸，一顿一顿吃饭，殊不知呼吸吃喝间，我们已把其中一个或多个器官置于危险之中。假如我们像某些哲学家错认为的那样，死抱住生命的抽象概念，或者像他们说的那样，对结束生命的颠覆性事件深感惧怕，那么号角尽可不停地吹，却不会有人响应号角奔赴战场；催人启航的蓝旗尽可在桅杆上飘扬，但是谁会愿意登船远航？试想一下，假如那些哲学家说对了，那么我们需要有什么样的精神准备，才敢面对源于餐桌的危险：餐桌要比史上任何的战场都危险，多少祖先悲惨地在战场上送了命！还有哪个女人会有结婚的愿望，因婚姻的危险远胜过惊涛骇浪？活到年老又会是何等境况？在人生的路上行走一段后，我们便会发现每向前一步，脚下的冰就变薄一点，环顾四周，放眼身后，同辈人失足掉在冰下的不在少数。活到七十多岁的人每向前一步就是一个奇迹；每天晚上老人拖着那副老骨头上床就寝，见不到天明的可能性非常大。在实际生活中，老人们会在乎这些吗？才不会呢！他们会活得很快活，晚上会喝一点小酒，讲几个风趣的故事；他们听到了同龄人去世的消息，有的甚至比他们还年轻，但他们没有兔死狐悲的感觉，相反，一想到比别人活得更久，反倒会像孩子那样一阵得意。当清风吹得他们如风前残烛，当意外摔得他们如玻璃破碎，他们那

fluttering candle, or a bit of a stumble shatter them like so much glass,[24] their old hearts keep sound and unaffrighted, and they go on, bubbling with laughter, through years of man's age compared to which the valley at Balaclava[25] was as safe and peaceful as a village cricket-green on Sunday. It may fairly be questioned (if we look to the peril only) whether it was a much more daring feat for Curtius[26] to plunge into the gulf, than for any old gentleman of ninety to doff his clothes and clamber into bed.

Indeed, it is a memorable subject for consideration, with what unconcern and gaiety mankind pricks on along the Valley of the Shadow of Death.[27] The whole way is one wilderness of snares, and the end of it, for those who fear the last pinch, is irrevocable ruin.[28] And yet we go spinning through it all, like a party for the Derby.[29] Perhaps the reader remembers one of the humorous devices of the deified Caligula: how he encouraged a vast concourse of holiday-makers on to his bridge over Baiae bay; and when they were in the height of their enjoyment, turned loose the Praetorian guards among the company, and had them tossed into the sea.[30] This is no bad miniature of the dealings of nature with the transitory race of man.[31] Only, what a chequered picnic[32] we have of it, even while it lasts! and into what great waters, not to be crossed by any swimmer, God's pale Praetorian throws us over in the end![33]

颗老年的心却能保持健康、处事不惊，老人们继续前行，笑声不断，年复一年，与这些相比，战事尤酣的巴拉克拉瓦峡谷就像乡村里周日板球绿茵场一样平静了。如果我们仅看危险这一端，那么我们大可心生疑问，古罗马库提乌司跳入广场裂缝救城和九十岁老人脱衣就寝，到底哪个堪称壮举？

确实这是一个值得反复思考的问题，人类是这样无忧无虑、欢快愉悦，沿死亡的幽谷忍痛前行。整个人生之路是布满陷阱的荒原，而对于那些惧怕终极痛苦的人，路的尽头就是有去无回的灭亡。可是我们在这条路上欢快地一路奔跑，恰如德比马会比赛。可能读者还记得被神化的卡利古拉的那出恶作剧：他鼓励度假者聚集在巴亚湾的桥上，但当他们游兴正浓时，卡利古拉却纵容罗马禁卫军，把这些人投入海中。这虽是一人的恶作剧，但小中见大，造化也正是这么弄人的。不同的是，我们人类的野餐不都是恶事充斥，也会好事相伴；上帝的禁卫军最终也会把我们投入大海，不同的是，海之广阔远胜巴亚湾，再好的水手也游不到岸边。

注 释

1. 这里的 final 表示"最后的,终结的",这个比较清楚,引申一下,说成"不可逆转的",也可考虑。但是 sharp 就比较模糊,因为这个词在不同语境中,意思会有些变化。这个词的本义是有图像的,如一把刀的锋利,其他意思都是从这个意思上引申出来的隐喻意思,比如 sharp turn 表示方向急剧改变,sharp pain 是突然和严重的,sharp sound 是突然和强烈的,等等。一般来说,这个词不管在什么语境中,似乎都有突然和严重的含义,所以译者可以据此选择一个符合语境的词,而不应该在这个词的翻译上有过多的规范。因同义词选项较多,本译文选用了"剧烈的"。另外,*so* sharp and final… *that* the thing stands alone 中确实有"如此……以至于……"这层表示程度的意思,但翻译时未必要表达出来。不是每一个英文的连接关系都要在译文中用一个连接的词表达。当然在实用的正式文本中则另作别论。

2. Thug 是指旧时印度部落中谋财害命的人,他们往往夜间杀人取财。根据《牛津英语词典》(*Oxford English Dictionary*,以后简称 OED),这个词也有 cutthroat 的意思。另外,这里是大写,所以可能不是泛指,而是特指印度部落中的盗贼。作者就是举一例子,说明普遍道理。

3. 在 a pin knocked out by which many subsidiary friendships hung together 中的 pin 很难明确断定是什么钉子,这就给译者造成了麻烦。这个句子的基本图像是由一个钉子把其他的东西都聚在一起了;也就是说,这个 pin 就是那个死去的人,knocked out 就是被除掉了,即死去了。但是由于 pin 是什么并不清楚,所以 knocked out 这个动作的意思也无法断定。另外 subsidiary 的意思是指朋友附属于那位逝者的意思。但这些细节并不重要，这句话的意思就是人一死，朋友也都散了。鉴于无法有把握地确定 pin 是什么钉子，可采用放弃细节的译法"人逝友散"。这个选择还基于另外一个判断，这里 pin 所营造的图像对于构成作者的风格没有特殊意义，尽管这确是一个作者使然的语言特点。当然也可以采取中间路线，保留一点原文的思路，却不完全采用原文的隐喻（"由死者维系的友情圈也随之而散"）。

4. 这里的 striking to the mind 表示对人的强烈影响（起到提醒人的作用），也就是说，下面的例子比如埃及法老的金字塔和中世纪欧洲的绞刑架给人强烈的印象，提醒人们记住。也可以和前面的联想起来，如法老生前地位显赫，死后也只能默默待在金字塔里，对应前面一句的 mocking 表达的对人的嘲讽，而中世纪欧洲处死人用绞刑架，死人挂在外边，不用多时就腐烂了，对应前面一句中的 "tragical, and soon intolerable residue"，当然这个 residue 应该解释得更宽泛，可以包括人们对死者的念想等抽象的东西，上面的仅是少数实体的例子。本句中的 from… to… 表示两个极端，一端是金字塔，是比较高端的一面，另一端是绞刑架，是比较低端的一面，在此之间还有很多不同程度的例子。dule trees 中的 dule 是苏格兰语，"悲痛"的意思。句子开头的 hence 是另外一个有关衔接的问题。这个词一般解释成 "consequently, as a result"，但这里的因果关系比较松散。根据上下文，可解释成 in order to bear up the situation of the death，灵活一点也可解释成 on the other hand，但是不管怎么解释，hence 应该和 residue 有衔接关系。

5. 这句是在说，前面那一长串有关死亡的仪式加上诗人唱诗等活动，虽说是各国文化习俗的不可缺少的部分，却并没有什么意思，甚至是错误的。作者对这类用死亡做文章的习俗采取完全否定的态度。

6. nay 一般表示 no 的意思，但在这里则不符合语境。这个词还有另外一个意思，即 and more than that，比如"He was grateful for and proud of his son's remarkable, nay, unique performance"。就是说，当你说了一件事，发现那个说法还不够正确，便用 nay 加以补充或更正。在我们的语境中，作者先说了 put humanity in error（简单说就是错误的），但作者认为那样说还没有说到位，他便补充说，有些哲学家甚至把这个错误说成如何符合逻辑，所以 nay 很像汉语中的"更有甚者"。至于 has been embodied 和 laid down 这两个动作应该和前面的有关，如形象的表达就可以说成是 embodied（express something abstract in tangible form），一般的平实表达就可以说是 laid down（described）。换句话说，错的东西会被说成是符合逻辑的。这两个动词本质上说的是一回事，但说法不同，一个是形象说法，一个是一般说法。若把词的色彩拿掉，就可合并说成是 described。最后，with every circumstance of logic 中的 circumstance 的用法和现代用法不同，很难确切讲清楚其含义，但是这个短语大致就是 logically，或者加上前面的动词，说成 has been set out in logical words。

7. 此处的 fearful whisperings 是指人们见到悲惨事件后的一种心态或反应，比如你刚刚听说了列车出事，于是你就会轻轻地对朋友或其他人说，你再也不乘火车了，你压低声音是因为惧怕。

8. impressed 这个动词现在常表示留下好的印象，比如"I am impressed by your English"，但这个词基本意思是中性的，可表达正面也可表达负面意思（OED: to produce a deep effect or

impression on the mind or feelings of），此处就是负面的，如表达惊扰、不安等意思。另外，这句中的 tremendous 在这个语境中虽有震颤的意思，但主要还是 astonishingly terrible 的意思。

9. 一般 delve 这个词当不及物动词用，如 delve into one's past。此处当及物动词使用，表示 digging 的意思。斯蒂文森曾在其他散文中也用到过这个词，但此词在美国英语中一般不用作及物动词。

10. 这个词一般表示 courageous behavior，比如"For his *gallantry* he was awarded a Victoria Cross"。但此处根据语境应该不是这个意思。OED 中还有两个古旧的词义和这个语境有关，如"fine or gay appearance or show, splendour, magnificence"和"amorous intercourse or intrigue"，而这两个定义中前者最合适，当然作者写作时第二个与性相关的词义也可能在其脑海闪过。应该指出的是，斯蒂文森在其写作中常喜欢将旧用法复活。

11. 这句中有三个地方需要解释。首先 living ruin 这个词可以有两层意思，一个可以是 ruin to all living things 的意思，但是在这里最合适的词义应该是流动的岩浆（lava flow），之所以是 living，是因为岩浆本身就是活动的，有其自己的"生命"。另外，句子中的 merry-making 应该表示寻欢作乐的意思，和上面的 gallantry 正好对应，正好是前者的具体内容，因为 merry-making 一般就是指吃喝玩乐的活动。最后，tumble...in the dust 翻译成"将……埋葬"，大意基本到位。译者若想再挖掘一下原文的意思，那么倒还真有可以补充的地方。"埋葬"仅仅是最后的结果，但是动词 tumble 则给人一种过程的印象，这个动词一般描写一样东西从较高处坍塌倒下的过程，所以译文中翻译成了"颠覆埋葬"。当然没有必要过度强调这个动作，译者可以根据自己的判断，选择添加这个动词表达的意思，但如前所说，不加也基本到位。

12. 这句中的 with umbrellas 需要解释一下。整个句子在说那些尊贵之人本该无胃口在可以望到火山的地方吃饭，因为很危险，万一火山爆发，逃离都困难。而这个 umbrellas 既可以看成是有身份人的装饰，更可以看成是为下雨备用，也就是提示这些尊贵之人总是有准备的。接下来一句的 high-handed debauch 可以解释为不顾别人的狂欢场合。

13. 这句是说，在这么危险的地方还吃得下饭、照常生活，常人是办不到的，只有心不在尘世的隐士或者整天喝酒不顾一切的人才能在那里生活。在翻译 hermits dwelling in prayer and maceration 时很难选择，因为作者头脑中想到的到底是什么样的 hermits，答案不同就有选词的差别。这个短语在这个语境中似乎既可以指东方宗教里的僧侣，也可指中世纪基督教中的修士。hermit 一词有两个意思，一个是和宗教无关的隐者（any person living in solitude），一个是和宗教有关的隐者（one of the early Christian recluses），这里应该是指后者。在东方宗教中，僧人念经吃素这类活动和句子中的 prayer and maceration 也有对应关系，但是我们翻译时是完全使用佛教语言体系中的词，还是使用形容基督教修士的词语，这会是一个需考虑的问题。根据语境判断，此处指基督教修士的概率应该远大于指佛教僧侣，所以避开明显的佛教用语会是我的选择。比方说，prayer 翻译成"诵经"是否合适，这就是个问题，因为佛教中这个词基本是以背诵、诵读为主，英文的 prayer 的诉求和佛教很不同，Collins 词典的解释是"Prayer is the activity of speaking to God"，而且还会外带出 a strong hope that you have as your prayer 的意思。maceration 翻译成"斋戒"

也会有东方宗教的味道,这个词在这里主要指为宗教目的而禁食(fasting)。所以挣扎一番之后,我选择了"潜心祈祷、虔修禁食的修士"。钱锺书欣赏黄克孙重译的《鲁拜集》,而黄译彻底归化成中国文化,甚至在诗中用了"碧落黄泉皆妄语,三生因果近荒唐"这样完全归化的语言。遵照钱先生的翻译观,我们也许应该为"诵经斋戒的高僧隐士"的译法点赞,译文简洁明快,重点突出,只是我总走不出那一步。

14. 这里的 pale figure 就是 faint image 的意思,其中的 pale 就是"弱"的意思。也就是说,火山下南美人处境所构成的一幅图像并不是一般人类处境的图像,与一般人类处境相比,南美人的险境算不了什么(pale figure for the state of ordinary mankind),因为火山下南美人虽然有灭顶之灾的威胁,但那毕竟不是每日发生的事,普通人却是每时每刻都面临危险。

15. 这里的 knock 指什么并没有明说,但是我们可以想到的也许是一颗流星。他这么说,是否是因为根据当时的天文知识,有人揣测会有流星撞击地球,我们不得而知,但是指流星的可能性最大。不过在翻译时是否要把 knock 换成流星,则是一个翻译的问题。原文的 knock 仅仅是个动作,并不是实体,所以在这个译文中就仍然保留了动作(无端而来的一击),不过翻译成实体也说得通(被流星一击)。两相比较,笔者更倾向不用实体,而用动作。

16. 这里短语 pathologically looked at 表示从病理学家的角度看人体,或者说从医生的角度看人体,看到的都是潜在的问题,都是危险,比如血压高就可能有潜在中风的危险,血脂高就有心肌梗死的危险,所以在他们看来,这个满是器官的人体就危机四伏了(a mere bagful of petards)。

17. 这句紧接着讲人体的上句，所以这里应该有局部和整体意思，也就是说，the least of these 是指局部的器官，而 the whole economy 就是指整个人体。另外，为了说明人体危险重重，作者将人体比作了装满炸药的船只。注意，下面的 powder-magazine 就是指弹药库，magazine 这个词还可以指子弹匣。
18. 这里的 clung 应该和后面的 to 连接（If we clung to the abstract idea of life），而 as devotedly as some philosophers pretend we do 则是插入部分，we do 就是 we cling 的意思。换个句型的话，就是 If we clung to the abstract idea of life as devotedly as some philosophers pretend we do。
19. 介词 for 应该和前面的 frightened 衔接，表示 frightened 的原因，而 as they make out we are 则是插入语。这个 for（because of）当然也可以用 by 替换（frightened by the subversive accident），但是 by 会给主语较强的被动含义。half as frightened as 这个结构中的 half 不应该解释为"一半"，因为这个句型的否定式是已载入字典的成语，如 "It's not half as easy as it looks"（not half = not nearly）。其实 not half 的意思和"一半"已经完全没有关系，仅表示 far from 的意思，或者就是 not at all 的意思（据 OED）。所以在我们的语境中是把否定反转成肯定，起到强调的作用，也就是说 half as frightened 不是表示 not nearly or far from frightened，而是表示 almost frightened。
20. 典自《圣经·哥林多前书》："For if the trumpet give an uncertain sound, who shall prepare himself to the battle?"（Corinthians 14: 8）
21. 这里的 the blue-peter 是指英国海军的旗语，主体为蓝色、中间白色的旗放在桅杆顶端，表示需要立即起航。这个旗语似乎并不局限在英国。

22. 在这一长句中，作者将 the dinner-table 和 any battlefield 做了隐喻对照，也就是说，餐桌和战场相比，餐桌更危险，每日就餐都会有死亡之危险。这里要注意的是，他并不仅仅是在说餐桌和就餐本身就有那么危险，而是说由用餐带来的后果可能会极其危险，比如说，吃多了东西，吃错了东西，造成的结果都可能是非常危险的，正是在这个意义上说餐桌是一个 deadlier spot，危险程度不亚于战场。这句后面的 left their bones 也提示战场。一般我们打仗在外，有时就回不来了，所以中文里有"何须马革裹尸还"的说法，这里的 left their bones 就是把骨头留在战场上的意思。此处翻译起来要保留原文的形象较困难，所以译文没有设法保留骨头的形象。

23. 本句意思还是比较清楚的，但说婚姻要比怒海更危险（so much more dangerous than the wildest sea）需要在理解上不局限于婚姻本身，而应该包括与婚姻相关的事件。婚姻本身（如婚礼）并不是作者要强调的，但由于婚姻而来的事件完全可能非常危险，比如女人生孩子就是非常危险的，特别是在医疗服务不发达的 19 世纪就更危险。总之，从 19 世纪的背景看，婚姻带给妇女的危险还是不难发现的。

24. 这一长句中有两个对老年人的比喻：一个是老人像风吹蜡烛一样，和汉语成语"风前残烛"较切合；另一个是把老人比喻成玻璃，一碰就碎，比如年纪老的人跌倒造成骨折，翻译时最好保留玻璃，因为很形象，而且也不难理解，甚至图像还能帮助理解。一开始用了"如玉盘破碎"，后来还是觉得不很妥当，因为原文就是玻璃，很普通的一个物品，玉盘尽管可以形成相同的破碎形象，但物件本身却有"珍贵"这个附带含义，而这是原文没有的。

25. 这个 Balaclava 指的是克里米亚战争中那次著名的巴拉克拉瓦战役，英、俄、土耳其等国参与了战斗。其间骑兵冲锋陷阵，伤亡惨烈，后来丁尼生有诗为证。斯蒂文森在这里使用对比的手法，将老年人遇到的危险与巴拉克拉瓦战役的危险做对比，相比之下，那次著名的战役就是小巫见大巫了，就只能是像乡村周日板球绿茵场那样平静。英国乡间的周日常会有板球比赛，但那项运动非常缓慢，甚至有些乏味。作者如此比喻显然是无限夸张了，而这也营造了些许幽默的气氛，可以看作是一个写作的特征，翻译时应该予以保留。

26. 这是指 Marcus Curtius。这位罗马士兵为了挽救罗马城，纵身跳进罗马城广场上的一个裂缝，结果他跳下去后，沟壑就合拢了，罗马城也得救了。这当然是一个需要事实根据证明的传说，作者把这个传说和九旬老人脱衣就寝相比，并认为老人之举动更可称为壮举，这显然是一个很夸张的写作手法，也构成他写作的特征，译者当然应该在翻译中保留下来。

27. 这个 Valley of the Shadow of Death 典自《圣经·诗篇》：Even though I walk through the valley of the shadow of death, I will fear no evil, for you are with me; your rod and your staff, they comfort me. (Psalm 23: 4) "我虽然行过死荫的幽谷，也不怕遭害，因为你与我同在，你的杖、你的竿都安慰我。"

28. 这一整句的隐喻基础是 Life is a journey，也就是说 the whole way 就是一生，the end of it 就是一生的结束，所以 irrevocable ruin 也就是指死亡，一种有去无回路程的结束。

29. 本句中的 it（go spinning through it all）到底指什么？在这个词前面有两个第三人称单数词，而且所指的是同一样东西，既可以指 the whole way，也可以指 one wilderness。但是介词 through 给了我们一个清晰的图像，动作是从一头到另一头，也就是说，这个 go spinning through it 的隐喻图像是 Life is a journey，因此把 it 理解成 the whole way 要比理解成 one wilderness 更便于与 journey 这个图像匹配。

30. 这一长句中有好几个要注释的地方。卡利古拉是罗马帝国的一个皇帝，在位时间为公元 37 年到 41 年，是出名的暴君，甚至自封为神，后被部下杀害。本文的故事是说卡利古拉诱惑度假的人到那不勒斯巴亚湾（Baiae Bay）的一座桥上去寻欢作乐，但当大家玩兴正浓时，他却纵容他的禁卫军（Praetorian guards）把这些人从桥上扔到海里。这句开头的 humorous 并不是我们一般意义上的幽默，因为卡利古拉的恶行不是幽默可以形容的，这对卡利古拉是幽默，对别人是一点都不幽默，所以翻译成"恶作剧"似乎比"幽默"更到位。至于 devices，最好理解成 game，也是一种把戏，这里就是"恶作剧"中的"剧"。

31. 这个 miniature 是拿来做比较的，一方面是卡利古拉的待人之道，另一方面是自然的待人之道，作者认为都一样，卡利古拉仅仅是更小的一个缩影，自然待人是更宏大的规模。翻译时最简单的办法就是和原文一样，前者是后者的一个缩影。但是也可以探索其他译法，比如避开"缩影"这个表达法。在这个过程中，可能想到不同的译法，如"宏观看人类，自然作弄我们也如出一辙""造化弄人在这个恶作剧中反映得惟妙惟肖""这个恶作剧恰是造化弄人的绝佳例证""这虽是一人的恶作剧，但小中见大，造化也是这么弄人的"，译文选了最后一个。其实，简单一点就用"缩影"也可以。这不是对错的选择，不同的译者会有各自的考虑，只要意思对了，还是建议给译者较大的选择空间。细心的读者也许看到这几个译文中漏掉了一些细节，比如 transitory 没有了，这个当然是漏译，只是"造化弄人"这个概念和原文的意思非常符合，但这个固定词组又不能添加 transitory 的意思，所以就忍痛割爱了。再比如 no bad 表示"不错的"的意思，但仅是一个程度词，翻译时未必就那么重要，所以也故意漏掉了。这两个词漏掉都是为了整体效果，但这样删掉并不影响句子的大意。在有些文本中，这样的删除也许不可原谅，但在另外一些场合，这样删除甚至不必有一丝遗憾，文本、目的不同，处理方法也不同。

32. 开头的 only 一词说明了造化弄人和卡利古拉恶作剧的不同之处。这里 chequered (picnic) 指的是生活的成功与失败或顺境与逆境。《剑桥高阶英语词典》(*Cambridge Advanced Learner's Dictionary*) 的定义是 having had both successful and unsuccessful periods in your past。Collins 词典则这样解释："If a person or organization has had a chequered career or history, they have had a varied past with both good and bad periods"。本译文根据这个定义略加发挥："我们人类的野餐不都是恶事充斥，也会好事相伴"。

33. 这句实际是在继续比较造化弄人和卡利古拉恶作剧的不同，也许水性好的人还可以游到巴亚湾的岸上，但是大自然把你投入的水域却无比宽广，水性再好也游不到岸边（not to be crossed by any swimmer），而且上帝的禁卫军最终肯定是会把人抛到海里去的。句子中的 over（throws us over）应该和桥的图像有关，因为在卡利古拉恶作剧中，禁卫军是把人从桥上扔过栏杆投入海里的，这个 over 就是假设造化弄人的相同情景（throws us over railings of the bridge）。至于 pale Praetorian 中的 pale 大概是形容这些士兵的脸色。

> 导 读

不畏生死见英雄

这篇《三重甲》（Aes Triplex）最初于 1878 年 4 月发表在颇负盛名的文学月刊《康希尔杂志》（*Cornhill Magazine*），后收入斯蒂文森散文集《童女与少年》（*Virginibus Puerisque*, 1881）。这个散文集收入的散文好多都是先发表在《康希尔杂志》上。此时他的散文在文学上已相当成熟。一般认为，斯蒂文森的散文承袭了兰姆（Lamb）和黑兹利特（Hazlitt）的风格，属于个人色彩浓厚的散文作品。

没有很多有关《三重甲》写作过程的资料，但是一般认为作者是在格雷兹（Grez）和伦敦写的这篇散文，以此推测大致的写作时间是 1877 年的 8 月到 11 月间。此时斯蒂文森和范妮已经相识交往。根据斯蒂文森的相关传记，他和范妮在这段时间里都病痛缠身，所以有些评论家认为这篇文章的内容多少也反映了他在疾病时的精神面貌。本书中收入的《黄金国》也是在同一段时间写的。

《三重甲》发表后广受好评。编辑兼批评家威廉·亨利在写给他的信中说："你这个聪明的年轻小鬼，真是堪称奇才。"斯蒂文森在文章里对生命展现出的积极态度受到很多人赞赏。普遍认为，这篇散文是他的散文代表作之一，在当时和后来都很受欢迎。据说在他所有的散文中，这篇的重印次数名列前茅。《三重甲》还被收入不同的文集中，甚至出单行本，如 1901 年《斯克里伯纳杂志》（*Scribner's Magazine*）专门为这篇出了一个单行本。1943 年，在第二次世界大战期间，红衣出版社（Redcoat Press）也专门为青年男子出了一个单行本，鼓舞风雷激荡岁月中的年轻人积极面对人生。可见斯蒂文森文中的现实主义深受广大读者的喜爱。这篇最初发表时仅获 6 英镑 6 先令报酬的短文居然有这么大的能量,足见此时的斯蒂文森已是不可小觑的作家了。

文章的题目 Aes Triplex 源自拉丁文,意为三重的黄铜(triple brass),也就是三重盔甲的意思。这个词有个典故,出自古罗马诗人贺拉斯《颂歌》(*Odes*)的第 1 章第 3 节(Illi robur et aes triplex | Circa pectus erat, qui fragilem truci | Commisit pelago ratem | Primus),英文大意就是"Oak and triple bronze encompassed the breast of him, whose frail craft he entrusted to the wild sea for the first time"。高健先生理解为"积极、乐观、无畏即是抵制甚至战胜死亡的三重铜甲"。斯蒂文森在这个时期的作品中,多次借用三重铜甲这个典故,比如在 *Edinburgh: Picturesque Notes* 中描写爱丁堡的市民:"triply cased in grease",在 *An Old Song* 中描写玛丽:"her treble armour of innocence, pride, and selfishness"。本译文把题目直译成"三重甲",但也可根据文章的意思自拟题目,比如高健先生意译成"生死之际"。

《三重甲》这篇散文主要是写死亡的。作者一开始就把这个令人生畏的题目摆在读者面前:"死亡造成的变化本身是剧烈、终极的,其后果可怖可悲,在人的经历中独一无二,没有什么意外事件可以与之相比。死亡超越所有人生中其他的意外,因为死亡之后再无意外。"死亡的危险每时每刻都伴随着我们,几乎与我们形影不离。他用生活在火山脚下的南美人来比喻潜在的危险:"脚底下大地颤抖,山体内咆哮怒吼,每一刻流动的岩浆都可能冲向月光满溢的天空,将人和他作乐寻欢的场面颠覆埋葬"。他还把我们满是器官的人体比作"装满爆竹的囊袋","它们中间最微不足道的一个器官就能危及整个机体,恰如船上的炸药库能危及整艘航船"。没错,我们人类就是生活在这样的环境里。如果你想焦虑,你有焦虑的理由，你想谨慎，你有谨慎的理由，你可以像扫雷士兵一样，跨出一步前做足功课，你甚至可以躲在家里足不出户，那样安全系数又可以提高不少。但那不是人生，那也不是大多数正常人的态度。你看那些火山脚下的南美人，即便是在那样的环境里，他们"也不会被死亡的严峻威胁而惊扰，也能像英国远郊绿野上的菜农一样过悠闲的生活"。他告诉我们，危险是生活的常态，"在人生的路上行走一段后，我们便会发现每向前一步，脚下的冰就变薄一点，环顾四周，放眼身后，同辈人失足掉在冰下的不在少数"，但是水手并不因此而不出海航行，青年男女并不因此而不结婚，老年人也并不因此而躺在床上不起来。

斯蒂文森要把生命落实在鲜活的生活里，他极不赞赏让生活龟缩在抽象的思维中："世上没有一个人能凌空飞至抽象的巅峰，对'生命'一词的意义有切实的揣摩。所有的文学，从约伯、奥玛珈音到托马斯·卡莱尔或沃尔特·惠特曼，都只是试图从这样宏观的角度观察人生，结果我们远离生活经历，去把玩生命的抽象定义"。这不是斯蒂文森想要的生活："我们尽可以用世间所有哲学流派做抽象思辨，但一个事实亘古不变：我们并不是为保余生、如履薄冰那样热爱生命；说得更确切些，我们毫不热爱抽象的生命，而是热爱具体的生活。"

斯蒂文森热爱生活，用火一般的热情拥抱实实在在的生活，那个不仅有开怀大笑也有切肤之痛的生活，那个充满危险也充满希望的生活。对于他来说，生命"自始至终是一个蜜月，一个算不上长的蜜月"。

他不怕危险，因而也胸襟宽广。斯蒂文森讨厌过度谨小慎微的人："一旦谨小慎微如阴郁的真菌开始在他头脑中滋长，慷慨大方的行动便开始消失。受害者的精神便开始萎缩。"他喜欢的人应该

"胸襟袒露，思维能敏捷应变，勇于将生命付诸使用，笑对危险"。他认为，"那些勇敢的有用之人也都会把恼人的危险踩在脚下，成功跨越谨小慎微在他们路上竖起的障碍"。他以词典学家约翰逊为例，说明他在一个巨大工程面前是如何不惧艰险，完成一部伟大的词典。于是斯蒂文森反问："如果一个人智慧谨慎、思前想后，谁还愿意做任何一项大于写明信片的工程？在萨克雷和狄更斯大作未成身先死之后，谁还会再来写连载小说？而假如人总让死亡萦绕，谁还会有勇气开启生活？"

他理想中的死亡是伴随搏击而来的。就算是在完成一个创举中他出师未捷，精神仍然可以长存，那样的死是壮丽辉煌的。"一边是浪花飞溅直冲断壁悬崖结束生命，一边是茫无目标在沙洲上痛苦前行了此一生，两相比照，哪个更精彩，岂不显而易见？"吊诡的是，他在文章结束时写的几句话，恰恰成为他出师未捷的写照："在人生激情四射的那一刻，他站在生命的巅峰上，一跃便到了另一世界。工作用的槌子和凿子声音犹在耳，战斗中的号角声仍在回响，身后是灿烂的云霞，这个心情快乐、精力充沛的精灵拔地而起，直冲向那个精神的家园。"1894年12月的一天，在毫无预兆的情况下斯蒂文森因脑出血英年早逝，年仅44岁，留下了《赫米斯顿的魏尔》(*Weir of Hermiston*) 这本被认为是斯蒂文森最好的小说，只可惜他没有写完，正应了"出师未捷身先死"这句话。

无论是在《三重甲》还是在《微尘与幻影》中，斯蒂文森都经常使用对立（antithesis）的手法，即把两个对立的概念用在一起，比如生和死，年老和年轻，勤奋和懒惰。这种对立造成的矛盾在斯蒂文森的散文中已成为一个广泛使用的技巧（Snyder, 1920），比如在这篇散文中，斯蒂文森把一种意义的活着看作是死亡，而把一般意义的死亡看作是活着："即便死亡能像一个大陷阱，在人们事业如日中天，眼前项目待举，正打算为巨大工程奠基动工时，在他们充满希望，口出豪言壮语时，把他们带走了，即便他们立马倒下，马上沉寂，即便是那样，你难道不觉得那样结束生命不乏英雄气概吗？"在斯蒂文森眼里，那个倒下的人仍活着。"一边是浪花飞溅直冲断壁悬崖结束生命，一边是茫无目标在沙洲上痛苦前行了此一生，两相比照，哪个更精彩，岂不显而易见？"而那个在沙洲上活着前行的人却已没有了生命。细心的读者不妨在阅读中慢慢去寻找这种对立矛盾的写法（paradox and antithesis）。此外，很多评论家认为，斯蒂文森在写作中经常使用典故，巧妙地利用语音的重复和变换，并在文章中模仿兰姆、蒙田等散文家。这些都是值得读者去挖掘的。由于本书的主要目的是翻译，所以这里就不说开去了。

参考资料

Robert Louis Stevenson, *Virginibus Puerisque and Other Papers*, ed. R. L. Abrahamson, Edinburgh University Press, 2018.

Roderick Watson, "Ginger beer and earthquakes": Stevenson and the terrors of contingency, *Journal of Stevenson Studies*, 8, 2011.

Alice D. Snyder, Paradox and Antithesis in Stevenson's Essays: A Structural Study, *The Journal of English and Germanic Philology*, Vol. 19, No. 4 (Oct., 1920), pp. 540−559.

Richard Dury, Stevenson's essays: language and style, *Journal of Stevenson Studies*, 2012.

高健，《枕边书与床头灯》，上海译文出版社，2012。

Aes Triplex (2)

We live the time that a match flickers;[34] we pop the cork of a ginger-beer bottle, and the earthquake swallows us on the instant. Is it not odd, is it not incongruous, is it not, in the highest sense of human speech, incredible,[35] that we should think so highly of the ginger-beer, and regard so little the devouring earthquake? The love of Life and the fear of Death are two famous phrases that grow harder to understand the more we think about them. It is a well-known fact that an immense proportion of boat accidents would never happen if people held the sheet in their hands instead of making it fast;[36] and yet, unless it be some martinet of a professional mariner or some landsman with shattered nerves, every one of God's creatures makes it fast. A strange instance of man's unconcern and brazen boldness in the face of death!

We confound ourselves with metaphysical phrases, which we import into daily talk. We have no idea of what death is, apart from its circumstances[37] and some of its consequences to others; and although we have some experience of living, there is not a man on earth who has flown so high into abstraction as to have any practical guess at the meaning of the word *life*. All literature, from Job and Omar Khayyam to Thomas Carlyle or Walt Whitman,[38] is but an attempt to look upon the human state with such largeness of view as shall enable us to rise from the consideration of living to the Definition of Life. And our sages give us

三重甲（二）

人生在世如火柴的微光瞬间即逝；我们正开着姜汁啤酒瓶，不远处的地震却大有顷刻间吞没我们之势。可我们居然把姜汁啤酒当回事儿，把吞噬人的地震不放在眼里，这难道不有点怪异，有点不着调，简直有点不可思议吗？贪生和怕死这两个人们最熟悉的词，我们越想越难理解它们。众所周知，大多数航船出事都是因为把控制船帆的缭绳绑了起来，若紧握在手中事故是不会发生的。但除非专业水手严守纪律或航海新手神经紧张，否则每一个上帝创造出来的人都会为了腾出手，把缭绳绑起来。这个奇特的例子说明人面对死亡是多么无畏勇敢！

我们在每天的交谈中都用一些玄而又玄的词，把自己搞得昏头转向。除掉死亡直观的证据和死亡对他人造成的后果，我们搞不清什么是死亡。尽管我们有些生活的经历，但是世上没有一个人能凌空飞至抽象的巅峰，对"生命"一词的意义有切实的揣摩。所有的文学，从约伯、奥玛珈音到托马斯·卡莱尔或沃尔特·惠特曼，都只是试图从这样宏观的角度观察人生，结果我们远离生活经历，去把玩生命的抽象定义。智者说生活是烟云，是戏剧，是无异于梦幻

about the best satisfaction in their power[39] when they say that it is a vapour, or a show, or made out of the same stuff with dreams.[40] Philosophy, in its more rigid sense, has been at the same work for ages; and after a myriad bald heads have wagged over the problem, and piles of words have been heaped one upon another into dry and cloudy volumes without end, philosophy has the honour of laying before us, with modest pride, her contribution towards the subject: that life is a Permanent Possibility of Sensation.[41] Truly a fine result! A man may very well love beef, or hunting, or a woman; but surely, surely, not a Permanent Possibility of Sensation. He may be afraid of a precipice, or a dentist, or a large enemy with a club, or even an undertaker's man; but not certainly of abstract death. We may trick with the word life in its dozen senses until we are weary of tricking; we may argue in terms of all the philosophies on earth, but one fact remains true throughout—that we do not love life, in the sense that we are greatly preoccupied about its conservation;[42] that we do not, properly speaking, love life at all, but living. Into the views of the least careful there will enter some degree of providence;[43] no man's eyes are fixed entirely on the passing hour;[44] but although we have some anticipation of good health, good weather, wine, active employment,[45] love, and self-approval, the sum of these anticipations does not amount to anything like a general view of life's possibilities and issues;[46] nor are those who cherish them most vividly, at all the most scrupulous of their personal safety.[47] To be deeply interested in the accidents of our existence, to enjoy keenly the mixed texture of human experience, rather leads a man to disregard precautions, and risk his neck against a straw.[48] For surely the love of living is stronger in an Alpine climber roping over a peril, or a hunter riding merrily at a stiff fence, than

的东西，这大概算是他们力所能及给我们的满意答案了。哲学以其更为僵硬的方式，世世代代做着这项解释生命的工作。无数的秃头哲人就这个问题摇头晃脑，著书立说，汗牛充栋的文字艰涩枯燥，置人于五里雾中，结果哲学十分荣幸、不无骄傲地在我们面前捧出它在这一议题上的贡献：生命就是永恒的感知可能性。真是一个不错的结论！一个人可能爱牛肉，或爱狩猎，或爱女人，但却肯定不会、绝对不会爱永恒的感知可能性。他可能怕断壁悬崖，怕牙医钻牙，怕手持武器的魁梧敌人，甚至怕殡仪馆的人，但是肯定不怕抽象的死亡。我们可以耍弄"生命"这个词的诸多含义，直到我们自己厌倦了那耍弄的把戏。我们尽可以用世间所有哲学流派做抽象思辨，但一个事实亘古不变：我们并不是为保余生、如履薄冰那样热爱生命；说得更确切些，我们毫不热爱抽象的生命，而是热爱具体的生活。没错，最粗心的人也会有某种程度的审慎与前瞻；没有一个人的眼睛完全盯着当前；对于好身体、好天气、好酒，我们确实有那么点期盼，也盼望有事做，有爱情，能自赏自傲，但所有这些前瞻期盼都不像生活的可能性和人生的议题这些宏观概念那么抽象；而且特别珍视这些期盼的人也绝不会为了自身安危而在人生路上如履薄冰。对生存的不测意外兴趣盎然，对人生的五味杂陈乐此不疲，这样的人就不会谨小慎微，而会置风险于不顾。阿尔卑斯山上命悬一线的攀岩者，骑马越障的愉快狩猎人，他们对生活的热爱

in a creature who lives upon a diet and walks a measured distance in the interest of his constitution.

There is a great deal of very vile nonsense talked upon both sides of the matter: tearing divines reducing life to the dimensions of a mere funeral procession[49], so short as to be hardly decent; and melancholy unbelievers yearning for the tomb as if it were a world too far away.[50] Both sides must feel a little ashamed of their performances now and again when they draw in their chairs to dinner. Indeed, a good meal and a bottle of wine is an answer to most standard works upon the question.[51] When a man's heart warms to his viands, he forgets a great deal of sophistry, and soars into a rosy zone of contemplation. Death may be knocking at the door, like the Commander's statue;[52] we have something else in hand, thank God, and let him knock.

Passing bells are ringing all the world over. All the world over, and every hour, someone is parting company with all his aches and ecstasies. For us also the trap is laid.[53] But we are so fond of life that we have no leisure to entertain the terror of death. It is a honeymoon with us all through, and none of the longest. Small blame to us if we give our whole hearts to this glowing bride of ours, to the appetites, to honour, to the hungry curiosity of the mind, to the pleasure of the eyes in nature, and the pride of our own nimble bodies.[54]

We all of us appreciate the sensations; but as for caring about the Permanence of the Possibility, a man's head is generally very bald, and his senses very dull, before he comes to that. Whether we regard life as a lane leading to a dead wall—a mere bag's end,[55] as the French say—or whether we think of it as a vestibule or gymnasium, where we wait our

远胜过为健康而饮食精挑细选、走路尺测丈量的人。

就此人生问题双方各有恶语胡言：一方是情绪激昂的神职人员把人生贬低为送葬列队那么点大的格局，狭隘得无法堪称人生；另一方神情忧郁的无神论者又渴望坟墓，总觉得那个死亡的世界太遥远。当他们坐下来用餐时，有时定会对自己的极端态度感到羞愧。真的，一顿佳肴、一瓶美酒就足以回答很多经典哲学著作讨论的这个难题。当一个人心系佳肴时，他准会忘掉那一大堆诡辩言辞，而会让思想畅游生活的梦幻之乡。死亡可能正在叩门，恰如《唐璜》中的雕像前来叩门一样；谢天谢地，我们手头有其他事可忙，且让它来叩门吧！

报丧的钟声在世界各地响起。在世界各地，每小时都有人与痛苦告别，和欢快分手。我们同样躲不开死亡的陷阱。但是我们热爱生命，没有闲心去把玩死亡的恐惧。生命对我们自始至终是一个蜜月，一个算不上长的蜜月。如果我们把心全给了我们这个光彩四射的新娘，给了欲望，给了荣耀，给了好奇，给了因饱览风光而生的快乐，给了对自身敏捷躯体的自尊自傲，也请不要责怪我们。

我们都喜爱切身去感知体验，但是"永恒可能性"这抽象的玩意儿，若不到头发已秃、感官迟钝，我们是不会去把玩它的。无论我们把生活看作是一条死胡同，用法国人的话说，仅是一个兜住底的袋子，还是把生活看成教堂更衣室或体育馆，我们在那里排队等

turn and prepare our faculties for some more noble destiny;[56] whether we thunder in a pulpit, or pule in little atheistic poetry-books, about its vanity and brevity; whether we look justly for years of health and vigour, or are about to mount into a Bath-chair, as a step towards the hearse; in each and all of these views and situations there is but one conclusion possible: that a man should stop his ears against paralysing terror,[57] and run the race that is set before him with a single mind. No one surely could have recoiled with more heartache and terror from the thought of death than our respected lexicographer;[58] and yet we know how little it affected his conduct, how wisely and boldly he walked,[59] and in what a fresh and lively vein he spoke of life. Already an old man, he ventured on his Highland tour;[60] and his heart, bound with triple brass, did not recoil before twenty-seven individual cups of tea.[61] As courage and intelligence are the two qualities best worth a good man's cultivation, so it is the first part[62] of intelligence to recognise our precarious estate[63] in life, and the first part of courage to be not at all abashed before the fact. A frank and somewhat headlong carriage, not looking too anxiously before, not dallying in maudlin regret over the past, stamps the man who is well armoured for this world.[64]

候，为更高尚的命运准备上场，抑或我们在讲道坛上高声咆哮，或在无神论的诗书里，就人生的虚荣与短暂而低声哭泣，抑或我们仅求数载体魄健康、活力充沛的人生，或者我们即将坐上轮椅，免得一步到位进入灵柩，不管是何种情况，只有一个可能的结果：一个人应该把令人发抖的恐惧抛诸脑后，专心地去跑完他眼前的赛程。没有人会像我们尊敬的词典学家那样因怕死而如此痛苦恐慌。可是我们都知道，他的行为很少受死亡影响，他生活的路走得既智慧又勇敢，说起生活来也轻松坦然。老年的他竟踏上了苏格兰高地之旅，他的心，像是被三重盔甲保护着，面对二十七杯茶水绝不畏惧退缩。勇气和智慧是好人教养中最值得培养的两种气质，所以认识到生命中的危险是最重要的智慧，而能坦然面对事实则是人最关键的勇气。性格坦率，略显冒失，前瞻不烦躁焦虑，后顾不伤怀悔恨，有了这些气质，就标志面对世界这个战场，他已盔甲齐备，可以上场了。

注 释

34. 这里的 a match flickers 本来有两个意思，一个是短暂，一个是不稳定，都源于火柴点燃后的形象。一般火柴划着后，一瞬间就烧到尽头，归于熄灭；另一个形象是燃烧的火苗摇摆不定。这两个意思在词典的定义中都有，如 Merriam-Webster 词典的一个定义就是："to appear or pass briefly or quickly"。Collins 词典的一个解释是："If a light or flame flickers, it shines unsteadily"。在我们的语境中都有些符合，但作者的用意似乎偏重形容人生短暂。

35. 这里的三个排比（Is it not…, is it not…, is it not…）构成了写作的一个局部特征，虽和文章的整体或主题无关，但仍有必要在翻译中保留排比。另外，这里的 in the highest sense of human speech 很难直译，因为那样读者会看不懂是什么意思。似乎没有其他人这么用过，与这个说法最接近的是 in the highest sense of the word，如 "Christ is called 'Saviour' in the highest sense of the word"，这话的意思是基督就是救星，就是这个词的本义，没有什么夸张忽悠的成分。所以我们可以根据这个，把这句改写成 in the highest sense of the word "incredible"，甚至可说成是 in the literal sense of "incredible"，因此这里翻译成了"简直有点不可思议"。

36. 这里的 the sheet 是指船上拿在手里控制风帆的绳子，因此后面的 making it fast 就是把这绳子绑起来，这样也就不会错误理解成"船跑得快"，因为是 make the sheet fast 和船没有关系。fast 这个词最常用的意思是 quick，但还有其他意思（firmly

fastened），如"I have seen the Mohawk River fast frozen on the 10th of November"或"Stand fast in the faith"等都表示稳固不动的意思。这个词到底是"快"的意思还是"稳"的意思，要看语境。

37. 后面的 consequences 比较好理解，就是死亡对他人造成的后果，但是前面的 its circumstances 翻译成"境遇""境况"等词典中常见的词都不怎么合适。这个词在这里指的是死亡的一些征象，很像法律用语中的 circumstantial evidence，可以理解成 evidence，就是说这些征象的出现证实了死亡，如没有呼吸、人体僵冷，等等。作者是想说，我们其实对于什么是死亡一无所知，仅仅能从这些征象或证据中断定人已经死了。

38. 这里点到的作家或作品都是很有名的。《约伯记》（The Book of Job）是《圣经》中的第一部诗篇性著作，也是《圣经》全书中最古老的书籍之一，大约写于公元前 2000 年至前 1800 年。奥玛珈音（Omar Khayyam）是中世纪时期的波斯诗人，同时也是数学家、天文学家、哲学家。他的《鲁拜集》（*Rubâ'iyât*）广为人知，经英国作家爱德华·菲茨杰拉德（Edward FitzGerald）翻译成英文后，在英语世界也享有盛名，汉译本多如牛毛，郭沫若、梁实秋等大家也都有译文，但是麻省理工学院物理学教授黄克孙的绝句体《鲁拜集》似乎影响颇大。托马斯·卡莱尔是苏格兰哲学家和作家，堪称 19 世纪英国散文的先驱者。沃尔特·惠特曼（Walt Whitman）是 19 世纪美国诗人，其《草叶集》（*Leaves of Grass*, 1855）是美国文学中有相当地位的作品，作者也因此诗集而声名鹊起。另外要注意的是，作者在这里点了四个作家的名字，来说明文学对生命的诠释，但是 from... to... 这个结构说明作者这里仅仅是举例，其实还有其他很多作家都在诠释生命，因此译文还是保留了"从……到……"这个结构。作者虽然非常喜欢这些作家，但是在这个上下文里，他仍然认为，这些文学对生命的诠释只从宏观着眼（with such largeness of view），太远离生活（rise from the consideration of living），太抽象（to the Definition of Life）。

39. 这个 about 表示的意思和 approximately 相同，就是说这些智者在他们力所能及的范围内给了我们最能让我们满意的有关生命的答案，但是作者毕竟不那么确定，所以他用了 about，也就是大致是最令人满意的智慧言论。这个和"I stayed in that house about three years"中的 about 是同样的意思。

40. 这里的 a vapour, or a show, or made out of the same stuff with dreams 是西方文学中常见到的，典故可追溯到西方经典作品，如《圣经》、莎士比亚戏剧等，如"For what is your life? It is even a vapour, that appeareth for a little time, and then vanisheth away."（James 4: 14），或"Life's but a walking shadow, a poor player, | That struts and frets his hour upon the stage, | And then is heard no more."（Shakespeare, *Macbeth,* V. 5. 23–5），再如"We are such stuff | As dreams are made on"（Shakespeare, *The Tempest,* IV. 1. 156–7）。

41. 这个 Permanent Possibility of Sensation 应该是出自约翰·穆勒（John Stuart Mill）的著作 *Examination of Sir William Hamilton's Philosophy*, Vol. I, Chap. XI: "Matter, then, may be defined, a Permanent Possibility of Sensation"。从这个引文中可以看出，穆勒是在定义 matter，并不是定义 life，但是作者借用来形容生命了。

42. 这句是说，我们当然热爱生命，但我们不贪生怕死，也就是说，否定的是后半句，是对 preoccupied about its conservation 的否定。我们并不是每分钟都在担心生命是否会失去，并不是谨小慎微，仅为着留住生命而活。

43. 这句中的 providence 当然不是上帝的意思，因为这个词的第一个字母没有大写，所以不是专有名词。这个词不指上帝或其他宗教意思时常表示"谨慎"的意思。但是如果我们把这句和下面一句"no man's eyes are fixed entirely on the passing hour"连起来看，这个 providence 的意思似乎还可以稍微扩大一下。后面那句的 passing hour 应该是指当下的时刻，而前句和后句是有逻辑联系的。所以我们可以将 providence 理解为审慎和前瞻，不只盯住当下（not fixed entirely on the passing hour），而是往前看（look ahead）。其实这两个词是有联系的，谨慎的人总是有前瞻性，把可能发生的事都放在计划中。Collins 词典中的一个定义把这两层意思都包括在里面："the foresight or care exercised by a person in the management of his affairs or resources"。OED 在解释这个词的意思时恰恰用了斯蒂文森的这句话做例子。

44. 上一注释中说过这个 passing hour 是表示 the present moment 的意思，而不是"流逝的时间"。只有这样理解才能和上下文连贯起来：前一句是说最不细心的人也会有前瞻计划（enter some degree of providence），接下来说没有人会完全只关注当下（not entirely fixed on the passing hour），再接下来转折一下说，尽管我们有些前瞻和期待（have some anticipation of good health...），可那种前瞻并不是抽象的宏观视野（the sum of these anticipations does not amount to anything like a general view）。

45. 这个 have active employment 表示有事做，特指为做事而做事，不是为报酬而做事。比如别人问你,今天下午有事儿吗?你可以回答说"I have some active employment. I am going to mow the lawn."。

46. 作者是不认同这个 a general view of life's possibilities and issues 的,因为这个宏观的观点太抽象,也就是前面那些智者的抽象定义。而所有那些对具体的好事物的期盼,比如期盼好身体、期盼好酒等等,虽然并不立足于当下,也是对未来的期盼,但却都是具体的,不是关于人生可能和人生议题这种不着边际的抽象概念。这句前面的 self-approval 可以理解为可以使自己得意骄傲的事物。

47. 这句的正常语序是 those who cherish them most vividly are not at all the most scrupulous of their personal safety。scrupulous 这个词有过度仔细的意思(extremely attentive to details),也可解释为 very concerned to avoid doing wrong,大意和汉语的"如履薄冰"很接近。最后,cherish them 中的 them 是指前面提到的 anticipations。

48. 没有查到这个词组,但就算是没有 against a straw 的可靠解释,根据上下文,还是能看出整个短语就是冒险的意思。

49. 这里想指出的是 reducing 和后面的 yearning 这两个非谓语动词形式。其实这两个词正好是冒号前面双方(both sides)说的恶言乱语(nonsense)的具体例子,所以分别在前面加上"一方面"和"另一方面"也未必不可。另外就是 tearing 这个词的意思怎么表达。这个词当然可以理解成流眼泪的意思,但是在使用这个词前,还得看看语境,看看在这个上下文中"流眼泪"是否最合适。根据上下文,似乎我们还应该再去寻找其他意思。查网上的牛津词典有这样一个定义:"violent;

extreme",给的例句是"he did seem to be in a tearing hurry"和"the tearing wind"。查 OED 则有些不常见的词义,如"headstrong, passionate; ranting, roistering; boisterous, rollicking, exuberant"。从这个语境看,ranting 这个词义比较合适(speaking at length in an angry and impassioned way)。其实这个词义和哭泣也是同源的,因为都是基于强烈的情绪。至于 the dimensions of a mere funeral procession 这个词组和前面的 Life 非常容易从 Life is a journey 这个角度理解,即送葬是一段路程,人生也是一段路程。但是这样理解不够准确,因为不是 reduce life to a funeral procession,而是 reduce life to dimensions,但 dimensions 是复数,不可能形成 journey 的图像。这里的 dimensions 应该理解成 sizes,那么认知图像就应该是立体的,而不是一条线。这样理解的话,后面的 so short 就应理解成 dimensions are so short,而不是 procession is so short,所以这个 short 在这个 dimensions 的语境中应该理解成 narrow,换句话说,送葬队伍(暗指人生之途)的"规模"是狭窄的。那么在什么意义上是"狭窄"的呢?斯蒂文森反对这种极端宗教的观点,因为在斯蒂文森看来,生活是繁复多趣的、广阔的,但是这些宗教人士却把生活看得非常狭窄,通往天堂的路也是非常狭窄(short)的,很多可以去尝试的事,在这些人眼里都是越了雷池,超出了那个可允许的范围。因此,在作者看来,广阔的人生被他们压缩在狭隘的空间里,实在很难堪称是人生了(so short as to be hardly decent)。至于 decent 一词最保险的译法就是"体面""有尊严",但它的核心词义就是达到或符合某事物的要求,可接受的,不错的,所以未必一定要用"体面"这样的词翻译,结合全句的意思,用"堪称"

似乎也可以，因为"堪称"就是达到一定要求的意思。

50. a world too far away 的解释应该是这样的：这些不信奉神的人渴望死亡（yearning for the tomb），所以这个 too far away 就是这些人的观点，由于他们渴望坟墓，所以就觉得 tomb 那个世界太远（too far away），真希望它早日到来。

51. 有 answer 就说明有问题。那么这到底是个什么问题呢？这个问题就是很多经典抽象著作（standard works）经常讨论的问题，即"What is life all about?"或"What is the purpose of life?"而答案就是佳肴美酒，就是从享用美酒佳肴而来的满足，那些哲学思辨见鬼去吧（forgets a great deal of sophistry），酒醉梦乡的满足（下一句的 rosy zone of contemplation）就是人生大问题的答案。这里 contemplation 应该不是以思考为主的精神活动，而是接近 daydreaming 的思维活动。另外，most standard works 应该理解为"most 'standard works'"，most 是数量的修饰（most works），而非程度的修饰（most standard），也就是说，作者没有把所有的 standard works 都看作是可以由美酒佳肴取代的。此处的 standard 最好不翻译成"标准的"，这个词就是指那些最受尊敬的、最被接受的抽象哲学或宗教著作，如休谟（David Hume）的著作。这里将 standard works 翻译成"经典著作"。

52. 这个 the Commander's statue 典自西班牙中世纪的民间传说，传说大致是这样的：唐璜曾诱惑一位来自贵族家庭的少女，并且杀害了她的父亲。然后唐璜在进入一处坟场时遇到贵族少女父亲的雕像，他邀请其回家与他吃晚餐，雕像就高兴地答应了邀请。贵族少女父亲的幽灵参加了晚餐，并请求与唐璜握手，当唐璜伸臂的时候，他就被拖下至地狱。这个故事在莫里哀的《唐璜》中也有讲述。但是有的文学研究者认为，斯蒂文森写这句话的时候，还可能想到了剧作家科利·西伯（Colley Cibber）写给小说家塞缪尔·理查森（Samuel Richardson）的信。这封信中有与本语境相关的文字："Though Death has been cooling his heels at my door these three weeks, I have not had time to see him. The daily conversation of my friends has kept me so agreeably alive, that I have not passed my time better a great while. If you have a mind to make one of us, I will order Death to come another day"。

53. 这里的 trap（For us also the trap is laid）指的就是死亡。前面说，全世界的人都在和痛苦和欢快告别，我们也不例外，我们也避免不了死亡，所以才说 also。

54. 这里的 small blame to us 是说，如果我们把心全给了我们这个光彩四射的新娘，给了我们热爱做的事，那也没有什么不对的，也不用责怪我们。这一长句中有好几个由 to 构成的短语（to this glowing…, to the appetites, to honour, to the hungry…, to the pleasure…），它们构成一种表达上的排比特征，所以在翻译时保留下来也是译者可以努力的方向，这里就用一系列的"给了"来反映这种排比（"给了我们这个光彩四射的新娘，给了欲望，给了荣耀，给了好奇，给了因饱览风光而生的快乐，给了对自身敏捷躯体的自尊自傲"）。

55. 这个 mere bag's end 是法语的隐喻，也就是 a dead wall 的意思，法语原文是 a cul de sac，汉语就是"死胡同"的意思。

56. 这句中的 vestibule 原本的意思是建筑物本体和建筑物外之间的一个小空间，是一个从外面进来或从里面出去过程中的一个过渡空间。这个词从词源上看，似乎有衣服的意思，vestibule

中的 vest 就是背心的意思，所以这个房间也常指教堂里供牧师上场讲道前更换衣服的地方，其功能和后面的体育馆中运动员在一个房间里更换衣服等待上场一样。总的来说，这就是一个等待的空间，这里是指有些哲学家把人的一生比喻成去更高尚之处（for some more noble destiny）的一个等待过程或言过渡空间。

57. 这里的 stop his ears 可以用一个动作表示，就是用手捂住耳朵，不让恐惧的声音进入耳朵（against paralysing terror）。

58. 这句中说的词典学家就是塞缪尔·约翰逊（Samuel Johnson），在鲍斯韦尔（James Boswell）的《约翰逊传》中，他多次提到约翰逊非常怕死亡，一想到死亡就惧怕无比（with more heartache and terror），本句就是说没有人会像他那样谈死色变。

59. 这句紧接上句。上句说约翰逊非常怕死，但即便是那样一个怕死的人也很少让死亡影响他的行动（how little it affected his conduct）。这里的 yet 是一个明确的转折词。至于说后半句的 how wisely and boldly he walked，仅从字面意思理解似乎不很合适，也就是说，这个 walked 所指的并非字面意义的走路，而是隐喻意义的走路，即他在人生的道路上走路，这样 wisely 和 boldly 解释起来都比较到位，这里翻译成"他生活的路走得既智慧又勇敢"。

60. 这里的 Highland tour 是指约翰逊 1773 年到苏格兰高地的访问。作者用这个例子说明约翰逊虽然很怕死亡，但是在行动上他仍然很勇敢，因为苏格兰高地环境严峻，一般上了年纪的人是不愿意去的。

61. 在鲍斯韦尔的传记中，他反复提到约翰逊喜欢大量喝水，所以这里的 twenty-seven individual cups 应该就是指他大量喝水。

这个数字 27 应该没有特殊意义，目前也没有查到 27 这个数字的出处。由于前面的动词是 recoil，所以面对 27 杯水的意思就是不畏惧（not recoil），而且这句前后都是在提约翰逊不怕困难，有勇气。关于喝水的杯数，有人在《纽约时报》（October 15, 1898）上发表过责怪斯蒂文森的文章，说应该是 24 杯，斯蒂文森凭空给加了三杯。另外这句中的 triple brass 正好是文章的题目，是全文中唯一一次用到的题目，表示有三重甲武装，就更不怕困难，不会退缩了。

62. the first part (of intelligence) 并不是表示具体的次序，而是表示重要性，也就是说 first in terms of importance（认识到生命中的危险是最重要的智慧）。

63. 在这个语境中，estate 表示 state 的意思。

64. 一般情况下，before 指时间常指过去，如 three days before，但此处 before（not looking too anxiously before）并不表示过去，而是表示未来，即看未来也不焦虑。这句下面的 well armoured，基本意思就指前面的 "headlong carriage, not looking too anxiously before, not dallying in maudlin regret over the past"，属于个人的性格和气质，那么 well armoured 可以意译成"修身完善"。但后来考虑到"修身"一词所具有的东方哲学含义（陶冶身心、涵养德性），加之本文的题目是"三重甲"，是以古代战争中的盔甲为隐喻基础的，所以最后还是用直译法保留了 well armoured 原文的隐喻（盔甲齐备），同时把 for this world 的隐喻明确化，点名这个世界是个战场。在"世界"前添加"战场"的依据恰恰是 armoured 这个词。不在战场打仗是不用穿戴盔甲的。当然也可以不添加，把联想的过程留给读者。

Aes Triplex (3)

And not only well armoured for himself, but a good friend and a good citizen to boot[65]. We do not go to cowards for tender dealing; there is nothing so cruel as panic; the man who has least fear for his own carcass, has most time to consider others. That eminent chemist who took his walks abroad in tin shoes, and subsisted wholly upon tepid milk, had all his work cut out for him in considerate dealings with his own digestion.[66] So soon as prudence has begun to grow up in the brain, like a dismal fungus, it finds its first expression in a paralysis of generous acts.[67] The victim begins to shrink spiritually; he develops a fancy for parlours with a regulated temperature, and takes his morality on the principle of tin shoes and tepid milk. The care of one important body or soul becomes so engrossing, that all the noises of the outer world begin to come thin and faint into the parlour with the regulated temperature; and the tin shoes go equably forward over blood and rain.[68] To be overwise is to ossify;[69] and the scruple-monger ends by standing stockstill. Now the man who has his heart on his sleeve,[70] and a good whirling weathercock of a brain,[71] who reckons his life as a thing to be dashingly used and cheerfully hazarded, makes a very different acquaintance of the world, keeps all his pulses going true and fast, and gathers impetus as he runs, until, if he be running towards anything better than wildfire,[72] he may shoot up and become a constellation in the end.[73] Lord look after his health, Lord have[74] a care of his soul, says he; and

三重甲（三）

　　而且他不仅自己装备齐全，还能成为别人的好朋友，国家的好公民。求仁义相待，是不能去求懦夫的；没有比大惊失色更残酷无情的了。一个人忘我才能利他。那位穿锡鞋在外行走，靠温奶维持生命的杰出药剂师已经有事忙了，他要细心周到地照料自己的消化过程，无心顾及他人。一旦谨小慎微如阴郁的真菌开始在他头脑中滋长，慷慨大方的行动便开始消失。受害者的精神便开始萎缩。他会迷恋起温控的客厅，遵循起穿锡鞋喝温奶者所崇尚的道德准则。他孜孜于一己之身躯与灵魂，以至于身外的喧嚣一经温室过滤，进入的噪音已相当微弱，结果穿锡鞋者居然不顾街上的血泊水坑悠然前行。过度聪慧谨慎的人会凝固不动。极度瞻前顾后的人最终反而寸步难行。一个人若胸襟袒露，思维能敏捷应变，勇于将生命付诸使用，笑对危险，那么他和这个世界的关系就大不同于前者了。这样的人矢志不移、情感激昂，一路走来，动力倍增，而只要他前进的目标并非幻象，那他就可能会直冲云霄，最终成为灿烂的星辰。他求上帝照顾他的健康，抚慰他的灵魂，接着他便直攻要塞，为达目的，一路上与逆境与危险死命拼搏。死亡带着锋利的兵刃，匍匐在他的四周，正如死

he has at the key of the position,[75] and swashes through incongruity and peril towards his aim. Death is on all sides of him with pointed batteries,[76] as he is on all sides of all of us;[77] unfortunate surprises gird him round; mim-mouthed friends[78] and relations hold up their hands in quite a little elegiacal synod about his path:[79] and what cares he for all this? Being a true lover of living, a fellow with something pushing and spontaneous in his inside, he must, like any other soldier, in any other stirring, deadly warfare, push on at his best pace until he touch the goal. "A peerage or Westminster Abbey!" cried Nelson in his bright, boyish, heroic manner.[80] These are great incentives;[81] not for any of these, but for the plain satisfaction of living, of being about their business in some sort or other, do the brave, serviceable men of every nation tread down the nettle danger,[82] and pass flyingly over all the stumbling-blocks of prudence.[83] Think of the heroism of Johnson, think of that superb indifference to mortal limitation that set him upon his dictionary, and carried him through triumphantly until the end! Who, if he were wisely considerate of things at large,[84] would ever embark upon any work much more considerable than a halfpenny post card?[85] Who would project a serial novel,[86] after Thackeray and Dickens had each fallen in mid-course?[87] Who would find heart enough to begin to live, if he dallied with the consideration of death?

And, after all, what sorry and pitiful quibbling all this is![88] To forego all the issues of living in a parlour with a regulated temperature[89]—as if that were not to die a hundred times over, and for ten years at a stretch! As if it were not to die in one's own lifetime, and without even the sad immunities of death! As if it were not to die, and yet be the patient spectators of our own pitiable change![90] The Permanent Possibility is preserved, but the

亡也在我们四周一样。他真是惊险环绕、祸患四伏；亲友们也一本正经地聚在一起对他之所为七嘴八舌故作忧虑状。他对这些作何反应呢？作为一个真正热爱生活的人，胸中涌动着激情，他就必须像任何其他战士一样，在任何其他一场殊死激战中那样，奋力冲锋向前，直到抵达目标。"不爵位加身，就西敏葬身！"纳尔逊在战前誓言高亢，语调中带着青春活力和英雄气概。上面这些都是激励人的高远目标；但任何国度里那些勇敢的有用之人也都会把恼人的危险踩在脚下，成功跨越谨小慎微在他们路上竖起的障碍，他们这样并不是为了达到那些高远的目标，而只是求生活的简单满足，求在平凡生活中打理营生的快乐。想想词典学家约翰逊的英勇之举，眼前是一个巨大的字典工程，他却体力不济，可他无视困境，坚持到底，终于成功！如果一个人智慧谨慎、思前想后，谁还愿意做任何一项大于写明信片的工程？在萨克雷和狄更斯大作未成身先死之后，谁还会再来写连载小说？而假如人总让死亡萦绕，谁还会有勇气开启生活？

但说到底，上面这些语焉不详的长篇大论该是何等地可悲可怜！让我们放弃生活在温控房间里的所有益处。在温控房子里你仿佛能一住十年，避开百余次死亡！仿佛能一生避开死亡，甚至无需死亡保护你，让你免遭痛楚。在温控房子里仿佛能避开死亡，还能耐心地旁观自己可悲的变化。永恒的可能性是被保留住了，但是体验感知却被精心地拒之门外，仿佛一个人在暗室里存着一张照相底片，根本就没

sensations carefully held at arm's length, as if one kept a photographic plate in a dark chamber.[91] It is better to lose health like a spendthrift than to waste it like a miser. It is better to live and be done with it,[92] than to die daily in the sickroom. By all means begin your folio;[93] even if the doctor does not give you a year, even if he hesitates about a month, make one brave push and see what can be accomplished in a week. It is not only in finished undertakings that we ought to honour useful labour. A spirit goes out of the man who means execution, which outlives the most untimely ending.[94] All who have meant good work with their whole hearts, have done good work,[95] although they may die before they have the time to sign it.[96] Every heart that has beat strong and cheerfully has left a hopeful impulse behind it in the world, and bettered the tradition of mankind. And even if death catch people, like an open pitfall, and in mid-career, laying out vast projects, and planning monstrous foundations, flushed with hope, and their mouths full of boastful language, they should be at once tripped up and silenced:[97] is there not something brave and spirited in such a termination? and does not life go down with a better grace, foaming in full body over a precipice, than miserably straggling to an end in sandy deltas?[98] When the Greeks made their fine saying that those whom the gods love die young,[99] I cannot help believing they had this sort of death also in their eye.[100] For surely, at whatever age it overtake the man, this is to die young.[101] Death has not been suffered to take so much as an illusion from his heart.[102] In the hot-fit of life, a tip-toe on the highest point of being, he passes at a bound on to the other side.[103] The noise of the mallet and chisel is scarcely quenched,[104] the trumpets are hardly done blowing, when, trailing with him clouds of glory,[105] this happy-starred, full-blooded spirit shoots into the spiritual land.[106]

有曝光。与其像守财奴那样白白浪费健康，还不如像挥霍者那样失去健康。与其每日在病房里慢慢死去，不如活出生命，潇洒走完一场。务必开始你的作品；就算医生说你活不到一年，甚至他不确定你还有一月，再去努力一搏，看看一周内能有何收获。我们不是仅用成果来表彰有益的劳动。放手去做的人是有精神的，而只要去做，即便出师未捷，精神仍可长存。意欲全心投入出色工作的人已做了出色的工作，尽管他们很可能看不到项目竣工。每一颗强力、愉快跳动的心都在这个世界里带出希望的脉动，改善人类的传统。而即便死亡能像一个大陷阱，在人们事业如日中天，眼前项目待举，正打算为巨大工程奠基动工时，在他们充满希望，口出豪言壮语时，把他们带走了，即便他们立马倒下，马上沉寂，即便是那样，你难道不觉得那样结束生命不乏英雄气概吗？一边是浪花飞溅直冲断壁悬崖结束生命，一边是茫无目标在沙洲上痛苦前行了此一生，两相比照，哪个更精彩，岂不显而易见？希腊人说得好，神爱的人早逝。我不禁觉得，他们说这话时想到的就是这种死亡吧！确实，不管是在什么年龄，要是这样热烈地死，那都堪称早逝。这样的人不会让死亡从他的心里带走什么，一个幻影都不让拿走。在人生激情四射的那一刻，他站在生命的巅峰上，一跃便到了另一世界。工作用的槌子和凿子声音犹在耳，战斗中的号角声仍在回响，身后是灿烂的云霞，这个心情快乐、精力充沛的精灵拔地而起，直冲向那个精神的家园。

注 释

65. 这里的 to boot 就是 in addition 的意思，比如 "She has a big house, an expensive car, and a holiday villa in Italy to boot."。

66. 这里的 that eminent chemist 是特指苏格兰医生兼化学家、化学元素镁的发现者 Joseph Black。此人谨小慎微，走路时在皮鞋外另套一双金属鞋，以保护自己，同时注意牛奶的温度，具体见 *Literary Gazette 1751*（10 Aug 1950, 564）。这个 work cut out for him 表示已经有做不完的工作等着他去忙了，什么工作呢？工作就是 considerate dealings with his own digestion，说明这位化学家会把精力都放在关心自己的消化上，没有时间或精力去照看帮助别人，前面那句恰恰是说会照顾别人的人（the man who has least fear for his own carcass, has most time to consider others）。这句有夸张幽默的味道。最后 walks abroad 就是在外边走，不要理解成到国外去。

67. 这句看上去很复杂，但其想表达的基本意思就是 as soon as one becomes prudent, one stops being generous。换句话说就是，一个人越谨慎，就越不慷慨。like a dismal fungus 是一个隐喻，暗示这个谨慎有蔓延的倾向。而 first expression 表示最先出现的迹象，和前面的 so soon as 相呼应，而 paralysis of generous acts 也是隐喻。paralysis 表示无力、软弱、瘫痪、不能行动的意思，提示不能做慷慨之事。

68. 这句中前面半句描写了一个与外界隔绝的环境，温控的房间里不受外界的影响，而后半句应该和前半句前后呼应。穿锡鞋的人向前走，但街上有雨水、有鲜血，但是即便这样他还是往前走，而且走得 equably，不受影响。equable 这个词在 Collins 词典中的解释是 "If you describe someone as equable, you mean that they are calm, cheerful, and fair with other people, even in difficult circumstances"，也就是说，能平静地走，不受外界（blood and rain）的干扰，和前半句与外界隔绝相呼应。至于最后的 over blood and rain 应该指街上坑中的水，还有地上的血。水的解释简单，是因为下雨，但是街上有血暗示社会革命，战斗中的流血。

69. ossify 这个词是变成骨头的意思（骨化），这里表示固化不动的意思，和后半句意思接近。而 to be overwise 除了表示过度聪明外，结合上下文，还可以引申出过度聪明的结果，即过度谨慎。添加这个语境意思估计不会偏离原文太远，但译者如果感到读者应该自己去理解，不想包办代理，那就不要添加。这也许就是让读者走近译者，还是让译者走近读者的选择吧？

70. 这个 has his heart on his sleeve 表示公开表达自己的意思，不隐瞒，见莎士比亚的戏剧："I will wear my heart upon my sleeve" (*Othello*, I. 1. 64)。

71. 这个 whirling weathercock of a brain 显然是个隐喻，weathercock 是房子上测定风速风向的仪器，看上去就是一只铁做的公鸡。OED 相关的隐喻定义是 "of persons; esp. one who is changeable or inconstant"，如 "He was a terrible weathercock in the matter of opinion"，但用在这里没有上面例句的负面意思，而是表示大脑能灵活反应，能对风（对环境）做出迅速的反应（receptive to the wind），可以翻译成"思维能敏捷应变"。

72. 本句中的 pulses going true and fast 很费解，因为有的词词义模棱两可。首先 pulses 在这个上下文中应该是当隐喻用，根据 OED 应该是指"something that denotes or indicates vitality, energy, tendency, or feeling"或者 the life force。但是后面的 true 比较麻烦。首先这个 true 和 fast 都是用来形容 pulses 的，也就是形容人的性格、情感、精神、精力。那么在 OED 中至少有两个定义都和这个语境有关，一个是"of a person, a person's character, etc.: honourable, virtuous, trustworthy; honest. Also of an action, feeling, etc.: sincere, unfeigned"；另一个是"of the wind: steady, constant, without variation in direction or force"。前一个更适合形容那个人的正直，后一个更适合形容那个人在这个语境中的特征。此人在本语境中是在向一个目标挺进（and gathers impetus as he runs… running towards anything better than wildfire），所以 true 就是在前进路上没有变化（without variation in direction），尽管有风浪（wind），仍然勇往直前。翻译时如果能把第一个定义也包含进去更好，但不必勉强。至于 fast 也会有不同解释，如有人认为是 securely 的意思（见本文注释 36），这样就和 true 有协同效果，两个词相辅相成。但这个词是在修饰 pulses，表示一个人的活力，而这个人正在向前冲，所以仍然觉得 fast 解释成最原本的意思"快速"更合理。整个一句处理成"这样的人矢志不移、情感激昂"，应符合原文的大意。这类文本已经穿越 100 多年的时空，解读起来有些歧义也不足奇，但译者还是应该尽量把意思搞清楚。建议多用 OED。另外，最后面的 wildfire 表示 illusion 的意思（real vs. fantasy），也就是你追求的目标只要是真实的目标，不是一个完全脱离现实的幻象（fantasy or illusion），那么你就能有所成就。

73. 这一句主要是说，只要你能像前面那么做，你就有可能做出令人瞩目的成就。这里的 a constellation 是指天上的星星。在 Collins 词典中也指 a gathering of brilliant or famous people or things；在有些民间传说或寓言中，成功的英雄会成为天上的星星。

74. 这里的 Lord have 应该看作是祷告语言，可以在前面加上一个 may（May Lord look after his health）。

75. 这里的 has at 是个词组，表示攻击的意思，就是 tackle or attack forcefully or aggressively 的意思，比如 somehow we thought we had to have at each other。介词 at 总会带有攻击性在里面。最好的一个例子就是 throw a ball to someone 和 throw a ball at someone 的区别，前者可带玩耍的意思，但是后面的介词 at 就暗含不友好、有敌意的意思在里面。另外这句中的 the key of the position 可指攻击的要害之处，如要塞，也就是你奋斗的主要目标。

76. 我们比较熟悉名词 battery，一般是指电池。但是这个词还有其他意思，比如它可以指 a range of something（children given a battery of tests），但在这里的 pointed batteries 是指对准敌人的大炮，泛指武器。

77. 这里的代词 he，按照语法应用 it，但是根据上下文语境，应该是指前面的 death，就是说，死亡不仅在他四周，也在我们四周。也许作者是将 death 拟人化，才用了 he。

78. 这里的 mim-mouthed 是苏格兰语，在《简明苏格兰语词典》（*Concise Scots Dictionary*）中是这样解释的：affectedly prim or demure in speaking or eating。指言语矫揉造作，故作惊讶状。

79. 这句表示他的亲朋对他这样一意孤行的态度，这些人的言谈做作，他们聚在一起（synod）对于他的前途（his path）深表忧虑（elegiacal）。hold up hands 是一种手势，用在悲伤等场合，向上伸出双手，表示无奈等心情。手势的文化特征很强，某个文化中的一个手势在另外一个文化中解读起来可能完全相反。翻译研究中的经典例子不少，如一般摇头表示否定的意思，但据说有的文化点头是否定。更著名的是奈达的握手和亲面颊的例子，西方人有些人握手打招呼，中东地方的一些男子见面亲面颊也是在打招呼，完全不同于西方男人的举动。我们不想笼统地谈手势等文化符号的翻译，而是倾向就事论事，看具体的语境，看这个手势符号是否有意义。比如这句中的 hold up 完全是用来表意的，符号形式本身虽提供原语文化的行为特点，但没有很大意义，翻译时就并非一定要保留。

80. 这里的 Nelson 就是英国最著名的海军将领纳尔逊（Horatio Nelson, 1758—1805），他雄心勃勃，在尼罗河战役（1798）前对下属说"Before this time to-morrow I shall have gained a peerage or Westminster Abbey"。这个 peerage 指爵位，而 Westminster Abbey 即威斯敏斯特教堂，也译西敏寺。这个教堂是英国国王或女王加冕的地方，但同时不少有身份的人也埋葬在这里。在纳尔逊这句话里，这个教堂就指在这里埋葬。这句话很像汉语中的"不成功则成仁"，但是是否可以使用这个中文的成语翻译，就值得仔细考虑。在这个问题上，可能会出现不同的意见，比如有人主张汉化，认为这样不仅意思正确，而且也大大提高了可读性，但很多人就可能持相反观点，认为汉化翻译会把原文的文化特征完全抹杀。我比较倾向于后者，但也觉得一字不变的翻译不能达到传达意义的目的（要么爵位，要么西敏寺），读者仍然不知道去西敏寺是干什么。所以不妨保留原文的爵位和西敏寺，但把去西敏寺的目的说出来：不爵位加身，就西敏葬身。另外，这句里的 boyish 如果翻译成"童稚"，表面很准确，但是在这个语境中未必合适。要知道他是在尼罗河战役前说的这话，当时他已 40 岁，接下来的词是充满英雄气概的 heroic，所以总觉得搭配欠妥。查在线牛津词典，有这样一个定义"of, like, or characteristic of a male child or young man"，也就是说它也可以指青年，换句话说，一个近 40 岁的人看上去仍然像个青少年，要比一个近 40 岁的人看上去仍像个男孩更符合语境，所以这里翻译成"青春"。其实原文的三个形容词 bright, boyish, heroic 未必需要还原成三个，这个译文中只用了两个（青春活力和英雄气概），但其实包含了三个形容词的意思（bright 对应活力，boyish 表示青春，heroic 对应英雄）。最后要说的是，这位纳尔逊在发誓"要么爵位，要么西敏寺"后确实因战功而获得爵位，但是七年后在另外一次西班牙的战役中战死，却没有安葬在西敏寺，而是安葬在伦敦的圣保罗大教堂。

81. 这个 great incentives 应该是指前面提到的大事业，比如像纳尔逊将军的事业，那种可以赌上一句"不成功则成仁"的大事业。接下来作者就要讲到普通人了。

82. 这句恢复到正常语序就是这样的：The brave, serviceable men of every nation tread down the nettle danger not for any of these, but for the plain satisfaction of living, of being about their business in some sort or other。这句就是在讲普通人。这里的 serviceable men 是指能积极做事的人。serviceable 在 Collins 词典中的解释是"If you describe something as serviceable, you mean that it is good enough to be used and to perform its function"，在线牛津词典中的定义是 functional and durable rather than attractive，有

一种中用未必中看的潜在含义。根据这些定义，这里可以解释成 active（people who are actively doing things or performing functions），甚至还可解释成 healthy（healthy enough to perform functions），把原定义中非主要潜在含义（rather than attractive）略去。另外 being about their business in some sort or other 就是指一个人日常生活中工作干事，也就是说，不用像纳尔逊那样求大功绩，就做好普通人该所的事，过普通人的生活，其中的 being about 是一个习惯用法，字典中有一个解释比较合适："to be actively engaged in something, especially a regular activity"。这句中的 satisfaction 最简单的译法就是满足，但由于出现两次，也许有的译者从行文考虑想变换一下，如前一个用满足，后一个用乐趣，这样似乎也可以，因为 satisfaction 的定义就是"<u>fulfillment</u> of one's wishes, expectations, or needs, or the <u>pleasure</u> derived from this"，其中包含 pleasure，但不要进一步过多引申，比如有的人加上"尝遍平凡生活中酸甜苦辣的满足"，尽管也不是完全离谱，因为原文的满足因人而异，未必都是快乐的事，但是这样添加似乎会有阐释过度之嫌。也许有人会允许这类添加，但我会在这种情况下"忍痛割爱"，译者有必要在翻译过程中时刻记住翻译和阐释间的一条线。至于 nettle danger 中的 nettle 是一种能刺痛人的植物，是讨厌恼人的意思，不过此句典自莎士比亚："Out of this nettle, danger, we pluck this flower safety"（从危险的荆棘里采下安全的花朵），见 Shakespeare, *1 Henry IV*, II. 3. 8-9。

83. 这里副词 flyingly 的本意就是"so as to fly; with light rapid movement"，说明动作轻盈迅速，提示轻而易举。但 Merriam-Webster 词典的一个定义更符合本文的语境，即 with flying

colors，就是 successfully 的意思。

84. 这里的 considerate of things at large 是指对生活的全面考虑（general view of life），或 in general、as a whole，也就是说方方面面都考虑到。这个 things at large 相对地就是针对一件具体的事。这部分大意就是，如果一个人聪明智慧（wisely）、仔细慎重（considerate）、全面考虑（at large），那他就不会动手去干某一项具体的事了。

85. 这个 a halfpenny post card 中的 halfpenny 就是半便士，表示明信片的价值很低，翻译的时候不译进去也不会影响大意，但会缺少细节。另外要注意这个明信片是放在萨克雷、狄更斯写作的语境中的，所以明信片在这里就是当一个写作的成果看待，即不费吹灰之力就能写一张明信片，与之相对的是经年累月写一本小说。

86. 这里的 serial novel 就是在报刊杂志上连载的小说。在狄更斯时代，普通人觉得整本的书太贵，所以喜欢每周或每月买份报刊阅读小说。

87. 萨克雷和狄更斯这两位大作家分别在 1863 年和 1870 年去世，身后分别留下两部未完成的著作，即萨克雷的 *Denis Duval* 和狄更斯的 *The Mystery of Edwin Drood*，这也就是这句话中说的著作未成身先死（fallen in mid-course）。有趣的是，后来斯蒂文森去世时也留下了一部未完成的重要著作，即 *Weir of Hermiston*，文学界普遍认为这是斯蒂文森最好的作品。

88. 在 what sorry and pitiful quibbling all this is 中的 all this 是指上面的整篇文字，作者认为这些话都是 quibbling，显然这个语气是自嘲。

89. 这句的动词 forego 没有主语，也可写成 forgo，表示 give up 的意思。注意这个词有不同的意思，我们这里是取其在本语境中的词义，表示作者理想中的生活，即放弃所有生活在空调房间里的好处。这里的 issues 在 OED 中的几个定义都有关，如 the outcome of an action or event; a result or consequence，其中一个例句就是"Monroe was sent to France, and the acquisition of Louisiana was the issue of his labour"，所以在这里根据语境解释成 benefits，就是作者希望放弃那些益处。

90. 这一部分一共有三个句子，都是以 as if 开头，都是假设句，都是与事实相反的。最要注意的是这几个 as if 的句子并不是修饰前面由 forego 引导的一个整句，而是仅仅和前句中 living in a parlour with a regulated temperature 有关，因为这几个句子都是在说住在温控空调房间里的人，不可能和 forego（放弃温控房子好处）这个词有关。也就是说，前句的主体是 To forego all the issues of living in a parlour with a regulated temperature，而破折号后面的几个 as if 从句仅仅是修饰前句中的动名词短语 living in a parlour。换句话说，在 as if that were not to die 或 as if it were not to die 中的代词 that 或 it 应该指 living in a parlour。这几句中的 as if 都是生活在温控房里的人的愿望，如能在温控房中一待就是 10 年，也不会死上数百遍，或一辈子不死，也不用死亡来保护你，或不会死，还会耐心地旁观自身的变化，但这些又不是真的。without even the sad immunities of death 中的 immunities 可以表示保护的意思，所谓死亡的免疫或保护就是说死亡可以让你免受那些痛苦，比如人一死，就不会感冒，就不会骨折，等等，都是死亡让人避免的。住在温控房里的人还以为在那里就可以避免本来只有死亡才能让你避免的，但实际是不可能的。而 spectators of our own

pitiable change 就是说温控房里的人可以自己旁观自己人生的变化，如人慢慢变老就是变化的一个例子。

91. 这个地方是将住温控房间的人比喻成在暗室中没有曝光的底片，没有曝光就没有任何图片，比喻人没有和社会有真正的接触，所以就没有任何意义，换句话说，人生就浪费掉了，恰恰是接下来那句所要说的。

92. 这个 be done with 是个习惯表达法，表示 to be finished with 或者 to be at the end of one's dealings with 的意思，比如"That is past and done with"或"I was done with love for ever"。

93. 根据下文，这个 folio 指书。作者在这里很可能想到了前面提到的一些作家，特别是那些在著作没有完成前去世的作家，所以指具体的书更合适，但也不排除通过隐喻解读法引申为篇章，即人生的篇章。但主要还是指具体的书。

94. 这里的 A spirit goes out of the man 表示精神出自把事情付诸实施的人，这个 execution 就是 carry out 的意思，其中的 which 指前面的 spirit。untimely 一般指不合时宜的死亡，但其实大部分情况下就是指过早去世。

95. 这句的主要意思就是强调意图、决定的重要性。也许你还没有开始做工作，但只要你在打算，你在计划，你决心要全心投入，那么这个打算本身就是出色的工作。

96. 这里的 to sign it 表示 to finish it 的意思，比如一个工程竣工，一个项目完成，一本书完稿，等等。

97. 这句非常不合语法规范。首先我们必须先搞清楚句子的结构。由 even if 引导的仅是分句（even if death catch people），其中的 like an open pitfall 是修饰前面的 catch people 的；句子中的"in mid-career, laying out vast projects, and planning monstrous

foundations, flushed with hope, and their mouths full of boastful language" 其实和 like an open pitfall 一样也是修饰语，但这些短语的逻辑主语都是 people。也就是说，前者是修饰 catch 的方式，后者是修饰 people 在被死亡抓去时的状态。问题出来了，这个"they should be at once tripped up and silenced"算是什么？你会发现这部分和前面是联系不起来的，看这架势本来是霸占着主句的位置，但读起来不通啊！tripped up 就是被绊倒、倒下的意思，而 silenced 就是没有声音了，或者说死了、沉寂了。可是这和前面的根本联不到一起。这里要想把意思说通，就必须找到真正的主句。其实真正的主句是冒号后面的问句："is there not something brave and spirited in such a termination?" 那么 "they should be at once tripped up and silenced" 也不能不去管它。一个解释就是，作者写作时思路快捷，没有在前面加上一个 even if。换句话说，这句中有两个 even if（Even if death catch people…, even if they should be at once tripped up…, is there not something…）。在 "they should be at once tripped up and silenced" 中的 should 应该是虚拟语气表达法，不是表示"应该"等有强制意思的词。这个 should 和前面 even if 从句中的 catch 同样表示虚拟语气，也即是说，你甚至可以在 catch 前面也放一个 should。原文的主语是第三人称单数（death）。若是陈述句，动词本该用 catches，用 catch 说明是虚拟语气。最后，中间的修饰部分（in mid-career, laying, planning, flushed, mouths full of…）都是在说人们被死亡抓走时的状态，如 in mid-career 应该是人在事业中段，不牵涉到事业干得如何，比如一个平庸的公务员在事业的中段离职（resign in mid-career），最保险的就是"在事业的中段"之类的译法，但根据上下文，后面都是在说此人如何成功，项目一大堆，计划也不少，还梦想连连，所以译文发挥了一下（事业如日中天之际）。再有 foundations 此处并非目前很常用的基金的意思，而是项目（建筑）的地基，至于 boastful language 也不应该解读成负面含义，这里还相当正面，比如一个作者的一些豪言壮语（我一定要写出一本在文学史上有地位的作品）。最后，at once 的意思是 immediately，尽管 simultaneously 也有可能，但前者更合语境。

98. 这里是两个对比的例子，前面一个是作者推崇的结束生命的方式，即 foaming in full body over a precipice，这是把生命的结束比作划皮划艇冲向悬崖瀑布，foaming 提示激流中的水泡沫。另一边完全相反，是没有目标的，困苦前行的，sandy deltas 是一个令人慵懒涣散的地方，和激浪奔腾的断壁悬崖完全对立。

99. 此句典自古希腊作家米南德（Menander）的作品（*Dis Exapaton*, 4），后来这句话在历代广为引用，已成经典。

100. 这句中的 eye 可以翻译成以思维为基础的词，如"想到"等。这个词表面虽是视觉，但往往可以转换成思维，在 OED 中就有一个定义"the eye regarded as an attribute of the heart, the mind, etc., imagined to possess powers of perception corresponding to sight; insight, awareness"（to witness facts with the eyes of reason）。另外，cannot help doing 这个结构常可译成"不禁……"。

101. 这句要特别警惕，若翻译成"在任何年龄死亡把你带走，都是早逝"就有问题。如果一个 90 岁的人被死神带走，不管怎么说都不是早逝。关键是这里的 it（it overtake the man）指什么？其实这个 it 应指作者上面说的那种结束生命的方式

(foaming in full body over a precipice)，只要是那样的死，那就无论年龄大小，都可以称为"早逝"，因为那样死的人内心都年轻；若是 miserably straggling to an end in sandy deltas 那样的死法，那绝不是作者认为的 die young。下面一句更印证了这里的年轻是从心理年轻的角度来界定的。

102. 这里的 suffered 是一种旧用法，是 allowed 的意思，类似的用法如 France will no longer suffer the existing government，或 They wouldn't have me tell thee before because of thy body's weakness, but now they suffer it。另外，这句后半部分的意思是说微不足道到连 illusion 都不允许拿走，隐含意思就是说要拿走他的激情就更不能。这里有一个惯用结构 not so much as，不过这句中表达否定的 not 和前面的动词 suffered 在一起。这个 so much as 有达到某种程度的意思，如 Without giving me so much as the least warning，就是连个最起码的警告都没给我，否定的意思融合在 without 里了。再比如 I should not expect any lady would so much as look at him，也是类似的意思。这个结构一般总是表达否定意思。这句话的大意就是死亡不能从他的心里拿走什么，哪怕是幻影也不许拿走。

103. 这句中的 a tip-toe 表示踮着脚尖（standing on one's toes），或者说就是站着，翻译时不明确表示出来，意思也一样。这个不同于 walking on the tips of one's toes，后者表示轻轻不出声的意思。这里排除轻轻不出声的意思很容易，因为接下来的动作显然不是轻轻的，at a bound 表示跳动的意思（jump），不是一个轻轻不出声的动作。也就是说，他一跳就从这个世界跳到了另外一边，恰如我们说从阳界一跃便到了阴界，也就是他死了。其实这最后一句正是作者自己的写照，预示了斯蒂文森自己的结局，他在44岁时，毫无预兆突然离开人世。

104. 这里的 mallet and chisel 代表工具，英美文化中常指木匠或石匠工作中用的工具，此处代表任何工作用的工具，noise scarcely quenched 象征临死前仍在工作。

105. 这个 trailing with him clouds of glory 出自威廉·华兹华斯（William Wordsworth）的诗 Ode: Intimations of Immortality（1807）。斯蒂文森本人多次在作品中引用这句诗，在本文中似隐含人所仍具有的本真率真的意思，也可解释为随死亡带走的辉煌成绩，甚至其他解释，所以以直译为上策，不宜过多解释。另详见"The Character of Dogs"篇注释10。

106. 最后一句理解应该没有大问题，但翻译时译者会遇到困难的选择。如果把原句解释一下，然后再安排一下句子中的语言单位，那么很有可能这句话并不是以 shoots into the spiritual land 结束。可是以 the spiritual land 结尾却是有意义的语言形式，甚至可以说，这是作者安排的一个形式结构，翻译时完全有必要复制。也就是说，在译文中和原文里一样，结尾的词是 the spiritual land，可参见译文。

Pulvis et Umbra (1)

We look for some reward of our endeavors and are disappointed; not success, not happiness, not even peace of conscience, crowns our ineffectual efforts to do well[1]. Our frailties are invincible, our virtues barren[2]; the battle goes sore against us to the going down of the sun.[3] The canting moralist tells us of right and wrong; and we look abroad, even on the face of our small earth, and find them change with every climate,[4] and no country where some action is not honoured for a virtue and none where it is not branded for a vice; and we look in our experience, and find no vital congruity in the wisest rules, but at the best a municipal fitness.[5] It is not strange if we are tempted to despair of good.[6] We ask too much. Our religions and moralities have been trimmed to flatter us, till they are all emasculate and sentimentalised, and only please and weaken.[7] Truth is of a rougher strain. In the harsh face of life, faith can read a bracing gospel.[8] The human race is a thing more ancient than the ten commandments; and the bones and revolutions of the Kosmos, in whose joints we are but moss and fungus, more ancient still.[9]

I

Of the Kosmos in the last resort, science reports many doubtful

微尘与幻影（一）

我们拼搏奋斗，希望有所回报，但总是非常失望；原本想行善有成，结果却有失圆满，没有成功，没有幸福，甚至没有良心的平静。我们的弱点战无不胜，我们的美德鲜少成果，战役打到夕阳西下时已败得落花流水。虚伪的道德家们总是大谈是非对错；可我们放眼望去，不说其他，就算是在这个小小的星球上，对错是非也会因文化不同而异；一个国家的美德在另外一个国家未必是德行，同理，恶行也并非放之四海而皆恶。反观我们自己的经历，各地的规矩就算定得充满智慧，也不能完全一致，能因地制宜，适用于当地环境就不错了。如果我们因此对善的存在感到绝望，那也不奇怪。我们奢求太多。宗教和道德已被调教得只知奉承，以致失掉阳刚之气，变得多愁善感，只会博人欢心，却使人虚弱。真实世界却是严酷的。在严酷的人生中，信仰能帮助人发现振奋人心的准则。人类这玩意儿要比十大诫命更远久，而宇宙中星球和天体的运行也比那诫命更远古，至于在宇宙这个大机体的关节间生存的我们，那就仅像青苔和真菌那样微不足道了。

一

关于宇宙，最近科学报道了许多令人生疑的事，件件让人胆

things and all of them appalling. There seems no substance to this solid globe on which we stamp: nothing but symbols and ratios.[10] Symbols and ratios carry us and bring us forth and beat us down;[11] gravity that swings the incommensurable suns and worlds through space, is but a figment varying inversely as the squares of distances; and the suns and worlds themselves, imponderable figures of abstraction, NH_3 and H_2O.[12] Consideration dares not dwell upon this view; that way madness lies;[13] science carries us into zones of speculation, where there is no habitable city for the mind of man. But take the Kosmos with a grosser faith, as our senses give it to us.[14] We behold space sown with rotatory islands; suns and worlds and the shards and wrecks of systems: some, like the sun, still blazing; some rotting, like the earth; others, like the moon, stable in desolation. All of these we take to be made of[15] something we call matter: a thing which no analysis can help us to conceive; to whose incredible properties no familiarity can reconcile our minds.[16] This stuff, when not purified by the lustration of fire,[17] rots uncleanly into something we call life; seized through all its atoms with a pediculous malady; swelling in tumours that become independent, sometimes even (by an abhorrent prodigy) locomotory; one splitting into millions, millions cohering into one,[18] as the malady proceeds through varying stages. This vital putrescence of the dust, used as we are to it, yet strikes us with occasional disgust, and the profusion of worms in a piece of ancient turf, or the air of a marsh darkened with insects, will sometimes check our breathing so that we aspire for cleaner places. But none is clean: the moving sand is infected with lice; the pure spring, where it bursts out of the mountain, is a mere issue of worms; even in the hard rock the crystal is forming.

寒。我们踩踏的这个地球好像并不存在物质,有的仅仅是符号与比例。这两样东西助我们前进,推我们创新,把我们打倒;引力将无比巨大的恒星和行星在宇宙间甩来甩去,而引力仅是虚构的抽象概念,表现为两个物体间距离的平方之反比;而恒星和行星本身则是不可想象的抽象数字,是化学符号 NH_3 和 H_2O。人的思考可不敢沿上面这个思路进行,那样思考的话,非疯了不可;科学把我们带入推测之境,在那里思想是无处安身的。但还有另外一种更为宏观的宇宙观,一种基于自己的感受所获得的观点。我们看到宇宙空间布满旋转的岛屿,恒星、行星、天体的残骸:有些(像太阳)仍然光耀无比,有些(如地球)正在腐烂,还有些(如月亮)在寂寞中稳定不变。我们认为所有这些都是由称为物质的东西构成的:何为物质,百般分析却仍不得其解,而物质的奇妙特征,就算我们再熟悉,也无法尽然掌握。这东西,若未经火的净化,就腐烂成肮脏的东西,即所谓生命。这东西虱子丛生,侵及细胞,或长成一独立肿突,有时甚至能动来动去,堪称吓人的奇物;随着这个病症发展阶段深入,一个分裂成百万,百万聚合成一个。这个由尘土组成的必不可少的腐烂之物,我们虽然已经见怪不怪,但有时还是让我们恶心。有时在一块古老的土壤上虱虫丛生,或是在草泽的上空昆虫盘旋,我们不禁喘不过气来,真向往一片净土。但是,没有干净的地方,流动的沙子也满是虱虫,山涧喷射出的泉水也有蠕虫滋生,甚至在坚硬的岩石里,水晶虽在那里慢慢形成,但虫患也如影随形。

In two main shapes this eruption covers the countenance of the earth: the animal and the vegetable: one in some degree the inversion of the other: the second rooted to the spot; the first coming detached out of its natal mud,[19] and scurrying abroad with the myriad feet of insects or towering into the heavens on the wings of birds: a thing so inconceivable that, if it be well considered, the heart stops.[20] To what passes with the anchored vermin, we have little clue:[21] doubtless they have their joys and sorrows, their delights and killing agonies:[22] it appears not how. But of the locomotory,[23] to which we ourselves belong, we can tell more. These share with us a thousand miracles: the miracles of sight, of hearing, of the projection of sound, things that bridge space;[24] the miracles of memory and reason, by which the present is conceived, and when it is gone, its image kept living in the brains of man and brute; the miracle of reproduction, with its imperious desires and staggering consequences.[25] And to put the last touch upon this mountain mass of the revolting and the inconceivable, all these prey upon each other, lives tearing other lives in pieces, cramming them inside themselves,[26] and by that summary process,[27] growing fat: the vegetarian, the whale, perhaps the tree, not less than the lion of the desert; for the vegetarian is only the eater of the dumb.[28] Meanwhile our rotary island loaded with predatory life, and more drenched with blood, both animal and vegetable, than ever mutinied ship,[29] scuds through space with unimaginable speed, and turns alternate cheeks to the reverberation of a blazing world, ninety million miles away.[30]

这一生物体之爆发以两种形态在地球上出现：动物和植物。而前者在某种程度上和后者正好相反：植物深植于一个地方，而动物出生后就离开出生的土壤，比如昆虫凭百足四处爬行，禽鸟借翅膀翱翔长空，当真不可思议。你若往深里想，定会十分震撼。这个卧地不动的生物到底在想些什么，我们不知道：无疑它们有喜有悲，有乐有痛，我们不得而知。但是对于那些走来走去的动物，我们所知略多，因为我们也属于那一类。它们和我们共有上千个奇异功能：也有视觉，有听觉，能发声，这些奇迹克服了空间的隔阂；还有记忆和说理的奇迹，借此"现时"的概念呈现在大脑里，而当现时成了旧时，其形象就长存在人和动物的脑海中。还有自身繁衍的奇迹，而这一繁衍的强烈欲望最终带出惊人的后果。而要把这一大堆令人生厌、不可思议的动物刻画得惟妙惟肖，最后还得加上一笔，他们相互把对方视为捕食的对象，把对方撕得粉碎，然后塞进自己的皮囊，就这样急匆匆往嘴里塞进去，结果使自己肥胖：素食者、鲸鱼，可能还有树，更不用说沙漠中的狮子都是这样；而素食者吃的也是生物，只是这些生物不会说话而已。同时，我们旋转的岛屿满载着猎杀捕食的生物，浸润着动物和植物的血液，远超过叛乱船上厮杀后的血液，这个岛屿以难想象的速度，穿行在宇宙空间，不停地让左右的脸颊轮番去迎接九千万英里外的一个炽热发光体射来的光芒。

注 释

1. 这一长句中有两个地方可以说明一下。首先 crown 这个词既表达工作努力后得到回报（to reward or honour a work with a prize），也表示事物完美结束（to be the triumphant culmination of something），但这里不必太计较，表达出大致意思就可以，比如下面的译法："我们拼搏奋斗，希望有所回报，但总是非常失望；原本想行善有成，却终落得事与愿违，没有成功，没有幸福，甚至没有良心的平静"，虽然没有 the triumphant culmination 的意思，但是基本意思到位。如果译者不愿意放弃"圆满地结束"这层意思，则也可应变补救（……原本想行善有成，结果却有失圆满，没有成功，没有幸福，甚至没有良心的平静）；总之，译者不要把这个词当作关注的焦点，只要把整句的意思翻译出来就可以了。另外，虽然现代英语中 do well 一般表示把事情做好，而 do good 表示做好事，但是本句以及本文中其他地方的 doing well 基于《圣经》（如本文最后一段：God forbid it should be man that wearies in well-doing），而《圣经》中的这个 do well 应该是 good 的意思。这可以从不同译本对这个词的修改看出来，如早期 King James 版本是"let us not be weary in well doing"，但 New King James 版本则是"let us not grow weary while doing good"，New International 版本是"Let us not become weary in doing good"，Good News 版本是"let us not become tired of doing good"，International Standard 版本是"Let's not get tired of doing what is good"，而 Contemporary English 版本则把话说得更清楚"Don't get tired of helping others"，但大部分的版本都是 doing good。将 do well 这个词组解释成做好事应该没有问题（见 OED: in accordance with a good or high standard of conduct or morality; in a way which is morally good）。当然在本语境中，也可以将做好事和做得好都包括进去，如"行善有成"。

2. 本句中的两个形容词意思应该很清楚，但从翻译的角度还是值得探讨的。首先，从认知隐喻的角度看，invincible 这个词的图像基础是战斗，也就是说，人在和 frailties 进行着战斗，但是人总是赢不了。而另一个词 barren 则能引出完全不同的图像，背后的认知基础是土壤生出果实（OED: unproductive of results; fruitless, unprofitable），就是说，在与我们的弱点的战斗中，我们的美德（virtues）没有给我们带来战果（这个和前面的 not success、not happiness 等前后呼应）。但是翻译时倒未必要沿着这个 fruitless 的隐喻思维走，只要说我们的弱点厉害，我们的美德在弱点面前总是失败，具体说法不用太细致规范，比如有学生用（美德）"乏善可陈"也大致到位。

3. 此处的 battle 刚好和前面的 invincible 相呼应，所谓的战斗就是前面半句中 invincible 一词所提示的战斗，即和自己的弱点的战斗。形容词 sore 或也可用 sorely，既可以有 extremely 的意思，也可有 badly 的意思。本句中的 to the going down of the sun 基本意思就是"到太阳下山"，所以其认知隐喻基础就是 A battle is a day。此处的 battle 似乎解释成与自己的弱点的战斗更合上下文。斯蒂文森总是喜欢提到人与自己的弱点战斗，比如我们决心不吃甜点，但是最后还是没忍住，这就是在与自己的 frailties 战斗中的失败。不过要注意这个 the battle goes sore against us to the going down of the sun 有宗教的背景，因这句出自《圣经》:"And the battle went sore against Saul"(1 Samuel 31: 3, King James)。sore 的意思可以在不同《圣经》的译文中反映出来，比如 "The fighting grew very fierce around Saul"(New Living Translation)，"The battle pressed hard against Saul"(English Standard Version)，"When the battle intensified against Saul"(Christian Standard Bible)，"the fighting was heavy around Saul"(Good News Translation)，"Saul himself was in the thick of the battle"(NET Bible)。我们可从不同的译文中看出翻译的差异，但是基本意思还是一样的，就是战斗激烈，而根据我们的上下文，这个战斗中我们人类是失败的一方。to the going down of the sun 也出自《圣经》:"and his hands were steady until the going down of the sun"(Exodus 17: 12, King James)，也有用 till sunset 或 until the sun went down，但基本意思就是"到日落的时候"。而此处的一天也喻指一生。

4. 这句里的 abroad 大意就是向四周看(look around)，而 change with every climate 中的 climate 可以换成环境或文化，就是说，你会发现对错是非这些概念在不同的文化或社会里会有不同的解读。

5. 这一长句很容易搞错。但是根据上下文，若错译的话，也很容易发觉。这前半句的意思应该是接应上面一句，就是说，对错是非会根据文化而异。那么接下来这句就应该不能和前一句矛盾。假如我们翻译成"任何一个国家善皆有善报，恶也得恶果"，那意思就和上面的连不起来。我们不要被句子的双重否定给迷惑住，这里想说的就是，有些行为在不同文化里会有不同解释，比如一夫多妻的行为在有些文化里就不是罪；同理，有些在一个文化里广泛认可和推崇的做法，在另外一个文化里却是不可接受的,比如复仇的行为在有些文化里是一种荣光之举,但在法治国家里是不被容许的。这句话的主要意图是承认文化相对论。这里的 no vital congruity 是说在各种不同的充满智慧的规则中是找不到一致性的,no congruity 可以解释成 no agreement。这句也是上面观点的延续,下面的 a municipal fitness 其实也是同样的意思,municipal 表示城市的,fitness 则是适应的意思,充其量也就是适用于当地,说得更广阔些就是要适合当地的情况,不是放之四海而皆准。vital agreement 中的 vital 是指 essential 的意思,这个词暗示不同社会还是在一些问题上相同的,但是这些 agreement 都无关紧要。可以说"无法取得基本的一致",若说成"不能完全一致"的意思,也大致到位。最后,at the best 似乎就是 at best 这个短语,一般不用定冠词 the,表示最理想的状态,暗示即使在最理想的状态,仍不够好。

6. 之所以说 despair of good,是因为我们对于 good 实在没有确定的定义,一个地方认为是好的东西,到另外一个地方却是不好的东西,而且你还不一定能善有善报,这就促使人对善的存在失去信心和希望,因此绝望也就可以理解了。这个 good 狭义可指本语境中提示的由我们的 virtues 驱动的 our endeavors(善举),但在 good 前没有定冠词 the,所以也可泛指世间普遍的"善"。后面一句"We ask too much."是在说人类要的太多,你不能每一个善举都要回报,那样就要的太多了。

7. 这一句中的 trimmed 可以解释成 adjusted,其隐喻图像是调整风帆(adjust the sails in relation to the direction of the wind)。这个词一般用作"修剪"的意思,隐喻图像是修剪树木,意为除掉多余的东西。在本句中似乎也不能排除这个意思,即宗教为了取悦信徒，不仅有所调整（adjusted），同时也会故意忽视、放弃一些东西（trimmed）。翻译时倒不必太计较，大意通了就可以，如调适、调教、形塑等均可。另外，emasculate 最基本的意思就是弱，但这个词还会有男性特有的强壮特征减弱的附带意思（deprive a man of his male role or identity），而 sentimentalised 和 emasculate 也很接近，有迎合人的情感、不自然、做作的意思（addicted to indulgence in superficial emotion）。

8. 这句的理解应和上面那句连起来看。上面是在说，宗教和道德女里女气（emasculate and sentimentalised），不能面对严酷的现实，而现实是艰难的（rougher）。正是在这个背景下，才引出 faith。在宗教和道德中，找不到告诉你在生活中该怎么办的东西，但是在艰难困苦的生活里，若有信仰，你就能从苦难中找到或者获得能在生活中让你振奋，告诉你该如何行动的东西（gospel = something that serves as a guide to human action）。这里的 read 不应该当一般的阅读解释，而应该是 "to make out, discover"（OED）的意思。就是说，在艰难的生活面前，信仰给我们机会发现人生的准则。句子里虽然没有人（we），但最后还是得落实在人的身上，信仰只是人依靠的对象。

9. 这里仍然要有逻辑上的连贯。这句仍然在贬低宗教和道德，他说人类要比十大诫命有更长远的历史，而宇宙的历史就更长了。这里的 bones 可以从隐喻的角度看，把宇宙当作人，而所谓的 bones 就是指宇宙中的实体，如各种星球等，而 revolutions 则是指宇宙的运转，具体的万物的运转（revolution = the apparent movement of the sun, a constellation, the firmament, etc., around the earth）。斯蒂文森不喜欢宗教和道德的教条，他更看重实际的宇宙、世界、生活等客观事实。另外，斯蒂文森是工程师出身，他对当时的科技和科学知识是很熟悉的，所以这个宇宙天体的比喻就可以理解了。至于说 in whose joints we are but moss and fungus 则也是隐喻，bones and revolutions 都是大结构大运动，而我们仅仅像是寄生于宏观大格局中的青苔和真菌（moss and fungus）那样微小，那样微不足道。这个 joints 给翻译造成了很大困难。首先若仅说宇宙，那么就很难和关节这个意象连起来。要和关节连起来，宇宙就必须被看作是一个大的机体（如人，因为人体有关节）。但也许你会说，原文就把宇宙和关节这个不合理的搭配交给了读者自己去处理，但是译者若稍微帮一把读者，读者理解起来就更省事儿些。所以，我们有两个选择，第一个是"在宇宙的关节间生存的我们"这个还原隐喻的译法，第二个是"在宇宙这个大机体的关节间生存的我们"，译者可以任意选择。后者抛弃了原文的隐喻，换成了明喻，理解起来更方便些。至于 moss and fungus，也以换成明喻为上策，且可以把微小的含义加进去（像是青苔和真菌那样微不足道）。当隐喻太突兀难以接受时，转换成明喻就可以降低突兀程度，有时不妨一试。

10. 这里的 symbols and ratios 泛指科学的典型代表数理化，这个可以从下面的例子说明。作者的观点是什么都能从科学的角度解释，具体见下一个注释。另外，这里的 in the last resort 好像不是在说最后的手段，last 可以解释成 latest，就是在最近的科学探索中。也不排除是笔误（report vs. resort）。

11. symbols and ratios 是当时的现代科学对人与客观世界的认识方式，人的一切可以用这些抽象的科学来解释。而这个"carry us and bring us forth and beat us down"和"gravity that swings… NH_3 and H_2O"应该相互关联起来理解。斯蒂文森

用分号分开的两个半句往往是互为关联的。这里斯蒂文森似乎在说，普通人和科学家看同一个世界的角度不同，科学家是用 symbols and ratios 等抽象概念看世界，而普通人则是用感官看世界。我们当然可从人出生到死亡的过程来解释这三个动作，如 carry 解释成 pregnant with offspring（OED: carry a child），bring forth 解释成 give birth，而 beat down 解释成 die。但是在这个语境中这样解释就显得比较狭窄。这三个动作既可以从字面意义上解释，也可以从隐喻意义上解释，所以包含的内容就更广泛。比如 carry 不仅可以解释成 pregnant with offspring，还可以解释成字面意义的携带；bring forth 不仅可解释成字面意义的 give birth，还可解释成隐喻意义的生成或产出（OED: He never thought of what the future might bring forth.）；beat down 既可以解释成字面意义的被击倒而死亡，但也可以是隐喻意义上被击倒（如被疾病击倒而死亡）。总之作者是想用抽象的科学概念来解释人生的现象，以便说明当时科学思维的盛行，而 symbols and ratios 仅是抽象科学的具体代表，所以翻译还是以不远离原文文字的本意为出发点，适当做些发挥与延伸。

12. 这里是在说，将星球甩来甩去的引力是虚构的一种概念，用抽象的物理学解释，就是反平方定律（inverse-square law），即牛顿定律。前半句是用物理和数学的抽象公式解释了宇宙间星球运转的现象。后半句 figures of abstraction 是用抽象的化学公式 NH_3（氨）和 H_2O（水）解释星球这些物质。

13. 这里作者又一次用动作当主语，而实际上人才是 dare 这个动作的实施者。上一段中，作者就用了 faith can read a bracing gospel，显然动词 read 的实施者并不是 faith 而是人。我们这句的意思也应该把这个实际实施动作的人带进去，也就是人不敢那么抽象地思考事物。这里的 dwell upon 可以解释成 linger over in thought。作者是在鼓励人真实地面对世界中的事物，而不是抽象地面对世界。比如一个人见到有人把手割破了，鲜血从手上流下来。此时谁还会去分析血的成分中包含水（H_2O），谁还会想到是物理学的引力使血液留下来？那样想的话，就会想疯了（"that way madness lies"，见 *King Lear*, III. 4. 21）。

14. 这句的理解仍然要紧紧地沿着上下的逻辑思路。注意这里有一个 but，说明有一个转折（but take the Kosmos with a grosser faith）。前面一句是说科学是推测的，而推测是抽象的（注意前面大半段都在说科学观的抽象思维），接着就是 but 这个转折，转到另外一个不同于科学的看宇宙万物的观点，就是用 a grosser faith 看宇宙的观点。此处的 faith 可以理解为 belief，或者根据上下文理解为 ways of looking at the world，是依靠自己的感官形成的一种想法。形容词 grosser 源于 gross，就是 gross national product 中的 gross，有总体的、宏观的等意思，在这个上下文里，有更接近主观感知的意思，因为我们的这个 faith，正是源于我们的感官的（as our senses give it to us）；也就是说，作者是在与前面的科学观相对照，前面的科学观是逻辑、抽象、微观的，而另外一个看世界的观点是更为粗略的、总体的、源于感知和体验的。

15. 这里的 something we take to be made of 可以理解为 something we regard as being made of，其中的 take 可以理解为 think、regard 等。下面一句也是同样的用法："They're just a bit of a joke," said one woman. "You can't really take it seriously."。

16. 这句里的 to whose incredible properties no familiarity can reconcile our minds，可以简化为 no familiarity can reconcile our minds to properties，基本结构是 A reconciles B to C。其实这句话的意思就是我们的大脑还是不懂什么是物质。类似说法英语里面常有，如 "How gradually does the eye grow reconciled even to a disagreeable dress" 或 "She had reconciled herself to never seeing him again"。这个结构中在介词 to 后面的东西一般都是不很招人喜欢的，如 a disagreeable dress 就是让人看不惯的，never seeing him again 也是不令人高兴的事。换句话说，当一个人 reconcile oneself to something，这个 something 一般是令人不快的事物，但是你接受这个事物。在这个例子中 to 后面的是物质的属性（properties of matter），在作者看来，这个物质的属性就不是一个令作者喜欢的东西，因为他搞不懂这物质是什么。翻译时完全不用死抠原文的结构，用解释的方法就可以。你若真翻译成"熟悉不能使我们的头脑与物质的惊人属性和解"，那就是典型的死译。

17. 这里的 this stuff 应该是指前面说的 matter，而根据前一句，这个 matter 就是构成宇宙中所有星球的物质（be made of something we call matter）。当作者说 when not purified by the lustration of fire，即是在说没有经过太阳的火净化（go through fire）。这里的背景仍然是宇宙的星球，所以当说 this stuff rots into life 时，我们想起前面的地球（some rotting, like the earth）。此时叙述的对象就在地球上了，就是地球上腐烂的有生命的东西（rots into life）。下句中事件的发生地点就是地球。

18. 到这里为止，此段的发展轨迹是这样的：the Kosmos (space) → rotatory islands → the suns, the worlds (such as the earth, the

moon) → matter → this stuff (matter) → life (this rotten stuff) → (life is) seized, swelling, splitting。这个过程反映了斯蒂文森受达尔文主义的影响，他甚至把这篇文章称为"达尔文思想的说教"。据此，这句可以扩展重写成"This rotten stuff is seized through all its atoms with a pediculous malady"。动词 seized 有 attacked 的意思，而 with 短语可以理解为 by，through (out) all its (the stuff's) atoms 是 attacked 触及的深度（侵及机体的细胞）。pediculous 是满是虱子的意思。这是一个非常恶心的图像，一个机体被满是虱子的疾病侵袭至身体的细胞。接下来 swelling 的主语也是 this stuff，而 tumour 一词在这里可以理解成 lump，但这个肿块游离于整体（independent），地球上的任何充满微生物的块状物都可以看作是这类肿块，比如果实、树木，这些块状物与大地不成一体（independent），但是甚至也可能是可以移动的（locomotory），如动物和人。至于 by an abhorrent prodigy 中的 by 似乎用 as 或 with 更合适，abhorrent prodigy 指的就是动物（包括人类），这些动物居然会动，所以是 prodigy（extraordinary thing）。而在这个 malady 的不同阶段，一个生物体分裂成百万，百万聚合成一个。这里指的就是生物或微生物。这几句的理解必须基于当时生物科学的发展，只有认识到显微镜技术的作用才能理解这几句。通过显微镜发现微生物一般认为是在 1676 年（发现者是 van Leeuwenhoek），到斯蒂文森时期已有快两百年的历史了，这几句的前提是显微镜技术发现微生物，而斯蒂文森的工科背景使他对一般的科学很熟悉，另外他本人疑似患肺结核病，也是他熟悉细菌的原因（见本文导读）。另外，我们上面的解读都是把主语理解成 this stuff，或者说是 life，而源头就是 the earth，但是作者用了与医学相关的词汇，如 malady、tumour、varying stages，所以解读时把主语看成人或动物，也可以是一个角度，而且再读下去时，下文确实提到人和动物（of the locomotory）。但是在这个阶段，范围应该要比人广，语法上的主语毕竟是 this stuff 或者 life，人只是其中之一。

19. 这几句中的一个标点需要说明一下（其实这个问题也包含在下文和其他文章里）。我们看到斯蒂文森连着用冒号，而这是很少见的，至少现代英语中罕见。斯蒂文森曾对编辑说，不要改动他的标点，他自有目的。但是在我们翻译时，译者还是需要考虑一下，到底是完全照搬原文的标点，还是根据现在汉语的习惯，对原文做些改动，本译文采取了后一种做法。但如要忠于原作者，就需要保留原文标点。另外，this eruption 指的就是前面一段描写的动植物在地球上的出现，显然作者沿用了达尔文主义的思路，把动植物的大量出现看作是进化过程中的 eruption。至于 out of its natal mud，也是一个很奇特的说法，mud 一词似乎可以联想到《圣经》中对人的描述，人是来自于尘土，所以动物的身体或人体也是泥土（mud）做成的。翻译的时候，可以抛弃"泥土"一词，如出生后就"离开母体""离开出生之处"，但也可以保留"土"字，如"离开出生的土壤"，各有得失。

20. 此处的 the heart stops 不能从字面意思理解，是感到惊恐害怕的意思。翻译的时候应该没有必要保留原文的比喻，不用翻译成"心脏停止跳动"，翻译出句子的实际意思就行，因为这个心脏的形象不是作者的写作特征，也没有什么特殊意义，就是英文的一个说法。

21. 前面总结性地介绍了两种生物，其实就是植物和动物。所以这里的 anchored vermin 指的就是植物，anchored 是说植物在一个地方不动，vermin 本来指那些讨厌的小动物，如鼠和猫。但这里用不动的生物，来指植物。

22. 在这里前面一对词 joys and sorrows 和后面一对词 delights and agonies 基本上就是同义词，并无特殊的区别特征，可以看作是行文的一种手段，所以翻译的时候还是以重现原文的重复为上策。但是后面一对中的 killing 在翻译时可能面临一个选择。这个词的基本意思是"难以容忍"，说成是 crushing，甚至 fatal 也不算错，但是基本就是 extremely 的意思。只是 killing 在这句中只起到修饰作用，放弃不说也不影响大意（有乐有痛）。

23. 这个 but of the locomotory 中的 locomotory 指的就是动物，而且作者认为人类本身就属于动物。传统基督教的观点是不会把任何动物放到同一个类别里去的，但是斯蒂文森显然是受到进化论的影响。

24. 这句中的 the projection of sound 指的就是发出声音的意思。本来可以用说话表示，但是这里描述的对象是动物，所以用发声更合适。至于 things that bridge space 中的 things 是指前面所有的 miracles，就是 sight、hearing、projecting sound。这三样能力可以搭架起空间之间的桥梁，这样两个人虽然不能触摸对方，但是却可以借助视觉、听觉和说话能力感知对方，正是在这个意义上说，视觉、听觉和说话的能力在两点的空间之间搭建起桥梁。

25. 这个短语 with its imperious desires and staggering consequences 和前面的 the miracle of reproduction 的关系可以理解成进一步追加说明的意思。中间的 its 指的就是 reproduction 的欲望，而这其中的一个欲望就是繁衍必不可少的性欲，而性欲造成的后果却是令人吃惊的。注意这里用的也是复数，所以不仅是一个后果，比如除一个活生生的动物生出来这一惊人的后果外，还会有与繁衍相关的情感方面的后果。但是上面这些理解和解读都不必在翻译中和盘托出，甚至没有必要把欲望换成性欲。译者需要在翻译和解释之间画出一道线，尽可能守住翻译的本位，不扩展到解释的领域内。

26. 前半句中的 this mountain mass 指的就是动物（包括人类），表示数量大，翻译的时候未必要翻译出 mountain 的意思来；而 cramming them inside themselves 就是把动物塞进嘴里去，动物吃动物，人类吃动物。

27. 这个 that summary process 中的 summary 可以理解为 "by a short method; done without delay"，类似的句子如 "he cleared the table by the summary process of tilting everything upon it into the fire-place"（Dickens, *Martin Chuzzlewit*, 1844, xiii. 177）。这里的代词 that 就是指前面的 cramming 这个动作（by the short and quick process of cramming）。

28. 这个 the eater of the dumb 就是指吃植物的人。前面给人的印象是吃动物，但作者认为素食者也是往嘴里塞生物，所以和吃动物一样。他在前面的举例中甚至提到树木（tree），因为树木也需要补充自己的营养才能长大。只要记住斯蒂文森自称这篇文章是"达尔文思想的说教"，所有这些就不难理解了。

29. 这里的 mutinied ship 是指在叛乱的战船上血流甲板的场景，主要是说到处都是血。但是作者使用的这个词（mutinied）是和他一些小说中的描写有互文关系的。在他著名的小说《金银岛》中就有叛乱船上流血的场景，而在他其他小说中也有船上哗变造成的流血情景。

30. 这句理解应该并不难，因为当译者看到 ninety million miles away 这个短语，大概就会想到太阳了，而看到 turns alternate cheeks 也自然会联想到白天和黑夜的交替。问题是翻译的时候是否有必要把所有这些都说出来，比方索性把 a blazing world 就说成是太阳，把 turns alternate cheeks 就转换成白天黑夜交替。这样解读当然是大大地帮助了读者，但是却有可能对不起斯蒂文森，因为这个具体的描述不像前面有的地方的描写属于语言体系，这里的描写纯粹是作者使然，加之就算是比较直接的翻译，也不至于看不懂，还是有必要让读者自己去解读。所以翻译时适当地做些有利于读者的归化应该可以，但是几个关键说法还是最好保留原文的特征。

导 读

苟且之身心亦高

斯蒂文森借用贺拉斯（Horace）的名句作为这篇散文的题目："Pulvis et umbra sumus"（We are but dust and shadow，我们只是微尘与幻影）。该文先发表于《斯克里伯纳杂志》（*Scribner's Magazine*, April, 1888），后又收入散文集《穿越平原》（*Across the Plains: With Other Memories and Essays*, 1892）。他在 1887 年 12 月写给文艺批评家西德尼·科尔文（Sidney Colvin）的信中提到《微尘与幻影》，说明该文写于 12 月前。从斯蒂文森的年表看，他 1887 年 8 月离开英国，9 月初抵达纽约。随后马上在 10 月初到萨拉纳克湖（Saranac Lake），在那里从事写作，一直到次年 4 月。这篇散文应写于萨拉纳克湖畔，时间是那年的秋冬之际。

当时斯蒂文森刚离开英国抵达纽约,健康状况仍不佳,所以他们一家人马上就离开了喧闹的纽约城,到纽约州北部的萨拉纳克湖小住。作者对自己的这篇散文显然非常满意,因他在写作中倾注了无限激情。在给西德尼·科尔文的信中他说:"这也就是一篇说教类文字……但却是倾注真情的,我觉得它能感动人,也让人受益,至少对我如此。我自觉这篇写得不错,文字贴切,饱含深意。"斯蒂文森认为这篇散文可称为"达尔文思想的说教"(Darwinian Sermon)。稍后在给阿德莱德·布多的信中,斯蒂文森也说,他是满怀深情写这篇散文的,他在文中描写的是他眼里的世界,而他也愿意在这样的一个世界里战斗,看落日残阳,在火炉旁不时听笑声爽朗。但斯蒂文森有自知之明,他知道文中的描写会让有些人不快,因为那些人会认为,像斯蒂文森那样看世界就会浇灭了人对上帝的信仰,也会剥夺了人的欢乐。他甚至说,假如他的文章让人不悦,他真希望没有发表这东西。但他真心觉得,他的这篇文章包含满满的允诺与希望。

那么他写了什么竟至于会冒犯他人?正如斯蒂文森自己所说,这篇文章不像有些散文那样有情景或人物的描述,更像是抽象的言说。宗教的说教常见于牧师的布道(sermon),人们常将这类文字冠以陈词滥调,教堂里的说教还会让你看到地狱的火焰,进而让你心生恐惧。但是斯蒂文森在本文里却恰恰相反,他的文字并不是陈词滥调,也不是训诫警言,而是振聋发聩的说教(sermon),比如下面这段话:"虚伪的道德家们总是大谈是非对错;可我们放眼望去,不说其他,就算是在这个小小的星球上,对错是非也会因文化不同而异;一个国家的美德在另外一个国家未必是德行,同理,恶行也并非放之四海而皆恶。"这种带有文化相对论的观点,避开了绝对的是非,当然会让那些原教旨主义者感到不快。他接着说:"宗教和道德已被调教得只知奉承，以致失掉阳刚之气，变得多愁善感，只会博人欢心，却使人虚弱。"这些话都和宗教的套话格格不入。

　　说到底，《微尘与幻影》说的是人在宇宙中的位置，说的是人的生命，以及生命的结局死亡。斯蒂文森紧跟时代的进步，在文中大量援引了18和19世纪天文学的发现和当时化学领域的前沿知识，来讨论人类居住的星球以及人类本身。他用崭新的天文学知识谈宇宙："引力将无比巨大的恒星和行星在宇宙间甩来甩去，而引力仅是虚构的抽象概念，表现为两个物体间距离的平方之反比"。他也用当时最前沿的知识，把动物和人看作是物质（matter），又认为由这物质构成的生物是腐朽肮脏的东西："这个由尘土组成的必不可少的腐烂之物，我们虽然已经见怪不怪，但有时还是让我们恶心。"在他眼里，人和动物没有本质的差别，"他们相互把对方视为捕食的对象，把对方撕得粉碎，然后塞进自己的皮囊，就这样急匆匆往嘴里塞进去，结果使自己肥胖"。为自己的生存去捕食、去杀戮，这些动物的本性人类同样也有。他认为，人和蚂蚁受制于同样的自然规律，也背负同样的罪恶。所以，他不以黑白对错看人说事。在斯蒂文森眼里，人是极不完美的动物："可怜的人啊，在世上如昙花一现，苦难缠身，但他的欲望总不切实际……，他身处野性世界，可自己也是野性物种的后裔，怎么都摆脱不了捕杀同伴的天生习性"。可他同时又觉得人的行为是会令人肃然起敬："在世界的任何角落，在历史的每个阶段，在任何不公的世道里，在所有失败的境遇中，没有希望，没人帮助，没人感谢，却为坚守道德，默默无闻地打着一场必输的战斗"，因为"无论在任何地方，不管是起于诚心还是装点门面，人都守着一点美德……坚守着那一点荣耀与尊严，他们那可怜的精神瑰宝"。在斯蒂文森眼里，人"这个高贵的猿猴……竟然放弃难得的快乐，在接踵而来的痛苦上再加痛苦，为一个理想而活，不管那个理想是如何不靠谱"。一个几乎可以说是恶贯满盈的人，比如说"在妓院，一个被社会抛弃的人，一个靠烈酒活着、饱受屈辱的女人，一个蠢人，扒手，扒手的朋友，就是这样一个人，仍守住一点尊严，保留着一丝同情，虽然世界蔑视她，可她却仍助人为乐，常坚守一点道德，也不在乎付出一些代价，拒财富于门外"。你看，斯蒂文森没有把人说得好如天使，也没有把人说得恶如坏蛋，而是把人描写成了一个矛盾的存在体，在身怀无限恶习的同时，也善良可爱，充满理想，这样就更接近事实。

斯蒂文森还认为，不仅是人的恶习与善行并存，动物也同样具备这种两重性，高傲的人其实无法撇清在原始微尘阶段与动物的亲缘关系。他的这种观点反映出他受当时达尔文思想的影响很深，这也就是他为什么说《微尘与幻影》这篇散文是达尔文思想的说教文字。人类既有人性也有兽性的特征使人在努力行善的过程中不停地施出恶行来，这种并存使人在不愧是英雄的同时也堪称恶魔。伟大的悲剧就能把这种既配上天堂也配下地狱的矛盾描写得淋漓尽致。好的作品不把人用善恶分得一清二楚，因为那极不真实。恰恰是因为人类有与生俱来的兽性，他怎么努力都甩不掉恶行，因此向人类求完美是缘木求鱼，人反倒值得同情可怜。这种态度显然受到进化论的影响，所以他担心文章会冒犯一些人也就并非没有根据了。

人的这种矛盾是斯蒂文森作品的一个重要特征，不仅存在于小说中，也存在于其他作品里。他最著名的《化身博士》就是这种双重性的典型写照。其实不仅作品的内容反映了这种矛盾，作品的语言似乎也与之相呼应。我们不妨粗略看看文章的语言特征。

在本文中，作者故意用一些与常理或传统观念相矛盾的词，比如"这东西，若未经火的净化，就腐烂成肮脏的东西，即所谓生命"（rots uncleanly into something we call life）。在这里故意用 rots 就和常理相碰撞，因为一般人认为生命是有活力的、健康的，而这个 rots 的使用就显出了矛盾，构成一定程度的"前景化"。这类矛盾修辞法（oxymoron）是斯蒂文森在本篇中常使用，如 this vital putrescence of the dust，也是自相矛盾的，因为既然是腐烂之物就该是坏东西，但作者却认为这是必不可少的（vital）。他有时甚至在语言形式上也表现出对立，比如有人认为"one splitting into millions, millions cohering into one"就是文字交错配列的一例（即所谓的 chiasmus），这里前半部分的首个词是后半部分的最后一词，而前半部分的最后一词是后半部分的首个词，这就形成了前后对立。此外，斯蒂文森还频繁使用隐喻，比如把人描写成为"一个尘土黏合成的病体"（the disease of the agglutinated dust），是"顶着一头毛发的尘土泡沫"（this hair-crowned bubble of the dust），说人有"一点荣耀与尊严，可怜的精神瑰宝"（some rag of honour, the poor jewel of their souls）。斯蒂文森还会过度使用连词，故意违反简洁原则，以便取得文学效果，比如"The canting moralist tells us of right and wrong; *and* we look abroad, even on the face of our small earth, *and* find them change with every climate, *and* no country where some action is not honoured for a virtue and none where it is not branded for a vice; *and* we look in our experience, *and* find no vital congruity in the wisest rules, but at the best a municipal fitness."，在这里作者连续不断地使用 and 这个连接词。

面对这些有一定意义的前景化语言表达法，译者应该采取什么办法呢？我的原则是，可能的话，尽量保留原文的语言特征，比如"一个分裂成百万，百万聚合成一个"就保留了原文词的交错配列。那个 rots 的隐喻也还原成"腐烂"；vital putrescence 当然可以很自然地翻译成"必不可少的腐烂之物"，保留那个矛盾；一系列的图像隐喻都尽可能还原，如"顶着一头毛发的尘土泡沫"等。但是译者却不应该过度在这些语言技巧上花太多精力。比如最后一个例子中频繁使用的 and，我在译文中就没有刻意去重复。斯蒂文森这篇散文中饱满的激情，不是形式对应的译法可以传达的。译者还得见机行事，在不影响散文总体效果的前提下，照顾到一些前景化的表达法就够了。

我不想以谈语言形式来结束这篇导读。分享这样一篇令人心潮起伏的散文，就得用令人心潮起伏的语言来收尾。还是回到令人心潮起伏的现实中来吧！看看眼前的世界，看看国与国间的纷争，看看你死我活的党争，看看尔虞我诈的商人，看看背信弃义的朋友，看看无家可归的穷汉，看看腰缠万贯的富人，我们身上兽性的一面是否过于膨胀了？我不奢望一个干干净净的"华胥国境"，因为人自己没有能力把身上的"兽性"斩尽杀绝。但我们至少能像斯蒂文森在本文中说的那样，"守着一点美德"，"保留着一点高洁的思想和行为"，"展现出一些善举"。我们和斯蒂文森有同样的愿望："我们这些活着的生灵，居住在这个充满恐怖的岛屿上，被握在死亡的巨掌中，置身如此境遇，上帝啊，千万不要让这个能站立、能理论、自觉聪慧的人在行善路上消磨了意志，不要让他因努力无果而灰心绝望、恶言抱怨。……毕竟并非所有的努力都是徒劳。"

让我用傅雷《约翰·克利斯朵夫》译者献辞中的几句话来结束这篇导读：

> 真正的光明决不是永没有黑暗的时间，只是永不被黑暗所掩蔽罢了。真正的英雄决不是永没有卑下的情操，只是永不被卑下的情操所屈服罢了。所以在你要战胜外来的敌人之前，先得战胜你内在的敌人；你不必害怕沉沦堕落，只消你能不断的自拔与更新。

参考资料

F. C. Riedel, A classical rhetorical analysis of some elements of Stevenson's essay style, *Style*, Vol. 3, No. 2 (Spring 1969), pp. 182–199, Penn State University Press (URL: http://www.jstor.org/stable/42945021).

Louise M. Rosenblatt, The Writer's Dilemma: A Case History and a Critique, *International Journal of Ethics*, Vol. 46, No. 2 (Jan., 1936), pp. 195–211, The University of Chicago Press (URL: http://www.jstor.org/stable/2989354).

Robert Louis Stevenson, *Essays of Robert Louis Stevenson* (Google Books), The Floating Press, Jan 1, 2009.

RLS website: http://robert-louis-stevenson.org/timeline/.

Pulvis et Umbra (2)

II

What a monstrous spectre is this man, the disease of the agglutinated dust,[31] lifting alternate feet or lying drugged with slumber; killing, feeding, growing, bringing forth small copies of himself; grown upon with hair like grass, fitted with eyes that move and glitter in his face; a thing to set children screaming;—and yet looked at nearlier, known as his fellows know him, how surprising are his attributes! Poor soul, here for so little, cast among so many hardships, filled with desires so incommensurate and so inconsistent,[32] savagely surrounded, savagely descended, irremediably condemned to prey upon his fellow lives:[33] who should have blamed him had he been of a piece with his destiny and a being merely barbarous?[34] And we look and behold him instead filled with imperfect virtues: infinitely childish, often admirably valiant, often touchingly kind; sitting down, amidst his momentary life, to debate of right and wrong and the attributes of the deity;[35] rising up to do battle for an egg or die for an idea; singling out his friends and his mate with cordial affection;[36] bringing forth in pain, rearing with long-suffering solicitude, his young. To touch the heart of his mystery,[37] we find in him one thought, strange to the point of lunacy: the thought of duty;[38] the thought of something owing to himself, to his

微尘与幻影（二）

二

人是多么可怕的怪物，是一个尘土黏合成的病体，用脚交替走，睡倒如酩酊；他杀戮，他吃喝，他成长，他复制出自己的下一代；长出的头发如野草，脸上的眼睛不停转动、闪闪发光；他让孩童见了大声惊叫；可若像同伴一样近距离去端详人，他的特征又是多么令人惊讶！可怜的人啊，在世上如昙花一现，苦难缠身，但他的欲望总不切实际，所望又出尔反尔，他身处野性世界，可自己也是野性物种的后裔，怎么都摆脱不了捕杀同伴的天生习性：若他天性使然野蛮依旧，谁又会责怪他呢？可我们看到的人虽不完美，却尽显美德：天真得堪比孩童，英勇得令人钦佩，善良得让人感动；一生虽短如瞬间，却要坐下来争个是非对错，要大谈神的属性特征；为一枚鸡蛋奔赴战场，为一个观念视死如归；对朋友和伴侣情有独钟；忍痛把孩子带到世上，又在无尽的焦虑牵挂中，将其抚养成人。我们探寻深藏人心底的秘密，发现他心怀一志，那志向奇特得极尽癫狂，竟是责任感，就是一种对自己、对邻居、对上帝负有债责的感觉，或者说这是一种理想，只要可能就会奋力向上，就要

neighbour, to his God: an ideal of decency,[39] to which he would rise if it were possible; a limit of shame, below which, if it be possible, he will not stoop.[40] The design in most men is one of conformity;[41] here and there, in picked natures, it transcends itself and soars on the other side, arming martyrs with independence;[42] but in all, in their degrees, it is a bosom thought:[43] —Not in man alone, for we trace it in dogs and cats whom we know fairly well, and doubtless some similar point of honour sways[44] the elephant, the oyster, and the louse, of whom we know so little: —But in man, at least, it sways with so complete an empire that merely selfish things come second, even with the selfish:[45] that appetites are starved, fears are conquered, pains supported; that almost the dullest shrinks from the reproof of a glance, although it were a child's; and all but the most cowardly stand amid the risks of war; and the more noble, having strongly conceived an act as due to their ideal, affront and embrace death.[46] Strange enough if, with their singular origin and perverted practice, they think they are to be rewarded in some future life: stranger still, if they are persuaded of the contrary, and think this blow, which they solicit, will strike them senseless for eternity.[47] I shall be reminded what a tragedy of misconception and misconduct man at large presents: of organised injustice, cowardly violence and treacherous crime; and of the damning imperfections of the best.[48] They cannot be too darkly drawn.[49] Man is indeed marked for failure in his efforts to do right.[50] But where the best consistently miscarry, how tenfold more remarkable that all should continue to strive; and surely we should find it both touching and inspiriting, that in a field from which success is banished, our race should not cease to labour.

If the first view of this creature, stalking in his rotatory isle, be

把人做得堂堂正正；抑或说这是他坚守的道德底线，只要能做到就决不堕落沉沦。大多数人的思维定势就是随大流；但少数精英会超越自己，不随波逐流，成为志士仁人，独立于芸芸众生；但是总而言之，这是一个深藏在内心的思想，各人程度不同而已。这个想法不仅人有，我们还可以在比较熟悉的狗和猫身上找到，无疑我们不怎么熟悉的大象、牡蛎和虱子也有几分荣誉感。但是至少人的荣誉感左右着他的行动，为了荣誉，纯粹的私事只能退居次位，就算是自私的人也会那么选择；为了荣誉，就算是饥饿，哪怕是恐惧，或者是疼痛都不在话下；为了荣誉，就算是最厚颜的人都怕外人投来责难的目光，即便那是孩子的目光；所有的人，除掉仅有的几个不可救药的懦夫，所有的人都会在战争的危险中屹立；更为高尚的人，因心怀理想，理想又孕育出行动，人便会坦然面对死亡、拥抱死亡。人源于兽，起源奇特，又劣迹斑斑，但他们仍相信自己会在来世得到回报，真可称奇；而如果他们根本就不信有来世，并认为此生历尽的苦难并不会给他带来永恒，却仍在尽责的路上自寻苦难，那就更称奇了。这使我想到，人总体上呈现给我们的是一个误解和误行的巨大悲剧：有组织的不公正、懦夫般的残暴、手段奸诈的犯罪，优秀者致命的不完美。把这些不完美描绘得怎么黑暗都不过分。人在努力行善时确实总有失误，这是命中注定的。但是虽然杰出者总是有失完美，可他们百折不挠的作风却更让人刮目相看。在一个成功完全无望的赛场上，我们人类竟然不懈努力，这怎能不让人感动，不让人精神振奋！

初看人类，这个在旋转岛屿上高视阔步的物种，会令勇者勇气

a thing to shake the courage of the stoutest, on this nearer sight, he startles us with an admiring wonder. It matters not where we look, under what climate we observe him, in what stage of society, in what depth of ignorance, burthened with what erroneous morality;[51] by camp-fires in Assiniboia, the snow powdering his shoulders, the wind plucking his blanket, as he sits, passing the ceremonial calumet and uttering his grave opinions like a Roman senator;[52] in ships at sea, a man inured to hardship and vile pleasures,[53] his brightest hope a fiddle in a tavern and a bedizened trull who sells herself to rob him, and he for all that simple, innocent, cheerful, kindly like a child, constant to toil, brave to drown, for others;[54] in the slums of cities, moving among indifferent millions to mechanical employments, without hope of change in the future, with scarce a pleasure in the present, and yet true to his virtues, honest up to his lights, kind to his neighbours, tempted perhaps in vain by the bright gin-palace, perhaps long-suffering with the drunken wife that ruins him;[55] in India (a woman this time) kneeling with broken cries and streaming tears, as she drowns her child in the sacred river;[56] in the brothel, the discard of society, living mainly on strong drink, fed with affronts, a fool, a thief, the comrade of thieves, and even here keeping the point of honour and the touch of pity, often repaying the world's scorn with service, often standing firm upon a scruple, and at a certain cost, rejecting riches:[57] —everywhere some virtue cherished or affected, everywhere some decency of thought and carriage, everywhere the ensign of man's ineffectual goodness:—ah![58] if I could show you this! if I could show you these men and women, all the world over, in every stage of history, under every abuse of error,[59] under every circumstance of failure, without hope, without help, without thanks, still

顿失，但近看人类，却令我们赞叹不已。不管你是在什么地方观察人，无论你是在什么环境下观察，还是在哪个社会阶段观察，无论你观察的人多么愚昧，心术多么不正，你都能看得肃然起敬；在加拿大阿西尼博亚的营火旁，一个人肩上飞雪如絮，寒风掀起他的披毯，在庄严的仪式中端坐，递过一个象征和平的烟斗，口中念叨着严肃的词语，活像个罗马元老；在行于大海的船上，一位曾历尽苦难，也苦中作乐的人，最让他欢快的愿望就是酒吧中有把提琴，有一位卖身取财的妓女相伴，而他，尽管苦难缠身，却仍像孩童一般简单、无邪、欢快、亲切，不停地辛劳，勇于为他人牺牲；在城市的贫民区，跟成百上千无动于衷的人，一起去干机械呆板的工作，未来没有改变的希望，现在少有快乐的时光，但他却德行依旧，良知未泯，仍旧善待邻里，在光鲜诱人的酒铺前抵挡住酒精的诱惑，仍守着酗酒成性的妻子，尽管那女人已让他饱受磨难，毁其一生；在印度，这回是一个女人，跪在地上，嗓音嘶哑，泪流满面，为取悦神灵，她正将自己的孩子淹死在圣河；在妓院，一个被社会抛弃的人，一个靠烈酒活着、饱受屈辱的女人，一个蠢人，扒手，扒手的朋友，就是这样一个人，仍守住一点尊严，保留着一丝同情，虽然世界蔑视她，可她却仍助人为乐，常坚守一点道德，也不在乎付出一些代价，拒财富于门外。无论在任何地方，不管是起于诚心还是装点门面，人都守着一点美德；无论在任何地方，人都保留着一点高洁的思想和行为；无论在任何地方，人都展现出一些善举，虽然这些善举总是徒劳。啊！让我向你展现人的光辉吧！让我为你展现这些男男女女吧！在世界的任何角落，在历史的每个阶段，在任何不公的世道里，在所有失败的境遇中，没有希望，没人帮助，没

obscurely fighting the lost fight of virtue, still clinging, in the brothel or on the scaffold, to some rag of honour, the poor jewel of their souls! They may seek to escape, and yet they cannot; it is not alone their privilege and glory, but their doom;[60] they are condemned to some nobility; all their lives long, the desire of good is at their heels, the implacable hunter.

Of all earth's meteors,[61] here at least is the most strange and consoling: that this ennobled lemur, this hair-crowned bubble of the dust, this inheritor of a few years and sorrows,[62] should yet deny himself his rare delights, and add to his frequent pains, and live for an ideal, however misconceived. Nor can we stop with man. A new doctrine, received with screams a little while ago by canting moralists, and still not properly worked into the body of our thoughts,[63] lights us a step farther into the heart of this rough but noble universe.[64] For nowadays the pride of man denies in vain his kinship with the original dust.[65] He stands no longer like a thing apart. Close at his heels we see the dog, prince of another genius: and in him too, we see dumbly testified the same cultus of an unattainable ideal, the same constancy in failure.[66] Does it stop with the dog? We look at our feet where the ground is blackened with the swarming ant: a creature so small, so far from us in the hierarchy of brutes, that we can scarce trace and scarce comprehend his doings; and here also, in his ordered polities and rigorous justice, we see confessed the law of duty and the fact of individual sin.[67] Does it stop, then, with the ant? Rather this desire of well-doing and this doom of frailty run through all the grades of life: rather is this earth, from the frosty top of Everest to the next margin of the internal fire,[68] one stage of ineffectual virtues and one temple of pious tears and perseverance. The whole creation groaneth and travaileth together.[69] It is the common

人感谢，却为坚守道德，默默无闻地打着一场必输的战斗，在妓院里，在断头台上，仍然坚守着那一点荣耀与尊严，他们那可怜的精神瑰宝！他们可以设法逃避，但他们不能逃避；这不仅是他们的殊荣，还是他们的命运；他们命中注定要保有一些高贵；在他们的一生中，行善的欲望和他们形影不离，恰似不获猎物誓不罢休的猎手。

所有在地球上转瞬即逝的动物里，人至少是最怪异也最令人欣慰的：这个高贵的猿猴，这个顶着一头毛发的尘土泡沫，这个传承了祖先寿命短暂、悲伤不断特征的人，竟然放弃难得的快乐，在接踵而来的痛苦上再加痛苦，为一个理想而活，不管那个理想是如何不靠谱。我们也不能仅把这些特征局限于人类。最近一个新的理论引得虚伪的道德家惊呼不已，至今还没有被我们的思想体系接受，却把这条坎坷却高尚的宇宙探索之路照亮一程。因为高傲的人现在已无法撇清与原始微尘的亲缘关系了。他已无法孤单而立。紧跟其后的就是狗，另一个天才王子。尽管狗不会说话，但在狗身上，我们照样看到了对无法达到之理想的膜拜，看到了在失败面前百折不挠的决心。难道只有狗是那样吗？我们看看脚下那块地上黑黑的一群蚂蚁：那可是极微小的生灵，在动物等级的排列上和人相距甚远，我们甚至对它们的所作所为无法察觉，很难理解；但就是在蚂蚁身上，在它们有序的组织结构和严密的公正体系里，我们也看到了责任的法则和个体的罪恶。那么这种现象仅到蚂蚁为止吗？绝非如此，这种想行善的欲望和总失败的厄运存在于所有等级的生物中：从珠穆朗玛峰的雪山顶，到地火的边缘，这个地球更像是一个舞台，台上的演员就想显出美德却总事与愿违，或像是一座庙宇，

and the god-like law of life. The browsers, the biters, the barkers, the hairy coats of field and forest,[70] the squirrel in the oak, the thousand-footed creeper in the dust, as they share with us the gift of life, share with us the love of an ideal: strive like us—like us are tempted to grow weary of the struggle—to do well; like us receive at times unmerited refreshment,[71] visitings of support, returns of courage; and are condemned like us to be crucified between that double law of the members and the will.[72] Are they like us, I wonder in the timid hope of some reward, some sugar with the drug? do they, too, stand aghast at unrewarded virtues, at the sufferings of those whom, in our partiality, we take to be just, and the prosperity of such as, in our blindness, we call wicked?[73] It may be, and yet God knows what they should look for.[74] Even while they look, even while they repent, the foot of man treads them by thousands in the dust, the yelping hounds burst upon their trail, the bullet speeds, the knives are heating in the den of the vivisectionist;[75] or the dew falls, and the generation of a day is blotted out.[76] For these are creatures, compared with whom our weakness is strength, our ignorance wisdom, our brief span eternity.

And as we dwell, we living things, in our isle of terror[77] and under the imminent hand of death, God forbid it should be man the erected, the reasoner, the wise in his own eyes—God forbid it should be man that wearies in well-doing, that despairs of unrewarded effort, or utters the language of complaint.[78] Let it be enough for faith, that the whole creation groans in mortal frailty, strives with unconquerable constancy: Surely not all in vain.[79]

庙里的生灵虔诚依旧，虽忍痛泪流，却坚韧不拔。凡受造之物都要一同呻吟劳苦。这是最基本的生命神律。靠嫩草为生的动物，咬人、吠叫的动物，田野森林中毛茸茸的动物，栖身橡树中的松鼠，地上行走的百足爬虫，都和我们人一样共享生命的礼物，都和人一样热爱理想，都和人一样努力要将事做好，也和人一样会在做事的奋斗中变得意兴阑珊；也和人一样不时会获得些受之有愧的东西而精神一振，会得到援助，会重拾勇气；他们也和人一样，逃脱不了在肉体欲望和个人意志间煎熬的命运。我不禁要问，他们是否也和我们一样，怯生生地希望有一些酬劳，希望吃一勺苦药时也有一匙糖？他们是否也和我们一样，以偏见盲从断善恶，觉得行善而无回报，觉得仁者受难、恶人发达，因而也会感到震惊不平？他们或许真和我们一样善恶分明，但动物该如何定夺善恶只有上帝知道。即便动物在分辨善恶时，即便它们在因错忏悔时，人都会用脚在地上踩踏这些千百生灵，猎犬在它们身上狂叫而过，子弹在它们身边飞驰；医生在动物解剖室内把刀加热消毒；夜幕降临，随着一天的结束，动物的一生也结束了。与这些生灵相比，我们的软弱已是它们的强悍，我们的愚昧已是它们的智慧，我们的一刹那已是它们的永恒。

我们这些活着的生灵，居住在这个充满恐怖的岛屿上，被握在死亡的巨掌中，置身如此境遇，上帝啊，千万不要让这个能站立、能理论、自觉聪慧的人在行善路上消磨了意志，不要让他因努力无果而灰心绝望、恶言抱怨。所有受造的生灵都是凡身肉体，受挫遭难，总会呻吟，但他们都不屈不挠、努力奋进，这足以撑起人的信心。毕竟并非所有的努力都是徒劳。

注　释

31. 在第一节对动物，特别是对人的描写后，斯蒂文森在这一节专门讨论人类。他开门见山的用词都是我们人类一般意义上的负面词，如 spectre 在 OED 中的解释是 "an apparition, phantom, or ghost, esp. one of a terrifying nature or aspect"，而 monstrous 一词也有贬义。而且沿袭上一节，他把人称为是一个疾病。这里的 agglutinated dust 使人联想到《圣经》中人由泥土而来，agglutinated 的意思就是黏合起来，此处是斯蒂文森自己选用的词，翻译的时候以按照原文翻译为上策。

32. 这一长句中的 here for so little 并不指数量的多少，而实际指时间长短，说明人活在人世的时间短暂。desires so incommensurate 主要是说超出一般欲望（out of proportion）。若翻译成"强烈的"表面上似乎也不错，但却还是脱离原文文字的意思。假如我们一般人有存款亿万的欲望，那就是 incommensurate 的意思，那欲望当然是强烈的，但是却不是这个形容词的意思，这个词总是暗示你的欲望不可能达到。而 inconsistent 的意思就是欲望之间有冲突，或者说今天想要什么，但明天又要其他东西了。这里译成"出尔反尔"，略有贬义，所以也可以用其他方法翻译这个意思，如欲望相互冲突。

33. 这个 savagely surrounded 是说野性物种包围着人，换个角度看，就是说人身处野性世界，而 savagely descended 则是说人是野性物种的后裔。显然斯蒂文森这里受到了达尔文进化论的影响，认为人来自猿猴，人与猿猴都充满野性。另外，condemn 这个词的意思不是我们常见的谴责之类的意思，这里是说命中注定要干某事的意思［to doom or devote to some (unkind) fate or condition; (in pass.) to be doomed by fate to some condition or to do something］。

34. 这句直接与上句衔接，人确实从野兽进化而来，所以假如他摆脱不了与生俱来的野性（with his destiny），而且在行为中表现出野性（merely barbarous），假如是那样的话，我们也不应该责怪他，原谅他的潜台词就是人毕竟是由野兽进化而来，所以斯蒂文森把这篇文章称为达尔文主义的说教。从语法上看，这句是与事实不符的虚拟语气。也就是说，他强调的是人其实并不是野蛮的。下面一长段，甚至到文章结束，作者都是在说人有别于野性的地方。另外 of a piece 这里是指人，就是具有某种特质的人（OED: applied to a person in whom some quality is exemplified or realized），比如"He was a piece of Perfection, noisy Perfection himself which I always recollect with regard."。最后，从翻译的角度看，merely 一词只是提示野性的程度，并不是非常重要的，所以从行文考虑，翻译时略去也不是大问题。merely 一词不只有一般我们熟悉的"仅仅"的意思，这个词还有 purely、entirely、absolutely、quite 等意思，可根据上下文选择。

35. 人们不仅就对错争论，而且还就 attributes of the deity 相互争论，这个短语实际就是在说人们还就有关神的题目争论，换句话说，即人类在神学方面的探索、讨论，乃至争论。

36. 这句中的 do battle for an egg or die for an idea 典自斯威夫特《格列佛游记》中的大蛋端和小蛋端。小说中，小人国为水煮蛋该从大的一端（big end）剥开还是小的一端（little end）剥开而争论，或者更确切地说为了一种想法而争斗。至于

singling out his friends and his mate with cordial affection 这部分，应该理解为人类不是不分青红皂白与所有人分享感情的，而是有选择性的，给某些人特殊感情。

37. 这里的 the heart of his mystery 典自《圣经》（1 Corinthians 15: 51）："Behold, I tell you a mystery"，或者源自 *Hamlet,* III, 2, 360："you would pluck out the heart of my mystery"（"你想要探出我的内心的秘密"——朱生豪译）。mystery 这个词在这里的意思就是 secret。从翻译的角度看，to touch 可以直接翻译成"触碰"，但是根据后面的动词 find one thought，这个 touch 翻译成"探索"也可以。为了保留原文的文字特色，可直译原词（如 touch、mystery）；但为了增加可读性，仍然是"探索心中的秘密"之类的译法更可取。

38. 学术界常把 the thought of duty 这个短语联系到康德的一些论说，如"Two things fill the mind with ever new and increasing admiration and awe, the oftener and the more steadily we reflect on them: the starry heavens above and the moral law within."（1788）。

39. 这是对前一句 the thought of duty 的进一步解释，就是你觉得对自己、邻居和神应该做些什么，owing to 也可以用 due to，或者说 You have to do something for them。在这里我们可以看出，斯蒂文森超越了进化论的观点，人不仅仅是以生物科学为基础的进化生物，他还有责任感、有廉耻（an ideal of decency 和 shame），他将在接下来的文字中大谈人的这个责任感，甚至说得让人流泪。

40. 这里的 rise 和 stoop 是从两个方面说同一个道理，为了这个 decency，人愿意起而奋斗，但是这是很不容易做到的，所以他又加了一句（if it were possible）。同理，那个羞耻感也是有限度的（a limit of shame），在这个限度之内（below which），可能的话，人是愿意挺直腰板的。在作者看来，夸下海口结果却做不到是没有意义的，所以他加了修饰语（"如果可能的话"）。

41. 这句的大意就是大多数人生来就是做大多数人做的事，一般不会做与众不同的事。句子中的 conformity 就是与别人一致（趋同）的意思。句子中的 design 一般语境里常会让人想起造物主的创造，但是这里提示 the way their mind works。

42. 前面一句是说大多数人的一生是随大流的，但不排除这里或那里（here and there），在几个优秀者（picked natures）中，人生的设计让这些精英超越随大流的倾向（the design transcends itself），做出与众不同的另类事（on the other side）。形容词 picked 在 OED 中有个定义（chosen, selected, esp. for special excellence, or for a definite purpose）适合这个语境，说明这样的人不是芸芸众生，而是少数精英。而 natures 这个词表示人（OED: a person of a particular quality or character）。it 和 itself 都是指 design，就是指一般人思维的方式（思维定势就是随大流）。这个 soars on the other side 就是指 other than conformity，就是不随大流，soars 这个词说明作者认为不随大流是高尚的，所以才有向上的方向，但一些细节翻译时未必需要包括进去。arming 的主语也是 the design，被武装的就是那些履行责任、守住道德底线的人，而 independence 就是指独立于随大流的倾向（independence from conformity）。

43. 这个 a bosom thought 就是指责任、原则、道德底线这些思想，bosom 表示深藏在心底的想法，和前面的 to touch the heart of his mystery 呼应，这种想法一般是深藏的秘密。in their degrees

表示这个深藏的秘密程度不同。

44. 这个 sway 的意思就是 to motivate、to govern、to influence，也就是说一种荣誉感控制或影响着大象等动物，或者说荣誉感是这些动物的动力。这句中的 honour 和前面的 duty 在内容上是同义的。此外，翻译的时候没有必要一定要保留 sway 这个动词，简单地说"大象等动物也会有荣誉感或责任感"也可以。

45. 在"But in man…"这一长句中，有两点要注意。在这里 sway 和前面一句用法不同。在前面 sway 的宾语是大象等动物，但是在这句里 sway 没有宾语，句子的主干就是"But in man, it sways with an empire"，也就是说，前面说在大象等动物中，荣誉有左右它们的作用，但是在人类，荣誉的作用更大。达到什么程度呢？这个程度就是 with 短语。empire 这个词虽然是帝国的意思，但是它的引申含义就是巨大影响的意思（OED: In extended use. Supreme command; complete or paramount influence, absolute sway; dominance, control）。作者还在这个短语中用了一个 so complete… that… 的程度修饰语（影响力如此之大，以至于……）。这个由 that 引导的程度短语有三个（so complete that merely selfish…, that appetite…, that almost the dullest…）。另外，merely selfish 中的 merely 用 only 解释不通，大意更接近 completely，比如在 OED 中就有"absolutely, entirely; quite, altogether"的意思。

46. 本句中的 ideal 根据上下文其实际内容就是上面一直在说的 duty 或 honour，译者当然可以用"理想"这个词，但换成"责任感"或"荣誉感"大意也差不多。而 affront 这个词确实有 face 的意思，但是不够到位。一般这个词总表示在逆境面前以一种毫不在乎的态度面对一个困难的局面，可以加一个副词，如坦然面对等。

47. 此处 strange 和 stranger 描写两种情况。第一种情况是人有一个源于动物的奇特起源（singular origin），因此人的行为做派也是道德上不堪的（perverted practice），这是达尔文主义人从猴子进化而来的观点。可如果这样的人仍觉得自己在来世会得到回报（rewarded in some future life），就不合常理，所以说是奇怪的（strange）。第二个情况是如果人恰恰相反，根本就不相信有来世（persuaded of the contrary），并认为在世上履行责任时所遭受的灾难（this blow）将剥夺他们相信永恒的观念（即不相信会有永恒），可是他们仍然在履行责任保持荣誉的路上自寻苦难（solicit this blow），那么就更奇怪了（stranger still）。这里 strike 的意思可以采用 OED 中下面的定义：to deprive (a person) suddenly of life, or of one of the faculties, as if by a physical blow. Often with complement, as to strike dead, blind, deaf, dumb。这句里的 strike them senseless for eternity 可以解释成 will deprive them of their sense of eternity，句型和 strike a person deaf 一样（verb-object-adjective）。

48. 这里的 organised injustice 指那些有组织的作恶而造成的不公平现象，比如由国家做出的移民政策使得有人不能和亲人团聚，就是有组织的不公现象。但斯蒂文森写这句话时心中想到的可能是爱尔兰的有组织的军事活动，这些行动在 18 和 19 世纪对英国的不少城镇或地标性建筑做过攻击。另外，下面的 imperfections of the best 主要是指人中间的那些优秀者所做的不良表现，斯蒂文森在他的作品中反复提到人的不完美，这是他作品的主题之一。另外，I shall be reminded 似乎可以基本理解为 This reminds me。

49. 注意这句中很容易把主语they理解成人，但这里的主语应该是imperfections，因为除了这个词，前面没有第三人称复数的名词。而cannot be too的基本意思就是怎么说都不过分，句型类似于成语"You can't be too careful."（怎么当心都不过分）。

50. 这里的marked有命中或事先决定的意思，比如我们可以说"The pig is marked for slaughter next week"。一般常跟for或to不定式。

51. 前面一句是说，人让我们惊讶赞叹。而这个It matters not就是说无论在什么情况下，人都让我们看得惊讶赞叹，虽然它只出现了一次，但它的连贯作用贯穿在下面一长段中。只有这样理解，才能把下面那么多的例子和前面的startles us with an admiring wonder有逻辑地联系起来，也就是说，无论在下面任何情况下，人都能让你惊讶赞叹。句中的in what depth of ignorance是说人不管有多么无知，无论是牛津大学的教授，还是根本读不懂《圣经》的文盲，都没有区别，都能让人惊讶赞叹。在burthened with what erroneous morality中的burthened是旧的拼写法，意思就是burdened，斯蒂文森在多处使用旧拼写法；另外这句话的意思就是不管一个人有多么错误的道德观，但人生来就有做善事的本性，比如一个江洋大盗也有让你赞叹的地方。

52. 这句最前面的Assiniboia是指加拿大马尼托巴以西的一个地方。calumet是印第安人用的一个象征和平的烟斗。这句在描写一个仪式，一位部落的头人将象征和平的烟斗递给别人，口中念念有词，活像个古罗马的元老。

53. 这句是描写在海上的一个人，这个人曾经经历过困苦（inured to hardship），同时也有过带苦味的快乐（vile pleasures），这个 vile 表示这种快乐和愉悦是不好的经历（vile=bad, nasty, obnoxious, unpleasant），比如因为没有钱而去喝劣质的烧酒等。

54. 从注释 53 开始，这很长的一句都是在描写 a man，而这个人所处的地点就是 in ships at sea，其余的都是围绕这个人展开的描写。其中的 for all that 就是 in spite of that 的意思。"brave to drown, for others"就是说这个在海上的人，他也许是个水手，虽然历尽艰难，但却愿意为别人牺牲，比如风暴来临、海涛汹涌，为了船上人的安全，他愿意爬到桅杆上去做一件事；若有人掉在海里，他会跳到海中去营救。

55. 这里的 lights 根据上下文理解成内心的良知（conscience）较合适，也就是前面一再提到的 duty、honour 等。原文中的 up to (his lights) 表示程度，有 as far as 的意思，暗示他尽其可能守护着自己的良知（lights）。tempted perhaps in vain 说明诱惑没有成功，而诱惑他的是一家光鲜的酒铺（bright gin-palace）。perhaps long-suffering with the drunken wife that ruins him 这部分仍然是在说这个蓝领工人，他家里有一个酗酒的妻子，让他长期受尽折磨，他的一生都毁了；此情此景，换一位男人也许早将妻子扫地出门，可他没有，也许谈不上善待，却未离未弃。没有抛弃妻子的意思并不在文字中，但是如果不加进去，句子就不符合逻辑，因为这一整句都是在说这位工人在艰难时刻的优良品质。

56. 这里描写的印度女人溺死自己孩子的做法是过去的历史，不是现在。当时，人们出于迷信，为了取悦神灵，平息神的愤怒，母亲会到圣河（恒河）去把自己的孩子溺死在水中。

57. 这句中的 the touch of pity 典自"No beast so fierce but knows some touch of pity."（*Richard III*, I. 2. 71）。这一句主要是在说妓

女，所以这个 (repay scorn with) service 很容易误解为妓女职业范围内的服务。那样理解是错误的，因为这里是在说人的优点，斯蒂文森从来都没有把妓女提供的服务当成优点。至于 (stand firm upon a) scruple 表示人的一点诚信或道德准则，比如说你答应给人一点微不足道的帮助，你不食言。再比如一个妓女原来和嫖客说好服务费是 10 英镑，可是嫖客错付给她 11 英镑，妓女绝不收多余的钱，尽管这个数字微不足道。也就是说，这个词不是指大原则，而是小原则，但再小也是原则。

58. 此处的 affected 可解释成"假装的"，说明那些有关德行的观念或举止是做给人看的（pretended），而前面的 cherished 则是发自内心的（authentically believed in）。本句点出了人类的实际情况，有些人是真心在实践德行，他们的德行不是口头，是发自内心的（cherish=to hold dear，cling to），但有些人的德行是表演出来的（affected），但不管怎样，人总是会觉得有德行是件光脸的事，就算不付诸行动，还是觉得那是好事，也得做些姿态（artificial gesture）。而且不管动机是什么，所做之事客观上毕竟都是善事（virtue）。

59. 在 under every abuse of error 中的 abuse 一般情况下都是"滥用"等意思，但此处似乎可以解释为 accusation，整个短语的意思大致就是用错误的依据来谴责别人（accusation against a person based on erroneous evidence）。比如说，反右斗争中有些知识分子的遭遇就是 under an abuse of error。其实本段中斯蒂文森提到的一些例子，那些被社会抛弃的边缘人物，那些被称为盗贼娼妓的人，之所以沦落到那种地步，是各有原因的，世道对他们的裁判是不公正的，因为世道裁判的基础是错误的。所以这个短语的深层含义就是不公正，就是指人在那种不公正的境遇中。

60. 这里的 not alone 一般常和 but 连用，alone 的意思和 only 接近，比如"They are not alone objecting, but also envisioning a better society"。

61. 这个 meteors 当然不能翻译成流星，因为这里是当隐喻使用的，指地球上的动物（包括人类）。该词的隐喻意思可有两层，首先是流星在宇宙间漫游（roaming），隐喻含义是动物在地球上漫游；第二个是流星转瞬即逝，隐喻含义是动物在地球上生存的时间短暂。翻译的时候不必面面俱到，详见译文。

62. 在 bubble of the dust 中的 dust 可追溯到《圣经》中上帝创造人类："And the Lord God made man from the dust of the earth, breathing into him the breath of life: and man became a living soul."(Genesis 2: 7) 另外，bubble 一词有一下子就破灭的意思，暗指人的生命短暂，和前面 meteors 的短暂呼应。这里的 inheritor 当然表示传承者的意思，所传承的就是 a few years 和 sorrows，也就是说，人只能活数年，人满是悲哀，这些特点都是从祖先那里继承来的，不是自己的选择。

63. 这个 a new doctrine 指的就是达尔文的进化论，也就是他在 1859 年出版的《物种起源》(Origin of Species)。斯蒂文森的这篇文章写于 1888 年，离《物种起源》出版没有几十年（a little while ago）。这个理论刚刚出来时受到保守势力的极力反对（received with screams），所以当时达尔文的观点还属于异端，还没有被纳入人类的思想体系（still not properly worked into the body of our thoughts）。

64. 这句的重点不是理解问题，而是翻译问题。lights us a step farther into the heart of this rough but noble universe 表示人在走路的时候看不清前程，点上一盏灯就亮了，就能走下去了，否则瞎走，其背后的概念隐喻是 exploring the universe is a journey，由于有 step 这个词，这个隐喻就确定无疑了。遇到这类不是非常显而易见的隐喻，我的翻译策略是，如果保留隐喻不影响阅读，最好不要换成非隐喻或其他隐喻。有些译者会调换隐喻，比如"that made their achievement a lamp to mankind for all the rest of history"这句，在吴文藻、冰心主译的《世界史纲》中译成"致使以后的历史，经常把这一时期所取得的成就，看成是人类智慧的源泉"，把原文灯照亮路的隐喻换成了源泉。其实你若深究，原文的 lamp 引发的隐喻是路，而泉源引发的隐喻是水。前者是帮助你认准方向，后者是给你水分和营养，在认知层面上是完全不搭界的。为什么不保留原文的灯呢？下面的翻译丝毫不影响阅读：其成就如一盏明灯，照亮日后人类的历史。

65. 人传统上总是觉得自己优于其他动物，所以要否认与动物的关系。但是由于进化论认为人源自猴子，人就无法否定（denies in vain）任何动物的亲缘关系了。这里的 the original dust 也是与《圣经》中上帝创造万物有关，动物也是由泥土（尘土）做成的。

66. 这句的基本结构是 we see the same cultus dumbly testified。testified 这个词当形容词用时表示"attested; made known, declared"的意思，甚至可以说成是 we see an example of the same cultus。而 dumbly 就是表示狗虽不会说话，但却在其行动中表现出来了 the same cultus。另外，cultus 这个词原本表示对某事物如信奉宗教一般尊崇（great respect）。若将 the same cultus of an unattainable ideal 翻译成"对无法达到理想的不倦追求"，大意虽勉强可以解释，不过还是背离原文文字的意思，最好还是从对无法实现的理想之膜拜这个思路翻译。

67. 这句中的 confessed 和前面的 testified 是相同的意思（made known, revealed, open to recognition）。作者也许觉得再用原来的词有重复之嫌，所以换用 confessed，但译者不必故意回避重复，汉语中仍然可以用"也看到"。

68. 这个 next margin of the internal fire 就是指地球中心的火，作者是在说地球的最高处（珠穆朗玛峰）和地球的最低处（大地深处）。

69. 见《圣经》："For we know that the whole creation groaneth and travaileth in pain together until now."（Romans 8: 22）在斯蒂文森的时代，会去读他作品的人不会对这个 1600 年代出版的钦定本《圣经》感到陌生，所以作者经常会引用旧版本的词句，但这并没有什么特殊意义，翻译时毫无必要用古旧文字去对应。

70. 这句在说各种动物，而 browsers 这个词表示一些吃嫩草的动物（OED: an animal which feeds on the young shoots, leaves, and twigs of shrubs and trees; a browsing animal），比如牛马等。

71. 现在 refreshment 一词常指茶歇时的茶水、糕点等，但其词义要比这个宽广。任何可以让人振奋的东西都是 refreshment（a thing or an action which refreshes; a means of refreshment），比如任何变化都是一个 refreshment，我们可以说"A hot bath is a great refreshment after a day's work"。在本句中，作者在说，人们不时获得一些受之有愧的东西（unmerited）。比如，在科级干部的位置上干了好多年，突然领导给你提副处级干部了，再比如你摆摊摆了好长时间，无人光顾，突然间出现了第一个客户，或者高温天你口干舌燥，突然别人给你一瓶可乐。

所有这些都可以是refreshment，而作者认为有时人生中获得的东西是受之有愧的。

72. 这里的double law 典自《圣经》："But I see another law in my members, warring against the law of my mind, and bringing me into captivity to the law of sin which is in my members."（Romans 7: 23）说的是两个法的冲突，一个是 the law of my mind（精神），一个是 another law in my members（身体）。注意members是指肢体，不是指成员。之所以被crucified是因为这两者的冲突，比如大热天思想上你仍想伏案写作，但身体上你希望到外边去乘凉。人总是在这类冲突中挣扎。

73. 这句还是将动物和人比照，在揣测动物的内心世界，stand aghast就是极度震惊的意思。是否见到好人无好报而震惊？是否见到善者遭难、恶者发达也会震惊？短语in our partiality 和 in our blindness的意思是类似的，就是说，我们认为那些人是正义的（we take to be just）或者是邪恶的（call wicked），那只是我们的一管之见（partiality），或说那只是我们的盲目推想（blindness），都是主观的，我们未必对。翻译时似乎可以灵活地处理blindness和partiality，比如可以把两个词合并起来（以偏见盲从断善恶）。

74. 这似乎是个不完整的句子，意思应该承接前面的句子。前面在说好人遭罪，坏人享乐，都是我们自己判断的。在这个语境下，我们接着说"It may be"，也许这表明作者对前面问题的肯定，也许它们还真能分辨善恶，但是只有上帝才知道动物（they）应该如何判断善恶（what they should look for）。

75. 这里的while they look似乎和前面一句的look for关联。甚至在动物也像人一样在寻求善恶的答案时，甚至在它们也像人一样对自己的错误有所忏悔时，它们的厄运也接连而至。作者是在用拟人说法，赋予动物人的能力，知道判断善恶，知道做错事后要忏悔，但该被踩踏照样被踩踏，猎狗照样在它们身上飞奔而过，猎手射杀动物的子弹照样在它们身边飞驰，解剖学家照样拿动物解剖开刀，这些事情照常发生。这个 the den of the vivisectionist 是指医生解剖动物的地方，而 the knives are heating 是把解剖动物用的手术刀烧热消毒。斯蒂文森对于解剖动物的看法还算温和，没有强烈反对。但在当时，有些著名作家极力反对这样对待动物，比如拉斯金（John Ruskin）和布朗宁（Robert Browning），前者甚至为此辞去牛津大学文学教授的职务，因为牛津大学允许解剖动物。

76. 露水是在夜晚时出现（降下）的，所以就是指夜晚到来了。虽然汉语露水和降下不算常用搭配，但英语的 dew falls 是个搭配，如《圣经》："And when the dew fell upon the camp in the night, the manna fell upon it."（Numbers 11:9）后面的 the generation of a day is blotted out 这句话的基础是 A day is a life，其中 the generation 是指动物，a day 就是一生，喻指短暂，也就是说，随着露水降临，一天结束，动物的一生也结束了。动词 blotted out 原义是消失（deleted），但在和主语动物搭配后，就转指死亡。这句的时间概念可能确实是基于某些昆虫，比如有一种飞虫叫 mayfly，学名 ephemeron 表示生命短暂，字面意思就是只持续一天（OED: an insect, which, in its winged state, lives but for a day），但这个昆虫却在短短的一天内完成一般意义上的一生活动，包括繁衍传代。这样就能接应下面一句，就是将这种生命短暂的动物（如昆虫）和人相比，虫世界中的一刻钟就是人世界里的数天，恰如"山中（虫世）方一日，世上（人世）已千年"，因此两个不同时空中概念的价值只能相对等值（weakness=strength, ignorance=wisdom, brief span=eternity）。

77. 参见罗伯特·赫里克（Robert Herrick）的诗歌 The White Island, or Place of the Blest: "In this world, the isle of dreams, / While we sit by sorrow's streams, / Tears and terrors are our themes"。

78. 此处的两个 God forbid 是重复的，也就是说，这句话的主要结构是 God forbid it should be man that wearies…, that despairs…，而后面的那个 God forbid 应该是作者重复的口气，也就是说，"the erected, the reasoner, the wise in his own eyes" 就是修饰 man 的。若合并成一个 God forbid 的话，就可以是这样的：God forbid it should be man (who is the erected, the reasoner, the wise in his own eyes) that wearies in well-doing, that despairs of unrewarded effort。另外这句可能有一个隐含语气很容易被忽视。最前面是 we living things，包括了动物和人类。在这样的语境下，作者说 "God forbid it should be man that wearies…, that despairs…"，这个 that 结构显然是个强调句型，强调的是人不能那样（暗示不是其他的动物），就像我们说 It is the old man that took the book，暗示不是 the young man，或不是 the woman。而此处强调是人不应该灰心丧气（wearies），而不是 all the living things，因为人是 "the erected, the reasoner, the wise"，这些都是使人优于其他动物的特征。这个潜台词理解时很容易漏掉，但翻译时倒未必要将这个强调的口气硬安排进去，因为毕竟只是个口气。至于句中的 God forbid 是说后面的事情千万不要发生，也就是说 that wearies 这类事不要发生在人类身上。这句一开始翻译成"千万不应是人消磨了斗

志",当时的考虑就是想把强调句式反映出来(不应是人,与所有生灵区分开的暗示较明显),同时也觉得 God forbid 只是一种感叹词,希望这种事不要发生,翻译时似乎没有必要让上帝参与进来。但是后来反复读译文,感到译文是在刻意把 God 排除在外,而这样避免是没有必要的,因为尽管 God forbid 这个短句确实是感叹词,已属于文化,但它毕竟是在对上帝说话(When we dwell, God, please do not...)。加之,有些人说斯蒂文森是在说进化论,就该排除上帝,但是斯蒂文森将本文称为 Darwinian Sermon,刻意用了 sermon 一词,而且在文章的结束段落里,他某种形式的宗教思想呼之欲出,所以在最后处理时还是把 God 用在了译文里,而由语言学形式结构反映出来的强调含义反而被淡化了(但仍可读出这层意思)。最后,有关 that wearies in well-doing 这句,见《圣经》:"And let us not be weary in well doing: for in due season we shall reap, if we faint not."(Galatians 6: 9)

79. 可以把 that the whole creation groans 这个分句看成是前面 it 的实际内容,即 it 是 let 的形式宾语,实际的宾语就是 that 从句。全部有生命的东西(all the living things)都受难呻吟,但都不屈服,这个事实足够砥砺你保住信心。也就是说,这些逆境是 faith 的基础。这个 mortal 一般翻译成"人的",但此处不宜,因它的意思是"subject to death, destined to die",有的地方指人,但也可以指动物,比如此处就包括所有的动物和人;frailty 一般翻译成"弱点",但说是因弱点而痛苦呻吟,意思有些勉强。所以最好不拘泥于字面意思,就说他们都是有血有肉的生灵,都挡不住痛苦呻吟之类的意思。

A Christmas Sermon (1)

By the time this paper appears, I shall have been talking for twelve months;[1] and it is thought I should take my leave in a formal and seasonable manner.[2] Valedictory eloquence is rare, and death-bed sayings have not often hit the mark of the occasion.[3] Charles Second,[4] wit and sceptic, a man whose life had been one long lesson in human incredulity, an easy-going comrade, a manoeuvring king — remembered and embodied[5] all his wit and scepticism along with more than his usual good humour in the famous "I am afraid, gentlemen, I am an unconscionable time a-dying."[6]

I

An unconscionable time a-dying — there is the picture ("I am afraid, gentlemen,") of your life and of mine. The sands run out, and the hours are "numbered and imputed,"[7] and the days go by; and when the last of these finds us, we have been a long time dying, and what else? The very length is something, if we reach that hour of separation undishonoured; and to have lived at all is doubtless (in the soldierly expression) to have served.[8] There is a tale in Tacitus of how the veterans mutinied in the German wilderness; of how they mobbed Germanicus, clamouring to go home; and of how, seizing their general's hand, these old, war-worn exiles

圣诞说教(一)

当大家见到这篇文章时,我应该已连续讲了十二个月了;人们觉得我该借圣诞时节见好就收,正式告别这次特邀连载。告别的话说得掷地有声者非常罕见,人之将死的话也常难讲得恰到好处。英王查理二世,一个足智多虑的人,给人们上了长长一课,让人们知道一个人缺乏信任竟至如此,不过他也不失为一个随和的友伴,一位善于操控的国王。他临死前那句"诸位,我这死怕是拖得太长了"已成经典,话中充满机智、疑虑,还有超常的幽默。

一

关于"死拖得太长",各位,你我脑海中恐怕都有那么一幅图画。沙漏中的沙子要走完了,我们"历数残生,功过在案",日子就这么一天天过去;于是当我们感到那最后一刻来临时,那就是"死拖得太长",还能是什么呢?如果我们活到要告别那一刻而仍然没有恶名昭著,那么徒增的年龄本身已相当了不起了;仅仅在人世上走了一遭就无疑像军人服过役一样不无荣光。塔西佗《日耳曼尼亚志》(*Germania*)中有个故事,说的是在日耳曼旷野中的

passed his finger along their toothless gums. Sunt lacrymæ rerum:[9] this was the most eloquent of the songs of Simeon.[10] And when a man has lived to a fair age, he bears his marks of service.[11] He may have never been remarked upon the breach at the head of the army; at least he shall have lost his teeth on the camp bread.

The idealism of serious people in this age of ours is of a noble character. It never seems to them that they have served enough; they have a fine impatience of their virtues.[12] It were perhaps more modest to be singly thankful that we are no worse. It is not only our enemies, those desperate characters—it is we ourselves who know not what we do;—thence springs the glimmering hope that perhaps we do better than we think: that to scramble through this random business with hands reasonably clean, to have played the part of a man or woman with some reasonable fulness, to have often resisted the diabolic, and at the end to be still resisting it, is for the poor human soldier to have done right well. To ask to see some fruit of our endeavour is but a transcendental way of serving for reward;[13] and what we take to be contempt of self is only greed of hire.[14]

And again if we require so much of ourselves, shall we not require much of others? If we do not genially judge our own deficiencies, is it not to be feared we shall be even stern to the trespasses of others? And he who (looking back upon his own life) can see no more than that he has been unconscionably long a-dying, will he not be tempted to think his neighbour unconscionably long of getting hanged?[15] It is probable that nearly all who think of conduct at all, think of it too much; it is certain we all think too much of sin. We are not damned for doing wrong, but for not doing right; Christ would never hear of negative morality; thou shalt

一批老兵如何群情激愤,直逼日耳曼尼库斯,吵着要回家,这些常年征战在外、饱经战事的老兵,拉着他们将军的手去抚摸自己已无牙齿的牙床。"泪流满面":这是西缅歌中最激昂的文字。一个人若活到了老年,那他就像士兵一样肯定留下了服过役的痕迹。也许人们没有看到他在战场上冲锋在前,但他至少啃军营的面包啃掉了牙。

在我们这个时代,严肃的人中盛行理想主义,那是一种崇高的人格。他们总觉得自己服务他人做得不够,对自己的德行要求过于苛刻。但也许还是降低要求更为谦虚,没做得更糟就已经万幸了。我们面对的不仅是那些穷凶极恶的敌人,更是我们自己,因为我们并不知道应该做什么;因此才冒出了一个微弱的希望,也许我们实际的表现要比我们想象的好,在这个无序随机的世界里跌打滚爬居然两手尚算干净,扮演男人或女人的角色尚属完美,还能常常抵御邪恶,而且一直抵御到最后,人这个可怜的战士表现得已是可圈可点了。要求见到努力的果实其实是在索求服务的回报,只是说得高尚些罢了,表面是小看蔑视自己,实则仅是贪求利益。

而如果我们要求自己这么多,对他人的要求会少吗?如果我们对自己的短处不那么和风细雨,恐怕我们对他人的过失也会严酷有加吧?一个人回首一生,若仅看到自己苟延残喘一无是处,那么他不是也会觉得他的邻居也同样一无是处早就该遭劫难呢?几乎所有思及品行的人大概都把品行看得过重;我们肯定都把罪恶看得过重了。我们不是因为做错了才受谴责,我们受谴责只是因为没做对;基督从不认同负面消极的道德说教;"你得"才是他的言语,他用

was ever his word, with which he superseded thou shalt not.[16] To make our idea of morality centre on forbidden acts is to defile the imagination and to introduce into our judgments of our fellow-men a secret element of gusto.[17] If a thing is wrong for us, we should not dwell upon the thought of it; or we shall soon dwell upon it with inverted pleasure.[18] If we cannot drive it from our minds—one thing of two: either our creed is in the wrong and we must more indulgently remodel it; or else, if our morality be in the right, we are criminal lunatics and should place our persons in restraint.[19] A mark of such unwholesomely divided minds is the passion for interference with others: the Fox without the Tail[20] was of this breed, but had (if his biographer is to be trusted) a certain antique civility now out of date. A man may have a flaw, a weakness, that unfits him for the duties of life, that spoils his temper, that threatens his integrity, or that betrays him into cruelty. It has to be conquered; but it must never be suffered to engross his thoughts. The true duties lie all upon the farther side,[21] and must be attended to with a whole mind so soon as this preliminary clearing of the decks has been effected.[22] In order that he may be kind and honest, it may be needful he should become a total abstainer;[23] let him become so then, and the next day let him forget the circumstance. Trying to be kind and honest will require all his thoughts; a mortified appetite is never a wise companion;[24] in so far as he has had to mortify an appetite, he will still be the worse man; and of such an one a great deal of cheerfulness will be required in judging life, and a great deal of humility in judging others.

It may be argued again that dissatisfaction with our life's endeavour springs in some degree from dulness. We require higher tasks, because we do not recognise the height of those we have. Trying to be kind and honest

这个说法替换了"你不得"。老把道德思考锁定在禁止做的事情上就会扼杀想象力，就会让我们在判断我们的同胞时幸灾乐祸。假如一件事我们认为是错的，那么我们连想都不要去想它；否则它就马上会盘旋在我们的思绪里，驱使我们幸灾乐祸。如果我们无法把这想法从思绪中驱散，那么就只有两个结果：要么我们的信条是错误的，那就必须重整信条；假如我们的道德是正确的，可我们却仗着正确不依不饶，表现得像患有精神病的罪犯，那就应该把我们自己控制起来。这种出发点正确但行事疯狂的分裂思维是极不健康的，而这种思维的一个表现形式就是特喜欢干涉别人："没有尾巴的狐狸"这则寓言就属于这一类，但是故事中的礼仪却有点陈旧过时（如果这故事可以相信）。一个人可以有劣迹，有弱点，使他不适合履行人生的职责，使他脾气拙劣，使他缺乏骨气，或使他显得残酷。没错，这些弊端都得克服改正；但千万不能允许这些盘踞人的思想。真正的职责并不是要洁身自好，而是全在身外，一旦自身的杂念得以清除，履行职责时才能心无旁骛。为了能履行待他人仁爱、诚实的职责，就有必要完全戒除自己的不良欲念；那就让他戒除，而且还得马上把戒欲之事忘掉。设法仁爱诚实需要全心投入；不能断绝欲望是不明智的；人只要还得扼杀残留的欲望，就好不到哪里去；这样的人，审视自己需多些欢乐，裁判他人要多些谦卑。

还可以这么说，在某种程度上，对自己的努力不满意是因为我们觉得生活百无聊赖。我们希望丰功伟业来挑战自己，殊不知我们面临的任务相当艰巨。对于英雄气概满怀的人来说，仁爱诚实似乎

seems an affair too simple and too inconsequential for gentlemen of our heroic mould; we had rather set ourselves to something bold, arduous, and conclusive; we had rather found a schism or suppress a heresy, cut off a hand or mortify an appetite. But the task before us, which is to co-endure with our existence, is rather one of microscopic fineness, and the heroism required is that of patience. There is no cutting of the Gordian knots of life;[25] each must be smilingly unravelled.

To be honest, to be kind—to earn a little and to spend a little less, to make upon the whole a family happier for his presence, to renounce when that shall be necessary and not be embittered, to keep a few friends but these without capitulation—above all, on the same grim condition, to keep friends with himself—here is a task for all that a man has of fortitude and delicacy.[26] He has an ambitious soul who would ask more; he has a hopeful spirit who should look in such an enterprise to be successful. There is indeed one element in human destiny that not blindness itself can controvert: whatever else we are intended to do, we are not intended to succeed; failure is the fate allotted. It is so in every art and study; it is so above all in the continent art of living well. Here is a pleasant thought for the year's end or for the end of life: Only self-deception will be satisfied, and there need be no despair for the despairer.[27]

II

But Christmas is not only the mile-mark of another year, moving us to thoughts of self-examination: it is a season, from all its associations,

太平凡普通，掀不起多大波澜；我们情愿去面对能让我们显出勇气、一举成名的艰难任务；我们情愿卷入对抗纷争，或镇压异端，或切断手臂，或扼杀欲望。但是我们眼前的任务却只与平凡的生活纠缠在一起，那是于细微处见英雄的任务，所需要的是忍耐。完成这样复杂的任务要的不是刚毅决绝，因为解决每个问题要的是充满温情。

要诚实，要仁爱，就要赚一点钱但花的比赚的少，总能让家人因你的出现而更快乐，需要时你应会放弃，放弃了又不耿耿于怀，得有几个朋友，但却不能因友失义，同理，你更需对己如友。要完成诚实仁爱的任务，一位既有硬骨又有柔肠的人就应具备这些气质。这个人心中有抱负，不满足于现状；他总希望在这样的事业中圆满成功。人类的命运中确实有这么个事实再浑然不觉的人也不会否认：我们意在做什么都行，就是不能意在成功；失败是命中注定的。这道理能在每一种艺术、每一个学问中印证；那么在这个自律节制、道德高尚的生活艺术中，就更要懂得这个道理。不管这是一年的结尾，还是一生的结束，下面这观点定能令人快乐：要想满足求完美的奢望只能自欺，绝了奢望的人就不会绝望。

二

但是圣诞不仅是岁尾年首的里程碑，催我们只去反躬自省是不够的。它是一个时令，让人想到与这时令相关的一切，无论它是让

whether domestic or religious, suggesting thoughts of joy. A man dissatisfied with his endeavours is a man tempted to sadness. And in the midst of the winter, when his life runs lowest and he is reminded of the empty chairs of his beloved, it is well he should be condemned to this fashion of the smiling face.[28] Noble disappointment, noble self-denial are not to be admired, not even to be pardoned, if they bring bitterness. It is one thing to enter the kingdom of heaven maim; another to maim yourself and stay without. And the kingdom of heaven is of the childlike, of those who are easy to please, who love and who give pleasure. Mighty men of their hands, the smiters and the builders and the judges,[29] have lived long and done sternly and yet preserved this lovely character; and among our carpet interests and twopenny concerns,[30] the shame were indelible if we should lose it. Gentleness and cheerfulness, these come before all morality; they are the perfect duties. And it is the trouble with moral men that they have neither one nor other. It was the moral man, the Pharisee,[31] whom Christ could not away with. If your morals make you dreary, depend upon it they are wrong. I do not say "give them up," for they may be all you have; but conceal them like a vice, lest they should spoil the lives of better and simpler people.

A strange temptation attends upon man: to keep his eye on pleasures, even when he will not share in them;[32] to aim all his morals against them. This very year a lady (singular iconoclast!) proclaimed a crusade against dolls; and the racy sermon against lust is a feature of the age. I venture to call such moralists insincere. At any excess or perversion of a natural appetite, their lyre sounds of itself with relishing denunciations;[33] but for all displays of the truly diabolic—envy, malice, the mean lie, the mean

你想到家庭或是想到宗教，都应带给你欢乐。一个人总觉得自己一事无成就自然会生出哀愁。正是隆冬之际，生命恰处于低潮，又看到了深爱之人坐过的那把空空的椅子，但此时是圣诞时节，他最好还是应一下景，尽力露出笑容。就算你在失望或自贬中有一丝高尚的情怀，也不该赞扬，而如果这样做会带来痛苦，甚至都不值得原谅。遍体鳞伤进入天国和自残自损不入天国那完全是两回事儿。天国属于孩子，属于那些一下子就能欢乐起来的人，属于充满爱，愿施乐的人。勇猛的人，那些习武的战士、构建伟业的人、领袖人物，他们活得长久，也历经艰辛，却仍然保有仁爱的性格。而在我们足不出户的狭隘生活中，关注着那些鸡毛蒜皮的小事，如果我们竟然丢失了这乐天的本性，那就太说不过去了。温存和乐天，这两样应该先于道德，是不折不扣的人生职责。道德之士的麻烦就是他们这两样一个都没有。基督不能容忍的恰恰是道德之士法利赛人。如果你的道德使你忧伤悲哀，让你离不开它，那么这道德就是错的。我倒不是说你应该"抛弃那些道德"，因为那也许就是你仅有的东西，但最好还是将其视为恶习，把它隐藏起来，免得这些道德把原本还算不错尚属单纯之人的一生给毁了。

有一种奇怪的心理诱惑着人：总是对各种欢乐疑心重重，甚至在欢乐与他无关时，也对欢乐心生警惕；他们动员自己所有的道德来对抗欢乐。就是在今年，一位女士（一位奇特的反对崇拜偶像的人）宣称要掀起对玩偶布娃娃的讨伐；言辞辛辣的反欲望布道正是我们这个时代的一个特征。我斗胆称这些道德家言不由衷。他们一见到天生的欲望有点过分或有点走火入魔，便痛快淋漓地大加

silence, the calumnious truth, the backbiter, the petty tyrant, the peevish poisoner of family life[34]— their standard is quite different. These are wrong, they will admit, yet somehow not so wrong; there is no zeal in their assault on them, no secret element of gusto warms up the sermon; it is for things not wrong in themselves that they reserve the choicest of their indignation. A man may naturally disclaim all moral kinship with the Reverend Mr. Zola or the hobgoblin old lady of the dolls; for these are gross and naked instances.[35] And yet in each of us some similar element resides. The sight of a pleasure in which we cannot or else will not share moves us to a particular impatience. It may be because we are envious, or because we are sad, or because we dislike noise and romping—being so refined, or because—being so philosophic—we have an overweighing sense of life's gravity: at least, as we go on in years, we are all tempted to frown upon our neighbour's pleasures. People are nowadays so fond of resisting temptations; here is one to be resisted. They are fond of self-denial; here is a propensity that cannot be too peremptorily denied. There is an idea abroad among moral people that they should make their neighbours good. One person I have to make good: myself. But my duty to my neighbour is much more nearly expressed by saying that I have to make him happy—if I may.[36]

挞伐；但是对于真恶魔的拙劣表现，比如嫉妒、歹念、卑鄙的谎言、恶意的沉默、虚假的真相、背后的中伤，小人的骄横、家中的蛮横，对于这些，道德家们却另有标准。这些当然都是恶行，他们也会承认，但是谈不上十恶不赦；对于这些，他们反对起来和风细雨，布道时也不会言辞猛烈激情奔放；他们把最为激烈的愤怒发泄在本身并不算错的事情上。一个人会自然地和左拉的道德观拉开距离，和执意反玩偶的老太划清界限，因为这些都是恶劣和显而易见的例子。但是在我们自己身上都有些类似的劣迹。有时我们眼睛看到了欢乐，可我们无缘或者说不愿去分享，于是心里就特别不爽。或许那是因为我们嫉妒，因为我们悲伤，因为我们过于精致，厌恶吵闹，也或许是因为我们思如哲人，深觉生命应该严肃；至少，当我们年岁渐增时，我们都忍不住对邻居的欢乐皱起眉头。人们当下很流行抵御诱惑；这就是一个我们要抵御的诱惑。人们也很流行自我否定，这就是一个很难一下子否定的天性。坊间道德之士中有这么个说法，他们应该让邻居变好。有一个人我确实得让他变好，那就是我自己。但我对邻居的责任似乎可以更准确地概括成下面这句话：我应该让邻居变得快乐，当然前提是我能够。

注 释

1. 有关本句的背景，请见本篇导读。

2. 这里的 seasonable manner，应该是说和某个时令相关，而在这里显然就是指和圣诞相关，也就是适合这个圣诞时节的。

3. valedictory eloquence 是某一个时节或重大活动结束时的讲话，也就是说，这是一种告别演讲。前半句是说，这种场合能讲得很棒的很少。后半句是说人临终的讲话，这种讲话不能 hit the mark of the occasion，就是说不能讲到非常适合这个时刻（occasion）。所谓的 occasion 就是死亡的时刻（occasion = occasion of dying）。

4. 查理二世（Charles II，1630—1685），斯图亚特王朝第十一位苏格兰国王（1650—1685）、复辟后的首位英格兰及爱尔兰国王（1661—1685）。其父查理一世被克伦威尔处死。这位国王不信任人，因此才有后边 one long lesson in human incredulity 的说法，incredulity 就是 not believing 的意思。

5. 这句的基本结构就是 The king remembered and embodied wit and scepticism in the famous line。remembered and embodied 未必要细分开，大意就是这位国王记得要在那句话中体现出 wit and scepticism（The king didn't complain, but remembered to be witty and graceful, and put or embodied all his wit and scepticism into his final remark）。翻译的时候最好不要纠结于细节，说出大意就可以了。

6. I am an unconscionable time a-dying 这句话非常有名，查理二世在临终前说这句话包含的信息量很大。unconscionable 表示过度的意思，如 unconscionable length 就是过度冗长；再如 He had stayed an unconscionable time—had made her quite a visitation.

但该词本意表示不顾别人感受，不顾对错（OED: of actions, behaviour, etc.: showing no regard for conscience; not in accordance with what is right or reasonable），所以 an unconscionable time a-dying 就有拖拖拉拉一直不死，给别人造成很多不便的隐含意思。查理二世确实在病床上拖了一段时间，所以临终说这句话的时候，他有些抱歉的口气，觉得麻烦了不少人。句中的 wit 表示风趣，因为临终的人居然还能这么逗趣地谈死亡，当然显得风趣和幽默（good humour）；至于说 scepticism（疑惑）则是透露出了查理二世对传统宗教生死观的不信任，居然这么随随便便地谈生死大事。当然最后一刻他还是请来了宗教人士为他的死亡祈祷。就翻译来说，这些解读出来的意思不应放到译文里，用原词 scepticism 就够了；换句话说，解读出来的东西是否部分或全部放到译文中是要谨慎的，如本句不加入译者理解的内容就给读者留下了自我思考解读的空间，就没有"越俎代庖"，但在不同场合，也许就可以添加，一切都要在特定的语境中决定，没有一个千篇一律的准则。

7. 这个 numbered and imputed 的主语是 the hours，也就是代表人度过的一生岁月。在临终时，人们回首这些日子，"衡量"了这些日子（numbered），同时将这些日子里我们的表现做了分类，哪段时间里干了哪些好事儿？也干了哪些坏事儿？（imputed, or to ascribe something to someone）也就是说，在人生即将结束来日无多时，得算个总账（counted and recorded）。这个词组中的词分别在《圣经》中多次出现，表达了与此处相近的意思。

8. 这个 served 原本是用在军人身上的词，表示服过兵役的意思。但是在这段中，斯蒂文森显然是将这个服兵役的词用在了我们普通人身上，合并使用了。所以翻译的时候就有必要把这个考虑进去。如果用隐喻处理，就容易把我们普通人的生活形容成军人的生活（在世上走了一遭就是服过兵役了？）；如果我们完全把军人服役拿掉，那么这段下面的军旅描述就完全被忽视了。所以，这里采用了将隐喻改成明喻的处理方法，并添加了原文表面没有但实际存在的意思（不无荣光）。其实本段下面的"He may have never been remarked upon the breach at the head of the army; at least he shall have lost his teeth on the camp bread."这句和这里一样，既是在描写军人，也是在描写我们普通人。

9. lacrimæ rerum 拉丁文，表示 tears of things，说明人生充满悲哀，源自罗马诗人维吉尔（公元前70—19年）的《埃涅阿斯纪》(The Aeneid)第一部中的第462行。

10. 见《圣经》中 The song of Simeon（Luke 2: 25-35），这段可以被看作是 Simeon 临死前的最后告别之言（Simeon's valedictory）。

11. 参考前面注释8。"he bears his marks of service"这句显然是在说我们普通人，但是它使用了 service 这个用在军人身上的词。加上下面的冲锋陷阵、军营面包，都是军用词，但却是在形容普通人。译者可以根据读者的理解能力，适当处理。比如这里译者就基本保留了原来的词（冲锋、军营、面包），但还是在用明喻（就像士兵一样）的前提下这样做的。

12. a fine impatience of their virtues 从语境看是指对于美德等的过高的要求（impatience of = intolerance of），fine 这个词可以解释为 over-precise，或者说 too impatient about their virtues, about not doing enough for others。这里的 doing enough for others（serving others）被认为是一种 virtue。

13. 我们这里是在说 serving for reward，这是一个不怎么高尚的动机，原来你在为别人服务是为了有所回报，但是你很机巧，以一种非常高尚的方式说出了不怎么高尚的动机。换句话说，有那么一点说得比唱得好听的味道。这里斯蒂文森是在讽刺那些嘴上说为别人服务，但实际并不是意在服务他人，而是有自己的小算盘的人。

14. 这里斯蒂文森是在批评那些虚伪的人，他们口口声声看不起自己（be contempt of self），觉得自己做得不够，但还是想获得一种有所回馈的感觉，我为别人做了一些事，我总得有些收获，至少能获得一种我为别人干了些什么的满足感，所以他小看自己最终还是为了某种自身的利益和满足（greed of hire）。注意，这里的名词 hire 就是 reward 或 payment 的意思。

15. 这里的 getting hanged 就是字面的意思（被吊死），但是根据上下文，我们也完全可以把它理解为被惩罚的意义（getting punished）。这句的基本意思就是，你对自己都那么严酷，那么你就更会惩罚他人了，甚至会用上最为严酷的惩罚手段（把人吊死）。

16. 我们可以看著名的"十大诫命"，都是用禁止人做某些事的形式言说的，都是以不可做某些事表述的（thou shalt not）。在《圣经·旧约》中和法利赛人的言说里，禁止是重要的表达方式。但是耶稣基督却是以你得做某些事来叙述的，是正面的言说。

17. 这个 a secret element of gusto 就是一种 zest，之所以是 secret 是因为这不是一种可以登大雅之堂的东西。比如说，你非常讨厌的一个人干了一件蠢事，你于是内心（secret）就会有一种快乐甚至激动的感觉，就是我们常说的幸灾乐祸的感觉。OED 解释 gusto 时就用了斯蒂文森的这个词组（No secret element of gusto warms up the sermon）。

18. 这个 inverted pleasure 就是指一种错误的快乐，就是上面说的那种幸灾乐祸的心理感受。

19. 这句的理解必须和整个大语境联系起来。这几句都是在说人应该把不正确的想法从思想中驱除出去。但如果不能驱除，那么就有两种情况。第一种是你的信条就错了，比如说，本书《被鄙视的种族》中坐火车的欧洲人认为华人肮脏，这个信条本身就是错误的。在这种情况下，你就应该改变你的信条（must more indulgently remodel it）。但是如果你的信条或道德并不错，比如说在新冠病毒流行期间，一个人见到好久没见面的朋友，马上走上前近距离攀谈，但这样却违反了当地要求人与人保持距离的行政命令。此时我们提出异议是正确的，因为我们的信条是对的（our morality be in the right）。但是如果你对这件事不停反复地强调，几天之后见到这个人还不停地说这事，到了不依不饶的地步，那么问题就在你了，这毕竟不是一件值得你这么大惊小怪的事件，所以你的表现说明你是一个疯人（criminal lunatic），而应相应受到管控，就像疯人院里的病人应该被束缚起来一样（should place our persons in restraint）。用 criminal lunatic 似乎太强烈了些，但基本意思还是合适的。正是这样的人才会不停地干涉他人的事务（A mark of such unwholesomely divided minds is the passion for interference with others）。另外，这个 criminal lunatics 是源自 1800 年大不列颠议会通过的一项法令。该法令规定了将精神病患者无限期拘留的程序，缘起于对詹姆斯·哈德菲尔德（James Hadfield）试图暗杀国王乔治三世的审判。

20. "没有尾巴的狐狸"（the Fox without the Tail），见《伊索寓言》。说这个寓言属于这类，就是说那狐狸为了自身的利益干涉别人的事务。

21. 这里说的 upon the farther side 是针对自身而言的。如果一个人老谈自己的修炼，自己思想的纯洁与否，那是没有抓到问题的实质。我们的责任主要应该在自身之外（the farther side），farther 指与自己相对应的地方，就是别人，换句话说，责任在为他人服务。

22. 这个 preliminary clearing of the decks 是一个隐喻，字面意思就是一艘船在海战前，先要清理甲板，这样才能集中精力战斗（Cambridge Dictionary: to remove unnecessary things so that you are ready for action goal by dealing with anything beforehand that might hinder progress）。同理，这里把履行职责（to be kind and honest）当作海战，那么你在干这件大事前就得先"清理甲板"，就是说要把不干净的念头都先清除掉，那样才能一心一意履行职责（with a whole mind）。

23. 这个 total abstainer 和前面的清理甲板有关。本来这个词组是指绝对戒酒的人。但是在我们这个语境中，仅仅局限于戒酒太狭窄。可以理解成戒除各种欲望，注意接下来就谈到欲望了（mortify an appetite）。

24. 这里的 mortified appetite 和下面的 the worse man 都是在说清除欲望不彻底的问题。the mortified appetite 说明欲望还在，仍然还得抑制扼杀欲望（in so far as he has had to mortify an appetite）。斯蒂文森甚至觉得，没有彻底清除的欲望更糟糕，所以才有 the *worse* man 这个说法。

25. Gordian 是 Gordius 的形容词，Gordius 是传说中小亚细亚的一个国王，他把一辆牛车的车辕和车轭用一根绳子系了起来，打了一个找不到结头的死结，声称谁能打开这个难解的 Gordian knot 谁就可以称王亚洲。这个结一直没有人解开。到了公元前4世纪，亚历山大大帝拔出佩剑，一下子就把这个死结斩开了。此后 Gordian knot 便用来指"难以解决的问题"，而 cut the Gordian knot 便指干脆利落解决复杂的问题。

26. 这里的 without capitulation 就是 without condition 的意思，也就是说这些朋友和你没有预设条件，不会因利益背叛你，而 to keep friends with himself 就是表示应该对自己如朋友，善待自己，不要对自己过于苛刻，这点也正是本文的中心思想。a man of fortitude and delicacy 是指一个人所具有的两种不同的气质，fortitude 强调一个人硬气的一面，比如在困难面前顶得住，不屈服，而 delicacy 则强调了一个人温柔的一面，有时光凭硬气不够，也许还要伸出一只手，给人以抚慰。也就是刚柔并存的人。另外，for all that a man has of fortitude and delicacy 可以改写成 for all (the qualities) that/which a man of fortitude and delicacy has，这样更容易理解。

27. 这句在下面的语境中理解会有帮助 (whatever else we are intended to do, we are not intended to succeed)。人们总希望成功，而且是圆满的成功。但斯蒂文森说，这世上唯独成功不可奢望。如果你要奢望成功，那么你的奢望就不可避免落空（绝望）。但是如果你没有了奢望，或者说，你成了绝了奢望的人（the despairer），那么你也就没有什么奢望可绝的了（no despair）。斯蒂文森在这里巧妙地把玩了这一对同源词。

28. "it is well" 可以理解为 it is a good thing 的意思。to be condemned to 基本意思就是 to be forced to，比如 to be condemned to prison。但是在这里，我们仅仅把它理解为需要做一件并不是很情愿做的事。这些心情不好，被悲观情绪左右的人，不是很容易高兴起来。斯蒂文森认为，他们即便不很愿意高兴起来，他们还是应该那么做，毕竟是圣诞时刻，不妨借这个时节露出一丝笑容，本来就是应该高兴的时刻嘛！the smiling face 就是表示笑脸，代表愉快。

29. a man of one's hands 就是 a man of vigour and courage 的意思。后面的三个就是这类人物的代表。the builders 的范围很广，但是在这个语境中不应该包括具体房屋的建造者，而应该是较为宏观意义上的建造者，比如帝国的建造者，大项目的建造者，若是在现代，就可以包括大公司的建造者，总之，建立的是宏观的大事业。至于 the judges 则肯定不是指现代意义上的法官，而指古代的领导人，特别是以色列的领袖（a leader in ancient Israel）。

30. 这个 our carpet interests and twopenny concerns 是在和前面的 a man of one's hands 相对应的语境中提出的。前面那些人可是大视野大格局大动作的人物，都有勇气。接下来我们要说的就是我们当中那些只有 our carpet interests and twopenny concerns 的人，这些人的格局就很小了，比如小到只有 carpet interests 和 twopenny concerns。比如我们说的 carpet knight 就是指不是因为战斗而是在房间里被授予骑士头衔的人，强调的是温室内的生活，不是跌打滚爬的生活。在这里应该也是类似的意思，就是兴趣或利益或关注的视野都在房间之内，也就是说，和前面的大格局刚刚相反。至于 twopenny concerns 那就很明显了，关注的事务仅仅值 twopenny，即关注的是小问题。

31. 有关耶稣基督谴责法利赛人，可在《圣经》中多处见到，如《马太福音》第 23 章。

32. 有关 share in 的意思，请参考本书"Despised Races"篇注释 25。

33. their lyre sounds of itself with relishing denunciations 是一种隐喻的说法，表达批评之声就像七弦琴发出的声音一样。在翻译时译者面临一个选择，到底要不要把七弦琴这个比喻表达出来。我们说，在有些文学作品中，这样直译的可能是有的，因为需要反映出原作者写作的特点。但是在这里，斯蒂文森修辞的特点意义不大，所以本译文采用了意译的方法（"便痛快淋漓地大加挞伐"），译文把原文中的主要意思都传达出来了，比如 relishing 就用了"痛快淋漓"。

34. the peevish poisoner of family life 主要指的是家庭生活中为了小事而大发脾气，结果破坏（poison）家庭气氛的事，比如丈夫对妻子的烹调不满意而大发脾气，这类事就属于 peevish poisoner of family life。

35. 这个 the hobgoblin old lady of the dolls 就是指前面提到的要和玩偶娃娃宣战的那位女士。至于这里的 the Reverend Mr. Zola，是指爱弥尔·左拉（Émile Zola，1840—1902），19 世纪后半叶法国重要的批判现实主义作家，其自然主义文学理论被视为是 19 世纪批判现实主义文学遗产的组成部分。但是左拉并不是宗教界人士（Reverend），斯蒂文森这么说是在讽刺法国人对左拉的无限崇拜。显然作者的这两个例子都是极端的，那位与玩偶宣战的女士过于保守，而左拉的观点（如对肉欲和妓女的观点）又是另外一个极端，所以人们比较容易撇清与这类极端例子（gross and naked instances）的关系。

36. 这个句子理解上没有问题，但是在翻译的表达上似乎可以推敲。其实 if I may 完全可以放到句子最后，就翻译成"如果我能的话"。但是读者会感到这样处理语言欧化的痕迹非常明显，因为我们汉语一般是不将"如果"这样的从句放到句子结尾的。按照汉语的行文习惯应该是"如果我能的话，我得让我的邻居快乐"，但这样就冲淡了这句话的核心内容——让邻居快乐，因为"如果"从句会把注意力吸引过去。正因此，这个译文（"当然前提是我能够"）仍然保留原文的语序，但做了些变动，避免了条件从句后置造成的翻译腔。

导　读

圣诞说教

《圣诞说教》这篇散文写于 1888 年春季，发表在《斯克里伯纳杂志》(*Scribner's Magazine*, Dec., 1888)，最后收入 1892 年出版的《穿越平原》。在文章一开头，斯蒂文森就说："当大家见到这篇文章时，我应该已连续讲了十二个月了"。这就解释了本篇为什么和圣诞有关，为什么发表在 12 月。其实作者和《斯克里伯纳杂志》签了一个合同，每月给杂志写一篇文章，而我们这篇《圣诞说教》就是那个合同要求的 12 篇文章中的最后一篇，所以他说他已经连续讲了十二个月。他并不是在教堂布道，而是在写文章，所以这不是一般的圣诞布道文，而是圣诞期间写的一篇说教文字。这十二篇发表在该杂志上的文章（本书选用了其中的两篇）分别是：

- A Chapter on Dreams（Jan. 1888）
- The Lantern Bearers（Feb. 1888）
- Beggars（Mar. 1888）
- Pulvis et Umbra（Apr. 1888）
- Gentlemen（May 1888）

- Some Gentlemen in Fiction（June 1888）
- Popular Authors（July 1888）
- Epilogue to an Inland Voyage（Aug. 1888）
- A Letter to a Young Gentleman Who Proposes to Embrace the Career of Art（Sep. 1888）
- Contributions to the History of Fife: Random Memories（Oct. 1888）
- The Education of an Engineer: More Random Memories（Nov. 1888）
- A Christmas Sermon（Dec. 1888）

写这篇散文时，斯蒂文森刚刚结束萨拉纳克湖的小住，来到了纽约。但他此时即将离开纽约西行去加州。他在 5 月 21 日写给好友查尔斯·巴克斯特（Charles Baxter）的信中说："还欠《斯克里伯纳杂志》两篇文章，但却只有 8 天时间，因为马上就要去旧金山了，不知道这任务怎么完成。"这两篇文债应该是 11 月份的 The Education of an Engineer 和 12 月份的 A Christmas Sermon。当然他后来还是及时交了文稿，可见斯蒂文森写作有多么快捷。

看文章的题目就知道，这篇散文是谈人生大道理的。整篇散文分四部分，分别是：

1. 一生不辱名声已万幸。不要老提道德和罪恶，温柔诚实更重要。
2. 人应欢快如孩童，应多做善事，应让他人快乐。
3. 人要善待邻居，邻居不伤害他人，就不要去纠正人家。
4. 一切如过眼烟云，所以要达观面世。

围绕这些题目，斯蒂文森娓娓道来，佳句连篇。比如他说："跌打滚爬居然两手尚算干净，扮演男人或女人的角色尚属完美，还能常常抵御邪恶，而且一直抵御到最后，人这个可怜的战士表现得已是可圈可点了"。你看他不是让人把理想设在高高的山巅，而是说做得不太糟就已很了不起。这种人生的态度，在任何时候都是很受用的。比如现在，我们都想让自己的孩子出人头地，仿佛进不了哈佛就是失败。斯蒂文森的话，也许会舒缓孩子在拼搏路上的那颗焦虑的心。斯蒂文森觉得伟大寓于平凡，不要一天到晚想着惊天动地："对于英雄气概满怀的人来说，仁爱诚实似乎太平凡普通，掀不起多大波澜；我们情愿去面对能让我们显出勇气、一举成名的艰难任务……。但是我们眼前的任务却只与平凡的生活纠缠在一起，那是于细微处见英雄的任务，所需要的是忍耐。"斯蒂文森还认为天国是属于孩子的，所以人应该留住孩子的天性，而孩子不是总愁容满面的："天国属于孩子，属于那些一下子就能欢乐起来的人，属于充满爱，愿施乐的人。"

斯蒂文森还告诉我们，这个世界尽管五光十色，但毕竟不是归宿之地："回首过去一年，看看我们多么无所事事，多么目标狭隘，多么胆小怯懦，多么畏缩不前，或又多么鲁莽轻率、愚笨介入；我们每日每刻都践踏着善良的准则；吊诡的是，在痛苦地发现这些不堪的同时，我们也有少许安慰。……在漫长的人生路途中，大多数时候人都深感惭愧、羞于昂首，……人有受不尽的回报，享不尽的快乐，他有幸见到晨曦破晓、明月升空，或会晤友人，或在饥饿时听到别人唤他用餐，人生充满惊喜，但是这世界仍不是久留之地。"所以在这个世上，我们"要诚实，要仁爱，就要赚一点钱但花的比赚的少，总能让家人因你的出现而更快乐，需要时你应会放弃，放弃了又不耿耿于怀，得有几个朋友，但却不能因友失义，同理，你更需对己如友。要完成诚实仁爱的任务，一位既有硬骨又有柔肠的人就应具备这些气质"。

看了这篇文章，读者马上就会感到这样的说教和宗教的布道不同，但又多少含有那么一点宗教情怀。我们读斯蒂文森的其他散文，比如《狗性》，总觉得他受达尔文思想影响颇深，是离经叛道者。没错，他确实在二十岁前后背叛了家庭的基督教传统，后来又接受了不少达尔文的思想，但他最终还是回归了基督教，正如他后来说："我确实紧抱住上帝。"与很多信徒不同的是，他把宗教落实在充满痛苦的人生路上，而不是脱离现实的平安之乡。在南太平洋居住的时期，他甚至对有组织的宗教活动持友善态度。

这篇散文发表后，反应毁誉都有。有的评论家认为作品散发着本能的道德观和仁慈的悲观主义（instinctive morality and kindly pessimism）。但也有人认为这篇散文是那本散文集中的败笔（the one mistake in this stimulating volume）。最负面的评论居然来自他曾经的好友威廉·亨利，此时他们的关系已经快要破裂了（详见导读《海角天涯了此生》）。但是普通大众还是很欢迎这篇散文的。斯蒂文森仁慈、善良、乐观的人生态度深得读者好评，一直到他去世后，都是不少人生活的指南。有人也常引用文章中的句子，特别是第一和第二节中的句子，以鼓励年轻人接受积极乐观的人生态度，反对消极的道德观。乔治·布朗在他的 *A Book of R. L. S.*（1919）中说："没有一篇文章能像这篇那样成功地把斯蒂文森对善的概念阐述得如此全面完整、积极向上。"由于文章广受欢迎，所以在1901年和1906年时出版了该文的单行本，而1925年在旧金山还出了限量版的单行本。在1948年时本文和另外一篇文章合起来也出过一个单行本。此外，这篇散文也被收入斯蒂文森的多个文集中。

有趣的是，这样一篇热销的作品，居然在1950年以后，没有收入任何文集，几乎消失了。这是什么原因呢？有些人认为，二战以后，世界变化很大，人们对道德等问题的观点，也逐渐发生了变化，特别是现代西方社会个人主义倾向严重，斯蒂文森19世纪的那一套道德情操，特别是他对仁慈、邻居、快乐的观点，都随着社会大环境的变化而失去了魅力，所以人们不仅是对他的这篇散文，就是对斯蒂文森的其他作品也都有不同的态度了。当然，有人认为本文失宠的另外一个原因是文中时而出现的悲观情调："回首过去一年，看看我们多么无所事事，多么目标狭隘，多么胆小怯懦，多么畏缩不前，或又多么鲁莽轻率、愚笨介入"。这些对人类的负面描写，也多少影响了读者的阅读兴致。

过去一个世纪，斯蒂文森散文的命运穿越时空起伏跌宕。而现在人类已进入人工智能的时代。他的作品会不会因为社会结构的变化，人类心理结构的变化，而重新散发出魅力，重新受到青睐，甚至再次受到追捧呢？我们拭目以待。

参考资料

RLS website: http://robert-louis-stevenson.org/.

Edrls: https://edrls.wordpress.com/2018/06/11/a-christmas-sermon-and-the-henley-quarrel/.

BROWN, George E., *A Book of R. L. S.: Work, Travels, Friends and Commentators*, New York: Charles Scribner's Sons, 1919. Illustrated.

Mary Thill, Robert Louis Stevenson's "A Christmas Sermon" December 24, 2009. https://www.adirondackalmanack.com/2009/12/robert-louis-stevensons-a-christmas-sermon.html.

"Truth Out of Tusitala Spoke", Stevenson's Voice in Post-Darwinian Christianity, by RLA.

A Christmas Sermon (2)

III

Happiness and goodness, according to canting moralists, stand in the relation of effect and cause. There was never anything less proved or less probable: our happiness is never in our own hands; we inherit our constitution; we stand buffet among friends and enemies; we may be so built as to feel a sneer or an aspersion with unusual keenness, and so circumstanced as to be unusually exposed to them;[37] we may have nerves very sensitive to pain, and be afflicted with a disease very painful. Virtue will not help us, and it is not meant to help us. It is not even its own reward,[38] except for the self-centred and—I had almost said—the unamiable.[39] No man can pacify his conscience; if quiet be what he want, he shall do better to let that organ perish from disuse. And to avoid the penalties of the law, and the minor capitis diminutio of social ostracism, is an affair of wisdom—of cunning, if you will—and not of virtue.[40]

In his own life, then, a man is not to expect happiness, only to profit by it gladly when it shall arise; he is on duty here;[41] he knows not how or why, and does not need to know; he knows not for what hire,[42] and must not ask. Somehow or other, though he does not know what goodness is, he must try to be good; somehow or other, though he cannot tell what will

圣诞说教（二）

三

　　虚伪的道学家们认为，幸福与善良成因果关系。可从来没有一件事比这更难证实，或者说更不可能发生。幸福从来不掌握在我们自己手里；我们的身体遗传自父母；我们受朋友的气、挨敌人的打；我们对鄙视或诽谤生来就异常敏感，偏偏又活在易受蔑视诽谤的环境中；我们的神经对疼痛本来就非常敏感，却偏患上疼痛难忍的病。德行不会帮我们，帮我们也不是德行的使命。施德行善甚至不能令我们自感满足，除非那人以自我为中心，看别人不顺眼。无人能安抚自己的良心；如果心的平静是人之所求，那么人最好还是不去搅动良心那官能，让它泯灭更好。要避免法律的制裁，避免受社会排斥而失去些许权利，就需要有一点智慧，也可以说得有一点精明，但和德行无涉。

　　那么人一生中就不该期盼幸福，只需在幸福降临时愉快地接受幸福给你带来益处就行；人在世上为的是担责任；他并不知道怎么担起让他人幸福的责任，也不知道为什么才担起这责任，但他不需要知道；他不知道担起这责任的回报是什么，但也没有必要去

do it, he must try to give happiness to others. And no doubt there comes in here a frequent clash of duties. How far is he to make his neighbour happy? How far must he respect that smiling face, so easy to cloud, so hard to brighten again? And how far, on the other side, is he bound to be his brother's keeper[43] and the prophet of his own morality? How far must he resent evil?

The difficulty is that we have little guidance; Christ's sayings on the point being hard to reconcile with each other, and (the most of them) hard to accept. But the truth of his teaching would seem to be this: in our own person and fortune, we should be ready to accept and to pardon all;[44] it is our cheek we are to turn, our coat that we are to give away to the man who has taken our cloak.[45] But when another's face is buffeted, perhaps a little of the lion will become us best.[46] That we are to suffer others to be injured, and stand by, is not conceivable and surely not desirable. Revenge, says Bacon, is a kind of wild justice; its judgments at least are delivered by an insane judge; and in our own quarrel we can see nothing truly and do nothing wisely. But in the quarrel of our neighbour, let us be more bold. One person's happiness is as sacred as another's; when we cannot defend both, let us defend one with a stout heart. It is only in so far as we are doing this, that we have any right to interfere: the defence of B is our only ground of action against A. A has as good a right to go to the devil, as we to go to glory; and neither knows what he does.

The truth is that all these interventions and denunciations and militant mongerings of moral hal-truths, though they be sometimes needful, though they are often enjoyable, do yet belong to an inferior grade of duties. Ill-temper and envy and revenge find here an arsenal of pious disguises;[47] this

问。可不知怎的，尽管他不知道什么是善，他必须尽力为善；不知怎么，尽管他不知道做什么才能为善，他必会努力让别人幸福。当然人承担不同的责任，相互之间无疑常有冲突。为让邻居幸福，他到底得走多远？为博取邻舍的笑脸，那张极易阴沉，很难灿烂的笑脸，他到底得做出多少让步？而另一方面，为了不纵容自己的兄弟，也为了坚守自己的道德，他只能退让几分？他也有责任憎恨邪恶，那么他又需憎恨到哪一步？

困难在于我们鲜有指导；在这问题上基督的话表面看相互很难自圆其说，而且那些话中不少也很难接受。但是基督教诲的真谛似乎是这样的：如果有人伤害了我们的身体，破坏了我们的财富，我们是应该接受并原谅这些的；因此是我们将自己的脸转过去让人家打，人家拿走了你的外衣时，是我们把内衣给他。但是当他人的脸被打时，我们最好应该显出些许强悍。遇他人受伤害却袖手旁观，那是不可想象，也肯定是不可取的。培根说，复仇是一种野性的正义；至少复仇时正义是伸张了，只是裁判者有点疯狂；纷争若与我们自己相关，那作为局内人我们看不清真假，拿不出明智举措。但纷争若涉及邻居，我们就该更勇敢些。一个人的幸福和另一个人的幸福同样神圣；我们若不能捍卫双方的幸福，那就让我们坚定地捍卫一方的幸福。只有这样，我们才有权干预：捍卫乙是我们采取行动反对甲的唯一理由。我们有权利走向光荣，但甲同样有权利走向邪恶；而其实双方并不知道他们之所为是对是错。

实情是，所有维护道德半真理的那些干预、谴责、好战行径，虽然有时也属必要，虽然常让你感到痛快淋漓，却只属于次等的责

is the playground of inverted lusts. With a little more patience and a little less temper, a gentler and wiser method might be found in almost every case; and the knot that we cut by some fine heady quarrel-scene in private life,[48] or, in public affairs, by some denunciatory act against what we are pleased to call our neighbour's vices, might yet have been unwoven by the hand of sympathy.

IV

To look back upon the past year, and see how little we have striven and to what small purpose: and how often we have been cowardly and hung back, or temerarious and rushed unwisely in; and how every day and all day long we have transgressed the law of kindness;—it may seem a paradox, but in the bitterness of these discoveries, a certain consolation resides. Life is not designed to minister to a man's vanity. He goes upon his long business most of the time with a hanging head,[49] and all the time like a blind child. Full of rewards and pleasures as it is—so that to see the day break or the moon rise, or to meet a friend, or to hear the dinner-call when he is hungry, fills him with surprising joys—this world is yet for him no abiding city.[50] Friendships fall through, health fails, weariness assails him; year after year, he must thumb the hardly varying record of his own weakness and folly.[51] It is a friendly process of detachment.[52] When the time comes that he should go, there need be few illusions left about himself. Here lies one who meant well, tried a little, failed much:—surely that may be his epitaph, of which he need not be ashamed. Nor will he

任。在这里，暴躁、嫉妒、复仇都会摇身一变，戴上道德的面具，各种邪恶的欲望都会粉墨登场。但是在几乎所有情况下，你只需略用忍、稍戒急，便能找到一种更温存、更智慧的方法；在私人生活中，我们用锱铢必较的激烈纷争武断解决问题，在公共事务中，我们也武断地谴责我们乐于称之为邻人罪恶的行为，但其实只要伸出一只同情之手，锁住的心结原本是可以解开的。

四

回首过去一年，看看我们多么无所事事，多么目标狭隘，多么胆小怯懦，多么畏缩不前，或又多么鲁莽轻率、愚笨介入；我们每日每刻都践踏着善良的准则；吊诡的是，在痛苦地发现这些不堪的同时，我们也有少许安慰。生命并不是为了满足人的虚荣而设计的。在漫长的人生路途中，大多数时候人都深感惭愧、羞于昂首，永远都像一个盲从的孩子。没错，人有受不尽的回报，享不尽的快乐，他有幸见到晨曦破晓、明月升空，或会晤友人，或在饥饿时听到别人唤他用餐，人生充满惊喜，但是这世界仍不是久留之地。友情会变味，健康会丧失，生活会变得百无聊赖；回顾自己的弱点和愚行，定是经年未改。这回顾成了温馨释怀的精神之旅。当一个人要离开时，有关自身的幻想已经所剩无几。这里就躺着一位，他一生意在为善、有所努力、失败连连：这真可以是他的墓志铭，但他却没有必要因此而羞愧。敦促战败士兵从战场上撤回的召唤来到

complain at the summons which calls a defeated soldier from the field: defeated, ay, if he were Paul or Marcus Aurelius![53] —but if there is still one inch of fight in his old spirit, undishonoured. The faith which sustained him in his life-long blindness and life-long disappointment will scarce even be required in this last formality of laying down his arms. Give him a march with his old bones; there, out of the glorious sun-coloured earth, out of the day and the dust and the ecstasy—there goes another Faithful Failure![54]

From a recent book of verse, where there is more than one such beautiful and manly poem, I take this memorial piece:[55] it says better than I can, what I love to think; let it be our parting word.

    A late lark twitters from the quiet skies;
    And from the west,
    Where the sun, his day's work ended,
    Lingers as in content,[56]
    There falls on the old, gray city
    An influence luminous and serene,[57]
    A shining peace.

    The smoke ascends[58]
    In a rosy-and-golden haze. The spires
    Shine, and are changed. In the valley
    Shadows rise.[59] The lark sings on. The sun,
    Closing his benediction,[60]
    Sinks, and the darkening air

时,他也不会抱怨:他战败了,没错,他若是《圣经》中的保罗或是罗马皇帝马可·奥勒留,那当然是战败了;但是在他那已经老去的精神世界里,若仍有一寸战斗的余地,他就仍会战斗到底、不辱荣耀。在他一生的盲从、一世的失望中,信仰支撑了他,但在这放下武器的最后仪式里,他甚至很少需要信仰的支撑。他会带着那副老骨头再次出征;离开了那阳光普照的大地,离开了白昼的光芒、离开了尘土、离开了欢欣,又一个忠贞不渝的失败者要再次出征了。

最近读过的一本诗集中有不少刚毅美妙的诗,且从中引来几行令人难忘的诗句,这诗说的要比我能说的好多了;读者诸君,就让这诗作为离别的话吧!

> 晚来天静,云雀声幽;
> 西坠的太阳,
> 一日劳作方休,
> 他心满意足,却欲走还留,
> 遂把霞光撒向旧城,
> 添一缕温馨宁静,
> 让平和柔光漫流。
>
> 炊烟起
> 映出金彩红艳,宛如雾游。
> 教堂的尖顶由亮转暗,
> 峡谷的幽影已然升浮。

Thrills with a sense of the triumphing night—[61]
Night, with her train of stars
And her great gift of sleep.

So be my passing!
My task accomplished and the long day done,
My wages taken,[62] and in my heart
Some late lark singing,
Let me be gathered to the quiet west,[63]
The sundown splendid and serene,
Death.[64]

云雀声中,太阳收起了祝福,
他已沉入夜幕,渐暗的空气,
拨动夜的心弦,完胜涌上心头。
夜,带着满天星斗,
送上安眠之礼丰厚。

但愿这是我的晚照!
我已事成功就,长日终到尽头。
劳作也获报酬,心底,
晚来的云雀一展歌喉,
死亡,
让我在宁静的西天与你聚首,
那儿已是霞光灿烂,静谧温柔。

注 释

37. 此处的 so built 和 so circumstanced 和前面的 inherit 和 stand buffet 相对应，前者强调的是先天的遗传因素，后者强调的是后天的环境因素。也就是说，人能不能幸福自己无法决定，天生就有容易生气的性格（先天），又偏偏处于能惹你生气的环境（后天），你的幸福不掌握在自己手里，比如说搞政治的人就会处于容易生气的环境。这里的 exposed to them 中的 them 应该指前面的 a sneer or an aspersion。尽管两个名词是用 or 连接起来的，按照语法应该属于单数，但这里作者用了复数的代词 them。

38. 这句是基于英语成语"Virtue is its own reward"。这个成语的意思就是一个人不应该做好事求回报，做好事有心理满足就不错了。但斯蒂文森在这里的意思是，做好事求自己满足都未必成立。

39. 这句中的 almost said 是一个习惯用法，表示想说但又有点犹豫，一种类似"欲说还休"的语境，但这个旧的表达法在这里分量极轻微，未必需要翻译出来。如果要表达的话，可以说"本不想说出来""本不想点名"等，但此处译者选择了放弃。另外，unamiable 这个形容词是由 amiable 派生而来，而后者既可以是 friendly、kind，也可以是"worthy to be loved, lovable, lovely"（OED）。所以在我们这个上下文中解释成 someone who is not kind 更合适，也就是说这个人不喜欢别人，总是对别人有敌意，比如本文中的那个要禁止木偶娃娃的女人就可归于这类人。

40. 这里的 the minor capitis diminutio of social ostracism 指法律之外的惩罚。除掉法律的惩罚(the penalties of the law),人也会希望逃避其他的惩罚,比如 social ostracism 就是一种惩罚,指将人排除在某些社会场合外,不让他参与某些活动。而这里的 capitis diminutio(diminished capacity)则是对人各种权利的剥夺,是古代罗马法惩罚人的尺度,一般分为三种:1. capitis diminutio minima(失去一个人的家庭联系); 2. capitis diminutio media(失去家庭成员的联系和公民身份); 3. capitis diminutio maxima(失去家庭、公民身份和个人自由),第一种失去的最少,第三种失去的最多。本文中作者没有具体指哪一种,仅仅说某种程度的权利丧失,但肯定是非重要的,因为用了 minor 一词,但译者没有必要去追究是上面三种中的哪一种。那么到底什么是所谓的 the minor capitis diminutio 呢?我们可以举个例子。如果一个人在对方不同意时强吻对方,那么那将招致 the penalties of the law。但是如果一个人满口种族歧视的语言,虽然很难用法律惩罚他,但是却可以受到另外一种惩罚,比如人们会疏远你(social ostracism),比如你若是一位表演艺术家,你的观众就会不去看你的表演,你进而受到惩罚。要想避免这种惩罚,那你就得有点智慧,更确切地说,得有点精明,比如你可以闭嘴不说种族歧视的话,但这个和美德无关,因为你之所以不说只是为避免惩罚的精明之举,不是因为你德行好。

41. 斯蒂文森在文章中多次提到 on duty。在本语境中他主要是在提人不要期待幸福(a man is not to expect happiness),紧接下来就是这句话(he is on duty here),所以说,这里的 duty 不是追求幸福,求幸福不是人的职责;再根据下面的句子,我们可以清楚地锁定这个职责就是为他人服务，为别人做好事。文中的 here 表示 in this world。

42. 见 153 页注释 14。此处的 hire 就是 reward 或 payment 的意思。

43. brother's keeper 典自《圣经·创世记》（4: 9）。该隐和亚伯是亚当和夏娃被上帝逐出伊甸园后最早生下的孩子。他们成年后，有次该隐和亚伯都向上帝献了礼物。可是该隐看到亚伯的礼物使上帝喜悦，而他的却未博得上帝的欢心，该隐出于嫉妒谋杀了他的兄弟。该隐谋杀他的兄弟亚伯后，上帝问他兄弟到哪里去了？该隐说："我不知道；难道我是看守我弟弟的吗？" the brother's keeper 就是要照顾到你兄弟，要为兄弟着想。在本文中，一方面，你的责任是要让你的邻居幸福，但另一方面，你也有责任为了你邻居的利益不能一味迁就下去，那样对你的邻居（兄弟）不好，但是你直言的话，就会冒犯你的邻居，你处于两难之中。这就是这段里说的 clash of duties。

44. 这句中的 pardon all 指的是所有对我们造成伤害的人和事，我们都要原谅。our own person 指与我们自身相关的，fortune 指与我们财富相关的。本句可以简单地理解为：We should be ready to accept and to pardon all injuries to our own person and fortunes。

45. 典自《圣经·路加福音》（6: 29）："有人打你一边的脸，把另一边也转给他打；有人拿你的外衣，连内衣也让他拿去。"

46. 这里的 lion 是作为隐喻使用的，比喻一个人的行动像狮子一样，有愤怒有勇气。这是说，当别人被打的时候，你应该有勇气站起来力挺弱者。

47. 这个 pious disguises 是说 ill-temper and envy and revenge 这些显

而易见的被人唾弃的行为会以完全不同的面貌出现，真的动机被遮盖起来了，遮盖它们的就是道德宗教（pious）等冠冕堂皇的东西，但实际它们真正的动机是后半句说的 inverted lusts，也就是 ill-temper and envy and revenge。比如说，我们有时会批评谴责比尔·盖茨，会从道德的角度批评他（pious disguises），但我们批评的实际动机是对他的巨富的妒嫉（envy=inverted lust）。

48. 这里的 knot that we cut 见本篇注释 25。fine heady quarrel-scene 中的 fine 不可能是正面的意思，因为整个短语的语境是激烈纷争（heady quarrel），所以 fine 也必须适合这个语境。似乎可以解释为对极细小（fine）事情也不放过的态度。

49. 这个 hanging head 是表示羞愧的动作（to lower one's head in shame or embarrassment），比如我们可以说"Don't hang your head over this loss—you ran an excellent race"。

50. no abiding city 典自《圣经·希伯来书》（13: 14），表示没有永恒的东西，任何地球上的东西都是转瞬即逝的。

51. 这个 thumb the hardly varying record 就是在一年的结束时（或一生的结束时）看一看自己的记录，一生的记录都是弱点和愚蠢的行为（weakness and folly），而且这些坏毛病并没有随着时间推移而有什么改善（hardly varying），上次表现得愚蠢，这次还是愚蠢。

52. 由于这句（It is a friendly process of detachment）是紧接着上句，所以这个 it 就可以理解成上句的 thumb the record。这里的 detachment 主要是表示人在人生的结束时，由于已经经历了无数，对于很多世事都能采取较为平心静气的态度，不像年轻时那么无法自拔，现在是可以超脱地（detachment）看待自己的弱点和愚蠢作为了。也正因此，这个回看自己斑斑劣迹的过程就是较为温和的（friendly）过程。

53. 这个 Paul or Marcus Aurelius 分别指《圣经》中的保罗和罗马皇帝马可·奥勒留。他们两位都努力追求德行完美，但都没有成功，所以这里说他们都是失败者。

54. 这最后一句的解读最好能最大限度地将语境考虑进去。这位已经在生命尾声的老者，带着那副象征身心疲倦、伤痕累累的老骨头（old bones），终于走在了回家的路上，战斗已经结束了，成败已不重要，当年多少次他就是靠成功的激励才战斗下去的，成功当时是非常重要的，但是现在已经不再重要。正如后面那首诗所说的，虽然饱经失败，但是他已经很满足了，而此时他正在离开那阳光普照的大地（go out of the glorious sun-coloured earth），在这片大地上其他人还在战斗，但那已经不是他的责任了；他正在离开那白昼的阳光（go out of the day），那阳光象征着在这片大地上的生活，尘世间的恩恩怨怨；他正在离开尘土（go out of the dust），尘土象征着肮脏的东西，但也让人联想到《圣经》中上帝创造万物用的尘土；他也正在离开一切给他带来激情欢乐的所有东西（go out of the ecstasy），他在这个世界上多少次被这种欣快影响，甚至忘掉了人生的方向；但他坚贞不渝，虽失败连连，却从不停止战斗（Faithful Failure）。句中的 the day 可以理解成 daylight，见 OED："figurative. Anything likened to daylight, esp. in terms of its clarity, purity, brightness, etc.; a light like that of day"，如 "We will all arise from the darkness of death unto the brilliant *day* of eternal life"。所有这几个 out of 后面的词都应借隐喻思维理解成物理实体才能建构出一幅隐喻图像，译者若仍停留在抽象思维里，就很难在翻译中表达，比如 the day 若理解成时间，就很难与 out of 结合，表达起来就困难了。这几个 out of 短语表示人即将离开这个世界，和下面那首诗的主题吻合。

55. 此诗出自 *A Book of Verses*（by William Ernest Henley, D. Nutt, 1888）。有趣的是，斯蒂文森用了作者的诗，却没有写上作者的名字。写本文这段时间，斯蒂文森和本诗作者的关系已经很紧张，后来诗作者对本文的差评也可证实这种紧张的关系。但此诗虽然是在说人生的结尾，作者还是流露出了对爱丁堡的眷恋，诗中的"the old, gray city"就是爱丁堡，诗人在那里生活工作患病，也在那里首次与斯蒂文森见面。斯蒂文森引用这首诗，也难免情系爱丁堡。还记得《被鄙视的种族》那篇里的故乡吗？（I beheld that old, gray, castled city）斯蒂文森对家乡爱丁堡有既恨又爱的情结。特别在此时，他结束了萨拉纳克湖的小住，来到了纽约。他即将横贯美国平原，去加州与范妮会面，有可能远赴南太平洋。他也许没有想到，这一去就是永远，他后来再也没有回到那个旧城古堡的家乡。本诗虽然分成三节，但可看作两部分，在"So be my passing!"之前是用拟人的手法描写落日，在这句之后，则是用隐喻的手法讲他自己的愿望，表示如何接受死亡，而整首诗的概念隐喻是 A life is a day。本诗的长处在意象和隐喻，如拟人化的太阳（lingers as in content）、拟人化的夜晚（her great gift of sleep），以及将人比成太阳、将一生比成长长的一日（the long day done），这些都是在翻译中应该尽量"维护"的东西；诗的形式为自由诗体（free verse），但诗的音律并不出彩。另需要说明的是，这首诗在文后附上，不仅没有说明作者，也没有题目，但这并不是说这首诗原来也没有题目。其实本诗的题目是拉丁语的 Margaritae Sorori，就是 Sister Margaret，是为了纪念作者五岁就死去的女儿。

56. "Lingers as in content" 是在说太阳。在黄昏时太阳可以缓慢地退下，历时很久，诗人在想，那太阳肯定很满足，不急于离开，这又折射到人的晚年，人也很满足，满足于现状，满足于一生的战斗，满足于虽败犹荣。

57. 这句的正常语序应该是 An influence falls on the old, gray city（指爱丁堡）。但这个 an influence luminous and serene 应该是指太阳的光线（晚霞），只有一个物理实体的晚霞才能 fall on a city。但是翻译时的角度却应该转换到晚霞的影响或效果上（influence），在晚霞的斜照下，我们看见的是房屋长长的影子，给人一种暖洋洋温馨宁静的柔光，因为 luminous 不是当空耀眼的烈日，而是已经快消失的余霞，所以译者在翻译的时候，可以根据语境选词，如用"柔光"，甚至用"温馨"来翻译 luminous 都未尝不可。

58. 这里的 smoke 应该主要指爱丁堡当地住家烟囱里冒出来的烟，可能是取暖的烟，但肯定也是烧饭时冒出来的烟，与汉语的炊烟似乎在文化意境上很接近，不妨借用一下。其实爱丁堡过去就有一个别称 the Auld Reekie，意思就是 Old Smokey。

59. "In the valley Shadows rise." 典自《圣经·诗篇》: Though I walk through the valley of the shadow of death, I will fear no evil: for thou art with me; thy rod and thy staff they comfort me.（Psalm 23: 4）

60. 这个 "Closing his benediction" 是说太阳要结束它的祝福了。在太阳没有落下前，太阳的祝福就是它温暖宁静的阳光，但现在太阳要沉下去了，所以说是 closing his benediction。

61. 这里的 thrill with a sense 只能和人的感官挂上钩，就是在那一刻，即白昼即将消失黑夜即将来临时人的一种感觉，也许似震撼，抑或是悸动，译者可调动活跃的想象思维，寻找合适的词。the triumphing night 中的 triumphing 应该是针对白昼而言的胜利，因为黑夜即将取代白昼。

62. 这个"My wages taken"是指他因一生的工作而得到的酬劳，包括他做的好事所得到的回报。但斯蒂文森主张，人为别人服务是不应该期待回报的。

63. be gathered to 这个表达法可追溯到宗教的源头，如《圣经·创世记》中的"I am to *be gathered unto* my people: bury me with my fathers in the cave that is in the field of Ephron the Hittite"（Genesis 49: 29）。根据《圣经》的这句，gathered unto 的后面是一群人，但是我们这首诗里是 the west，既是一个地点，也象征死亡，而诗人正是在对 death 做拟人的讲话。

64. death 在这里较合适的一个解释就是，诗人是在对 death 说话，这在翻译时会造成一点困难。这个点睛之"词"在原文是放在最后的，有一定形式上的意思。强调语言形式的人会尽量把这个词也放在最后，但汉语放到最后就比较困难，还是应该根据整体的诗意考虑来决定。

Crabbed Age and Youth (1)

"You know my mother now and then argues very notably; always very warmly at least. I happen often to differ from her; and we both think so well of our own arguments, that we very seldom are so happy as to convince one another. A pretty common case, I believe, in all VEHEMENT debatings. She says, I am TOO WITTY; Anglice, TOO PERT; I, that she is TOO WISE; that is to say, being likewise put into English, NOT SO YOUNG AS SHE HAS BEEN."

—Miss Howe to Miss Harlowe, *Clarissa*, vol. ii. Letter xiii.[1]

There is a strong feeling in favour of cowardly and prudential proverbs. The sentiments of a man while he is full of ardour and hope are to be received, it is supposed, with some qualification. But when the same person has ignominiously failed and begins to eat up his words, he should be listened to like an oracle. Most of our pocket wisdom is conceived for the use of mediocre people, to discourage them from ambitious attempts, and generally console them in their mediocrity. And since mediocre people constitute the bulk of humanity, this is no doubt very properly so. But it does not follow that the one sort of proposition is any less true than the other, or that Icarus is not to be more praised, and perhaps more envied, than Mr. Samuel Budgett the Successful Merchant.[2] The one is dead, to be sure, while the other is still in his counting-house counting out his money;[3] and doubtless this is a consideration. But we have, on the other hand, some

倔老头与年轻人（一）

你知道，有时我母亲辩论起来语惊四座，每次总是至少争得异常激烈。而我又常与她意见相左；我们两人都觉得自己的观点正确无比，结果就很少能有那种说服对方的快乐。我想，所有的激辩一般都是这么个套路。她说，我太风趣诙谐，其实就是说我没大没小，我则说，她太智慧，其实说白了就是说她已经不再年轻。

——"豪伊小姐致哈洛小姐"，《克拉丽莎》，第2卷，第13封信

有人强烈主张为人要奉行懦弱谨慎的格言。说是一个人踌躇满志时的情感不可全信。但是若同一个人灰头土脸失败后开始悔尽前言，他的话反倒应奉为圭臬。大多数我们听到的简语哲言都是说给平庸者听的，旨在为雄心壮志泼冷水，是在安抚他们满足中庸的现状。鉴于芸芸众生大多平庸，所以如此安抚无疑也恰到好处。但却不能说只有上述训教才是人生真谛，总不能说飞向太阳的伊卡洛斯就不如成功商人塞缪尔·巴基特更值得赞扬，更应被人羡慕。没错，他们一个已经死去，另一个还在守着账簿数钱；这个差别无疑是个考虑的因素。但是另一方面，我们也有一些性情高贵、志存高远者的豪言壮语，这些言语大谈失败者令人仰慕的品格，声称他们

bold and magnanimous sayings common to high races and natures, which set forth the advantage of the losing side, and proclaim it better to be a dead lion than a living dog.[4] It is difficult to fancy how the mediocrities reconcile such sayings with their proverbs. According to the latter, every lad who goes to sea is an egregious ass; never to forget your umbrella through a long life would seem a higher and wiser flight of achievement than to go smiling to the stake;[5] and so long as you are a bit of a coward and inflexible in money matters, you fulfill the whole duty of man.

It is a still more difficult consideration for our average men, that while all their teachers, from Solomon down to Benjamin Franklin and the ungodly Binney,[6] have inculcated the same ideal of manners, caution, and respectability, those characters in history who have most notoriously flown in the face of[7] such precepts are spoken of in hyperbolical terms of praise, and honoured with public monuments in the streets of our commercial centres. This is very bewildering to the moral sense. You have Joan of Arc,[8] who left a humble but honest and reputable livelihood under the eyes of her parents, to go a-colonelling,[9] in the company of rowdy soldiers, against the enemies of France; surely a melancholy example for one's daughters! And then you have Columbus,[10] who may have pioneered America, but, when all is said,[11] was a most imprudent navigator. His life is not the kind of thing one would like to put into the hands of young people; rather, one would do one's utmost to keep it from their knowledge, as a red flag of adventure and disintegrating influence in life. The time would fail me if I were to recite all the big names in history whose exploits are perfectly irrational and even shocking to the business mind. The incongruity is speaking;[12] and I imagine it must engender among the mediocrities a very peculiar attitude, towards the nobler and showier sides of national life.[13]

宁为死狮不做活狗。很难想象平庸者如何将这类壮语和他们的哲言都接纳。平庸者的观点是,奔赴大海的年轻人都是愚蠢透顶的家伙;能一生始终不忘带伞似乎是更高尚更智慧的成就,远胜于带笑走向火刑柱;只要你有那么一点胆小谨慎,在钱财上一丝不苟,你就担起了人的全部责任。

虽然所有的导师,从所罗门,到本杰明·富兰克林,再到不信神的宾尼,都向我们灌输风度、谨慎、尊严这些完美的观念,但有些与这类观念格格不入的历史人物却被赞扬得上了天,还在商业区的街上为他们竖碑立像,这对于我们一般人来说就更想不通了。这现象令持传统道德观的人百思不得其解。历史上有法兰西的圣女贞德,离开了父母的垂顾,放弃了简朴但体面的生活,为了法国率军作战,与粗鲁的士兵一起抗击敌人;女流如此,真是女儿们悲壮的楷模。接着是哥伦布,他也许是发现美洲的先驱,但不管怎么说,也是个最爱冒险的航海者。他的一生并不是人们喜欢推荐给年轻人的;人们反倒会尽力不让年轻人知道他的生平,会把那样的人生当作是冒险、失败的警钟。如果要我举出历史上的名人,数落他们那些在商界人士眼里堪称毫无理性,甚至十分震惊的作为,那么我可能没有足够的时间。平庸者常会表里不一,结果我想就肯定会酝酿出一种很独特的态度,一种对更高尚、更光辉的国家叙事采取事不关己的态度。他们把在书中读"巴拉克拉瓦战役"和在剧院看"里昂邮件"的表演一视同仁。这些看戏的富足人士手拿一份显示身份

They will read of the Charge of Balaclava in much the same spirit as they assist at a performance of the Lyons Mail.[14] Persons of substance[15] take in the Times and sit composedly in pit or boxes according to the degree of their prosperity in business. As for the generals who go galloping up and down among bomb-shells in absurd cocked hats—as for the actors who raddle their faces and demean themselves for hire upon the stage—they must belong, thank God! to a different order of beings, whom we watch as we watch the clouds careering in the windy, bottomless inane, or read about like characters in ancient and rather fabulous annals.[16] Our offspring would no more think of copying their behaviour, let us hope, than of doffing their clothes and painting themselves blue in consequence of certain admissions in the first chapter of their school history of England.[17]

Discredited as they are in practice, the cowardly proverbs hold their own[18] in theory; and it is another instance of the same spirit, that the opinions of old men about life have been accepted as final. All sorts of allowances are made for the illusions of youth; and none, or almost none, for the disenchantments of age.[19] It is held to be a good taunt, and somehow or other to clinch the question logically, when an old gentleman waggles his head and says: "Ah, so I thought when I was your age." It is not thought an answer at all, if the young man retorts: "My venerable sir, so I shall most probably think when I am yours." And yet the one is as good as the other: pass for pass, tit for tat, a Roland for an Oliver.[20]

"Opinion in good men," says Milton, "is but knowledge in the making." All opinions, properly so called, are stages on the road to truth. It does not follow that a man will travel any further; but if he has really considered the world and drawn a conclusion, he has travelled as far. This does not apply to formulae got by rote, which are stages on the road to

的《泰晤士报》，根据事业上成就的不同，或从容地坐在楼下前排或悠闲地坐于楼上包厢。至于那些戴着难看的三角帽在枪林弹雨中冲锋陷阵的将军，就像那些为了在舞台上谋得一个角色而涂脂抹粉极尽自毁形象之能事的演员，谢天谢地，他们肯定属于另一类人，我们这些富足人士看他们，就像看天上长风流荡、浮云过眼，就像读浩瀚古卷中的人物，与我们毫不相干。但愿我们富足人士的后代不会想去模仿将军的行为举止，也不会因读了英国史课本第一章中承认的一些脱衣涂漆的轶事，而去模仿古人将衣服脱掉，把蓝色的漆也涂在身上。

在生活实践中，这些懦弱谨慎的教训名誉扫地，但在理论中却寸步不让；比如老年人有关生活的意见仍被奉为圭臬就是又一例证。人们总把年轻人异想天开当作幼稚而予以宽恕，但是对于老年人缺乏理想，却几乎从不用去找理由去为他们开脱，老年人的话总是对的。若一位年老的绅士摇着头说："我在你那个年龄也是这么想的"，这话会被认为答得好，符合逻辑。但如果年轻人顶回去说："尊敬的先生，我若到你这年龄时很可能也会这样想"，就会被认为完全算不上是个答案。但实际是，两个答案无优劣之分。

弥尔顿说："好人的意见经年累月后就是知识。"所有的意见（且这么称之）都是达到真理途上的一个个阶段。这并不是说每个人都一定会前进；但一个人若洞察世事，从中得出结论，那么他就在通往真理的路上前进了。但不假思索因循守旧却使你茫然不知所

nowhere but second childhood and the grave. To have a catchword in your mouth is not the same thing as to hold an opinion; still less is it the same thing as to have made one for yourself. There are too many of these catchwords in the world for people to rap out upon you like an oath and by way of an argument. They have a currency as intellectual counters;[21] and many respectable persons pay their way with nothing else. They seem to stand for vague bodies of theory in the background. The imputed virtue of folios full of knockdown arguments is supposed to reside in them, just as some of the majesty of the British Empire dwells in the constable's truncheon.[22] They are used in pure superstition, as old clodhoppers spoil Latin by way of an exorcism.[23] And yet they are vastly serviceable for checking unprofitable discussion and stopping the mouths of babes and sucklings.[24] And when a young man comes to a certain stage of intellectual growth, the examination of these counters forms a gymnastic at once amusing and fortifying to the mind.

Because I have reached Paris, I am not ashamed of having passed through Newhaven and Dieppe.[25] They were very good places to pass through, and I am none the less at my destination. All my old opinions were only stages on the way to the one I now hold, as itself is only a stage on the way to something else. I am no more abashed at having been a red-hot Socialist with a panacea of my own than at having been a sucking infant.[26] Doubtless the world is quite right in a million ways; but you have to be kicked about a little to convince you of the fact. And in the meanwhile you must do something, be something, believe something. It is not possible to keep the mind in a state of accurate balance and blank; and even if you could do so, instead of coming ultimately to the right conclusion, you would be very apt to remain in a state of balance and blank to perpetuity.[27]

向，会把你带回幼稚的童年或带向坟墓。嘴中喊几句口号和持一种意见不可同日而语；但持一种意见仍不如形成自己的意见。这世界上有无数口号，有时它们表现为誓言或出现在争论中，喋喋不休地敲打着你。这些口号被人们广泛用来当作舌战的武器；许多有头有脸的人就是利用这种东西一路顺畅的。这些口号似乎代表了背景中虚无缥缈的理论，寓于其中的是权威经典中能助你辩论取胜的智慧，人们坚信这些口号，就像他们坚信寓于警棍中的是大英帝国的威严一样。人们以纯粹迷信的态度使用这些口号，就像装神弄鬼的人用语无伦次的语言驱散鬼魂时迷信不疑。但是它们却能用于阻止毫无用处的讨论，堵住儿童和婴儿的嘴巴而已。一旦年轻人的智力成长到一定阶段，他们就会思考审视这些口号，这种思维的激荡既为年轻人增添了乐趣，也为他们加固了思想。

鉴于我已经抵达巴黎，所以我并不羞于曾途经纽黑文和迪耶普。经过这两个地方应是快事，不管怎么地，我已经达到目的地。所有我过去的看法都是我一路走来的阶段性看法，正是这些看法把我引导至我目前所持的看法，而我目前的看法也只是抵达另外一种看法路上的一个阶段。我并不羞于曾经是一个手握万灵药激情满怀的社会主义者，就像我也不羞于我曾是个吃奶的婴孩一样。毫无疑问，这个世界有千万个对法；但是要想认识到这点，你必须碰得头破血流。同时，你得有所作，有所成，有所信。不可能让你的思维保持在某个平稳有序的状态，就算你能做到，你可能最终还是无法

Even in quite intermediate stages, a dash of enthusiasm is not a thing to be ashamed of in the retrospect: if St. Paul had not been a very zealous Pharisee,[28] he would have been a colder Christian. For my part, I look back to the time when I was a Socialist with something like regret. I have convinced myself (for the moment) that we had better leave these great changes to what we call great blind forces: their blindness being so much more perspicacious than the little, peering, partial eyesight of men.[29] I seem to see that my own scheme would not answer; and all the other schemes I ever heard propounded would depress some elements of goodness just as much as they encouraged others. Now I know that in thus turning Conservative with years, I am going through the normal cycle of change and travelling in the common orbit of men's opinions. I submit to this, as I would submit to gout or gray hair, as a concomitant of growing age or else of failing animal heat;[30] but I do not acknowledge that it is necessarily a change for the better—I daresay it is deplorably for the worse. I have no choice in the business, and can no more resist this tendency of my mind than I could prevent my body from beginning to totter and decay. If I am spared (as the phrase runs) I shall doubtless outlive some troublesome desires; but I am in no hurry about that; nor, when the time comes, shall I plume myself on the immunity just in the same way, I do not greatly pride myself on having outlived my belief in the fairy tales of Socialism. Old people have faults of their own; they tend to become cowardly, niggardly, and suspicious. Whether from the growth of experience or the decline of animal heat, I see that age leads to these and certain other faults; and it follows, of course, that while in one sense I hope I am journeying towards the truth, in another I am indubitably posting towards these forms and sources of error.

达到正确的结论，而会永远卡在那个静止不动的状态中。即便是在某个中间阶段，短暂的热情爆发事后看来也不是件可耻的事：如果圣保罗不是一个非常狂热的法利赛人，那他就会成为一个冷漠的基督徒。就我来说，我回首那段热衷社会主义的时光，多少有些后悔。我（此刻暂且）说服了自己，我们最好还是将这些社会巨变留给我们称之为"盲从的伟力"来定夺。这种驱动历史进程的巨大力量尽管盲从，但还是要比眼光局限的人看得更清楚。我似乎看到我自己的计划并不是答案，而所有其他提出的计划则总会激励一些义举，却压制另一些善行。现在我知道，随着年龄增长我变得保守了，其间我所经历的是一个人观点演变的正常周期和常见轨迹。我屈服于这个变化，恰如我屈服于痛风和白发，这是年龄增长必然随之而来的，或者说是生理热情减弱的自然结果；但我并不承认这种变化一定是变好，我敢说，很可悲那是变坏。这事儿我别无选择，就像我无法阻止我自身步履蹒跚变得老朽一样，我也无法抗拒我思维的转变。如果我有幸活下去，我无疑可能摆脱一些讨厌的欲望，但是我不急于摆脱它们，当时间到来时，我也不急于自夸我有免疫力抵抗欲望，同理，我也不觉得我摆脱了社会主义的童话有什么值得骄傲的。老年人有老年人的毛病。他们总是比较怯懦、小气、多疑。不管这是起于经验增长，还是源于生理热情减弱，反正我觉得年老总会带出这类毛病；当然在某种意义上我希望自己正朝真理迈进，但在另一种意义上无疑自己也正奔向形形色色的谬误。

注　释

1. 这段正文前的文字选自英国作家塞缪尔·理查森的《克拉丽莎，或一位年轻女士的历史》(*Clarissa Harlowe, or the History of a Young Lady*)，具体出自哈洛小姐的密友豪伊小姐致哈洛的一封信。理查森的这本小说被认为是英国小说中最长的一本，共7卷，长达1534页，2015年英国BBC把这本小说排在100本英国小说榜中的第14位。据信斯蒂文森是在写这篇文章后读这本小说的，所以作者把本应为后语（afterthought）的这段文字放到了卷前引语（epigraph）的位置上了。这段中的warmly不能望文生义，解释成"温顺地"，而应该解释成with controversial ardor、fervently或fiercely。

2. 伊卡洛斯（Icarus）是希腊神话中代达罗斯的儿子，与代达罗斯使用蜡和羽毛造的羽翼逃离克里特岛时，他因飞得太高，双翼上的蜡遭太阳融化跌落水中丧生，被埋葬在一个海岛上。这里的Mr. Samuel Budgett the Successful Merchant是指英国商人塞缪尔·布吉特，他去世后出版的*The Successful Merchant* (by William Arthur)一书畅销英国内外，也使他远近闻名。斯蒂文森在这里提到他时没有任何介绍，说明作者认为这是家喻户晓的人物。

3. 这里的counting-house就是指商人存放账簿文件等的办公场所。"The one is dead,… the other is"当然分别指伊卡洛斯和巴基特。虽然这句表面看是表述事实，但是根据语境，斯蒂文森对前者褒奖有加、对后者不以为然的态度还是很清楚的。另外in his counting-house counting out his money应该与儿童歌曲的歌词有互文关系。（见Sing a Song of Sixpence: The king was in his

counting-house / Counting out his money.）

4. 这句出自《圣经·传道书》（Ecclesiastes 9: 4）："For to him that is joined to all the living there is hope: for a living dog is better than a dead lion."（与一切活人相连的，那人还有指望，因为活着的狗比死了的狮子更强。）斯蒂文森在这里反其意而用之。

5. 这句里有两处应该解释一下。首先 a higher and wiser flight of achievement 中的 a flight of 在一般情况下解释为 a group of，后面跟飞禽，如 a flight of birds 等。但在这里似乎没有 a group of 的意思，而有 flying high 的含义，和前面的 high 一同起到协同作用。另外一个就是 the stake 的翻译。这个词指把人绑在上面去处死（a post upon which persons were bound for execution, esp. by burning）。最原始的是用火烧死，基本就是去死的意思，如"I know I would go to the stake for you"。一开始想到比较具体的"断头台""刑场"等，但是都觉得不很合适。尽管都是表示去死，但"断头台"的形象和一个人绑在一根木头的柱子上还是很不一样，"刑场"更容易联想起射杀而死。虽然这里仅指赴死，但 stake 这个词现在仍有柱子的形象，加之，后面提到的圣女贞德就是绑在柱子上烧死的，所以最后还是用了"带笑走向火刑柱"。

6. 此处的 Solomon 就是指圣经中《箴言》的作者所罗门。Benjamin Franklin 指本杰明·富兰克林（1706—1790），是美国政治家和科学家，美国独立战争中非常重要的人物，而作为美国启蒙运动的领袖，他也影响了欧洲的科学家。the ungodly Binney 在有的版本中用的是 the infamous Budgett，指 Thomas Binney，即托马斯·宾尼牧师，是19世纪英国公理会的神职人员。

7. 这个 fly in the face of 过去常用来表示 oppose 或 attack 的意

思，比如下面这句1891年的句子："He had to fly in the face of adverse decisions."（OED）但是这个短语目前主要表示 in contradiction with 的意思，比如 "The findings fly in the face of the myth that chocolate is an antidepressant"（2006）。在本句中就是这个意思，即表示这些历史人物和上述的观念相悖。

8. 圣女贞德，出生在中世纪法国的一个农民家庭。她相信上帝选择了她，要她带领法国在与英国的长期战争中取得胜利。在没有任何军事训练的情况下，她说服了四面楚歌的查尔斯王储允许她率领一支法国军队前往被围困的奥尔良市，在那里她取得了的重大胜利。但后来在战争中她被英国军队俘虏，受审后于1431年被烧死在火刑柱上，当时只有19岁。她后来在1920年被正式封为圣女，是法国统一和民族精神的持久象征。注意前面提到的 go smiling to the stake 就是与圣女贞德的典故有关。圣女贞德正是 the nobler and showier sides of national life 的一个例证。

9. 短语 go a-colonelling 表示率领军队打仗的意思，colonelling 一词源自名词 colonel（上校），当动词用表示 to make a colonel of、to play the colonel 的意思。在前面用连字符再加上一个字母 a 使文字略添古雅的味道，如 "Here we go a-wassailing among the leaves so green"。under the eyes of her parents 中的 under 在这句中有长辈对孩子关怀照顾的意思。而 humble but honest and reputable 则表示她的家境，她出身普通农民家庭，humble 表示简朴，而 honest and reputable 大致就是还不错的意思，即一般体面的小康生活。

10. 这里的 Columbus 是指 Christopher Columbus（克里斯托弗·哥伦布，1451—1506），意大利探险家、殖民者、航海家，大航海时代的主要人物之一。下面的 pioneered America 指的就是发现美洲大陆。

11. 这个 when all is said 有时还可写成 when all is said and done，基本意思就是 when you are about to tell someone the most important fact they should remember in a situation（Cambridge Dictionary），或 when everything is taken into account（Online Oxford）。但是这个词组已经成为惯用说法，一般解释为 in the end、ultimately，可翻译成中文的"说到底""毕竟""归根结底"。任何其他和上面解释的意思一致的翻译都可以。

12. the incongruity 这个词表示自相矛盾的意思（OED: want of self-consistency; incoherence. Also something incoherent or not self-consistent），如 the incongruity of his fleshy face and skinny body disturbed her。在这里就是指那些平庸者对待事物明显矛盾的态度，比如，人们嘴上赞扬英雄人物（比如圣女贞德、航海家哥伦布），把他们的雕塑放在街上，但却不希望子女步英雄后尘。speaking 这里表示 significant、noticeable、remarkable 等意思，如 "This recovery seemed to be speaking, as to the point I was concerned about."（OED）此话是说平庸者对事件的态度表里不一。

13. 这后半句，就是前半句（The incongruity is speaking）的具体例子，所以这个 it 就是指前面半句中的 the incongruity，或者说这种表里不一必定会在平庸者中间营造出一种态度。什么态度呢？就是对 the nobler and showier sides of national life 的特殊的态度，之所以独特是因为心口不一到不合常理的地步。那么什么是 the nobler and showier sides of national life 呢？斯蒂文森在这里在强调国家、社会、文化象征符号的重要性。他觉得平庸者只顾赚钱，而对于一个国家更高尚的、更为灿烂的宏观叙事却不感兴趣，具体的例子就是前面的圣女贞德等，和下面对"巴拉克拉瓦战役"和"里昂邮件"的态度。斯蒂文森似乎觉得历史大叙事（圣女贞德、巴拉克拉瓦战役）很重要，一般消遣的戏剧（里昂邮件）不能与其同日而语。

14. 这个 Balaclava 指的是克里米亚战争中那次著名的巴拉克拉瓦战役［详见"Aes Triplex"篇注释 25］。这里的 Lyons Mail 指 1854 年查尔斯·雷德（Charles Reade）的戏剧《里昂信使》（*The Courier of Lyons*），这是维多利亚时代非常流行的舞台剧。一个是有历史意义的宏观历史叙事，另一个仅仅是供消遣的流行戏剧，但这些富足之士把读历史大叙事和观赏消遣戏剧一样看待，说明这些人没有宏观视野。注意，这里的 assist 不是帮助的意思，而是出席、参加的意思（to attend, to be present at），一般常和 at 连用，如 OED 中的例句："The dinner at which we have just assisted"，或 "And assisted—in the French sense—at the performance of two waltzes"，但这些用法都比较古旧，目前已经不常用了。

15. persons of substance 中的 substance 有不同的意思，比如其中一个意思就是 quality of being significant，所以初一看我们这个短语译成"重要人物"似乎也不错。但是这个词也表示富贵的意思，如在线牛津词典就有一个定义 wealth and possessions，而且马上就给了一个例句 a woman of substance，所以后者更符合我们的语境。其实前面那个"重要人物"的定义也不错，只是根据上下文，强调"富有"更合适。

16. 这一长句中有好几处需要解释。首先，有两种人，一种是打仗的将军，还有一种是舞台上粉墨登场的演员。这个 demean themselves 就是自己糟蹋自己的意思（Collins: If you demean

yourself, you do something which makes people have less respect for you）。for hire upon the stage 就是希望找到一个舞台上的角色。这两种人（将军和演员）是这句的主语（we）喜欢的职业吗？由于是 we，所以读者很容易理解为作者以及他所代表的大众。但是我们都知道本文中斯蒂文森的态度不是站在富贵者一边的，可是句子中偏偏有个"thank God!"，马上就暴露了主语 we 的态度，因为当人们说"thank God"时，一般总是说自己幸运了，不幸的事总算没发生，如"Thank God you arrived safely"。可是在我们这句中，作者在说，谢天谢地，将军（和演员一样）和我们不是同一类人，我们不喜欢与这些人为伍。但是我们接下来却发现，这个不喜欢将军的态度，不像是我们（斯蒂文森及其所代表的大众）的态度，而像是有钱人的态度。其实这里作者的口气完全转换了。作者让富有之人以我们的身份在说话。因此用"我们"翻译 we 虽然非常准确，但是却把这个麻烦留给了读者。译者面临三个选择：1. 翻译成"我们"；2. 翻译成"富足人士"；3. 翻译成"我们富足人士"。最能反映作者写作特点的是 1，最能把意思交代清楚的是 2，两者尽量都照顾到的是 3。我们这里选择 3。后半句就是表达了我们富足人士对将军的态度。句子中有两个比喻的动作，一个是"watch the clouds careering in the windy, bottomless inane"，另一个是"read about like characters in ancient and rather fabulous annals"。我们富足人士看将军（像看演员一样）如同看浮云和读古书，结合上面几句和下面一句，我们知道看云和读书是可欣赏但不必认真对待的事，而在这些富足人士的生活里，当将军（像当演员一样）也只能与看云读书一样无足轻重。下面一句正好证实了这点。

17. 这句中的 let us hope，和前面的一样也是我们富足人士的希望（更说明前一句我们判断的准确）。我们希望什么呢？就是希望我们的后代 would no more think of copying... than doffing...。第一个 copying their behaviour 是将军的行为，儿孙们别学；第二个 doffing their clothes and painting... 是演员的行为，儿孙们也别学。句中的 in consequence of 可以理解为 because of，或 as a result of，就是后面的部分（certain admissions in the first chapter of their school history of England）是前面 doffing 的原因。in the first chapter of their school history of England 是指英国学校的历史课本，而 certain admissions 就是指历史课本里的一些 facts。古代英国人打仗前会先脱掉衣服，用蓝漆涂在身上，然后冲锋陷阵。这些 facts 也是人们读了历史书了解后会模仿的，当然富足人士不希望他们的后代去模仿。至于 admissions 一词可以用 OED 中的一个定义（2a）："acknowledgement of something as valid or true; concession of a fact; acceptance, approval"。所以 certain admissions 就是 certain facts that are admitted to be true in the history book 的意思（关于 admissions 的复数形式及其意义，见"Despised Races"篇注释 30）。之所以要用 admitted，也许是因为这些祖先们干的脱衣涂漆的事儿实在不登大雅之堂，姑且承认了，有一点幽默的味道。

18. hold one's own 是一个成语表达法，表示在阻力面前顶住（to maintain one's situation or position, especially in spite of opposition or difficulty），比如"The Frenchman held his own against the challenge"。

19. 这句确实很难理解。根据上下文，可以说，作者想说的是人们总是否定年轻人的行为，而接受老年人的观点。但是如果我们把下面这句纳入这个理解思路，往往和字面意思对不起来，比如把 make allowances 理解成 forgive 的话，这句就是"人们总是原谅年轻人的幻想，却几乎不原谅老年人的幻灭"。这显然和语境不符。查《朗文当代英语辞典》，发现 allowance 有一个定义符合这里的语境："to let someone behave in a way you would not normally approve of, because you know there are special reasons for their behavior"，如例句：Dad is under a lot of pressure, so we have to make allowances for him。也就是说，爸爸由于压力大，就算有些不很得体的行为（比如脾气大），我们也得原谅他，但是发脾气这行为我们认为还是错的。回到我们这句，什么是年轻人的 illusions 呢？比如花天价的钱去买一个乐器，因为想成为小提琴演奏家，这就可能是一种 illusion。人们对这种异想天开的行为往往会给予原谅（make allowances），因为毕竟年轻嘛！但人们是既原谅又否定的。那么什么是老年人的 disenchantments 呢？用同一个例子，老年人则会对年轻人的异想天开持现实态度，否定他天价买提琴的想法，因为他们是过来人，知道大多数年轻人的梦想最后都不了了之，什么小提琴演奏家，都是实现不了的目标，这是因为老年人心中缺少热情，没有理想（disenchantments），总把事物往消极方面想。也就是说，社会对年轻人是虽否定但原谅，对老年人则不是虽否定但原谅，而是不假思索地接受。翻译的时候不能被原文文字牵绊，应该允许使用解释性的翻译，在不违背原文的情况下，做一点添加也是可以的。

20. 这里的 a Roland for an Oliver 是指两位中世纪著名的骑士罗兰和奥利弗，他们为查理曼大帝而战，能力不相上下。前面的 pass for pass 和 tit for tat 也是不相上下的意思。换句话说，斯蒂文森在这里用了三个同义短语。从翻译的角度看，若要完全重现作者的写法，三个都用中文的同义词表达。但是一般情况下，译者完全可以用一个译法把三个短语的意思都包括进去（如"两个答案无好坏之分"）。典故不用直译过来，因为如果没有注释，读者根本看不懂"罗兰和奥利弗"是什么意思。当然，如果要反映原文的特色，就应该都翻译出来，只是关心到这种细节的读者，往往都可以读原文。

21. 这个 currency 是广为接受的意思，如 "His theory of the social contract had wide currency in America"。而 counters 就是对批评等不同意见的回应（something that you say to reply to a criticism or argument），比如 a counter to unfair criticism。这里就是指那些 catchwords。

22. 这句中的 folios 应取其隐喻的意思（a volume made up of sheets of paper folded once; a volume of the largest size）。knockdown arguments 中的 arguments 由于是复数，所以可以指权威经典（folios）中可用于辩论的语言；而 knockdown 本来指拳击中把人击倒，但这里当形容词用，是 overwhelming 或 powerful 的意思（比如 a knockdown fight）。imputed 源于动词 impute，表示赋予价值，在这句中，就是人们赋予这些 catchwords 以智慧美德（people impute the virtue or wisdom without any evidence that the wisdom exists）。换句话说，这个 virtue 并非是斯蒂文森认为的 virtue，而是使用这些口号的人赋予它们的。

23. 这后半句的 as old clodhoppers... 就是在举例说明，用这些口号的人是以迷信的态度使用它们的，就像一些愚昧无知的老农民（old clodhoppers）搞的驱散鬼神的迷信活动（exorcism），他们在驱鬼的过程中口中念念有词，但说出的话都是不标准的，是变异了的话语（spoil Latin）。就像中国北方农村的跳大神，两个人嘴里念念有词。spoil Latin 就是 corrupt Latin 的意思，就是说驱鬼念咒时用的语言不是标准的拉丁语而是变异的。

24. the mouths of babes and sucklings 出自《圣经》：Out of *the mouth of babes and sucklings* hast thou ordained strength because of thine enemies, that thou mightest still the enemy and the avenger.（Psalm 8:2）

25. Newhaven（纽黑文）和 Dieppe（迪耶普）是英吉利海峡两端的海港城市，纽黑文在英国一侧，迪耶普在法国一侧。从英国到法国当时必须经过这两个城市，假如目的地是巴黎，那么就一定要途经这两个不甚有名的港口。斯蒂文森是在比喻，假如你想抵达一个认知的目的地（巴黎），那你就必须要经过一些中间的认识阶段（纽黑文和迪耶普），不可能一步到位。

26. sucking infant 见《圣经》：Can a woman forget her *sucking child*, that she should not have compassion on the son of her womb?（Isaiah 49:15）

27. 这句话的意思参考译文应该已经说得很清楚了，但要解释一下 a state of accurate balance and blank。由于这个平衡是 accurate，这说明这个状态稍一不慎就会失去。这是个平衡的状态（balance），而平衡必须有两端，保持了平衡就处在中间（注意斯蒂文森在说平庸之辈）。至于 blank 应该也是类似的意思。OED 有这么个定义："the white spot in the centre of a target; hence figurative anything aimed at, the range of such aim"，可见是一个瞄准的目标，也是一个稍有不慎就会失去的东西。当然也有人说，这两个词是财会报表上的词，但不管怎么说，这个 a state of accurate balance and blank 是表示一个不偏不倚的、有序的、理想的状态，但在斯蒂文森看来那是不可能的状态。就算你能达到那个状态，你也追求不到真理，而只会永远停留在那个所谓的有序状态，不会进步，不会靠近真理（the right conclusion）。

28. St. Paul 指《圣经》中的使徒保罗，原来是法利赛人（Pharisee），迫害基督徒，后归顺耶稣，成为耶稣基督的忠实门徒，详见《圣经·使徒行传》。

29. 这里的 blind forces 应该是指宏观社会历史的趋势。作为曾经的社会主义者，斯蒂文森此时认识到与其高喊变革变革，不如让历史的进程顺其自然。他虽然也认为这个巨大的力量（great forces）是盲目的，但是比起人来还是更敏锐的（perspicacious），因为人的眼力（判断力）实在是视野太小（little），像从门缝里看那么点视野（peering），看得也非常局限（partial），也就是说，这三个形容词大致是差不多的意思，翻译时未必要翻译成第三个，合并成一个也行（眼光狭窄局限等）。

30. 这个 failing animal heat 指的就是人生理的衰退。由于年老，人很自然会变得缺乏热情。这个 heat 就是一种隐喻思维，因为人体热度高时，一般都比较喜欢活动，都有热情，反之亦然。相关的概念隐喻有：Emotion is heat、Excited activity is heat、Criticism is heat，而在思维中有了这些概念隐喻，就能写出语言隐喻，如"George was wounded in the *heat* of the battle"。

导读

自古少壮胆气豪

这篇《倔老头与年轻人》发表在1878年3月号的《康希尔杂志》(*Cornhill Magazine*)上，署名R. L. S.，后收入斯蒂文森散文集《童女与少年》(*Virginibus Puerisque*, 1881)。本书从这本散文集中选了三篇，分别是《三重甲》、《黄金国》和本篇。根据他给友人的信件，我们大致可以判定本文写于1877年7月和8月，当时他在爱丁堡和英国海边小镇彭赞斯（Penzance）居住。斯蒂文森那时已认识了范妮，但仍没有结婚。据说，斯蒂文森获稿费9英镑9先令。本文的题目源自莎士比亚的一首诗（Crabbed Age and Youth Cannot Live Together, by Shakespeare, *The Passionate Pilgrim*, XII. 1.），这里的 crabbed age 指的就是脾气不好的老年人（age），a crabbed person 类似英文中常说的 sour person。莎氏原诗如下：

Crabbed Age and Youth Cannot Live Together

Crabbed age and youth cannot live together:
Youth is full of pleasance, age is full of care;
Youth like summer morn, age like winter weather;
Youth like summer brave, age like winter bare.
Youth is full of sport, age's breath is short;
Youth is nimble, age is lame;
Youth is hot and bold, age is weak and cold;

Youth is wild, and age is tame.

Age, I do abhor thee, youth, I do adore thee;

O my love, my love is young.

Age, I do defy thee. O, sweet shepherd, hie thee,

For methinks thou stays too long.

我们在《三重甲》和《微尘与幻影》中，看到了斯蒂文森使用对立（antithesis）这个手法，即把两个对立的概念用在一起。在本文中作者又一次使用这个手法把老年和青年对立起来。可见这种将矛盾对立起来的方法是作者在散文写作中常用的手段。

斯蒂文森觉得这个世界总是倚重老年人的意见，而他认为，人一到年老就缺乏斗志，少有勇气，趋于平庸。让老年人来指导年轻人会使有血气的年轻人丢掉勇气，变得平庸。在某种意义上，说老年没有勇气也不仅是因为生理衰退使然，更是因为人生积累的经历让老年人谨小慎微，而这种胆量的丧失，又和人地位的变化有关。当你一无所有时，你当然舍得一身剐，但你渐渐积累了人生的财富后，就开始保守了，因为你怕失去你已拥有的。你看他把有地位的人说得："平庸者常会表里不一，结果我想就肯定会酝酿出一种很独特的态度，一种对更高尚、更光辉的国家叙事采取事不关已的态度。他们把在书中读'巴拉克拉瓦战役'和在剧院看'里昂邮件'的表演一视同仁。这些看戏的富足人士手拿一份显示身份的《泰晤士报》，根据事业上成就的不同，或从容地坐在楼下前排或悠闲地坐于楼上包厢。"这些人关心的是盘点自己已经获得的物质成就，才不会让他们的子女做"飞向太阳的伊卡洛斯"，因为他更想让孩子翻开账簿数钱。

斯蒂文森认为，获得真理不可能一步到位，最终的真知灼见都是一步一步在探索中积累起来的。他说："所有我过去的看法都是我一路走来的阶段性看法，正是这些看法把我引导至我目前所持的看法，而我目前的看法也只是抵达另外一种看法路上的一个阶段。"他认为人不可能一下子就寻得真谛，每个人都是在"试错"过程中不停地否定自己前一阶段的认知，一步一步抵达目的地的。斯蒂文森现身说法："我回首那段热衷社会主义的时光，多少有些后悔"，但也"不觉得我摆脱了社会主义的童话有什么值得骄傲的"。当时对一种主义的热衷是那个阶段的认识，假如没有那些热情，没有现在看来并非完美的观点，也不会有今天的更为完美的观点。 不过他认为，一个人观点的演变是"正常周期和常见轨迹"。他屈服于这个改变，恰如他屈服于痛风和白发一样。

他说的演变就是成长。他把人生比作一条奔腾湍急的河流，人在里面无法自在悠闲，因为这个河流太湍急："我们不妨把飞逝的人生路比作湍急的巨流河，人们在河中载沉载浮，时而撞向巨石，时而抓住一线水花求瞬息依托；但最后还是被甩了出去，淹没在黑暗无底的海洋中"。这条人生的河是瞬息万变的："但是在这风驰电掣的人生路上，我们一转眼已从儿童变为成人，刚刚还在恋爱此刻已步入婚姻或已各奔前程，一转眼已离开一个年龄段而步入另一段人生，刚刚还年富力强，一转眼就年老力衰走向坟墓"。"在这样一个凌乱飞逝的人生中，试图寻求稳定清晰的观点是注定要失败的。"一个人若以不变应万变是不行的，人必须不停参照自己的境遇，选择应对策略。斯蒂文森用航海来说明这个道理："（这）就像一位船长要从伦敦的码头启程去印度；启航时拿的是泰晤士河的地图，而整个航程硬是全用这张导航图，其余什么都不用。"我们在一生中不能老用旧地图来指引新航程。

所以他提倡不断学习不断进步的人生，而不是因循守旧的人生。他鼓励年轻人趁风华正茂，遍尝人生："要想攀登勃朗峰或要想看一看伦敦东区小偷藏身的地方，若想穿潜水衣下海，坐热气球上天，那么就趁年轻勇敢去做"，因为你现在不去尝试，那么"有朝一日，我们做什么事都会如履薄冰，走路也会因关节病一瘸一拐"。

年轻人在尝试人生的过程中，会有出格的观点与举止。但是斯蒂文森认为，"那些行为举止自有其道理，是年轻人特有的，表达了他们的态度和激情。不过你的那些行为可不仅与你自己相关，它们牵涉到你周围的事物，反映了你对当时现状的批判"。他正确地指出："年轻人反社会的举止说明我们的社会有毛病。"

斯蒂文森在文章快结束时，又把老年和青年这一对对立的概念呈现在我们面前："老年可能有一种观点，但是青年肯定会有另一种观点。最确定的是两种观点都对，但也可能两种皆错。"斯蒂文森在文中最后说的话令人深思，同时也会使人茫然："这个神秘的东西是没有答案的，不过你也可以说，你想让它有多少答案就有多少答案。"也正因此，他主张生活在地球上的人必须学会"客气礼貌地同意可以保留分歧"，也许这是唯一能让这个世界安宁和平的办法，因为"这个迷宫是没有中心的，就像这个著名的天体一样，任何一处都是中心"。老年和青年，都不要觉得自己握有绝对真理。所以，当今世界上任何两种对立的观点，无论是政治的、经济的、文化的、社会的，双方都不要认为自己握有绝对真理，对方绝对错误，因为真理的判定是困难的。也因此，某种程度的妥协是必要的，因为那是安宁和平的前提。

参考资料

Robert Louis Stevenson, *Virginibus Puerisque and Other Papers*, ed. R. L.

Abrahamson, Edinburgh University Press, 2018.

Claire Harman, *Myself and the Other Fellow: A Life of Robert Louis Stevenson*, Harper Perennial, 2006.

William Shakespeare, Crabbed Age and Youth (https://genius.com/William-shakespeare-crabbed-age-and-youth-annotated).

Crabbed Age and Youth (2)

As we go catching and catching at this or that corner of knowledge, now getting a foresight of generous possibilities, now chilled with a glimpse of prudence,[31] we may compare the headlong course of our years to a swift torrent in which a man is carried away; now he is dashed against a boulder, now he grapples for a moment to a trailing spray; at the end, he is hurled out and overwhelmed in a dark and bottomless ocean. We have no more than glimpses and touches; we are torn away from our theories; we are spun round and round and shown this or the other view of life, until only fools or knaves can hold to their opinions. We take a sight at a condition in life, and say we have studied it; our most elaborate view is no more than an impression. If we had breathing space, we should take the occasion to modify and adjust; but at this breakneck hurry, we are no sooner boys than we are adult, no sooner in love than married or jilted, no sooner one age than we begin to be another, and no sooner in the fulness of our manhood than we begin to decline towards the grave. It is in vain to seek for consistency or expect clear and stable views in a medium so perturbed and fleeting.[32] This is no cabinet science, in which things are tested to a scruple; we theorise with a pistol to our head; we are confronted with a new set of conditions on which we have not only to pass a judgment, but to take action, before the hour is at an end. And we cannot even regard ourselves as a constant; in this flux of things, our identity itself seems in a perpetual

倔老头与年轻人（二）

我们试图抓住些片鳞半爪的知识，时而见到机遇欲进取，时而预见险情就畏缩。如此，我们不妨把飞逝的人生路比作湍急的巨流河，人们在河中载沉载浮，时而撞向巨石，时而抓住一线水花求瞬息依托；但最后还是被甩了出去，淹没在黑暗无底的海洋中。我们得到的也仅是些零星的所见所感；结果就只好放弃我们原有的那一套套理论。我们一生如蓬转，见到五花八门有关人生的观点，直到最后只有傻瓜或不诚实的人才会死抱住自己的观点。我们看到生活中的某种状态，于是便说，自己研究过那状态；殊不知我们的观点虽缜密得无以复加却也仅是一种印象。如果有喘息的时间，我们应该借机把自己的观点修正调适一番；但是在这风驰电掣的人生路上，我们一转眼已从儿童变为成人，刚刚还在恋爱此刻已步入婚姻或已各奔前程，一转眼已离开一个年龄段而步入另一段人生，刚刚还年富力强，一转眼就年老力衰走向坟墓。在这样一个凌乱飞逝的人生中，试图寻求稳定清晰的观点是注定要失败的。若是实验科学，万事都要验证个水落石出，但人生不是实验科学；我们大谈人生理论时手枪正顶着我们的脑袋；我们面临一系列新环境，而对这些环境，只做判断是不够的，还得采取行动，免得一切都太晚了。我们甚至不能把自己当作是稳定不变的；在这个万物都瞬息万变的

variation; and not infrequently we find our own disguise the strangest in the masquerade.[33] In the course of time, we grow to love things we hated and hate things we loved. Milton is not so dull as he once was, nor perhaps Ainsworth so amusing.[34] It is decidedly harder to climb trees, and not nearly so hard to sit still. There is no use pretending; even the thrice royal game of hide and seek has somehow lost in zest.[35] All our attributes are modified or changed and it will be a poor account of us[36] if our views do not modify and change in a proportion. To hold the same views at forty as we held at twenty is to have been stupefied for a score of years, and take rank, not as a prophet,[37] but as an unteachable brat, well birched and none the wiser. It is as if a ship captain should sail to India from the Port of London; and having brought a chart of the Thames on deck at his first setting out, should obstinately use no other for the whole voyage.[38]

And mark you, it would be no less foolish to begin at Gravesend with a chart of the Red Sea.[39] *Si jeunesse savait, si vieillesse pouvait*, is a very pretty sentiment, but not necessarily right.[40] In five cases out of ten, it is not so much that the young people do not know, as that they do not choose. There is something irreverent in the speculation, but perhaps the want of power has more to do with the wise resolutions of age than we are always willing to admit.[41] It would be an instructive experiment to make an old man young again and leave him all his savoir. I scarcely think he would put his money in the Savings Bank after all; I doubt if he would be such an admirable son as we are led to expect; and as for his conduct in love, I believe firmly he would out-Herod Herod,[42] and put the whole of his new compeers to the blush. Prudence is a wooden juggernaut,[43] before whom Benjamin Franklin walks with the portly air of a high priest, and after

世界里，我们自己的身份也永远在变换；在这个人人带假面具的社会舞会上，我们常会发现自己的装扮竟是如此奇特陌生。随着时间的推移，我们会慢慢爱上曾恨之入骨的东西，也会渐渐憎恨曾爱恋至深的事物。弥尔顿现在已不像当年那么味同嚼蜡，而安斯沃思的小说也不像过去那么令你兴致盎然。年龄渐增，爬树无疑变得更为困难，静止不动就容易多了。这些因年老造成的变化是掩盖不了的；即便是捉迷藏这种曾深爱的游戏你慢慢也会失去兴趣。我们所有的属性和特征都会修正或改变；若我们的观点不相应有所改变，那么我们的一生就会一败涂地。若四十岁时仍持二十岁时的观点，那这几十年就白活了，那就说明我们所持的观点毫无先见之明，我们无异于不可教的孺子，苦头吃得不少，但没有变得聪明。这好有一比，就像一位船长要从伦敦的码头启程去印度；启航时拿的是泰晤士河的地图，而整个航程硬是全用这张导航图，其余什么都不用。

请注意，反过来也有一比，从英格兰的格雷夫森德启程时却拿一张快到站的红海导航图同样愚不可及。"要是年轻人能懂，老年人能做，那该多好！"这个法语的谚语愿望良好，却未必是事实。十个例子中有五个证明，与其说年轻人不懂，还不如说他们不选择那么做。下面的推测可能略有不敬，但老年人稳妥智慧的决定可能只是因为他们想做却力有不逮，只是我们不愿意承认罢了。让一个老年人返老还童但却保留他的智慧，这会是一个令人颇有感悟的实验。我想那老人是不会把钱全放在储蓄账户中的；我觉得他也不会成为我们预期的孝子贤孙；至于说男欢女爱之事，我坚信他会把爱

whom dances many a successful merchant in the character of Atys.[44] But it is not a deity to cultivate in youth. If a man lives to any considerable age, it cannot be denied that he laments his imprudences, but I notice he often laments his youth a deal more bitterly and with a more genuine intonation.

It is customary to say that age should be considered, because it comes last. It seems just as much to the point, that youth comes first. And the scale fairly kicks the beam,[45] if you go on to add that age, in a majority of cases, never comes at all. Disease and accident make short work of even the most prosperous persons; death costs nothing, and the expense of a headstone is an inconsiderable trifle to the happy heir. To be suddenly snuffed out in the middle of ambitious schemes, is tragical enough at best; but when a man has been grudging himself his own life in the meanwhile, and saving up everything for the festival that was never to be, it becomes that hysterically moving sort of tragedy which lies on the confines of farce.[46] The victim is dead—and he has cunningly overreached himself: a combination of calamities none the less absurd for being grim. To husband a favourite claret until the batch turns sour, is not at all an artful stroke of policy; and how much more with a whole cellar—a whole bodily existence![47] People may lay down their lives with cheerfulness in the sure expectation of a blessed immortality; but that is a different affair from giving up youth with all its admirable pleasures, in the hope of a better quality of gruel in a more than problematical, nay, more than improbable, old age. We should not compliment a hungry man, who should refuse a whole dinner and reserve all his appetite for the dessert, before he knew whether there was to be any dessert or not. If there be such a thing as imprudence in the world, we surely have it here. We sail in leaky bottoms

发挥得淋漓尽致，让他的同辈人汗颜。谨慎就像是游行花车队伍中木制的神龛偶像，在它前面带路的是威风凛凛的本杰明·富兰克林，在它后面跟随的是一批成功商人，他们都像吕底亚王国的阿特斯那样如履薄冰。但是人在青春年少时要培育的不是膜拜神明。如果一个人已经有一把岁数，无可否认，他会历数过往的鲁莽之举而追悔莫及，但是我发现更让他追悔、真令他悲叹的是蹉跎了青春岁月。

都说老年应备受尊重，因为它是人生中最后一站。但同理，青年也应受尊重，因为它是人生最先一站。如果你考虑到大多数情况下，人都活不到老年，那么就更说明年轻人举足轻重了。疾病和意外常使人的宏图大业戛然而止；死亡却是免费的，儿孙作为你财产的继承人为你竖块墓碑花费微薄，何乐不为。人在雄心勃勃事业未竟时，突然离世至多也只是悲惨之事，但一个人同时又把自己的生命都搭上，为了那个永不会到来的盛会省吃俭用，那种悲剧才让人疯狂，令人动容，却也多少有点滑稽可笑。受害者死了，他谋划过度，引来的灾难实在悲惨却也荒唐。守着一坛好酒不忍品尝，直到酒变酸，这可不是好的存酒之道；那么就像不能让一窖的酒都这么浪费一样，也不能让整个人生这么浪费掉！人们坚信会蒙福而得永生，便可以带笑放弃生命；但这完全不同于放弃青春带来的无尽快乐，以期在问题百出甚至未必到来的老年获得一杯质量尚好的羹。人要是不知道是否会有餐后甜点，就放弃整顿晚餐，把好胃口留给那悬在空中的甜点，那么这样的饿汉不值得赞扬。如果说在这个世界上确有轻率鲁莽之举，那么我们身边就有。我们人类驾驶着一条

and on great and perilous waters; and to take a cue from the dolorous old naval ballad, we have heard the mer-maidens singing, and know that we shall never see dry land any more. Old and young, we are all on our last cruise. If there is a fill of tobacco among the crew, for God's sake pass it round, and let us have a pipe before we go![48]

Indeed, by the report of our elders, this nervous preparation for old age is only trouble thrown away. We fall on guard,[49] and after all it is a friend who comes to meet us. After the sun is down and the west faded, the heavens begin to fill with shining stars. So, as we grow old, a sort of equable jog-trot of feeling is substituted for the violent ups and downs of passion and disgust; the same influence that restrains our hopes, quiets our apprehensions; if the pleasures are less intense, the troubles are milder and more tolerable; and in a word, this period for which we are asked to hoard up everything as for a time of famine, is, in its own right, the richest, easiest, and happiest of life. Nay, by managing its own work and following its own happy inspiration, youth is doing the best it can to endow the leisure of age. A full, busy youth is your only prelude to a self-contained and independent age; and the muff inevitably develops into the bore. There are not many Doctor Johnsons, to set forth upon their first romantic voyage at sixty-four.[50] If we wish to scale Mont Blanc or visit a thieves' kitchen in the East End,[51] to go down in a diving dress or up in a balloon, we must be about it[52] while we are still young. It will not do to delay[53] until we are clogged with prudence and limping with rheumatism, and people begin to ask us: "What does Gravity out of bed?"[54] Youth is the time to go flashing from one end of the world to the other both in mind and body; to try the manners of different nations; to hear the chimes at

漏水的破船，在波涛汹涌的海上行驶，这就非常轻率鲁莽了；且引用航海者忧伤歌谣里的话，我们听到了美人鱼在歌唱，知道我们再也见不到陆地。诸位，不管你是老年还是少年，我们都是在最后一趟航船上。海员中哪位有一斗好烟，千万传过来让大家都吸上一口，然后再走。

确实，据老一辈人说，为老年焦虑地做准备实属徒劳。我们警惕防范，但是来与我们相见的毕竟是一位朋友，不需要准备防范。加之，此时太阳已经下了山，西天已经暗下去，苍穹已是满天星斗。所以，随着我们渐渐老去，一种平稳缓慢的情绪取代了我们内心的不平与块垒；这就是那种会淡化我们的希望、舒缓我们忧虑的心情；如果快乐不是异常强烈，那么麻烦也会相对缓解、更可忍受；简单地说，我们总是被要求，人生的这段时期要尽量有所囤积，就像为应付饥荒而未雨绸缪，殊不知，这段人生本身却是最富有、最悠闲、最幸福的大好时光。其实，若年轻人掌控自己的作为，追随自己愉快的心灵，那他就是在竭尽全力为自己送上晚年的悠闲与安逸。一个充实忙碌的青春是自足独立晚年的唯一前奏；谨小慎微的平庸之辈晚年时不可避免会感到百无聊赖。像约翰逊博士那样在64岁时才开始首次传奇之旅的人并不多。要想攀登勃朗峰或要想看一看伦敦东区小偷藏身的地方，若想穿潜水衣下海，坐热气球上天，那么就趁年轻勇敢去做。有朝一日，我们做什么事都会如履薄冰，走路也会因关节病一瘸一拐，别人会问你"你起来干什么？"，待到那时再去做想做之事就晚了。青春时，你的思想和身体都需要从世界的一端飞奔到另一端；你需要欣赏万国风采，狂欢

midnight; to see sunrise in town and country; to be converted at a revival;[55] to circumnavigate the metaphysics, write halting verses, run a mile to see a fire, and wait all day long in the theatre to applaud *Hernani*.[56] There is some meaning in the old theory about wild oats;[57] and a man who has not had his green-sickness and got done with it for good, is as little to be depended on as an unvacciated infant. "It is extraordinary," says Lord Beaconsfield,[58] one of the brightest and best preserved of youths up to the date of his last novel *Lothair*, "it is extraordinary how hourly and how violently change the feelings of an inexperienced young man." And this mobility is a special talent entrusted to his care; a sort of indestructible virginity; a magic armour, with which he can pass unhurt through great dangers and come unbedaubed out of the miriest passages.[59] Let him voyage, speculate, see all that he can, do all that he may; his soul has as many lives as a cat;[60] he will live in all weathers, and never be a halfpenny the worse. Those who go to the devil in youth, with anything like a fair chance, were probably little worth saving from the first;[61] they must have been feeble fellows—creatures made of putty and pack-thread, without steel or fire, anger or true joyfulness, in their composition; we may sympathise with their parents, but there is not much cause to go into mourning for themselves; for to be quite honest, the weak brother is the worst of mankind.

至午夜钟鸣；在城镇乡野看旭日东升；听牧师激情讲道而心回意转，畅游抽象世界的琼楼玉宇，写它几句歪诗，跑上一里路去看大火熊熊，等上一整天去为《埃尔纳尼》鼓掌赞叹。古往今来都说年轻人放荡不羁，但这放荡不是没有道理的；一个人从没患过萎黄病就永远与这病绝缘，这就像没有接种疫苗的婴孩一样不可靠。比肯斯菲尔德勋爵本杰明·迪斯雷利首相刚出版了《洛塞尔》，记述了一个最聪颖、青春活力保留得最佳的洛塞尔，也正是小说问世时作者的写照。作者说，一个未经世事的年轻人在几小时内大改自己的心情，这可是极不寻常的。这种动态的心情是他独享的天赋；是一种不受世俗玷污的清纯；是一副神奇的盔甲，戴上它就可过险境而无损，出淤泥而不染。让这年轻人去航行，去思索，去阅尽人间冷暖，去做他之所能；他的灵魂就像猫一样有许多条命，能应对许多险境；他将在各种各样的环境中生活，却都不逊色。那些在年轻时就去拜见魔鬼的人，也有过成功的机遇，他们可能从一开始就不值得拯救；他们想必都是弱者，是由柔软材料做成的人，性格中没有钢铁，也缺少烈火，不会义愤填膺，也难有真正快乐；我们可以同情他们的父母，但是没有什么理由为他们哀悼；因为坦率地说，懦弱的兄弟是人类家庭中最糟糕的一员。

注 释

31. 这句的理解是要抓住两个对立的人生态度，就是 generous possibilities 和 prudence，而根据上下文，我们已经知道前者是年轻人的人生态度，后者就是老年人的态度。这个 generous 的意思和我们一般用的不完全一样，但也有联系。OED 中有一个解释是 "gallant, courageous, valiant"，还有个例子 "He had in himself a salient, living spring, of generous and manly action"。根据我们的上下文这个词可以解释为 outgoing, warm-hearted, courageous。而 prudence 就是谨小慎微的意思，反映了老年人在生活中如履薄冰的态度。动词 chilled 表示的意思和前面的 warm-hearted 正好也相反。至于其他词译者可以根据大意自由安排一下，不要一个词一个词地去翻译，比方说 generous possibilities 和 prudence 就不对等，说 prudence possibilities 才和前面的 generous possibilities 对等，但加 possibilities 就有搭配问题。另外还有个小问题，catching at 中的 at 表示目标，但动作没有涉及结果，对照一下 catch something 和 catch at something 的区别。
32. 这里的 medium 代表人或人的一生，是把人生当作一个媒介了。
33. 这个 the strangest 是表示和化装舞会上的其他人格格不入的意思，请注意，这句话虽然是在泛指，但可能完全是源于斯蒂文森自己的经验。他在生活中经常得不到社会的认同，这就促使他感到 the strangest。显然这里的化装舞会是隐喻，暗指社会。
34. Milton 是指约翰·弥尔顿（John Milton，1608—1674 年），英国诗人，曾在英格兰国务委员会担任公职，后来也在奥利弗·克伦威尔（Oliver Cromwell）领导下的政府担任公务员。

他在宗教和政治动荡的历史大背景下写作，以史诗《失乐园》（1667）闻名于世。Ainsworth 指威廉·哈里森·安斯沃思（William Harrison Ainsworth，1805—1882）是当时很受欢迎的英国历史小说家。

35. 这句和前后句都在强调一个主题，就是变化。人老了，爬树难了，静静地坐着不难。这种老起来的变化是挡也挡不住的，当然装也装不了（There is no use pretending），然后他就给了一个例子，你看就连当年最喜欢玩的捉迷藏的游戏，到最后老年人还是失去了兴趣。

36. to give a good account of 可以看作是个成语，基本意思就是 to be successful with; do one's duty by（OED）。所以我们这里的 to be a poor account of us 就可以解释成不成功的意思。

37. take rank 可以和前面的 to hold the view 看作是并列的，所以这里 take rank, not as a prophet 就可以解释成 to hold the view not as a prophet。

38. 这一长句背后的认知隐喻就是 life is a journey，把人生当作了一个旅途，从伦敦出发到目的地印度，用这个隐喻暗指从孩童到老年，用伦敦的航海图就像是在说用年轻人的经验，一路都用伦敦航海图就是用隐喻的方法指一生都以年轻人的经验作为指导。显然本文的目的和这句话刚刚相反。接下来的那句才是作者的真正意图。

39. Gravesend 是离伦敦不远的一个小镇，是航程的起点；但这回的目的地是红海，所以这个英国的小镇就是人生的起点，红海就是终点，拿红海的航海图就像是拿老年人的经验来指导一生，包括指导青少年。作者认为，这和前面那个例子虽然相反，但一样荒唐。"And mark you"这个用法目前已经显得很古旧了，基本意思就是please notice this point。mark这个词表示pay attention to的意思目前已基本消失。

40. "Si jeunesse savait, si vieillesse pouvait"是法语中的一个谚语，基本意思就是，要是年轻人能有知识懂世事，而老年人也能做事儿，那该多好。这恰恰击中了年轻人和老年人的弱点，因为年轻人缺的就是经验，老年人少的正是活力。句子看上去似乎没有主句，但是这是法语的习惯表达法。

41. 这句中的wise resolutions of age显然是在说老年人所做的决定。我们年轻人突发奇想，会突然决定去旅游，而且没有详细的具体方案；但老年人却会详细制定旅游计划，所以说他们的旅游决定是智慧的（wise resolutions）。再比如老年人不会在路面滑的地方散步，年轻人就未必，所以说老年人又显得智慧（wise）。斯蒂文森在说，别以为这是智慧，其实这种智慧的决定背后隐藏的实际原因是want of power。这个want不是需要的意思，而是缺乏的意思（lack of power），说明老年人其实是缺乏能力，比如他们已经没有年轻人那种游历世界的体力了，在滑的路面上摔一跤，也可能因骨折而一病不起，不像年轻人，跌一跤爬起来继续走，老年人可没有这种能力。但是我们传统上是不肯承认这是老年人缺乏能力的结果。

42. 这是一个成语，源自莎士比亚的《哈姆雷特》("I would have such a fellow whipp'd for o'erdoing Termagant; it out-Herods Herod."），但典自《圣经》。根据《圣经·新约》，希律王（Herod）下令杀死所有男婴以便能杀害耶稣。所以Herod这个词表示做事都做到了极致，而out-Herod Herod则表示做得更甚。鉴于我们是在说老年人，而且是在谈爱这个语境中，所以说老年人out-Herod Herod就是说他们也会把爱发挥得淋漓尽致。

43. 这个juggernaut原指印度教在节日游行时的神龛木偶像,一般情况下在偶像前有一个有地位的宗教人物带路,其后面跟随的是一批信众。在我们这个语境中,斯蒂文森把老年人奉为神明遇事谨慎的态度比喻成了这个神龛偶像,把主张应该谨慎的富兰克林比喻成在神龛前带队的地位高上的宗教人物,而把一大批信奉这种人生哲学的人(在这里主要是成功的商人)比作跟在神龛后面的信众。但是juggernaut这个词解释成泛指(不强调印度教)似乎更合适,也就是任何游行花车队伍中抬着宗教或民俗偶像的场景。

44. 这个Atys是指吕底亚王国的阿特斯。吕底亚是小亚细亚中西部一古国。阿特斯的父亲是吕底亚王国的最后一代国王克洛伊索斯。有一天他做了个梦,梦见他儿子阿特斯被一长枪所毙,于是他就百般谨慎,尽力避免让儿子处于危险之中,但还是在一次意外事件中被保护他儿子的保镖意外用长枪击毙。这里强调了这些成功商人为保护住自己的所得所采取的谨慎态度。

45. 前一句是youth comes first,然后就是这句scale fairly kicks the beam,显然是和年轻人的重要性有关。kick the beam是成语,一般的解释是to be so lightly loaded that it flies up and strikes the beam,但也解释成to be greatly outweighed,还是强调分量重的意思,特别是斯蒂文森用了一个fairly,更强调了greatly的意思,因为在苏格兰英语中fairly常表示强调。

46. 这句基本是在说我们观看时会大笑,觉得滑稽荒唐,但静下心来一想又实在觉得可悲。on the confines也是一个习惯表达法(borders的意思),比如"It is no more a happiness, than it is

an unhappiness; upon the confine of both, but neither"（OED），在我们这句中就是表示近乎 farce 的意思。

47. 这一长句中有几个地方需要说明。首先 cunningly overreached himself 就是在说那些老年人谋划得过分，他们居然计划到几十年后的事儿（overreached），而 cunningly 就是计划、计算（老谋深算）。另外这里的 none the less 就是 no less 的意思。这句还是和上句有联系，这个 grim 是让人们感到悲惨的事，而 absurd 是让人感到笑的事，而 absurd 一点都不比 grim 分量轻（none the less）。下面一句作者用一坛酒，进而讲到一窖酒，转而谈到人的一生（a whole bodily existence）。译文已经解释得很清楚了。

48. 这里的 before we go，若解释成 go on traveling，似乎不很合适。所以还是把这个 go 看作是隐喻，当死亡解释更合适。鉴于汉语"走"也有表达死亡的意思，翻译时采用了直译。

49. 这里的 fall on guard 是击剑术语。这个 fall on guard = nervously prepare for old age, feeling threatened by it，但是前面一句已经说过这个 trouble (or efforts) to nervously prepare for old age 是没有必要的（trouble thrown away），也就是说，必须把 fall on guard 和前面一句联系起来，才能厘清和后半句的关系（后半句说我们迎来的是个朋友，所以 fall on guard 是没有必要的）。

50. 约翰逊的苏格兰高地之旅见"Aes Triplex"篇注释 60。

51. 这是指历史上的伦敦东区，这个地区以其严重的贫困以及相关的社会问题而臭名昭著。这导致了东区激烈政治活动的出现。而这个 thieves' kitchen 就是指伦敦东区的贫民窟，犯罪活动频发的地方。

52. to be about it 是一个成语，表示的意思很广泛，但基本意思就是在有一定困难情况下坚持去做某件事（exhibiting extreme courage and bravery in times of stress or overwhelming odds），比如"Even though there have been threats of violence against our peace rally, be about it when we march"。在我们这里，就是让我们必须在仍然年轻的时候去从事那些看似较困难的活动。

53. 这个 will not do to delay 也应该看作是个成语，表示做某事不合适（used for saying that a particular situation or way of behaving is not sensible or suitable），比如"It does not do to dwell on dreams and forget to live."。我们这句就是说推迟不好。

54. "What does Gravity out of bed?"这句源自莎士比亚戏剧："What doth Gravity out of his bed at midnight?"（*1 Henry IV*, II. 5. 270），大意就是"格拉维特这老头半夜不睡觉干什么？"本句中是说等到你老了，别人总会觉得你不躺在床上起来干什么？说明那时你已经离不开床了。

55. a revival 是一种特殊的宗教布道仪式，由牧师做激情讲道，信众会站起来和布道者一起赞颂耶稣基督（a reawakening of religious fervor, especially by means of a series of evangelistic meetings）。斯蒂文森是说年轻时，人也应有这种经历，听了牧师的布道而皈依宗教（converted）。他是在举例，人应该有各种各样的经历，包括这种宗教的思想转变。另外，前半句中的 to hear the chimes at midnight 表示和友人狂欢到午夜的意思，而且也有典故，见莎士比亚戏剧："We have heard the chimes at midnight"（*2 Henry IV*, III. 2. 197）。

56. *Hernani* 指法国浪漫作家维克多·雨果的一部戏剧《埃尔纳尼》。题目源自西班牙小镇埃尔纳尼。这是一出悲剧，后成为新浪漫主义的代表作品。

57. (sow one's) wild oats 是指那些在没有改邪归正前行为反叛，性生活混乱的青年人（to engage in rebelliousness or promiscuity, typically in one's youth before settling down），如"he sowed his wild oats before settling down"。

58. Lord Beaconsfield 指的是英国保守党领袖兼首相本杰明·迪斯雷利（Benjamin Disraeli，1804—1881），他同时也是小说家，*Lothair* 就是他写的一本自传式小说。

59. indestructible virginity 应该是指年轻人未经世俗污染的状态，作者认为这种状态是不会被击败的，直接翻译成"不会被毁坏"的话，汉语搭配不合适，可以理解为不会被世俗侵袭。至于下面的 pass unhurt through great dangers and come unbedaubed out of the miriest passages，其实是同义的并列结构，前面一个强调 unhurt，是以伤害为基础的，后一个强调 unbedaubed，是以污染为基础，但是基本意思相近。

60. 民间都说猫有九条命，说的是这个动物能应变。猫在空中坠落时灵活转换身体能应对不同的着陆可能。在我们这句中，作者是说年轻人也能适应各种不同的环境。

61. go to the devil 也是一个成语，有特殊的意思。根据 OED 的解释这个词组的意思是："to go to ruin, fail completely; to be damned"。斯蒂文森在这句中说的年轻人是他鄙视的，因为他们在年轻时就 go to the devil 了，把自己给搞砸了，把生活弄得一塌糊涂，而这些人并非注定要结局惨淡，因为他们也有成功的机遇（a fair chance）。这个 fair chance 就是 a reasonable probability of success 的意思，是18世纪时较流行的用法，源自赌博用语，是说参与赌博的人机会均等。

诸位，不管你是老年还是少年，我们都是在最后一趟航船上。

——《倔老头与年轻人》

Crabbed Age and Youth (3)

When the old man waggles his head and says, "Ah, so I thought when I was your age," he has proved the youth's case. Doubtless, whether from growth of experience or decline of animal heat,[62] he thinks so no longer; but he thought so while he was young; and all men have thought so while they were young, since there was dew in the morning or hawthorn in May;[63] and here is another young man adding his vote to those of previous generations and rivetting another link to the chain of testimony. It is as natural and as right for a young man to be imprudent and exaggerated, to live in swoops and circles,[64] and beat about his cage like any other wild thing newly captured, as it is for old men to turn gray, or mothers to love their offspring, or heroes to die for something worthier than their lives.

By way of an apologue[65] for the aged, when they feel more than usually tempted to offer their advice, let me recommend the following little tale. A child who had been remarkably fond of toys (and in particular of lead soldiers) found himself growing to the level of acknowledged boyhood without any abatement of this childish taste.[66] He was thirteen; already he had been taunted for dallying overlong about the playbox; he had to blush if he was found among his lead soldiers; the shades of the prison-house were closing about him with a vengeance.[67] There is nothing more difficult than to put the thoughts of children into the language of their elders; but this is the effect of his meditations at this juncture:

倔老头与年轻人（三）

老年人摇着头说"我在你那个年龄也是这么想的"，他这样说正好为年轻人的观点提供了佐证。毫无疑问，不管是因为经验的积累，还是生理功能的衰退，他现在已经不再那么想了。但是他年轻时确实是那么想的；而且所有的人在青春年少时都那么想，远自早晨有露水，五月有山楂时起就是那么想的。这里我拿下面这个年轻人的故事作例证，为一代代年轻人的行为再添一例。年轻人有点轻率放荡，有点言过其实，活得横冲直撞，就像刚被抓住的野兽在笼子里乱蹦乱跳，这是很自然很不错的，就像人会满头银发，母亲会爱子心切，英雄为珍视人生价值会放弃生命一样都很自然。

老年人有个习惯，总喜欢向年轻人进言。那么让我来讲下面这个小故事，权当是一则说给老年人的寓言。一个特别爱玩具的小孩（特喜欢铅做的士兵）自觉已成长为公认的少年，却对孩童时的爱好丝毫不减。他已经十三岁了，说他玩物丧志的指责不绝于耳。要是在玩铅做的士兵时被人发现，他会感到脸红；牢房般的阴影在他四周恶狠狠地逼向他。把孩子的思想用老年人的话说出来是最难不过了，但是还得把这孩子思考的结晶概括如下："显然此刻我得放弃我的玩物，才能免遭无端嘲笑。同时，我也坚信玩物是人生中不

"Plainly," he said, "I must give up my playthings, in the meanwhile, since I am not in a position to secure myself against idle jeers. At the same time, I am sure that playthings are the very pick of life; all people give them up out of the same pusillanimous respect for those who are a little older; and if they do not return to them as soon as they can, it is only because they grow stupid and forget. I shall be wiser; I shall conform for a little to the ways of their foolish world; but so soon as I have made enough money, I shall retire and shut myself up among my playthings until the day I die." Nay, as he was passing in the train along the Esterel mountains between Cannes and Frèjus,[68] he remarked a pretty house in an orange garden at the angle of a bay, and decided that this should be his Happy Valley.[69] Astrea Redux; childhood was to come again![70] The idea has an air of simple nobility to me, not unworthy of Cincinnatus.[71] And yet, as the reader has probably anticipated, it is never likely to be carried into effect. There was a worm i' the bud,[72] a fatal error in the premises. Childhood must pass away, and then youth, as surely as age approaches. The true wisdom is to be always seasonable, and to change with a good grace in changing circumstances. To love playthings well as a child, to lead an adventurous and honourable youth, and to settle when the time arrives, into a green and smiling age,[73] is to be a good artist in life and deserve well of yourself and your neighbour.

You need repent none of your youthful vagaries. They may have been over the score on one side, just as those of age are probably over the score on the other. But they had a point; they not only befitted your age and expressed its attitude and passions, but they had a relation to what was outside of you, and implied criticisms on the existing state of things, which you need not allow to have been undeserved, because you now see that

可取代的；所有的人都出于对年岁略大者的敬畏与尊重而放弃玩物；如果他们不尽快重新捡起那些玩物，那只是因为他们变傻了，忘掉了。我会更聪明些；我会对大人的愚蠢规范暂做妥协，但是等我赚够了钱，我就退休不干，躲在屋里与玩物为伴，直到死去。"这孩子坐着火车行驶在戛纳和弗雷瑞斯间的埃斯特尔山脉下，突然在海湾的一角处看到一幢漂亮的房子，还有一个橘黄色的花园，不行，他转念一想，觉得这地方才是他实现梦想的快乐谷。像希腊神话中正义纯真女神阿斯翠亚重现一样，童年又将再来。我觉得，那孩子的想法里透着一股朴实高尚的气质，让人想起功成身退的古罗马将军辛辛纳图斯。但是，读者也许已经猜到，他的想法不可能付诸实施。恰如花蕾中有一个虫子必将毁掉玫瑰，这个想法中也有个致命的错误。童年那一页必须翻过去，紧接着是青年，而且老年必至。真正的智慧应该是与时俱进的，任由时过境迁，总能处之泰然。童年时玩得尽兴，青年时活得真诚、敢于闯荡，上了岁数却能安然服老，但也朝气不减、笑对人生，这才是生活的艺术，这才对得起你自己，也不负你周围的人。

  对于年轻时的奇异行为，你无需有忏悔之意。也许从一方面看，你确实玩过了；另一方面，老者又何尝没有过分之处？但那些行为举止自有其道理，是年轻人特有的，表达了他们的态度和激情。不过你的那些行为可不仅与你自己相关，它们牵涉到你周围的事物，反映了你对当时现状的批判。你现在知道了那些批判相当片面，但你却不必因此而否定当时的批判。所有的错误，不仅是错误

they were partial. All error, not merely verbal, is a strong way of stating that the current truth is incomplete. The follies of youth have a basis in sound reason, just as much as the embarrassing questions put by babes and sucklings. Their most antisocial acts indicate the defects of our society. When the torrent sweeps the man against a boulder, you must expect him to scream, and you need not be surprised if the scream is sometimes a theory. Shelley, chafing at the Church of England, discovered the cure of all evils in universal atheism. Generous lads irritated at the injustices of society, see nothing for it but the abolishment of everything and Kingdom Come of anarchy. Shelley was a young fool; so are these cocksparrow revolutionaries. But it is better to be a fool than to be dead. It is better to emit a scream in the shape of a theory than to be entirely insensible to the jars and incongruities of life and take everything as it comes in a forlorn stupidity. Some people swallow the universe like a pill; they travel on through the world, like smiling images pushed from behind. For God's sake give me the young man who has brains enough to make a fool of himself! As for the others, the irony of facts shall take it out of their hands, and make fools of them in downright earnest, ere the farce be over.[74] There shall be such a mopping and a mowing[75] at the last day, and such blushing and confusion of countenance for all those who have been wise in their own esteem, and have not learnt the rough lessons that youth hands on to age. If we are indeed here to perfect and complete[76] our own natures, and grow larger, stronger, and more sympathetic against some nobler career in the future,[77] we had all best bestir ourselves to the utmost while we have the time. To equip a dull, respectable person with wings would be but to make a parody of an angel.[78]

的批评，都强烈地说明当时的真理并不全面。年轻时的愚行自有一定道理，就像婴孩提出让人难堪的问题一样也自有其道理。年轻人反社会的举止说明我们的社会有毛病。当巨流把人冲向岩石时，那人自然会叫出声来，这种尖叫有时会是一种理论，你不必感到惊讶。雪莱不满于英格兰教会的约束，在泛无神论中发现了一切恶的解药。勇敢的年轻小伙子见社会的不公而愤愤不平，他看到的解决之道就是砸烂一切，不惜未来世界天下大乱。雪莱当时是个傻气十足的年轻人；这些吵吵闹闹的革命者也同样够傻。但是做一个傻人总比做一个死人要好。与其漠然面对生活的不和谐，照单全收枯燥人生的一幕幕，还不如大声疾呼出一个理论。有些人把世界当药丸吞下；他们在这个世界上穿行，却像从后面被人推着前行的木偶人像一样表面有张笑脸，实际完全木然。看在上帝的面上，给我一个有足够大脑能出些洋相的年轻人！至于其他人，现实的讽刺就是，他们安分守己，但世事总使他们无法招架，让他们出尽洋相，直到这场闹剧结束。对于所有那些自视高尚，却没有从青春年少那里学到癫狂一课的人，都会在最后时刻显出一副哭脸，露出尴尬和茫然的面容。如果我们来到这个世界确实是为了完善我们的天性，确实是为了要在未来一场更为高尚的事业中变得更强大、更有同情心，那么最好在我们仍有时间时，尽情地让身心活跃到极致。为无聊透顶的尊贵人士插上翅膀学天使无异于让他们邯郸学步。

简言之，假如年轻人的观点不很正确，那么极有可能老年人的也正确不到哪去。不灭的希望和坚定的信念总同时主宰我们的思

In short, if youth is not quite right in its opinions, there is a strong probability that age is not much more so. Undying hope is co-ruler of the human bosom with infallible credulity. A man finds he has been wrong at every preceding stage of his career, only to deduce the astonishing conclusion that he is at last entirely right. Mankind, after centuries of failure, are still upon the eve of a thoroughly constitutional millennium.[79] Since we have explored the maze so long without result, it follows, for poor human reason, that we cannot have to explore much longer; close by must be the centre, with a champagne luncheon and a piece of ornamental water. How if there were no centre at all, but just one alley after another, and the whole world a labyrinth without end or issue?

I overheard the other day a scrap of conversation, which I take the liberty to reproduce. "What I advance is true," said one. "But not the whole truth," answered the other. "Sir," returned the first (and it seemed to me there was a smack of Dr. Johnson in the speech),[80] "Sir, there is no such thing as the whole truth!" Indeed, there is nothing so evident in life as that there are two sides to a question. History is one long illustration. The forces of nature are engaged, day by day, in cudgelling it into our backward intelligences.[81] We never pause for a moment's consideration but we admit it as an axiom. An enthusiast sways humanity exactly by disregarding this great truth, and dinning it into our ears that this or that question has only one possible solution; and your enthusiast is a fine florid fellow, dominates things for a while and shakes the world out of a doze; but when once he is gone, an army of quiet and uninfluential people set to work to remind us of the other side and demolish the generous imposture. While Calvin is putting everybody exactly right in his Institutes, and hot-headed Knox

想。一个人可以觉得人生走过的每一步都是错的,却得出了惊人的结论,原来他的结局竟是完全正确。人类在那么多世纪的失败后,仍处在天下大治的黄金时代的前夜。我们在这迷宫中探索如此之久却毫无结果,于是人类因为本身的局限错误地认为,我们不必再探索下去了;认为我们肯定离中心近在咫尺了,不妨倒上香槟摆上美食,再点缀些流觞曲水庆祝一番。可是万一这个世界根本就没有中心,有的只是一条接一条的街巷,整个世界就是迷宫,没有边界,也没有出路,那该如何是好?

前几天,我无意中听到些片言碎语,容我在这里复述一下。一位说,"我这里推崇的是真实";另一位说,"但不是完全的真实";前面那位回答说,"先生,根本就没有完全的真实!"(我觉得,一句"先生"就让人想起詹姆斯·鲍斯韦尔书中约翰逊博士的口气。)确实人生中显而易见的就是任何问题都有两面。历史是一个漫长的叙事。日复一日我们所处的环境中有无数的事例不停地敲打我们冥顽不化的头脑,促使我们接受凡事都有两面的事实。我们从来不停下来做片刻的思考,但却接受它是至理名言。鼓动你的人恰是通过无视凡事有两面这一伟大真理,往我们的耳朵里反复灌输,让大家认为某个问题只有一个可能的解决方案,就这样把我们人类给左右了;那位鼓动者是花言巧语的能手,一时间把世事左右,把世界从昏睡中震醒;但是当他离开后,众多平时沉默、威望有限的人开始不停地提醒我们关注完全相反的一面,并将喋喋不休的欺骗者否定。当加尔文把每个人都框在他的教义中,诺克斯在讲道坛上布道

is thundering in the pulpit, Montaigne is already looking at the other side in his library in Perigord,[82] and predicting that they will find as much to quarrel about in the Bible as they had found already in the Church. Age may have one side, but assuredly Youth has the other. There is nothing more certain than that both are right, except perhaps that both are wrong. Let them agree to differ; for who knows but what agreeing to differ may not be a form of agreement rather than a form of difference?

I suppose it is written that any one who sets up for a bit of a philosopher, must contradict himself to his very face. For here have I fairly talked myself into thinking that we have the whole thing before us at last; that there is no answer to the mystery, except that there are as many as you please; that there is no centre to the maze because, like the famous sphere, its centre is everywhere;[83] and that agreeing to differ with every ceremony of politeness, is the only "one undisturbed song of pure concent"[84] to which we are ever likely to lend our musical voices.

声如雷鸣时,蒙田已经在法国南部佩里戈尔的书斋里探讨着问题的另一面,并预测,就像他们在教会中会因很多事争论不休,他们也会因《圣经》中的很多话而各执己见。老年可能有一种观点,但是青年肯定会有另一种观点。最确定的是两种观点都对,但也可能两种皆错。让他们同意保留分歧吧,因为谁能说这不是一种同意而是一种分歧呢?

常言道,一说哲学话题总免不了自相矛盾。在本文中,我也努力说服自己接受下面的矛盾哲理:全部的现状最终总算呈现在我们面前;这个神秘的东西是没有答案的,不过你也可以说,你想让它有多少答案就有多少答案;这个迷宫也没有中心,因为像这个著名的天体一样,中心无处不是;客气礼貌地同意可以保留分歧是仅有的"一首不被干扰的纯粹和谐的歌",一首我们每个人都能参与演唱的歌。

注 释

62. 这里的 animal heat 就是指 body heat（OED: the heat generated within the bodies of living animals）。但是这里主要是说人到了年老时生理功能的衰退，因为生理代谢的衰退总是和人体的温度下降成正比的。

63. 这个 dew in the morning or hawthorn in May 表示 since time began 的意思，但是翻译时会面临选择，到底是直译成"自从早晨有露水，五月有山楂"，还是意译成"自古以来""自开天辟地以来"等。其实两个各有利弊。如果直译，读者得费些脑筋，因为有人会觉得突然蹦出了露水和山楂不好理解。但是如果翻译成"自古以来"，理解是好理解了，但斯蒂文森的语言特色就完全没有了。最后决定保留原文的语言特色，尽管这个语言点也未必有什么大价值。还是让读者有个锻炼脑筋的机会吧！

64. 可以将 swoops and circles 当成一个较为固定的词组看待，意思就是两个动词动作的综合，比如说"The mind makes curious swoops and circles. It touches the point of pain or interest, then sweeps away again in a cycle"，或"This large transitional chandelier loops, swoops and circles overhead"。这里翻译成"横冲直撞"，没有去追求两个动作的精准吻合，因为这里只求大意即可。

65. 这里的 an apologue 实际是一个小故事（OED: an allegorical story intended to convey a useful lesson; a moral fable），一般指有一定哲理的小故事，这里指下面有关那个小男孩的故事。

66. 这个故事中的小男孩，其实就是斯蒂文森自己。他在这里将自己儿童的经历奉献给大家。由于他自己没有说明这是自己的经历，读者更容易觉得这个故事带有普遍意义。

67. shades of the prison-house 见华兹华斯的诗："Shades of the prison-house begin to close / Upon the growing boy"（William Wordsworth, *Ode: Intimations of Immortality*）。这句的 shades of the prison-house 指社会中传统势力对他的约束。

68. 这个 Esterel（埃斯特尔）是指位于法国东南部地中海沿海的山脉，而后面的 Cannes（戛纳）和 Frèjus（弗雷瑞斯）都是这一带沿海的城市。上面讲过，这个男孩就是斯蒂文森自己，所以这里男孩乘坐从戛纳到弗雷瑞斯之间火车的感受也就是斯蒂文森的感受。

69. his Happy Valley 似乎没有什么特指的背景，但是在这里代表了斯蒂文森当时的十分幼稚的理想境地，他希望这个"快乐谷"就是他未来要回归的地方。

70. Astrea Redux 是拉丁语（the restoration of Astrea）。Astrea（阿斯翠亚）是希腊神话中的女神，象征纯真、无邪、正义。后半句刚好解释了这个拉丁语词组的意思，即童真无邪的儿童时代的回归。翻译的时候最好把希腊神话的背景知识添加到译文中："像希腊神话中正义纯真女神阿斯翠亚重现一样，童年又将再来。"

71. Cincinnatus（辛辛纳图斯，拉丁语：Lucius Quinctius Cincinnatus, 519—430 BC），古罗马共和国时期的英雄，其事迹在古罗马广为传颂。公元前 458 年时任执政官的米努基乌斯所统率的罗马军队遭到意大利埃奎人的包围，退隐务农的辛辛纳图斯临危受命担任罗马独裁官，以保卫罗马。退敌 16 天后，他辞职返回农庄。斯蒂文森说这男孩日后要回归 Happy Valley 的天真想法，颇有一点辛辛纳图斯功成身退的高尚情操。

72. 这个 a worm i' the bud 表示一个隐藏的虫子毁坏了玫瑰，喻指年轻的女人。这里取其一个错误毁坏整体的含义。这个表达法典自莎士比亚戏剧（Shakespeare, *Twelfth Night*, II. 4）: "She never told her love, But let concealment, *like a worm i' the bud*, Feed on her damask cheek. She pined in thought, And with a green and yellow melancholy"。

73. 这个 green 的意思似乎现代人是可以根据颜色正确联想出来的，就是青春焕发之类的意思。OED 适合这个语境的定义是：of a person: young, youthful; not advanced in years。比如 "Your greener age and robust constitution promise longer life"，或 "Tho' his body was wither'd his heart was aye green"。

74. 这句是说那些因循守旧之辈的。斯蒂文森认为，这些人才算是真正地出洋相呢（make fools of them in downright earnest）。这个 in downright earnest 表示 in an extremely serious manner 的意思。out of their hands 就是 out of control 的意思。至于说 the farce be over，是一种隐喻的说法，暗指人离开这个世界。

75. a mopping and a mowing 是表示面部的表情（OED: to make a grimace, to make faces. Chiefly in to mop and mow）。但问题是这个面部的表情是什么表情，暗指什么？我们无法从这个成语中引申出来，还得看上下文。根据下文（blushing and confusion），这里的 mopping and a mowing 也是一种嘲弄的感觉（mocking），所以也可能是这些人的自嘲表情。另外这个词组典自莎士比亚的戏剧（"Each one, tripping on his toe | Will be here with mop and mow" ——Shakespeare, *The Tempest*, IV. 1. 46–7）。

76. perfect and complete 这两个词本身就有近义，且有相互补充的作用，应该看作是一种修辞手段。但这个词组也有《圣经》语言的影子，如："And let steadfastness have its full effect, that you may be *perfect and complete*, lacking in nothing."（James 1: 4, English Standard Version）但斯蒂文森在世时的《圣经》语言略有不同。（如 King James Version: "But let patience have her perfect work, that ye may be *perfect and entire*, wanting nothing."）但不管怎么说，这两个词连在一起容易唤起《圣经》的联想，应该是站得住脚的。鉴于是同义词，翻译的时候就未必要用两个词去反映这个有文化背景的典故了。

77. 要注意句子里 against 的意思（against some nobler career in the future）。这个介词并不是我们一般说的"反对"的意思，而是引出一个场景或目标，表示 in preparation for 的意思。

78. make a parody of 是个成语（OED: a poor or feeble imitation of something），有明显的贬义，如"May is a pious fraud of the almanac, / A ghastly parody of real Spring"。如你说"A is a parody of B"，那么你是在批评 A，认为 A 不如 B（it is a very poor example or bad imitation of that thing）。在本句中，斯蒂文森在说，如果你给那些无聊的人安上翅膀，但那些人仍然成不了天使。一般认为天使是带翅膀的。

79. 这句中的 millennium 不能按照我们现在一般理解的那样翻译成"千禧年"。在这个语境中主要是指一个乌托邦似的理想境地（OED: a period of peace, happiness, prosperity, and ideal government, esp. a future utopia, typically ushered in by violent events accompanying the end of the existing world order）。至于这个 constitutional，一般表示"机体的"（of, belonging to, or inherent in, a person's constitution of body or mind），但这里似

乎表示法律的有序治理，特别是这个例子中 constitutional 有一个修饰它的形容词 thoroughly，这就给我们理解提供了一点帮助。这个 constitutional 可以是彻底的（thoroughly），但也可能是不彻底的，也就是说，这个词所代表的状态是可以处于不同程度的。constitutional 毕竟来自 constitution，而后者的主要特征就是通过规则法律有序治理。所以在本句中，这两个词暗指一种治理完善的理想时代，而人类仍处于这种理想国之前夜（on the eve of the golden age in which all things are ordered according to the constitution）。下面的句子告诉我们，人类的探索也许永远都没有尽头，但人们太急了，仿佛认为那理想的境地马上就会到来。不过斯蒂文森发问：可万一这个世界根本就没有中心，有的只是一条接一条的街巷，整个世界就是迷宫，没有边界，也没有出路，那该如何是好？这些话否定了乌托邦的存在，这种观点和本书第一篇的"黄金国"完全一致。

80. 这个 a smack of Dr. Johnson 是指约翰逊讲话的口气。詹姆斯·鲍斯韦尔（James Boswell）写过一本 *Life of Samuel Johnson*，书中记述约翰逊强势回应别人时，总是以 Sir 开头，所以这里的 a smack of Dr. Johnson 就是指这个，因为前面那句中说话的人也是以 Sir 开头。

81. 这句中的 the forces of nature 不能翻译成"自然界的各种力量"。这句必须要从上下文来理解。前面一句说凡事都有两面，世间并不存在全部的真理（the whole truth）。接下来就是我们这句。forces of nature 应该指我们所处的环境（我们的周围）有许许多多的事例，这些事例每天不停地将凡事都有两面这个事实（it）敲打入我们的保守、愚笨、不接受事实的大脑（backward intelligences）。forces 在很多时候都不能翻译成"力量"，这里是指具体的一个一个可以证实凡事都有两面的例子。

82. 约翰·加尔文（John Calvin, 1509—1564）是法国新教改革时期的神学家、牧师和改革家，创建加尔文主义基督教神学体系的主要人物。他的那本 *Institutes of the Christian Religion*（1536）奠定了基督教新教神学的基础。约翰·诺克斯（John Knox, 1514—1572）是苏格兰牧师、神学家和作家，该国宗教改革的领导人，苏格兰长老会的创始人，确立了苏格兰宗教改革的原则。米歇尔·德·蒙田（Michel de Montaigne, 1533—1592）是法国文艺复兴时期最重要的哲学家之一，他在佩里戈德庄园（Perigord）写了《蒙田随笔集》，该书内容包罗万象，融书本知识和生活经验于一体，是 16 世纪各种知识的总汇，有"生活的哲学"之称。这里斯蒂文森说，当前面两个人在说宗教问题的一个方面时，蒙田已在关注问题的另外一面了。

83. 《圣经》中上帝存在于所有的地方："I am a God who is everywhere and not in one place only."（Jeremiah 23: 23）这个 famous sphere 可以指那个无边无际的天体，所以也可以指上帝。这个主题（God is an infinite sphere, the centre of which is everywhere）反复出现在多种文学作品中，所以我们这句应该也有《圣经》的文化背景。

84. one undisturbed song of pure concent，典自弥尔顿的"At a Solemn Music"，这个歌指的是天堂里天使和谐的声音。concent 一词就是 harmony 的意思。

The Character of Dogs (1)

The civilisation, the manners, and the morals of dog-kind are to a great extent subordinated[1] to those of his ancestral master, man. This animal, in many ways so superior, has accepted a position of inferiority, shares the domestic life, and humours[2] the caprices of the tyrant. But the potentate, like the British in India, pays small regard to the character of his willing client,[3] judges him with listless glances, and condemns him in a byword.[4] Listless have been the looks of his admirers, who have exhausted idle terms[5] of praise, and buried the poor soul below exaggerations. And yet more idle and, if possible, more unintelligent has been the attitude of his express detractors; those who are very fond of dogs "but in their proper place"; who say "poo' fellow, poo' fellow,"[6] and are themselves far poorer; who whet the knife of the vivisectionist or heat his oven;[7] who are not ashamed to admire "the creature's instinct"; and flying far beyond folly, have dared to resuscitate the theory of animal machines.[8] The "dog's instinct" and the "automaton-dog," in this age of psychology and science, sound like strange anachronisms. An automaton he certainly is; a machine working independently of his control, the heart like the mill-wheel, keeping all in motion, and the consciousness, like a person shut in the mill garret, enjoying the view out of the window and shaken by the thunder of the stones;[9] an automaton in one corner of which a living spirit is confined: an automaton like man. Instinct again he certainly possesses. Inherited

狗性（一）

狗类的文明、举止、道德，很大程度上屈从于人的那套规矩，人类自古都是狗的主子。这个动物在很多方面优于主子，却甘当劣等，放弃野外与人共居，主子嬉笑怒骂，它却俯首帖耳。但是这个位高权重的主人，恰如在印度的英国人对待当地人一样，对百依百顺的狗之习性却不屑一顾，看它时态度爱理不理，责骂时也漫不经心。那些羡慕狗的人也总是一副爱理不理的样子，用尽一切赞扬狗的空洞言词，用誉美夸张的话将其埋葬。至于那些直言贬低狗的人，他们的态度更无价值，可能也更无知愚钝。那些人喜欢狗却与狗保持距离，认为"狗应待在狗该待的地方"；他们整天说"可怜的狗狗，可怜的狗狗"，但自己其实更可怜；他们为活体解剖动物而磨刀霍霍或为满足食欲而点燃烤炉；他们不羞于赞扬"动物的直觉"，甚至愚不可及，竟然重弹动物是机器的老调。在这个心理学和科学昌明的时代，"狗的直觉"和"狗是机器"这种观点听起来与时代背道而驰。没错，狗确实是一台机器；是一台不受自己控制而运行的机器，它的心脏就像磨轮，牵引一切不停运转，它的思维就像关在磨坊楼中的人，欣赏着窗外的风景，被磨轮转动发出的巨响吓得发抖；但在狗这台机器的一个角落却有一个鲜活的精神，这

aptitudes are his, inherited frailties. Some things he at once views and understands, as though he were awakened from a sleep, as though he came "trailing clouds of glory."[10] But with him, as with man, the field of instinct is limited; its utterances are obscure and occasional;[11] and about the far larger part of life both the dog and his master must conduct their steps by deduction and observation.

  The leading distinction between dog and man, after and perhaps before[12] the different duration of their lives, is that the one can speak and that the other cannot. The absence of the power of speech confines the dog in the development of his intellect. It hinders him from many speculations, for words are the beginning of metaphysic. At the same blow[13] it saves him from many superstitions, and his silence has won for him a higher name for virtue than his conduct justifies. The faults of the dog are many. He is vainer than man, singularly greedy of notice, singularly intolerant of ridicule, suspicious like the deaf, jealous to the degree of frenzy, and radically devoid of truth. The day of an intelligent small dog is passed in the manufacture and the laborious communication of falsehood; he lies with his tail, he lies with his eye, he lies with his protesting paw; and when he rattles his dish or scratches at the door his purpose is other than appears. But he has some apology to offer for the vice. Many of the signs which form his dialect have come to bear an arbitrary meaning, clearly understood both by his master and himself; yet when a new want arises he must either invent a new vehicle of meaning or wrest an old one to a different purpose; and this necessity frequently recurring must tend to lessen his idea of the sanctity of symbols. Meanwhile the dog is clear in his own conscience, and draws, with a human nicety, the distinction between

是一台和人一样的机器。没错,狗也确有动物直觉。它有遗传而来的能力,或言遗传而来的弱点。有些东西它一看即懂,就像它在睡眠中惊醒一般是本能使然,就像华兹华斯诗中说"随身而来的灿烂云霞"来自本能。但是在狗身上,也和人一样,本能起作用的领域是有限的;狗凭直觉告诉我们的事意思含糊不清,而且也为数不多;在生活的更广泛的领域里,狗和它的主人都得依靠推论和观察举步前行。

狗和人的寿限不同也许是他们之间的主要区别,但一个能说话一个不能,这个区别可能也重要得不相上下。语言能力的缺如限制了狗智力的发展。这使得它不能进行很多推断思考,因为词语是形而上思考的第一步。但同时这也使得它免遭迷信思想的干扰,而它的沉默为它赢得了美名,尽管它的行为还够不上那名声。狗的缺点很多。它要比人更虚荣自负,拼命寻求关注,绝对受不了嘲弄,如聋人一样疑心重重,妒忌起来无以复加,根本没有一丝真实。一只智慧的小狗一天中不停制造虚假,努力传播谎言;它用尾巴说谎,它用眼睛说谎,它用抗议的爪子说谎;而它拨动碟盘或用爪子抓门时,目的并非显而易见。不过对此虚假谎言的恶行,狗自有它的辩护之词。许多构成狗语的符号都有固定的意思,它的主人和它都懂;但是要表达新意思时,狗就得创建意义的新载体或寓新意义于旧载体;而这一必要性反复出现,结果符号的神圣性便在它头脑中弱化了。同时狗的心里清清楚楚,能和人一样精准地把实实在在的真实和装装样子的姿态分开。狗娴熟恰当地运用符号,将一个动作

formal and essential truth.[14] Of his punning perversions, his legitimate dexterity with symbols, he is even vain; but when he has told and been detected in a lie, there is not a hair upon his body but confesses guilt.[15] To a dog of gentlemanly feeling theft and falsehood are disgraceful vices. The canine, like the human, gentleman demands in his misdemeanours Montaigne's "je ne sais quoi de genéréux."[16] He is never more than half ashamed of having barked or bitten; and for those faults into which he has been led by the desire to shine before a lady of his race, he retains, even under physical correction,[17] a share of pride. But to be caught lying, if he understands it, instantly uncurls his fleece.[18]

Just as among dull observers he preserves a name for truth, the dog has been credited with modesty.[19] It is amazing how the use of language blunts the faculties of man—that because vainglory finds no vent in words, creatures supplied with eyes have been unable to detect a fault so gross and obvious.[20] If a small spoiled dog were suddenly to be endowed with speech, he would prate interminably, and still about himself; when we had friends, we should be forced to lock him in a garret; and what with his whining jealousies and his foible for falsehood,[21] in a year's time he would have gone far to weary out our love. I was about to compare him to Sir Willoughby Patterne, but the Patternes have a manlier sense of their own merits; and the parallel, besides, is ready.[22] Hans Christian Andersen, as we behold him in his startling memoirs, thrilling from top to toe with an excruciating vanity, and scouting even along the street for shadows of offence—here was the talking dog.[23]

It is just this rage for consideration that has betrayed[24] the dog into his satellite position as the friend of man. The cat, an animal of franker

赋予双重意义，这方面狗甚至有几分自鸣得意。但是当它说谎被揭时，它身上没有一根毫毛不惭愧内疚。对于一个心怀绅士情操的狗来说，偷窃和虚假是十分丢脸的恶行。绅士一般的狗，和人类社会中的绅士一样，希望主子对自己的小错能海量放宽。它因此对自己狂吠或咬人之行径，从来没有觉得非常丢脸；狗有时在母狗面前想显摆一下，于是做了那些不当之举，对此，尽管有时硬被阻止，但还是有那么一丝骄傲。但是若觉得自己说谎被抓现行，那就马上会感到无地自容。

狗在缺乏洞察力的人那里拾得一真诚的美名，同样还获得一个谦卑的称号。让人惊异的是，语言的运用使人的感觉功能退化，结果由于狗没有语言来表达自负虚荣，有眼睛的人就一直没能发现狗身上这个错得如此离谱的恶习。要是一个惯坏了的小狗突然被授予言语功能，那它就会胡言乱语喋喋不休，而且肯定都是胡吹自己；当我们有朋友时，我们会不得不把它关到小屋子里去；因为它嫉妒起来总要叫，还有喜欢扯谎作假的毛病，不出一年时间，它就会折腾过度，失去我们的宠爱。我本想把它比作自负的威洛比·帕特纳爵士，但人家的优点中毕竟也不乏几分男子汉的气质，所以还是不想拿来比较；当然可比之人并非没有。比如汉斯·克里斯蒂安·安徒生，他在惊人的回忆录里从头到脚都散发着虚荣，甚至会因街上一些微不足道的小事而感到冒犯。论及虚荣，这位安徒生与狗倒好有一比，只是他会说话。

正是这求关注的强烈渴求，才把狗引入歧途，成了人的朋友，

appetites,[25] preserves his independence. But the dog, with one eye ever on the audience, has been wheedled into slavery, and praised and patted into the renunciation of his nature.[26] Once he ceased hunting and became man's plate-licker, the Rubicon was crossed.[27] Thenceforth he was a gentleman of leisure; and except the few whom we keep working, the whole race grew more and more self-conscious, mannered and affected. The number of things that a small dog does naturally is strangely small. Enjoying better spirits and not crushed under material cares,[28] he is far more theatrical than average man. His whole life, if he be a dog of any pretension to gallantry, is spent in a vain show, and in the hot pursuit of admiration. Take out your puppy for a walk, and you will find the little ball of fur clumsy, stupid, bewildered, but natural. Let but a few months pass, and when you repeat the process you will find nature buried in convention.[29] He will do nothing plainly; but the simplest processes of our material life will all be bent into the forms of an elaborate and mysterious etiquette. Instinct, says the fool, has awakened.[30] But it is not so. Some dogs—some, at the very least—if they be kept separate from others, remain quite natural; and these, when at length they meet with a companion of experience, and have the game explained to them, distinguish themselves by the severity of their devotion to its rules.[31] I wish I were allowed to tell a story which would radiantly illuminate the point; but men, like dogs, have an elaborate and mysterious etiquette. It is their bond of sympathy that both are the children of convention.[32]

屈居附属地位。猫这动物的所欲所求较为直爽，因而保留了独立性。但是狗，由于一只眼睛总盯着观众，经不住诱惑，而沦为奴隶，几句甜言蜜语，几下轻拍柔摸，就让它放弃了本性。狗一旦不再狩猎，就只能舔人给它的盘子，这就像恺撒跨过了卢比孔河，不再有回头路了。从那时起，它已是有闲的绅士；除掉极少数我们仍然让它们干活，整个狗类都变得越来越具自我意识，越注重举止，越矫揉造作。一只小狗自自然然做的事极其有限。它开心愉快，食宿无忧，为博欢心，表演起来要比人强多了。如果一只狗深谙殷勤博欢之道，那么它就会在虚荣的舞台上表演一生，热追热捧。只要带你的小爱犬出去一溜，就会发现这毛茸茸的小球尽显拙笨、愚蠢、迷惑，但却本真自然。只消几个月时间，当你再带它出去遛弯儿，就会发现这狗已不再自然，而变得矫揉造作起来。它已经不会简简单单地做事；我们物质生活中一件件简单之极的事，也都被歪曲成了繁复神秘的礼仪套路。愚蠢者说，狗的本能这样才算被唤醒。但实际不然。有些狗，至少是有些狗，如果和其他的狗分开，会继续保持天性；这些狗若最后遇到了一个经验丰富的同伴，并深得后者在游戏规则方面的指点，结果便会成为不折不扣循规蹈矩的典范。但愿我能讲一个故事，来栩栩如生地说明这一点；但人和狗一样，也有繁复神秘的一套礼仪规范。这恰恰是因为人和狗都有情感，所以都受制于一套规则。

注 释

1. 这个 subordinated 表达的关系是狗的行为、道德体系从属于人的行为、道德体系，就是说狗那一套得听从人那一套。比如说，你领狗出去时，狗冲着另外一只狗叫起来，但是你马上阻止它，对狗说："别叫，那样不好！"狗于是就听从你，不再叫喊。其实狗见到另外一只狗叫喊可能就是狗文化（civilization）中的正常举动（manners），但是在人的社会规范中就不正常了，狗最后就只能屈从于人的规范。注意，dog-kind 估计是斯蒂文森自己创造出来的词，与 mankind 对应。本句中 the civilisation、the morals 的使用有幽默夸张的效果，因狗是没有文明和道德体系的，至少我们不知道。另外，这里的 his ancestral master 的代名词是 his，而不是 its，这说明一般是可以用指代人的代词（he、she、his、her 等）来指代动物的。这篇文章里作者都是用一般指代人的代词来指狗，这点请读者注意。在翻译的时候，译者倒是可以换成汉语一般指代动物的代词（它），因为这样可以避免与人之间称呼的混乱。
2. 这个 humour 当动词使用时，一般表示"迁就"的意思，甚至有逆来顺受的意思，比如这句"she was always humoring him to prevent trouble"，就有姑息、迁就等意思。
3. 在目前商业社会中，client 的意思几乎毫无例外地解释成"客户"，但是在本文中这个词的意思其实是 a person depending on another's patronage 的意思，也就是受人保护，跟随依靠别人。这里用在狗身上，表达了狗与人的关系。
4. 这个 byword 经常解释为"代名词"，但是这里的意思不同，它基本上和前面的 listless 是呼应关系，with listless glances 和 in a byword（in a casual manner）。也就是说，可将 in a byword 这个短语解释为 casually，有别于"正式地、庄重地"，比如你坐的位置挡住了我看电视的视线，我于是就对你说"Could you move to the left a little?"，这么随随便便一说，就是 in a byword，不是形式正规的请求。

5. 在这里 idle 并不表示"懒惰，闲置，无事可干"等意思，而是表示无实质意思（of actions, feelings, thoughts, words, etc.: void of any real worth, usefulness, or significance）。所以常用的词若解释不通，最好去查查词典，有时会有新的发现。

6. 这个 but in their proper place 是在说那些人虽然口口声声说喜欢狗（fond of dogs），但是却不让狗接近自己，换句话说，狗毕竟是狗，还是待在狗该待的地方。在翻译时，为了把话说清楚，可以添加一些符合语境的文字，比如参考译文就添加了原文文字没有的"却与狗保持距离"，然后再把原文引号中的文字直接翻译过来"狗应待在狗该待的地方"，这样既保留了原文的文字，又把话说清楚了。接下来的"poo' fellow, poo' fellow"是直接引用了那些人的话，口气就像对小孩说的话一样，所以翻译时最好也有一点像大人对孩子说话的口气，如"可怜的狗狗"。在后半句的翻译时，也和前面一样添加了原文没有的文字。若按照原文翻译，就应该是：他们整天说"可怜的狗狗，可怜的狗狗"，自己其实更可怜。但为了告诉读者为什么更可怜，这里添加了"但没有了狗带来的欢乐"，这应该是说他可怜的原因。但是这个完全可以不加，以留给读者自己去寻找可怜的原因。这种根据语境的添加，完全得由译者自己判断，主观性较强，判断错了，添加的内容也就错了，所以必须谨慎。

7. 动物活体解剖在当时的19世纪引起过很大争议，有些人强烈反对，有些人支持，很多文学家都卷入了这场争论。斯蒂文森在这个问题上的观点比较中立，见"Pulvis et Umbra"篇注释76。

8. 这里的 the theory of animal machines 是当时的一个哲学观念，源于笛卡尔，他认为动物是机器，不会思考，而这就和人有了本质的区别。斯蒂文森在本文中要说的就是动物和人有很多相近的地方，人有思维，动物也有思想。笛卡尔的观念目前已经站不住脚了，斯蒂文森认为，在科学时代那种观点和时代不符（见下句 like strange anachronisms）。在这个 who 引导的从句中有两个动作，一个是 are not ashamed to admire (instinct)，另一个是 have dared to resuscitate (the theory)。这两个动作显然都强调动物不会思考，只凭本能直觉，斯蒂文森不同意这种观点。我们借这个机会把这部分梳理一下：这部分的领头词是 those，后面跟着三个 who 引导的从句。其中第一个从句 who are very fond of dogs "but in their proper place"，说的是嘴上喜欢狗，却敬而远之；第二个从句 who say "poo' fellow, poo' fellow"，也是说这类人仅口头上爱狗；第三个从句 who whet the knife... heat his oven，表示这些人残忍地对待狗；第四个分句就是我们刚讲过的（admire instinct and resuscitate the theory）。这四个分句合起来就是在说 those，而 those 就是前面的 his express detractors，所以这个部分是在贬低狗，狗只是动物，有直觉，但无思想，狗毕竟是狗，人不用和狗太亲近等。

9. 这一长句都是在做铺垫，在承认狗确实是一台机器（An automaton he certainly is），而后面分句中的都是机器的例子，比如拿磨盘做比喻就是狗是机器的例子，而这里的 shaken by the thunder of the stones 是在说磨盘在旋转过程中磨石发出的声音，thunder 一词的使用有夸张的效果。注意，此处的铺垫就是想说明接下来一句的狗不仅仅是机器，还是有生命有精神的动物（of which a living spirit is confined），这句中 confined 可以解释成"存在"的意思。而且在接下来的那句中，斯蒂文森把狗比作了人（an automaton like man），是像人一样的狗，这就完全与当时的 the theory of animal machines 相反，和笛卡尔的观念对立。顺便提示一下，automaton 本来的意思和我们今天说的 robot 差不多，但是现代读者概念中的 robot（机器人）都是电子指令驱动的，用到 19 世纪的语境中似乎不很合适；当然可以说成是"机械人"，但鉴于作者本人的解释就把 automaton 定义为 machine，所以此处仍用"机器"翻译 automaton。

10. 上面是在围绕 automaton 表达观点，在这个注释里，作者要向第二个"狗是机器"的观点开炮。但是和上面一样，他一开始是承认部分事实，也是一种铺垫，最后点名狗可不仅仅是机器。他先说 Instinct again he certainly possesses，他无意否认狗的直觉本能，没错，狗在很大程度上是凭直觉行事，而直觉是遗传承袭下来的（inherited），有些事狗是一看就懂（once views and understands），不需要掂量思考的，就像 were awakened from a sleep，是一种本能直觉的反应，就像 trailing clouds of glory 一样，显然这个短语和直觉有关。如果你已读过本书中的"Aes Triplex"，就会在文章的结束处看到这个短语，该语出自威廉·华兹华斯的诗 Ode: Intimations of Immortality（1807）。在华兹华斯的原诗中，这个 glory 是天堂的象征，未经世事的人保留着很多由本能指使行事的能力，trailing clouds of glory 大意就是人（这里指狗）与生俱来的那点仍然存在的凭直觉做出反应的能力。一直到这里，作者仍然是在肯定狗的行为有直觉驱动的领域。但是铺垫到此结束，接下来的连接词 but 引导的文字才是作者真正的意图，也就是直觉起作用的领域是有限的（the field of instinct is limited），在很多方面，狗和人都依靠推论和观察（must conduct their steps by deduction and observation）。

11. 注意这里的 its（its utterances are obscure and occasional）不应该是指狗，而应是指前面的 field 或 instinct。也就是说，这些 utterances 是由直觉驱动或者是凭直觉告诉我们的事情。比如，狗发出的声音就是一种直觉反应，表达喜欢或不悦等，但是直觉驱动的这种情感表达并不多（occasional），而且意思也不清晰（obscure），人类难免需要猜测狗的这种表达的意思。另外注意，作者在本文里一般都是用 his 来指代狗，不用 its 指代狗，这也是一个帮助译者决定 its 所指的线索（参考本文注释1）。

12. 作者在这里是指能说话的重要性，而这个 after and perhaps before 也是指重要性的排序，人和狗的主要区别是寿命长短还是说话能力？哪个排在后（after）哪个排在前（before）？作者用了 perhaps，说明他并不确定。但此处作者的意图很清楚，想说明说话能力的重要性，所以翻译时未必要直接把 after 和 before 这两个词都翻译出来。

13. 这里的 at the same blow 就是 by one action 的意思。

14. 狗是会区别 formal and essential truth 的。比如我们有时到别人家做客，客人问你要不要来一杯果汁，你也许并不想喝果汁，但是出于礼貌你说"好啊"，这句话就不是 essential truth，而仅仅是 formal truth，是流于形式的一种姿态（gesture），而此时的 essential truth 其实是"不想喝果汁"。而 with a human nicety 就是 accurately，也就是洞悉一切细节的意思。

15. 这里在说够能将一个动作赋予多个意思（punning perversions），这种能熟练使用符号的能力（dexterity）是无可厚非的（legitimate）。而对于自己的这个能力，狗还是很自负的（vain）。但是如果一旦狗发现自己撒谎被看穿了，便一下子就承认了（not a hair upon his body but confesses guilt），换个说法就是 every hair confesses his guilt，换句话说，He completely confesses his guilt。翻译的时候未必需要使用隐喻的修辞手法，但是译者如果愿意保留隐喻，大部分读者应该也能理解。译者可以根据自己假想的读者做决定。

16. 这句"je ne sais quoi de genéréux"引自蒙田的随笔，表示一点点慷慨宽容的意思。也就是说，这个绅士一样的狗，对于自己的小毛病（his misdemeanours）是希望主子能给它一点点宽容（genéréux），请高抬贵手。换句话说，错误有大有小，有些小错，您就别太计较了。这绅士一般的狗自己也不很在乎这些小事，如狂吠或咬人之类的行径（barked or bitten），不仅不感到羞辱（never more than half ashamed），有时甚至还不无骄傲（a share of pride）。但是说谎被抓可就不同了，那种行径丢脸可就丢大发了。斯蒂文森深受蒙田随笔的影响，详见"Books Which Have Influenced Me"篇注释15。

17. 这个 even under physical correction 是指被狗主人纠正，比如一只公狗在母狗面前显摆，被主人制止，physical 暗指硬性的阻止，如用牵狗的绳子硬拽回来，在某些文化里，甚至打狗都属于 physical correction。另外，shine 在这里就是 show off 的意思（OED: to be radiant or brilliant with high colouring, rich array, or the like; to be effulgent with splendour or beauty; to make a brave show）。

18. 这句中的 instantly uncurls his fleece 是指狗感到羞愧的意思，没有必要把字面的意思说出来，uncurls his fleece 指狗舒展开皮毛，比如狗会耷拉下耳朵和尾巴等，但实际是感到羞愧，参考译文翻译成"感到无地自容"基本到位。当然也可以两个都说。
19. 这句在理解上没有大问题，但是在表达时，译者会遇到一个问题，就是到底以什么做主语？若以人做主语，那么这个句子就可以这么写："就像观察不敏锐的人总认为狗是坦诚的一样，不明真相的人们也送给狗一个谦卑的美名。"这样处理就语义来说应该可以。但是这句话言说的核心并不是人，而是在说狗，所以以狗为主语，更能突显出原文言说的主体："狗在缺乏洞察力的人那里拾得一真诚的美名，同样还获得一个谦卑的称号。"参考译文原来是选择前面的译法，但最后选用了后一个译文。
20. 这句的逻辑是这样的：首先人使用语言反而使得人的感官迟钝，因此人（creatures supplied with eyes）就不能察觉到狗的一个显而易见的恶习（a fault），也就是说，狗的虚荣恶习（vainglory）不能用语言表达（finds no vent in words）出来，而人只善于用语言交流信息，狗却不会语言，人就没法察觉到狗的恶习了。本句的结构（It is amazing how…，—that because…）有些难解释，这主要是因为这个破折号（—）。根据一般英文标点符号的规则，破折号有引导类似同位语的作用，类似冒号，如"He is afraid of two things—spiders and senior prom"。所以这里"it is amazing how the use of language blunts…"和破折号后的"that because vainglory finds…"意思相近，也就是说，可以这样重组句子：*It is amazing* how the use of language blunts the faculties of man, and *it is amazing* that because

vainglory finds no vent in words, creatures supplied with eyes have been unable to detect a fault。换句话说，blunts the faculties 和 unable to detect 是同义的。当然也应看到，前面的 blunts 是总体地说，后面的 unable to detect 是前面的具体例子。也正是这种总体和具体的关系排除了把后面的 that 从句解释成为语法上的结果状语；不过仅就语义来说，确实有逻辑上的因果关系，正因为是 blunts the faculties，结果才 unable to detect。

21. 这句前面的 what with 是一个习惯表达法，就是 because of 的意思。注意，这句和前面那句都是表示与事实相反的虚拟语气。
22. Sir Willoughby Patterne 是 *The Egoist*(《利己主义者》)中的人物。*The Egoist* 是乔治·梅瑞狄斯（Meredith，1828—1909）的一个作品，此人极端自私虚荣自负。斯蒂文森在他的 "Books Which Have Influenced Me" 中也提到过，请参考该文注释 50。作者这里本来想把狗拿来与这位梅瑞狄斯比较，但是转念一想，这位威洛比（Willoughby）不管怎么说对自己优点的理解还是有一点像男子汉的，所以觉得这一对比不合适。这个 manlier sense of their own merits 需要解释一下。先说这个名词 sense。此词在词典中有很多不同的词义，但是大意都差不多，都是对某事某物某等等的感觉、理解。在这个例子中大致可以解释成 "a faculty, esp. of an intuitive nature, of accurately perceiving, discerning, or evaluating. Frequently with of"（OED），类似的例句有："*Her sense of right and wrong* was confused by a passion to which she had so madly surrendered herself.", 或 "A good translator… must have *a quick and delicate sense of what is proper and becoming*… that he may perceive the beauties of the original."。在本句中是说威洛比这个人对于 merits 的理解或评价是 manlier 的（in a manlier

way）。有必要说一下manly这个词，因为在不同时代，人们对这个词的理解是不同的，比如我们这个时代，不少人会把"霸气"当作一个很正能量的词，就有可能把"霸气"当作manly的含义。但是在作者生活的维多利亚时代，只有荣誉、礼貌、坦诚、勇气、责任等才构成这个词的核心词义。the Patternes have a manlier sense of their own merits 就是说，the Patternes 这类人理解评价自己的优点（merits）时是会用维多利亚时代的标准，即manlier的标准。翻译时译者面临两个选择，要么直接翻译manlier，要么把这个词在维多利亚时代的内容翻译出来。一开始翻译成"但人家毕竟把勇敢坦诚等看作是自己的优点"，好处是没有用"男子汉"这个会被不同时代的人赋予不同意义的词，但是这样翻译的问题是，译者不得不在具体的男人的气质中挑来挑去，到底把哪几个气质放到"篮子"里呢？上面的译文用了"勇敢和坦诚"，但是这个词在OED中的定义是"courageous, strong, independent in spirit, frank, upright, etc."。你看说不全了就只能用etc.了。最后还是选择了相对比较靠近原文的译法"但人家的优点中毕竟也不乏几分男子汉的气派"。这里，译者为了前后逻辑通顺，原本想添加几个原文没有的词（"帕特纳那类人虚荣自负不假"），但后来谨慎起见，还是没有添加。接下来的"the parallel, besides, is ready"应该是说除了这个威洛比外（besides），可以比较的人物唾手可得（ready），也就是下面那句里的Hans Christian Andersen。

23. 这个Hans Christian Andersen是中国读者都很熟悉的安徒生，他的童话可谓家喻户晓。但是这位大作家也有生活中的弱点，比如有一次他到英国住在狄更斯家，但是住得太久，惹得狄更斯家人不快，据说被下了逐客令，两位文学家的关系就此中断。在安徒生的回忆录 The Story of My Life 中就有他非常自负的例子。这里的 scouting even along the street for shadows of offence 就是在说安徒生故意找茬儿。动词 scout 的意思是 search，一般的用法是 scout some place for something，比如"I wouldn't have time to scout the area for junk"。这里就是在街上寻找 shadows of offence。这个 shadows of offence 可能指他访问英国的小插曲。他在大街上故意问别人是否知道他，尽显虚荣；等到别人说不知道他时，他就非常不快（offence）。shadows 的意思是不明显的或者说是微量的（OED: a slight or faint appearance, a small insignificant portion, a trace），比如我们说"There is not a shadow of evidence that Harold ever reigned as Under-king in England"。在这里是指那些微不足道、吹毛求疵的小事，他会因这些小事而不快，比如在街上别人不知道他，他就很不高兴。

24. 这里的 betray 并不是我们一般常使用时的意思，而是引导人误入歧途的意思（OED: to lead astray or into error, as a false guide; to mislead, seduce, deceive），比如说"Pride and self-confidence betray man to his fall"。

25. 这个 franker appetites 直译就是"更为坦率的食欲"，或者意译成"想吃什么就要什么"等也对。我们可以看出，这个直译在汉语中不是很合适，而第二个意译似乎就更接地气，较符合散文的语言。但是由于这里是和狗相比较，所以才有了比较级（franker），结果第二个译文（想吃什么就要什么）就没有了比较级，结果参考译文就采用了另外一种保留隐含比较的方法（猫这动物的所欲所求就不那么羞羞答答）。

26. 这句若翻译时受被动语态牵制，摆脱不了三个动词的束缚，像下面这样译，译文的意思应该也可以，但却留有太多原文的痕迹："但是狗，由于一只眼睛总盯着观众，就被诱惑而成为奴隶，被表扬、被抚摸得放弃了本性。"应该说这也是一种译法，也不无灵活之处，但是散文翻译似乎仍然给译者更大的活动空间，仍然可以大胆地触碰一下底线："但是狗，由于一只眼睛总盯着观众，经不住诱惑，而沦为奴隶，几句甜言蜜语，几下轻拍柔摸，就让它放弃了本性。"

27. 这里的 ceased hunting 到 plate-licker 使人想起杰克伦敦的小说《野性的呼唤》(*The Call of the Wild*)，小说中一只经文明驯化的爱犬，被卖到阿拉斯加，成了一条拉雪橇的狗，在主人的逼迫下重返野蛮。这句中 Rubicon 的意思就是 a point of no return，类似于汉语的破釜沉舟，是决定性的一步。这个词的典故源自古罗马恺撒率领军队渡过卢比孔河回到意大利北部的事件，显示了恺撒决定自己掌权的决心。在本文中更符合语境的解释应该是 a point of no return。

28. crushed under material cares 是一个富含隐喻意义的词组，动词 crushed 就像是一幅图画，狗被压垮，但是压垮它的是 cares，即使它担忧的事儿，而且是使它担忧的物质的事儿，比如我们人类的那些油盐酱醋的生活方面的担忧。若比较贴近原文翻译的话（不被物质的担忧所压榨），虽然未必就不行，但是从散文行文简洁考虑，还是有些欠缺，因此这里简单地翻译成"食宿无忧"，不去过度关注动词 crushed 的词义。这种省去一些词义的做法在政经法文本的翻译中似乎应该更谨慎些，但是在散文等软文本的翻译中，是可以经常想到的一种选择。

29. 此处的 convention 指的是 convention of showing off，就是狗原

本的自然完全被要显摆的做法所埋葬了,而这恰都是人类驯养的结果,这个 convention 也就是下面一句中的 etiquette,或言 mannerism。这句直接翻译虽不错,但这个 buried 并没有什么大意义,所以参考译文翻译成"(你)就会发现这狗已不再自然,而变得矫揉造作起来"。动词被故意忽略了。

30. 注意,这里 Instinct has awakened 是那些傻瓜们说的话,作者显然不同意,作者接下来说 "But it is not so"。那些傻瓜们才认为,狗这样表现是唤起了狗的天性,但作者不同意这种说法。

31. 这句中的 a companion of experience 是指那些跟人有过很多来往的狗(experience with human beings),或者说已经被人驯化的狗。另外这句中的 distinguish themselves 应该看作是成语表达法,意思就是使自己与众不同、鹤立鸡群的意思(Collins: If you distinguish yourself, you do something that makes you famous or important)。而 severity 这个词指对规则遵守的严肃程度,或言狗不折不扣遵守人规定的那套(an almost religious seriousness)。换句话说:Dogs become excellent in religiously following the rules。

32. 这里的 their bond of sympathy 是指可以将狗和人联系起来的东西,就是 sympathy;而这里的 convention 就是指人和狗都有的各自的一套社会规范,而 children of convention 就是受规则规范制约的意思(it is the bonds of feeling and sympathy that create conventions which both are subject to...)。就像我们说 children of a father 可以表示父亲制约孩子(孩子得听命于父亲),这里的 convention 也制约着 children。但这一长句中的 but 应该注意。作者先说 "I wish I were allowed to tell a story which would radiantly illuminate the point",接着他马上说了 but,显然他是

不会讲这个有关狗的故事的，因为他未被允许讲（I wish I were allowed）。那么到底是什么不让他讲出来的呢？下面一句中的 convention 应该就是原因。也就是说，狗有狗的规则，人也有人的禁忌，在有些场合有些话是不应该说的。

导 读

人狗原本一纸隔

《狗性》（The Character of Dogs）一文写于 1884 年，收入三年后出版的《回忆与肖像》（Memories and Portraits）。斯蒂文森从 1884 到 1887 年期间身体非常不好，所以他和范妮便离开爱丁堡，到英国南部的海岸城市伯恩茅斯（Bournemouth）居住。虽然疾病缠身，有时甚至不能离开住房，但他仍顽强写作，完成了不少有分量的作品，包括那两部著名的小说《化身博士》和《绑架》，以及散文集《回忆与肖像》。这篇写狗的文章就收在这本散文集中。

现在养狗的人不少，不管自己有钱没钱都会养狗。对有闲阶级，养狗代表身份与时尚；对没钱的人，养狗是为找个伴，排遣寂寞。19 世纪的欧美，养狗同样是有闲阶级养尊处优的标志，无异于坐在包厢里听歌剧，获邀在宫廷露面。有身份的女人要是没有这宠物就太掉份儿了。当然和现在一样，当时的普通人也养狗，比如斯蒂文森一家就算不上达官贵人，但也养有几只狗，他文中的言谈描写不少就是观察自家狗的结果。你看他是这么形容狗的："在异性面前展绅士风度本身并非酷林的目的，那只是一种为它赢得尊敬的行为，尽管这种行为也使它失去不少自由。""要作为酷林的偶像，挂个名是不够的；它严苛起来像位死板的家长；它尊崇的那个人一有轻浮之举，它就大声疾呼美德不再、地陷天崩。"这是斯蒂文森在描写他家里名叫"酷林"的那只狗，你是不是觉得他在描写人不在描写狗？斯蒂文森总用拟人的手法描写狗，觉得狗也有思想情操，仿佛狗就是人："狗跳不出封建等级思想，也惯于膜拜神明；由于受制于驱不散的多神观念，一面是人这个拿着鞭子的奥林帕斯之神统治着狗类，但另一面，狗与狗之间在外形、力量上极大的差异，也彻底防止了民主观念的形成，结果就有了狗自己的神"；他家的酷林对不同人有不同态度："感激程度的深浅，拜访时间的长短是明显不同的。促使它厚此薄彼的原因肯定与本能相去甚远"。在这里，狗和人一样都有思想，都有价值判断，而这种判断仅凭直觉是做不到的。他说："在狗身上，也和人一样，本能起作用的领域是有限的；狗凭直觉告诉我们的事意思含糊不清，而且也为数不多；在生活的更广泛的领域里，狗和它的主人都得依靠推论和观察举步前行"。

斯蒂文森把狗和人一视同仁的态度在其他作品中也有反映，比如在《微尘与幻影》中他把人类善恶的两重性和动物的两重性相提并论。这种对动物的态度多少受当时社会思潮的影响。英国生物学家达尔文在1859年出版了著名的《物种起源》一书，赫胥黎在1863年出版了《人在自然中的位置》(*Man's Place in Nature*)，他的《进化论伦理学》(又译《天演论》)也是在1893年出版的。也就是说，在斯蒂文森生活的英国，进化论是当时的重要思想。斯蒂文森对狗的拟人描述可能正是由这种思想驱动的。也正是这种思想使他认为狗的行为举止不仅是直觉使然，狗还是会思考的。他在本文中就极力批判狗仅是机器的观点："他们不羞于赞扬'动物的直觉'，甚至愚不可及，竟然重弹动物是机器的老调。在这个心理学和科学昌明的时代，'狗的直觉'和'狗是机器'这种观点听起来与时代背道而驰"。他甚至认为狗不仅有思想，狗还是社会的动物,具有狗社会的一套独特的规则:"人和狗一样,也有繁复神秘的一套礼仪规范。这恰恰是因为人和狗都有情感,所以都受制于一套规则"。狗有思想和情感,所以就不仅有高尚的举止,也有卑下的表现。他说他家中的两只狗骗术高超:"酷林一直到最后仍是一个小偷;轻罪数不胜数,外加一只全鹅、一条冷羊腿让它羞不胜羞;但是沃格斯这只狗,就是我前面提到过的那只讨好母狗未果而伤透心的狗,目前所知偷窃的勾当仅有两次,算是高尚地抵御了诱惑"。在他笔下,狗能察言观色,还会势利待人:"至少在与人的来往中,它们不仅有性别的考虑,也有地位的掂量。而且是狗眼看人,势利之极;穷人的狗并不讨厌看到富人,它会把所有的丑恶心情留着发泄给比它主子更贫穷或更衣衫褴褛的人。而且狗还会为不同的地位配以相应的举止"。你看这是在说狗还是在说人呢?

斯蒂文森除了对狗有这类深刻的描写外,他也对狗采取更为人道的态度。文中他谴责活体解剖动物(vivisection)。针对这个议题,在19世纪中叶前后,英国出现过一场大辩论,支持和反对的双方各持己见。其实动物活体解剖在当时已存在几百年,不是新现象,但由于19世纪自然科学进步迅速,医学科学更是蓬勃发展,动物活体解剖实验就变得非常普遍。结果大量动物(特别是狗)被送进了实验室。在这个问题上,当时科学界的重量级人物达尔文也处于左右为难的境地。一方面作为科学家,他支持动物实验,但另一方面,他也强烈反对残酷对待动物。就在斯蒂文森写这篇文章前后,要用人性对待动物的讨论方兴未艾,英国立法机构还制定出保护动物的相关法律。文学界的人也参加了这场热议。有些作家坚决反对活体解剖动物,比如拉斯金(John Ruskin)和布朗宁(Robert Browning),前者为此还辞去了牛津大学文学教授的职务,因为牛津大学允许解剖动物。斯蒂文森对这个问题的态度没有那么激进,和达尔文相近，但他也强烈反对残酷对待动物。

　　本文开头，作者用生动的语言，概述了人类的这个宠物："狗类的文明、举止、道德，很大程度上屈从于人的那套规矩，人类自古都是狗的主子。这个动物在很多方面优于主子，却甘当劣等，放弃野外与人共居，主子嬉笑怒骂，它却俯首帖耳。"显然在作者看来，狗虽是我们的附庸，但也是有思想、有道德、有文明的动物，和我们没有本质的区别："我见过狗，也见过学校中的英勇男孩，他们之间，除了一个有毛，一个无毛，还真很难分辨；如果我们意欲了解中世纪的骑士风范，那就一定得到学校的操场上或群狗聚集的垃圾场去一睹风采。"

　　我们未必能在狗是否通人性这个问题上取得一致，但是我们至少可以在更人道地对待动物这个问题上站在一起。人若能对狗少一分残忍，那么可能对同类也会多一分怜悯。这也许是我们读斯蒂文森这篇散文的一大收获。

参考资料

Pascale McCullough Manning, The Hyde We Live In: Stevenson, Evolution, and the Anthropogenic Fog, *Victorian Literature and Culture* 46 (01): 181–199, March 2018.

Eric Michael Johnson, Charles Darwin and the Vivisection Outrage, *Scientific American*, October 6, 2011.

Harriet Ritvo, Plus ça Change: Anti-Vivisection Then and Now, *Science, Technology & Human Values*, Vol. 9, No. 2 (Spring, 1984), pp. 57–66, Sage Publications, Inc.

RLS website: http://robert-louis-stevenson.org/timeline/.

The Character of Dogs (2)

The person, man or dog, who has a conscience is eternally condemned to some degree of humbug;[33] the sense of the law in their members fatally precipitates either towards a frozen and affected bearing.[34] And the converse is true; and in the elaborate and conscious manners of the dog, moral opinions and the love of the ideal stand confessed.[35] To follow for ten minutes in the street some swaggering, canine cavalier, is to receive a lesson in dramatic art and the cultured conduct of the body; in every act and gesture you see him true to a refined conception; and the dullest cur, beholding him, pricks up his ear and proceeds to imitate and parody that charming ease. For to be a high-mannered and high-minded gentleman, careless, affable, and gay, is the inborn pretension of the dog. The large dog, so much lazier, so much more weighed upon with matter, so majestic in repose, so beautiful in effort, is born with the dramatic means to wholly represent the part.[36] And it is more pathetic and perhaps more instructive to consider the small dog in his conscientious and imperfect efforts to outdo Sir Philip Sidney.[37] For the ideal of the dog is feudal and religious; [38] the ever-present polytheism, the whip-bearing Olympus of mankind, rules them on the one hand; on the other, their singular difference of size and strength among themselves effectually prevents the appearance of the democratic notion.[39] Or we might more exactly compare their society to the curious spectacle presented by a school—ushers, monitors, and big and

狗性（二）

无论一个人还是一只狗，只要他有道德良知，就永远逃不脱耍些花招骗术的命运，程度不同而已；它们凡胎肉体的弱点不可避免地使它们的行为表现得极度僵硬做作。但反之亦然，在狗繁复做作的行为里，道德和理想这些高尚的精神也昭然若揭。在大街上跟随大摇大摆风度翩翩的狗走上十分钟，你定能学得一套表演艺技，知道怎样的行为才是有教养；看它一摇头一抬腿，都透着高雅的格调；最愚笨的劣等狗，看着这只派头十足的狗，也会竖起耳朵，开始模仿起来，要把那副自在得意的样子学个惟妙惟肖。可不是，要当一个举止高雅、思想高尚的绅士，要显得满不在乎、和蔼友善、欢乐快活，这扮演学样的本领可是狗与生俱来的。大狗较慵懒，体重更肥胖，仪态更威严，努力时尽显优美，天生一副演绅士的本领。相比之下，小狗虽也认真模仿，誓要超越有典范绅士之称的菲利普·西德尼爵士，但总是学得不伦不类，让你看得更心生不忍，不过也使你受教不浅。狗跳不出封建等级思想，也惯于膜拜神明；由于受制于驱不散的多神观念，一面是人这个拿着鞭子的奥林帕斯之神统治着狗类，但另一面，狗与狗之间在外形、力量上极大的差异，也彻底防止了民主观念的形成。或者可更准确地将学校奇观与狗类社会相比较。学校有助理、班长，还有大小男孩，唯一不同的是学校没有女孩，狗社会却有母狗。无论是狗还是男孩，我们都能

little boys—qualified by one circumstance, the introduction of the other sex.[40] In each, we should observe a somewhat similar tension of manner, and somewhat similar points of honour.[41] In each the larger animal keeps a contemptuous good humour; in each the smaller annoys him with wasp-like impudence, certain of practical immunity;[42] in each we shall find a double life producing double characters, and an excursive and noisy heroism combined with a fair amount of practical timidity.[43] I have known dogs, and I have known school heroes that, set aside the fur, could hardly have been told apart; and if we desire to understand the chivalry of old,[44] we must turn to the school playfields or the dungheap where the dogs are trooping.

Woman, with the dog, has been long enfranchised. Incessant massacre[45] of female innocents has changed the proportions of the sexes and perverted their relations. Thus, when we regard the manners of the dog, we see a romantic and monogamous animal, once perhaps as delicate as the cat, at war with impossible conditions.[46] Man has much to answer for; and the part he plays is yet more damnable and parlous than Corin's in the eyes of Touchstone.[47] But his intervention has at least created an imperial situation for the rare surviving ladies.[48] In that society they reign without a rival: conscious queens;[49] and in the only instance of a canine wife-beater that has ever fallen under my notice, the criminal was somewhat excused by the circumstances of his story. He is a little, very alert, well-bred,[50] intelligent Skye, as black as a hat, with a wet bramble for a nose and two cairngorms[51] for eyes. To the human observer, he is decidedly well-looking; but to the ladies of his race he seems abhorrent. A thorough elaborate gentleman, of the plume and sword-knot order,[52] he was born with the nice sense of gallantry to women. He took at their hands the most outrageous treatment;[53] I have heard him bleating like a sheep, I have seen

见到成员间类似的紧张关系，相近的一套行为准则。较大的总在温顺友善中带一点傲慢；较小的总像黄蜂一样无理取闹惹恼大的，却又确信自己不会惹麻烦；无论是狗还是男孩，我们都能见到双重生活造就的双重性格，四面出击、喧哗吵闹的英勇行为和出于谨慎的一点胆怯心态总是同时存在。我见过狗，也见过学校中的英勇男孩，他们之间，除了一个有毛，一个无毛，还真很难分辨；如果我们意欲了解中世纪的骑士风范，那就一定得到学校的操场上或群狗聚集的垃圾场去一睹风采。

至于说到狗，母狗早就享有很大自由了。那么多无辜的母狗被残杀，结果改变了性别比例，也颠倒了公狗和母狗间的关系。所以，当我们观察公狗的举止时，我们看到的是这个充满浪漫、至死不渝的动物，这个曾可能和猫一样温柔的动物，正在不堪的处境中拼命挣扎。而狗处在这个境地全得怪人；人在这里扮演的角色要比莎士比亚《皆大欢喜》里试金石眼中科林的作用更危险更可咒。但人的介入至少为幸存下来的少数母狗创造了一个绝佳的环境。在狗的社会里，母狗权势炎炎，没有竞争对手，是个自命不凡的女王；仅有的一例"狗打妻"引起了我的注意，但那位打妻狗由于它特殊的经历而被免于惩处。它是一个身体不大、非常机警、很懂规矩、聪明智慧的斯凯梗良种狗，黑得像头上戴的礼帽，有一个湿湿的黑莓果样的鼻子，两只黄宝石样的眼睛。在人的眼中，它绝对是长得好看的；但在母狗的眼里，它似乎有些可恶讨厌。它是一个浑身都透着绅士气息，挂有羽毛与剑结的狗，生来就有阿谀母狗的绝佳本能。但母狗待它极其恶劣；我听见它像羊一般颤抖哭泣，我看

him streaming blood, and his ear tattered like a regimental banner; and yet he would scorn to make reprisals. Nay more, when a human lady upraised the contumelious whip against the very dame who had been so cruelly misusing him, my little great-heart gave but one hoarse cry and fell upon the tyrant tooth and nail. This is the tale of a soul's tragedy.[54] After three years of unavailing chivalry, he suddenly, in one hour, threw off the yoke of obligation; had he been Shakespeare he would then have written Troilus and Cressida[55] to brand the offending sex; but being only a little dog, he began to bite them. The surprise of the ladies whom he attacked indicated the monstrosity of his offence; but he had fairly beaten off his better angel, fairly committed moral suicide;[56] for almost in the same hour, throwing aside the last rags of decency, he proceeded to attack the aged also. The fact is worth remark, showing as it does, that ethical laws are common both to dogs and men; and that with both a single deliberate violation of the conscience loosens all. "But while the lamp holds on to burn," says the paraphrase, "the greatest sinner may return."[57] I have been cheered to see symptoms of effectual penitence in my sweet ruffian;[58] and by the handling that he accepted uncomplainingly the other day from an indignant fair one, I begin to hope the period of Sturm und Drang[59] is closed.

All these little gentlemen are subtle casuists. The duty to the female dog is plain; but where competing duties rise, down they will sit and study them out like Jesuit confessors.[60] I knew another little Skye, somewhat plain in manner and appearance, but a creature compact of amiability and solid wisdom. His family going abroad for a winter, he was received for that period by an uncle in the same city. The winter over, his own family home again, and his own house (of which he was very proud) reopened, he found himself in a dilemma between two conflicting duties of loyalty and gratitude. His old friends were not to be neglected, but it seemed hardly

过它体有血迹，耳朵像破损的军旗；但它却不屑于对母狗报复。不仅如此，当一个女人傲慢地举鞭抽打那只曾残忍待它的母狗时，我那个子很小心胸广大的狗怒吼一声，爪牙齐上，直扑向施暴者。但下面发生的是一个"伤心的悲剧"。在施展骑士风范三年无甚收获后，它竟在一小时内，抖落了责任的枷锁；它要是莎士比亚的话，一定会写《特洛伊罗斯与克瑞西达》这样的悲剧去挞伐多有冒犯的母狗；但是由于它仅是一只小狗，便开始咬起她们来。被它攻击的母狗大惊失色，足以说明它冒犯严重；但是它心中善的天使几近杀绝，道德几近自毁；因为大概就在同一个小时里，它抛弃了仅存的一点尊严，也开始攻击起老狗来。这现象值得一提，它说明道德法则对狗和对人都一样，违反良知的事只要一开头，就会一发不可收拾，人狗皆然。但恰如借圣经典故的诗行所说："只要灯盏不灭，浪子总会回头。"我高兴地在我那可爱的恶棍身上看到了真正忏悔回头的迹象；某日一只气势汹汹的母狗又残忍地对待起它来，可它却毫无怨恨地接受了这遭遇。就凭这点，我开始希望狗身上那阵暴风骤雨般的坏脾气已经过去了。

所有这些小绅士们都是注重细节的道德审判高手。对母狗的责任算是简简单单的；但是若其他责任同时出现，它们就会坐下来，像听忏悔的神父一样把这些责任细细掂量一番。我还知道另外一只斯凯㹴小狗，它举止与外貌都并不惊人，但是却可爱至极，绝顶智慧。它的家人到外地去度冬日，它就到同城的一位叔叔家客居数日。冬去春来，它又回到了自己的家里，它对自己的住处非常自豪，小房子又开门迎接它回来。可是它感到要把忠诚与感恩分给两

decent to desert the new. This was how he solved the problem. Every morning, as soon as the door was opened, off posted Coolin to his uncle's, visited the children in the nursery, saluted the whole family, and was back at home in time for breakfast and his bit of fish. Nor was this done without a sacrifice on his part, sharply felt; for he had to forego the particular honour and jewel of his day—his morning's walk with my father. And perhaps, from this cause, he gradually wearied of and relaxed the practice, and at length returned entirely to his ancient habits. But the same decision served him in another and more distressing case of divided duty, which happened not long after. He was not at all a kitchen dog,[61] but the cook had nursed him with unusual kindness during the distemper; and though he did not adore her as he adored my father—although (born snob) he was critically conscious of her position as "only a servant"—he still cherished for her a special gratitude. Well, the cook left, and retired some streets away to lodgings of her own; and there was Coolin in precisely the same situation with any young gentleman who has had the inestimable benefit of a faithful nurse. The canine conscience did not solve the problem with a pound of tea at Christmas. No longer content to pay a flying visit,[62] it was the whole forenoon that he dedicated to his solitary friend. And so, day by day, he continued to comfort her solitude until (for some reason which I could never understand and cannot approve) he was kept locked up to break him of the graceful habit. Here, it is not the similarity, it is the difference, that is worthy of remark; the clearly marked degrees of gratitude and the proportional duration of his visits. Anything further removed from instinct it were hard to fancy;[63] and one is even stirred to a certain impatience with a character so destitute of spontaneity, so passionless in justice, and so priggishly obedient to the voice of reason.[64]

个主人实在左右为难。旧主人当然不能忽视，但新主人也岂能抛弃。它是这样解决这个难题的！每天早上，房门一开，小狗酷林就跑到叔叔家，去看看孩子，向全家致敬，而后及时赶回家吃早饭，吃它那点鱼。它这么两头跑也不是没有代价的，这个代价它也深有感受；因为它得在和父亲晨间散步前去拜访叔叔一家，而和父亲一起晨间散步是一种殊荣，是一天的精华所在。也许正是因此，它慢慢热情逐减，去叔叔家的次数越来越少，最后完全恢复了老习惯。但是此后不久，同样的决定却使它比这次更深受侍二主之苦。它根本不是喜欢在厨房转悠的那种狗，但是厨娘在犬瘟热时对它呵护有加；它也很喜欢厨娘，当然和父亲比还是差远了，它毕竟生来就有一副势利眼，厨娘只是仆人这点它看得非常清楚，不过它对厨娘还是有一份特殊的感情。后来，厨娘不干了，但就住在几条街外的屋子里。这位厨娘之于酷林恰如尽职的保姆之于一位青年男子，都曾给予对方百般照顾。面对这样的境遇，狗并不会像人一样在圣诞日送上一磅茶叶以表寸心。酷林觉得蜻蜓点水似的探访是不够的，所以它把整个上午都奉献给了它这位孤独的朋友。它就这样日复一日地去排遣厨娘的孤独，直到有一天它因某个原因被关了起来，才不得不终止这已成习惯的善举，而我就是不能理解关它的原因，当然也不认同对它这样做。本例中值得关注的不是和上面拜访叔叔家例子的相似，而是不同。感激程度的深浅，拜访时间的长短是明显不同的。促使它厚此薄彼的原因肯定与本能相去甚远；面对这样一个既缺乏自然举止，又对正义无动于衷，却对理性百依百顺的动物，你甚至真会有点不耐烦了。

注　释

33. 这里的 person 指单一的个体，无论是人还是狗。这个词一般用在人身上用惯了，一下子指代狗我们有点不习惯。注意在这个语境中 man 只是个陪衬，整段都在讲狗，所以接下来句子中的 their 就是指代狗的。另外 condemned 这个词一般有被谴责、被判罪的意思，但是在这里有表示逃脱不了某种命运的意思（OED: to be doomed by fate to some condition or to do something），比如"Men that are condemned to be rich"，或"Reindeer are tamed; one sort being condemned to the Sledge, others to carry burden"。翻译的时候有时可用"命运"一词来表明这层意思，但有时就不应表明，因为这个词有时的背景是命运（fate），有时则是条件（condition）等。当然忽视这个词也行（总免不了会要些"花招骗术"），可由译者选择。

34. 这句中有几个问题需要解释。首先是 the sense of the law in their members 这部分的意思。这个短语其实有《圣经》的典故："But I see another law in my members, warring against the law of my mind, and bringing me into captivity to the law of sin which is in my members."（Romans 7: 23）可见这里将 the law in their members 和 the law of my mind 对立起来，前者负面，后者正面。their members 原本指人的肢体，喻指肉身的弱点（"I am speaking in human terms because of the weakness of your flesh".— Romans 6: 19）。另外，这句中的 precipitates 原意有两层，一层意思是造成某事发生: A slight mistake could precipitate a disaster，另一层意思是表示降落: The hurricane will also

precipitate a lot of water in the form of rain。有趣的是，语言中向下降落的东西常会有负面的含义，比如上面的 a disaster 就是负面的意思；介词 towards 则有目标的意思；接下来的 bearing 表示人的行为（behavior），而修饰 bearing 的 frozen 有冷漠的意思，affected 则有虚假做作的意思。而这个 bearing 显然是人不好的行为，促成这个行为的原动力就是前面人的弱点（the sense of the law in their members）。本句大意就是"Human weaknesses cause that type of behavior to happen"，翻译时贴近原文的译法很难传达原文实际的意思，所以解释性的意译是不可避免的。另外还有一个语法问题，就是不要误解句中 either 和 and 的关系。我们也许一下子就发现这个错误的搭配，因为正确的搭配应该是 either 和 or 连用，表示选择关系，但实际这样理解是错误的。根据意思 frozen and affected 是并列关系，前面的 either 并不是与 and 搭配的连接词，而是指无论是人还是狗，理解成副词更合适。

35. 这个 the converse is true 把后半句与前半句对立起来。前面是基于人体的弱点（the weakness of your flesh），是作者不认同的；而接下来的是相反的（converse），是正能量了，而且是基于精神的（the law of my mind）；确实 moral opinions and the love of the ideal 都属于精神领域的，类似后面提到的 high-mannered and high-minded，这些在狗的行为中（in the elaborate and conscious manners of the dog）清晰可见（stand confessed）。也就是说，在狗的身上这两种相反的东西都有所体现。翻译的时候译者仍然可以对具体词视而不见，比如 moral opinions and the love of the ideal 的粗略大意就是有道德和理想，所以翻译的时候就未必一定需要将 opinions 和 love 这两个词翻译出来。

36. 这里的 more weighed upon with matter 虽然理解成"心头重压着心事"也未必就完全错误，但是根据上下文，理解成是在描写体重更合适。接下来的 represent the part 是指扮演的角色，也就是扮演 a high-mannered and high-minded gentleman 的角色。注意，dramatic 这个词有两个意思，一个是指和戏剧相关的（related to drama），另一个是惊人的或令人激动的。在我们这句里，应该是指前者（扮演学样）。

37. 菲利普·西德尼（1554—1586）是伊丽莎白一世时期的廷臣、政治家、诗人和学者，几乎无懈可击，被认为是当时绅士的典范。在这里狗把西德尼当作是仿效的目标。这句的翻译也可以探索一下。原文的 his conscientious and imperfect efforts to outdo Sir Philip Sidney 若直译就可以翻译成"在它超越西德尼的认真和不完美的努力中"。但是这样翻译似比较适合正式文本的翻译，在散文翻译中总有些生硬的感觉。参考译文采用了比较大胆的方法，把 imperfect 单独拿出来处理。所谓 efforts 就是模仿绅士，所谓 imperfect 就是学得不成功，所以译者把 imperfect 翻译成"学得不伦不类"，也就是"邯郸学步"的意思。后者存在过于明显的中国文化特征，这里没有选用，但并非所有语境中都不能用。

38. 这句直译就是"狗的理想是封建的和宗教的"，应该说是一个可以接受的译文。我们这里想探索的是更自由一点的译法。若是在经济论文、法律文书、政治宣言里，译者并没必要舍近求远。但是在文艺文本的翻译中，再伸展一下"拳脚"，争得一点自由至少是应鼓励的。那么这里的 feudal 为什么不能让译者满足呢？因为这个词包含的面比较宽，仅仅一个"封建"不能很好地与我们这个语境无缝对接；同理，将 religious

翻译成"宗教"也会有同样的问题，说狗的理想是封建的和宗教的，读者完全可能读不懂这话的意思。但只要我们将语境考虑进去，去寻找这两个词在本段中的意思，然后再微调译文，译文就会更明朗。这句接下来的文字就是狗受制于人，没有民主思想，又讲到学校里孩子得听孩子王的，这些正是 feudal 和 religious 这两个词的语境，那么译者就可以在不含语境的词义基础上做一下语境微调，如"封建等级""膜拜神明"，这样整句就更具可读性："狗跳不出封建等级思想，也惯于膜拜神明"。

39. 这里的 polytheism 指的就是多神的意思，在本句中指狗所面临的两个神：一个是人这个神，另外一个就是在狗中间树立起来的神。前者就是 whip-bearing Olympus of mankind，作者将人比成希腊神话中的奥林帕斯天神，这里的 whip-bearing 就是 whip-carrying 的意思。原句中在 on the other 后面仅仅说了民主不能出现，没有提到另一个神的存在，但是根据上下文，在提到多神后，提到一方面的人类这个奥林帕斯天神，再提到另一方面的无民主观念，第二个神其实已呼之欲出。可以在句子结尾处添加"狗类自己的神"，但不添加更保险。

40. 这里的 ushers 指学校里类似校长助力的职务（OED: an assistant to a schoolmaster or head-teacher; an under-master, assistant-master）；而 qualified (limited) by one circumstance 就是说有一个不同的地方，即 the introduction of the other sex。换句话说，在学校里没有女性，但在狗的社会里就两性都有了。这主要是因为本文的背景是 18 和 19 世纪的欧洲，学校里都是男孩，就像中国古代，外出读书的都是男的。

41. 这里的 similar tension of manner 是指无论在人的社会还是狗的

群体里，成员之间都有一定程度的紧张关系，每个人都要提防另外的人，每只狗也得提防其他的狗；而 similar points of honour 则是指狗和人都有的一套类似的行为准则，比如说小偷也有小偷的准则——相互不拆台（Thieves' honour recognizes a principle which the thief applies only to his fellow-thieves）。这个 points of honour 此处暂且翻译成"行为准则"。

42. 这里的 certain of practical immunity 是说那个小狗（the smaller one is certain of practical immunity），换句话说，the smaller one is certain that it is practically immune from trouble。

43. 这句是在对照 heroism 和 timidity，也就是上面说的 double characters，即在一个人身上有两个相反的特征，一方面有那种大胆的英勇大胆的行为，一方面也有胆怯的行为，而 excursive and noisy 是描写英勇行为的，如学校的孩子打来打去四面出击（excursive）吵吵闹闹（noisy）。

44. 这个 the chivalry of old 指欧洲中世纪的那种骑士行为。

45. 在解释 massacre 这个词前，应该看一下前面那句："Woman, with the dog, has been long enfranchised"。这里的 with the dog 可解释为 in the case of dog，所以这里的 woman 其实指母狗（本文中作者常用指人的词来指代狗，如母狗称为 ladies），也就是说母狗早就获得了自由。到底是哪方面的自由文中没有说，但应该和接下来的事有关。接下来的这个 massacre of female innocents 毫无疑问就是在说母狗的死亡。母狗死得多了，就变得公多母少（changed the proportions of the sexes）。至于母狗被杀害的原因，可能是人类为避免过多狗崽子的出生，便杀掉不少母狗。这和后面的（Man has much to answer for）也相符。

46. 上面一句是在说，母狗的死亡改变了公母的比例，颠倒了公母间的正常关系，使得母狗获得自由（enfranchised）。母狗之所以获得自由是因为数量少了，身份抬高了，甚至可以说这种自由也体现在选择公狗上的自由，因为选择余地大了。接下来就是"when we regard the manners of the dog, we see…"这句。这里的 the dog 是指公狗（不包括母狗），也就是指下面的 a romantic and monogamous animal；这个公狗在和不堪环境争斗（at war with impossible conditions）。这个 impossible conditions 到底是什么？在这里没有交代。但是我们希望下面几句的语境能对这个状态有所暗示。

47. 这句对理解上句中不明确的地方有帮助。"Man has much to answer for" 应该就是对前面的 impossible conditions 要负的责任。answer for 就是对某些不良的事要负起责任（to accept responsibility for one's misdeeds），比如"Now that he's been caught, the thief will answer for his crimes"。配合语境，这句是说公狗所处的不堪处境该由人类负责。接下来的 the part he plays 则进一步说明这个责任，其中的 he 是指人，the part 是人在促成 impossible conditions 中的角色，而这种角色是危险可咒的，然后作者把这种危险可咒的角色和莎士比亚《皆大欢喜》中的剧情比较（见 *As You Like It*, III. 2: "Sin is damnation: Thou art in a parlous state, shepherd."）。句子中的科林是牧羊人，而 Touchstone 是一个弄臣。但是到这里为止，我们仍然不是很清楚这个 impossible conditions 到底是什么？

48. 这句似乎给出了理解 impossible conditions 的关键信息。首先这个 but 就很主要。前面在说是人把公狗置于不堪的处境，这个 but 就转折了，要说人类所做的事儿也有好的一面，即

狗性（二）

created an imperial situation for the rare surviving ladies。这里可以看出这个好事儿是对 the rare surviving ladies 而言的,是对母狗的好事,对公狗仍然是不堪处境。这里的 surviving 给出很多信息,似乎暗示人类做的事儿促成很多母狗死亡,只有这样才能用 surviving 这个词。对于没有死亡的母狗,这可是 imperial situation,为什么呢?因为物以稀为贵,数量少了,公母比例变化了,变得对母狗有利了(imperial),变得对公狗不利了(impossible)。文中没有直接说明人类是怎么造成母狗死亡的,所以我们翻译的时候也不能言之凿凿地说人类残杀了母狗,不过这却是个很合理的猜测。

49. 到这里母狗的 imperial situation 就很清楚了,imperial 就是当皇后了,无人可以挑战它们,而且它们还是 conscious queens。这个 conscious 就是说这些母狗对自己的优越处境是有意识的(aware of their own queen's position or imperial situation)。翻译时能表达出类似的意思都可以。

50. 这里的 well-bred 怎么翻译需要斟酌一下,原因是这个词有两层意思,一个是生物种类优良,另外一个是有好的调教、教养好、较文明、懂规矩。在这里似乎都能搭上边儿,因为 Skye 也算是一种品种优良的狗。参考译文都包括进去了(懂规矩的良种狗),但是仅保留有调教的意思应该也基本到位。这句中说的狗在后文会受到母狗的欺负,应该也就是上句中打妻狗被免于惩罚的原因。

51. 这是在用比喻的手法来形容鼻子的形状,像黑莓果的鼻子。bramble 是一种短小灌木,上面长的果实叫 bramble berry。而形容眼睛也是比喻说法,cairngorms 本来是指苏格兰的山脉,此处指一种淡黄色的烟熏石英,可当作宝石用。翻译时不必求矿物科学的对等，就说是黄宝石（"两只黄宝石样的眼睛"）就差不多，未必需要把苏格兰山脉等背景信息都翻译进去。

52. 这里的 order 就是 particular type 的意思，比如 "We accept that peaceful protest should be allowed, but this is something of a very different order"，就是 different type 的意思。

53. 这句中的 he 指的就是公狗，也就前一句中的 gentleman，而 at their hands 中的 their 应该是指前一句中的 women，整句是说这只公狗在母狗那里受到极其恶劣的待遇。这里代词的使用不是很清楚，到底是人的女性（women）还是母狗（female dog）？但根据上下文，我们还是把这里的 women 看作是比喻，不是指女人而是指母狗。接下来当作者确实想指人类的女性时，他用了 human lady 这个词组，但在文中的其他地方 women 还是指人。接下来的几句基本不用注释，读参考译文就能搞清楚了。

54. 这里的 a soul's tragedy 是指罗伯特·布朗宁的作品《一个灵魂的悲剧》(A Soul's Tragedy)。但是和本文没有很重要的联系，所以简单地说成"下面发生的事是一个悲剧"，基本反映出句子的大意。注意这句中的 "This is the tale" 中的 this 应该不是前指，而是后指，就是指后面这只狗疯狂地咬起母狗来了。一般代词 this 用作前指更普遍。

55. Troilus and Cressida 是莎士比亚的一个悲剧，但是这个剧饱受批评。故事中描述的男性（特洛伊罗斯）对女性（克瑞西达）的失望和挞伐是作者将其用在本语境中的原因，因为这里公狗对母狗也失望，本该也可以写上一大篇来谴责母狗，就像莎士比亚的这个剧中的特洛伊罗斯谴责克瑞西达一样。当然狗不会写，所以就攻击母狗了。这句中的 the offending sex 就是指母狗。

56. 这里的 better angel 是基于西方基督教文化的 shoulder angel，与之相反的是 shoulder devil。better angel 促使人行善，worse angel 促使人作恶。句中的 fairly 表示程度很大（very great degree）的意思，在这个语境中甚至可以解释成 almost completely。也就是说，这只狗几乎完全把善的一面给击败了，所以才干出了下面攻击老狗的事儿。fairly committed moral suicide 也是类似的意思，就是几乎完全道德自杀或死亡了。

57. 这句"But while the lamp holds on to burn, the greatest sinner may return"是源自以撒·华滋（Isaac Watts，1674—1748）的诗句：

> Life is the time to serve the Lord,
> The time to insure the great reward;
> And while the lamp holds out to burn,
> The vilest sinner may return.

之所以说这是 paraphrase，是因为这最后两句的典故来自《圣经》（Luke 15: 11-32），就是著名的浪子回头的故事（the Parable of the Prodigal Son），这诗行不是《圣经》原样的照搬，仅仅是 paraphrase。the lamp holds out to burn 喻指人只要活着，就像《圣经》里那儿子最终还是回来一样。用灯盏的灭与不灭喻指生命的存在与消亡，在中国文化也是可以理解的。

58. 这里的 my sweet ruffian 就是指那只想做绅士却没有结果，最后去咬人的狗，但它后来改邪归正忏悔了。作者看到了忏悔的种种表现，也觉得很欣慰："I have been cheered to see…"。

59. 这一句就是这狗忏悔的一个表现。这个 the handling 就是指母狗对待它的 bad treatment，而 fair one 就是指母狗（OED:

applied to a woman or to women collectively, as expressing a quality considered as characteristic of the female sex. In earlier use frequently in *fair one*）。句子里的 Sturm und Drang 是德语词，翻译成英文就是 Storm and stress，也就是那只狗短期出现的疯狂咬母狗的情况。这句中的"the period of Sturm und Drang is closed"，是说那只狗的疯狂期结束了，浪子回头了。但这个 Sturm und Drang 的概念在德国乃至欧洲 18 世纪末形成了文学领域的一种风潮，以过度情感的宣泄为特征，最著名的一个作品就是歌德的《少年维特之烦恼》。

60. Jesuit 就是 Society of Jesus，是罗马天主教的一个组织，而 confessors 就是指听忏悔的神父。这一比喻是想说明，在出现双重责任时，狗是会非常认真地掂量两个责任孰轻孰重的，认真得就像神父倾听别人的忏悔一样。

61. 此处 a kitchen dog 是指经常在厨房内外逛来逛去求食物的那类狗。另外，有关 kitchen dog 的更多内容，可参考维基百科的 turnspit dog 词条。

62. flying visit 就是指非常短暂的访问，就像这只狗前面拜访作者叔叔家的那类访问，类似于蜻蜓点水一类的停留访问。

63. 这句恢复正常语序的话就是"It were hard to fancy anything further removed from instinct"。这里的关键是要先搞清楚在这个语境里，作者想说什么？斯蒂文森在说，那只狗对待去客居过的叔叔家和对待照顾过它的厨娘明显不同（it is the difference），对待后者的"礼遇规格"高多了。正是在这个语境中作者说这句话的。其实这句话的意思就是，这种礼遇不同的原因不是直觉而是思想。但作者是用了一个弯弯转转的口气说的。"A is further removed from B"就是 A 与 B 是相距甚远的（distant from），或者说是和 B 不同（unlike B），比如"I wasn't even in the office that day, so I'm the furthest removed from this situation"。也就是说狗之区别对待是出于一种和 instinct 完全不同的原因（unlike instinct; distant or remote from instinct），这种东西和 instinct 已经相去甚远，已经远到很难想象（fancy 或者 imagine）的程度了（it is hard to picture any kind of connection between it and instinct）。但作者没有在这里指出这是什么，而只用了 anything。若贴近原文翻译成"很难想象出任何一个比直觉更为不同的原因"，估计很容易把读者给绕糊涂了，所以结合上下文，译者甚至可以更灵活一点，如"促使它厚此薄彼的原因肯定与本能相去甚远"。

64. 这句是在说，面对这样一只狗，人难免会有些不耐烦。那么到底是什么样的一只狗呢？原来这只狗（a character）竟是如此缺乏自然举止（destitute of spontaneity），对正义无动于衷（passionless in justice），对理性死板顺从（priggishly obedient to the voice of reason）。没错，狗的理性、责任等都是好品质，但无论是人还是狗，都别弄得太过火，履行起责任来竟然这么一丝不苟（每日雷打不动地去看望退休的厨娘），这么死板难免让人有点不耐烦（a certain impatience）。

我从陪伴我们的宠物身上看到了和我们一样的推理过程，看到了同样古老且致命的是非间的冲突，还看到了自由的天性和死板的习惯间的冲突；我在它们身上看到了我们人类的诸多弱点，比如虚荣、虚假，虽偶尔与贪婪为敌，却不能一以贯之；也和我们一样，靠着那一点美德，追求梦想矢志不渝……

——《狗性》

The Character of Dogs (3)

There are not many dogs like this good Coolin. and not many people. But the type is one well marked, both in the human and the canine family. Gallantry was not his aim, but a solid and somewhat oppressive respectability.[65] He was a sworn foe to the unusual and the conspicuous, a praiser of the golden mean, a kind of city uncle modified by Cheeryble.[66] And as he was precise and conscientious in all the steps of his own blameless course, he looked for the same precision and an even greater gravity in the bearing of his deity, my father. It was no sinecure to be Coolin's idol; he was exacting like a rigid parent; and at every sign of levity in the man whom he respected, he announced loudly the death of virtue and the proximate fall of the pillars of the earth.[67]

I have called him a snob; but all dogs are so, though in varying degrees. It is hard to follow their snobbery among themselves; for though I think we can perceive distinctions of rank, we cannot grasp what is the criterion. Thus in Edinburgh, in a good part of the town, there were several distinct societies or clubs that met in the morning to—the phrase is technical—to "rake the backets" in a troop.[68] A friend of mine, the master of three dogs, was one day surprised to observe that they had left one club and joined another; but whether it was a rise or a fall, and the result of an invitation or an expulsion, was more than he could guess. And this illustrates pointedly our ignorance of the real life of dogs, their social

狗性（三）

像酷林这样的好狗不多，这样的好人也很少。但此类生灵特征明显，人狗皆然。在异性面前展绅士风度本身并非酷林的目的，那只是一种为它赢得尊敬的行为，尽管这种行为也使它失去不少自由。酷林是异类犬和出众狗的死敌，它赞扬中庸，有点像狄更斯小说中切尔以布兄弟那样助人为乐的城市大叔。在它无懈可击的一生中，一步步都走得准确无误、严肃认真，因此它也要求我父亲的行为同样精准，甚至更为认真，尽管我父亲是它膜拜的神！要作为酷林的偶像，挂个名是不够的；它严苛起来像位死板的家长；它尊崇的那个人一有轻浮之举，它就大声疾呼美德不再、地陷天崩。

我称它为势利之徒，但所有的狗都势利，只不过程度不同。要想理解狗与狗之间的势利非常不易；因为尽管能看出狗的等级不同，但划分等级的标准是什么我们却不得而知。所以在爱丁堡，城里一个不错的地段，有几个独特的狗社团或俱乐部，在那里狗上午聚在一起挑拣废物垃圾。我的一个朋友，养了三条狗，一天惊讶地发现，他的三条狗一起退出一群，再入另群；但是这一退一入到底是高升还是低就，是因新群邀请还是旧群驱赶，他毫无所知。这显然说明我们对狗的真实生活、社会抱负、社会等级并无所知。至少在与人的来往中，它们不仅有性别的考虑，也有地位的掂量。而且

ambitions and their social hierarchies. At least, in their dealings with men they are not only conscious of sex, but of the difference of station. And that in the most snobbish manner; for the poor man's dog is not offended by the notice of the rich, and keeps all his ugly feeling for those poorer or more ragged than his master.[69] And again, for every station they have an ideal of behaviour, to which the master, under pain of derogation,[70] will do wisely to conform. How often has not a cold glance of an eye informed me that my dog was disappointed; and how much more gladly would he not have taken a beating than to be thus wounded in the seat of piety![71]

I knew one disrespectable dog. He was far liker a cat;[72] cared little or nothing for men, with whom he merely coexisted as we do with cattle, and was entirely devoted to the art of poaching. A house would not hold him, and to live in a town was what he refused.[73] He led, I believe, a life of troubled but genuine pleasure, and perished beyond all question in a trap. But this was an exception, a marked reversion to the ancestral type;[74] like the hairy human infant. The true dog of the nineteenth century, to judge by the remainder of my fairly large acquaintance, is in love with respectability. A street-dog was once adopted by a lady. While still an Arab,[75] he had done as Arabs do, gambolling in the mud, charging into butchers' stalls, a cat-hunter, a sturdy beggar, a common rogue and vagabond; but with his rise into society he laid aside these inconsistent pleasures. He stole no more, he hunted no more cats; and conscious of his collar he ignored his old companions. Yet the canine upper class was never brought to recognize the upstart, and from that hour, except for human countenance, he was alone. Friendless, shorn of his sports and the habits of a lifetime, he still lived in a glory of happiness,[76] content with his acquired respectability, and

是狗眼看人，势利之极；穷人的狗并不讨厌看到富人，它会把所有的丑恶心情留着发泄给比它主子更贫穷或更衣衫褴褛的人。而且狗还会为不同的地位配以相应的举止，对此狗主人也只能屈尊，知趣地和狗一样按地位定举止。不知有多少次狗的冷眼告诉我，它失望了；它是更乐于挨一顿痛打，也不想看到它膜拜的主人让它失望，使它心中受伤！

我知道有那么一只不在乎体面的狗。它更像猫，对人几乎毫不关注，与人在一起仅是共存，就像人与牛共存一样，它完全专注于窃取。一间房屋圈不住它，一座城镇它也嫌不够大。我相信，它虽不无糟心之事，但却过着真正快乐的生活，后来显然是被捕捉其他动物的夹子给夹死了。但这是个例外，那狗完全回归了野性，就像长毛发的婴儿一样。我还观察过很多我不很熟悉的狗，得出的结论是，真正19世纪的狗都爱体面顾尊严。某次一位女士收养了一条街上的流浪狗。流浪街头时，这狗和所有的流浪狗一样，在泥巴里乱跑，直冲入肉铺，还捉猫，乞食，整个一个歹徒。可一旦它进入上等人的狗圈子，就把这些曾给它带来快乐却与其新身份不符的恶习抛弃了。它不再偷窃，也不再捉猫；意识到项圈在身，它便开始无视那些老玩伴了。但是狗的上流社会却从来不接纳它这个新贵。从那一刻开始，除了人的垂顾，它十分孤独。它没有朋友，没有捕抓猎物的机会，也不能回到原本习惯的生活，可它却仍然生活在快乐之中，满足于赢得的体面与尊严，并庄严地维护这份尊严，其他的它毫不在乎。我们是要谴责这只靠自己赢得尊严的狗还是要赞扬

with no care but to support it solemnly.[77] Are we to condemn or praise this self-made dog? We praise his human brother. And thus to conquer vicious habits is as rare with dogs as with men. With the more part, for all their scruple-mongering and moral thought, the vices that are born with them remain invincible throughout; and they live all their years, glorying in their virtues,[78] but still the slaves of their defects. Thus the sage Coolin was a thief to the last; among a thousand peccadilloes, a whole goose and a whole cold leg of mutton lay upon his conscience;[79] but Woggs, whose soul's shipwreck in the matter of gallantry[80] I have recounted above, has only twice been known to steal, and has often nobly conquered the temptation. The eighth is his favourite commandment. There is something painfully human in these unequal virtues and mortal frailties of the best.[81] Still more painful is the bearing of those "stammering professors"[82] in the house of sickness and under the terror of death. It is beyond a doubt to me that, somehow or other, the dog connects together, or confounds, the uneasiness of sickness and the consciousness of guilt.[83] To the pains of the body he often adds the tortures of the conscience; and at these times his haggard protestations form, in regard to the human deathbed, a dreadful parody or parallel.[84]

I once supposed that I had found an inverse relation between the double etiquette which dogs obey;[85] and that those who were most addicted to the showy street life among other dogs were less careful in the practice of home virtues for the tyrant man. But the female dog, that mass of carneying affections,[86] shines equally in either sphere; rules her rough posse of attendant swains with unwearying tact and gusto; and with her master and mistress pushes the arts of insinuation to their crowning point.

它呢？同样的情况，我们是会赞扬它人类的兄弟的。可见不管是人是狗，战胜恶习者仅是凤毛麟角。不仅如此，它们虽考虑周全、有道德考量，但那些与生俱来的恶习其实是它们始终都无法战胜的；它们一生都因自己的美德而自鸣得意，但却仍是自身瑕疵的奴隶。因此圣者酷林一直到最后仍是一个小偷；轻罪数不胜数，外加一只全鹅、一条冷羊腿让它羞不胜羞；但是沃格斯这只狗，就是我前面提到过的那只讨好母狗未果而伤透心的狗，目前所知偷窃的勾当仅有两次，算是高尚地抵御了诱惑。"十大诫命"中的第八条是它的最爱：你不可偷窃。就算是在最优秀的狗身上，美德和弱点一强一弱地并存，这一来透露出狗有人性，也不免让人为狗而悲哀。而更令人看了悲哀的是，狗在病痛缠身、面对死神恐吓时的行为。毫无疑问，我觉得不知怎么的，狗既有肉体的痛苦，也有良心的煎熬。它常在肉体的痛苦之上再加上良心的煎熬；而在这种受痛苦受煎熬的时刻，狗忍受肉体或心灵折磨的痛苦状和人之将死时的痛苦状真像得令人可怕。

我曾觉得狗在街上和家里的行为恰恰相反；和其他的狗相比，那些酷爱街上多彩生活的狗不会一丝不苟地去实践严酷的人所立下的家庭美德。但是母狗，那个善于讨好会耍手腕的动物，却在街上和家里同样表现出色；她不断地以老练和热忱掌控着那一群会闹腾的跟班公狗；而在她的主人和主妇那里，又会把曲意奉承的艺术发挥到极致。人的垂顾和其他狗的关注似乎同样能让狗得意洋洋；但如果我们能读懂狗的内心，我们也许就能发现它们阿谀奉承的程度

The attention of man and the regard of other dogs flatter (it would thus appear) the same sensibility; but perhaps, if we could read the canine heart, they would be found to flatter it in very marked degrees.[87] Dogs live with man as courtiers round a monarch, steeped in the flattery of his notice and enriched with sinecures. To push their favour in this world of pickings and caresses is, perhaps, the business of their lives; and their joys may lie outside. I am in despair at our persistent ignorance. I read in the lives of our companions the same processes of reason, the same antique and fatal conflicts of the right against the wrong, and of unbitted nature with too rigid custom; I see them with our weaknesses, vain, false, inconstant against appetite, and with our one stalk of virtue, devoted to the dream of an ideal;[88] and yet, as they hurry by me on the street with tail in air, or come singly to solicit my regard, I must own the secret purport of their lives is still inscrutable to man. Is man the friend, or is he the patron only? Have they indeed forgotten nature's voice? or are those moments snatched from courtiership when they touch noses with the tinker's mongrel,[89] the brief reward and pleasure of their artificial lives? Doubtless, when man shares with his dog the toils of a profession and the pleasures of an art, as with the shepherd or the poacher, the affection warms and strengthens till it fills the soul.[90] But doubtless, also, the masters are, in many cases, the object of a merely interested cultus, sitting aloft like Louis Quatorze,[91] giving and receiving flattery and favour; and the dogs, like the majority of men, have but forgotten their true existence and become the dupes of their ambition.[92]

是明显不同的。狗与人同住，恰似臣子围绕于君王，因深得主子关注而开心，同时也获利颇丰。在这个用尽手段邀宠获利的世界里，尽量受惠也许是它们的生存之道，求快乐反倒不在这营生之内。我们对此竟持续无知，这实令我绝望。我从陪伴我们的宠物身上看到了和我们一样的推理过程，看到了同样古老且致命的是非间的冲突，还看到了自由的天性和死板的习惯间的冲突；我在它们身上看到了我们人类的诸多弱点，比如虚荣、虚假，虽偶尔与贪婪为敌，却不能一以贯之；也和我们一样，靠着那一点美德，追求梦想矢志不渝；可是，看着它们在大街上急冲冲在我身边走过，尾巴翘到天上，或独自走过来邀我的关注，我必须承认，它们生活的秘密目的对于人来说仍然是高深莫测的。人类到底是它们的朋友，还是说只是恩主？难道它们真的把天性泯灭殆尽？难道当这些尊贵的狗和铁匠的杂种狗鼻子相碰时，它们暂已摆脱了看地位、求尊贵那一套，在矫揉造作的生活中享受起短暂的欢愉快乐？无疑，当人和狗分担职业的艰辛或分享艺技的快乐时，就像牧羊人和狗或偷猎者和狗同担艰辛或同享快乐一样，定会生出深深的感情。但是同样无疑的是，在很多情况下，主人才是唯一膜拜的对象，他像路易十四那样高高在上地坐着，有时说几句奉承话，施舍些恩惠，当然也有满耳的奉承，满满的收获；而狗，就像大多数的人一样，早已忘掉了自己真正的身份，为成就抱负而沦为任人摆布的傀儡。

注　释

65. 这个 a solid and somewhat oppressive respectability 很不好翻译，原因是首先它很不好理解。这个词组在语境中是这样的"Gallantry was not his aim, but a respectability"。显然在这里 respectability 是可数的，是一种"东西"，由于我们还无法界定这到底是个什么东西，数量词是什么也不清楚，暂且用"一种"。我们在"Despised Races"一文的注释30讲到过动词转变成名词的两种情况：一种仍然保持较多动词特征（像活动的电影），另外一种已完全获得了名词特征（像静止的照片），可以加上冠词或变成复数。我们这里的 a respectability 就是可数的。那么这个 respectability 到底是什么？译者可以从前面的主语那里得到启发，gallantry 是生活行为，所以 respectability 也是一种行为，这种行为是可以受 respect 的。确实 gallantry 是一种受人尊敬的行为。那什么是 oppressive respectability？这里我们发现奈达的"解包袱法"非常有用（参见叶子南《高级英汉理论与实践》，58页）。如果这个名词的源头是及物动词（respect），那么就可以找出逻辑的主语和宾语。也就是说，谁尊敬谁？在这里受到尊敬的是 gallantry 这个行为，尊敬来自人，或者说在那个维多利亚时代，这种行为是人们期待的，因而受到尊重。用同样的思路，oppressive 这个形容词也有其逻辑的主语和宾语，也就是这个 respectability 的行为是压迫的源头（注意是 oppressive，不是 oppressed），被压迫的是做出这种行为的人。那么做出这种行为的人怎么会感到受压迫呢？因为 gallantry 不是一种放松自己的自由行为,是社会规范下的做作举止,导致人的天性和社会规范之间出现张力。举例来说,当时的社会绅士得戴手套,但不喜欢社会规范的人就是不喜欢戴手套,他们会说,我只在天冷时戴手套。严守社会规范的人就会在某种意义上受到约束(oppressed),而那个社会的规范就是 oppressive 的。那什么是 solid respectability?可以将 solid 解释为 firm,即赢得这种尊敬是较稳当的,换句话说,狗已经彻底按社会规范行事,因此无疑会获得尊敬(you have followed all the required "rules" and so you are now unquestionably "respectable")。这样,a solid and somewhat oppressive respectability 就得到了合理的解释,翻译的时候译者有很大的活动空间:"在异性面前展绅士风度本身并非酷林的目的,那只是一种为它赢得尊敬的行为,尽管这种行为也使它失去不少自由。"

66. 这一句进一步说明这个酷林狗是什么样的狗。有些狗是 the unusual and the conspicuous,也就是说,那些狗不同于一般的狗,而是与众不同的异类,酷林是那些狗的死敌。同时它也主张做事要规矩,不过分(the golden mean),加之,它就是 a kind of city uncle modified by Cheeryble。city uncle 是城市(此处也许特指伦敦)中有一定地位、乐于为别人建言的好人,Cheeryble 则指狄更斯小说《尼古拉斯·尼克尔贝》(*Nicholas Nickleby*)中的孪生兄弟,为人古道热肠,是助人为乐的典范。这里的 modified 表示 city uncle 的为人特征也被后面的孪生兄弟的行为所"修正",可以说成是兼有后者古道热肠气质的城市大叔。

67. 这一长句主要是说酷林见不得它尊敬的人犯错,一旦看到自己膜拜的对象干出什么不当的事儿,就像我们一般说的,那是天塌下来了。

68. 这里的 backets 是苏格兰语，指装东西的容器，也就是目前常说的垃圾箱之类的东西，rake the backets 就是在挑垃圾里可以吃的东西，in a troop 就是指群狗。至于 the phrase is technical 这部分可以不翻译，因为这个短语在当时是所谓的"技术用语"，但在当前的语言中已失去其专业的意义了。

69. 这里的语言问题需要指出。这个开头的 and 是起到承接前面一句的作用，而接下来的 and that in the most snobbish manner，是在说前面 their dealings with men，也就是说，在与人打交道时，显得最为势利。而接下来的 for the poor man's dog… 就是具体的势利做法了。另外要注意这个分号。斯蒂文森在写作中大量使用分号（；），这也许是维多利亚时代一些作者的写作特征，但是目前在同样的场合，一般会使用逗号（，）。译者翻译的时候，可以根据情况自由处理，不排除在有些场合保留分号，但是不少场合，换成逗号更合适。

70. 这里 derogation 有贬低自己的意思（OED: falling off in rank, character, or excellence; loss of rank; deterioration, debasement），也就是说，主人也只能像狗一样 conform to an ideal of behaviour for every station，即像狗一样势利，这显然是痛苦的（under pain）。

71. 这一长句包含两个以 how 开头的分句，但这都不是问句。这句本来并不难理解，可是由于用了 not 一词，结果很可能造成理解错误。其实这话的意思是它失望了、受伤了。这种有否定词，却没有否定意思的表达法，在当时维多利亚时代的作品中不少，斯蒂文森的作品中也常见，比如，"what a strange dissimilarity must there not have been in these pictures of the mind"

的意思也是相反的（详见"Despised Races"篇注释 23）。这句中的 in the seat of piety 是在说狗，说狗情愿挨一顿揍，也不想在 the seat of piety 的位置上受到伤害。piety 就是指狗对斯蒂文森父亲的那种虔诚近乎宗教。若翻译成"在虔诚的位置上受到伤害"意思并不错，但是比较费解，为了帮助读者，参考译文采用了解释性的译法："也不想看到它膜拜的主人让它失望，使它心中受伤！"目前文学译文中常可见到这类看似很准确，但是非常难懂的句子，一般的建议是：最好抛弃 in the seat of piety 的形式特征，采用读者容易懂的译法，毕竟这个语言形式无大意义。

72. 这里的 far liker 可能是笔误，或是作者自己的一种不规范的写法。其实这句的基本意思就是"He was very much like a cat"。

73. 这句是在说，这狗嫌屋子小，也嫌城镇小，它希望更广阔的乡村旷野，即仍然保有野性。句中的 to live in a town 有人认为有《圣经》语言的影子（"Then they will have towns to live in and pasturelands for the cattle they own and all their other animals."— Numbers 35: 3）。

74. 这个 ancestral type 指的是 the original type，也就是"原始的、野性的"意思。说明这只狗又返回到了（reversion to）被家养前的状态，就像人一样，我们身上都不长毛，但是如果一个人身上长起毛来（like the hairy human infant），那也是返回到原始的状态。

75. Arabs 一般可以指无家可归的人，特别是孩子（A homeless child or young person living on the streets），有时也叫 street Arab 或叫 city Arab，此处则指流浪狗。

76. in the glory of happiness 在这里的基本意思就是 enjoying happiness。

有一个短语 bask in the glory of something，意思就是 enjoy something。这里虽然没有 bask 这个词，但大意也是接近的。其实 glory 当动词用时也是这个意思（to take great pleasure or pride in something）。译者没有必要硬去把 glory 这个词翻译出来。

77. 这里的 it（support it solemnly）指前面的 respectability。这里的 but（but to support it）是 except 的意思。

78. 这里的 glorying in their virtues，就是 take great pleasure in something，比如"He just glories in all the attention he is getting"。（参考注释 76）

79. 这句中的 among 可以说一下。这个介词有多个意思，但有两个意思需要区分一下。其中一个是表示在某人或某物之内的，是其中的一员（If someone or something is among a group, they are a member of that group），如"Also among the speakers was the new American ambassador to Moscow"。还有一个意思是被什么包围（surrounded by; in the company of），比如"you're among friends"，you 本身不在朋友之列。我们这个句子应该是后者的意思，因为 a whole goose and a whole cold leg of mutton 应该不是 peccadilloes。

80. 这个 Woggs 是斯蒂文森最心爱的一只狗。作者和这狗的感情颇深，后来狗死了，斯蒂文森从此不愿意再养狗。这句中的 shipwreck 是隐喻说法，就是一样东西毁坏、失去了等意思，如"The only Plank left me in the Shipwreck of my Soul"或"Agrippina was maddened by the shipwreck of her ambition"，都说明一样东西（soul 或者 ambition）毁坏了、没有了。如果说精神或灵魂 shipwrecked，可以看作是受到伤害、毁坏、失去功能，就像船在大海中坏掉一样。在这个语境中，翻译时故意去保留这个船坏了的隐喻是没有意义的，建议这类情况都可采用解释性的意义。那么不翻译隐喻怎么把 shipwreck 的意思说出来呢？由于泛指的 shipwreck 在现实中可以延伸解释的范围很广，具体怎么选词就得和具体的语境联系起来。作者在这句中提到了这只狗遭遇 shipwreck 的事件是 in the matter of gallantry，也就是前面提到的那只可以在母狗面前表现优秀，却不招待见的那些事儿，这狗后来突然还发了一阵脾气，但还是改过来了，又善良起来了。这就是它的 shipwreck，它是求尊重不得，伤心之极啊！所以可以将这个词集中浓缩成 heart broken。假如翻译成"在讨好母狗的过程中精神受到毁坏"，读者是看不懂你在说什么的。所以还是不用脱离语境的译法，改成结合语境的译法更好："就是我前面提到过的那只讨好母狗未果而伤透心的狗"。

81. 我们经常见到用副词修饰形容词的结构，有些较容易翻译，有些就得琢磨一下，比如这里的 painfully human 就需要琢磨一下。首先 there is something human in these virtues and frailties，直接说就是，在狗的这些美德和弱点中有人的东西，大白话就是见了狗的这些美德和弱点，觉得这和人一样啊！狗居然和人一样能彰显人性，也能暴露人一样的弱点。那么为什么是 painfully human 呢？痛在何处？这至少可以从两方面解释，首先可悲可痛之处就是让人感到狗也和人一样有痛苦的经历（接下来的句子就是讲狗的痛苦），其次让人感到悲痛的是，狗和人一样总是战胜不了自己的弱点，也就是说美德和弱点，总是弱点多于美德，也就是这里说的 unequal virtues and mortal frailties。这个 unequal 在语言上会有歧义，到底是 virtues 或 frailties 内不平等呢，还是 virtues 和 frailties 之间不平等？参考译文采用第二种解释，即美德和弱点之间的不平衡。考虑到这篇文章中多次提到狗和人一样总是战胜不了自己的弱点，所以这个 unequal 还是理解成 frailties 强于 virtues 更合理些。这样解释也符合本句的语境，人悲痛的一个原因也可以是看到了邪强正弱（unequal）的结果。翻译时若求稳妥，可以翻译成"美德和弱点不平衡地并存"。若大胆一点把语境考虑进去，也可以翻译成"美德和弱点一强一弱地并存"。参考译文在处理这句时采用了比较自由的方法，加大了解释的力度："在最优秀的狗身上，美德和弱点一强一弱地并存，这一来透露出狗有人性，也不免让人为狗而悲哀"。悲哀的原因上面解释了，但是这些具体的解释内容不宜引入译文，这一来是因为都是主观的揣测，二来也是为了坚守翻译的基本定义，译者仍然希望在翻译和阐释之间画出一条界线，尽管这条线译者偶尔也会迈过去。

82. 注意此处的 stammering professor 是指狗，professor 的词义和教授没有任何关系，因这个词还可以指 "a person who makes open profession of religion, esp. a professing Christian"。在我们这个语境中词的表面意思是指基督徒，但由于有引号，所以在指狗，有比喻的意思。至于 stammering 这个词，它是以一种调侃的语气形容那类宗教人士讲话时的迂腐样子。在这类翻译中直译实在无必要，译成狗更清楚。这句中的 the bearing 是指狗的行为举止。

83. 这里的 the consciousness of guilt 是指狗在作恶后内心有的负疚感，比如偷食了东西后的负疚感。当然这些都是作者自己的揣测。另外，这句和下面那句（To the pains of the body he often adds the tortures of the conscience）意思基本是类似的。

84. 首先是这个 haggard protestations，这个名词来源于动词 protest，有对某事表示抵抗的意思。在这个语境中，狗显然在抵抗一些东西，比如和其他狗打架时腿被咬伤了，疼痛难忍，此时抵抗的就是病痛（the pains of the body）；或一块羊排放在厨房的桌子上，主人刚好不在，实在想吃，但又觉得吃了有损尊严，此时抵抗的是欲望（the consciousness of guilt）。这些"抵抗"的结果最后都反映在脸部或其他肢体动作上。鉴于修饰这个名词的 haggard 一般都形容脸部表情，所以 protestations 解释成脸部表情（a look resulting from protesting/resisting）似乎合理。这种动词变名词的特征在认知语言学上有很好的解释，在本书多处都提到，可参见注释65。另外这里的 a dreadful parody or parallel 也需要解释一下。parody 或 parallel 一般不可能单独存在，应该有和这个词对应的词，也就是 protestations form a parody or parallel 后面跟的是什么（form a parody of something 或 form a parallel to something）？此句的意思就是狗的悲痛表情和人的表情非常相像，所以这里的 in regard to the human deathbed 似乎是比照对象（the protestations form a dreadful parody of, or parallel to, the human deathbed）。最后，dreadful 是修饰 parody 或者 parallel 的，说明可怕的是狗和人看上去非常相像（what is dreadful is the way the dog looks like a human being on a deathbed）。这也反映了整篇散文的目的，狗和人在多方面是相似的。

85. 这里的 the double etiquette 就是下面那半句中的 addicted to the showy street life 和 in the practice of home virtues 这两项活动。如果在街上（street life）和在家里（home virtues）都是一样积极，那就不是这里说的 inverse。但显然这里是在街上积极，

在家里急慢，才称之为 inverse relation。此句的翻译也需要译者掂量，如果直译成"双重礼仪之间的反向关系"，更像科技译文的语言，而且读者估计也看不懂是什么意思。就算是看到下面一句看懂了这句，也会十分吃力。参考译文选用了意译的方法，简单明白："狗在街上和家里的行为恰恰相反"。

86. 这个 the mass 指的是 the female dog，后面的 carneying affectations 都是修饰这母狗的。形容词 carneying 和我们熟悉的 carnival 同源（A carnival of something such as colours or sounds is a bright or exciting mixture of them），但在这里词义略不同，表示忽悠哄骗的意思。而名词 affections 也是虚假做作的意思，两个词生动地刻画了会耍手段的母狗。

87. 首先这里的 it（flatter it in very marked degrees）指的是前面的 heart。这个 marked 的意思就是 noticeable，但说的是两种情况的明显不同（注意这里是复数的 degrees）。也就是说，人的关注和其他狗的关注所产生的作用是不一样的，所以可以看成是 different 的意思。

88. 梳理一下这句的语法结构对翻译有好处。句子的主干是"I see them with our weaknesses"，后面的应看作是具体的 weaknesses，但是这些具体的弱点都是以形容词或分词的形式出现的（vain、false、inconstant against、devoted），但是后面两个词都带一个短语（前一个是 against appetite，后一个有两个短语 with our one stalk of virtue 和 to the dream of an ideal），所以翻译的时候应该扩展成句子才能表达清楚。

89. 这句是在说那些脱离了野性的狗（forgotten nature's voice）。动词 snatched from 表示"被拿走"的意思。tinker's mongrel 是一种地位非常低下的杂交狗，tinker 在过去常是居无定所的人。

当一个对尊贵孜孜以求的狗在街上和一个被人看不起的杂交狗鼻子碰鼻子时，那个为求尊贵而养成的习惯（courtiership）就那么短暂地被去掉了（snatched from）。

90. 这里的 as with the shepherd or the poacher 千万不要和前面的 shares with 连起来，因为这个和前面的 shares 无关。这个应该理解成 as with the case of the shepherd or the poacher。这句的意思是说，人和狗在工作和愉悦过程中会产生情感，就像牧羊人和狗或偷猎者和狗在他们的互动中会产生情感一样。牧羊人在把羊群圈起来的过程中就常与狗互动，偷猎者在偷猎的过程中也和狗有互动，比如狗帮助他把猎物拿到手，同时偷猎者也会分享一些食物给狗，这个过程中有 toils，也有 pleasures，进而产生了情感。说明狗是有人性的，这也正是本文的主题。

91. 这是指法国的统治者路易十四，他在位时无视人民的疾苦，也因此为后来的法国革命埋下伏笔。前一句作者在说人和狗之间的亲密关系（affection warms and strengthens），但是作者马上补上这句，他同样确信（doubtless, also），人这个主子在很多场合对于膜拜他们的狗是不在乎的，就像路易十四高高在上（sitting aloft like Louis Quatorze）不在乎人民一样。

92. 如果直译 the dupes of their ambition 的话，就是"它们雄心的傻瓜"，显然这样会给读者造成不少困难。为了使表达符合汉语习惯，进而提高可读性，我们不应停留在直译的层面，而应该把词之间蕴含的意思补充进去，比如加几个词："为成就抱负而沦为任人摆布的傻瓜"。

Books Which Have Influenced Me (1)

The Editor has somewhat insidiously[1] laid a trap for his correspondents, the question put appearing at first so innocent, truly cutting so deep[2]. It is not, indeed, until after some reconnaissance and review[3] that the writer awakes to find himself engaged upon something in the nature of autobiography[4], or, perhaps worse, upon a chapter in the life of that little, beautiful brother[5] whom we once all had, and whom we have all lost and mourned, the man we ought to have been, the man we hoped to be. But when word has been passed (even to an editor), it should, if possible, be kept; and if sometimes I am wise and say too little, and sometimes weak and say too much[6], the blame must lie at the door of the person who entrapped me.

The most influential books, and the truest in their influence, are works of fiction. They do not pin the reader to a dogma, which he must afterwards discover to be inexact; they do not teach him a lesson, which he must afterwards unlearn. They repeat, they rearrange, they clarify the lessons of life; they disengage us from ourselves, they constrain us to the acquaintance of others; and they show us the web of experience, not as we can see it for ourselves, but with a singular change—that monstrous, consuming ego of ours being, for the nonce, struck out[7]. To be so, they must be reasonably true to the human comedy; and any work that is so serves the turn of instruction[8]. But the course of our education is answered best by those poems and romances where we breathe a

那些影响了我的书(一)

编辑先生为作者设了个套,提的问题乍一看很简单,但实则令人伤痛。作者是在做了一番回顾与思考后,才突然如梦初醒,原来自己是被要求写自传类的东西,甚或更糟,明明是写人生的一章,而写的是那位英俊青年,那位我们曾经有过,现在失去、已在哀悼的年轻人,那个我们本应就是、希望能是的人。不过,一言既出,岂能反悔(即便是向编辑的承诺也该信守)。假如有时我精明老成,守口如瓶,或有时疏于自控,滔滔不绝,读者诸君千万要把牢骚发向给我设套的那位。

最有影响的书,最有真正影响的书,是小说。小说不把读者绑在教条上,而教条你定会在日后发现并不正确;小说也不为你说教上课,而那些说教日后都得抛弃。小说重复、重组、澄清人生的教训;小说让人走出自己的生活,去熟悉他人的世界,向我们展示错综复杂的人生经历,却不用我们亲身目睹体验,而是做一个角色转变,暂且甩掉那巨大强烈的自我意识。要这样做,小说就必须真实反映这个人间喜剧。任何这样的作品都能起到教育人的作用。但是最能教育人的作品却是诗歌与传奇作品,读这类作品能让我们呼吸高尚思想的空气,邂逅慷慨虔诚的人物。莎士比亚最使我受

magnanimous atmosphere of thought and meet generous and pious characters. Shakespeare has served me best. Few living friends have had upon me an influence so strong for good as Hamlet or Rosalind. The last character, already well beloved in the reading, I had the good fortune to see, I must think, in an impressionable hour[9], played by Mrs. Scott Siddons. Nothing has ever more moved, more delighted, more refreshed me; nor has the influence quite passed away. Kent's brief speech over the dying Lear had a great effect upon my mind, and was the burthen[10] of my reflections for long, so profoundly, so touchingly generous did it appear in sense, so overpowering in expression[11]. Perhaps my dearest and best friend outside of Shakespeare is D'Artagnan—the elderly D'Artagnan of the *Vicomte de Bragelonne*. I know not a more human soul, nor, in his way, a finer; I shall be very sorry for the man[12] who is so much of a pedant in morals that he cannot learn from the Captain of Musketeers. Lastly, I must name the *Pilgrim's Progress*, a book that breathes[13] of every beautiful and valuable emotion.

But of works of art little can be said; their influence is profound and silent, like the influence of nature; they mould by contact[14]; we drink them up like water, and are bettered, yet know not how. It is in books more specifically didactic that we can follow out the effect, and distinguish and weigh and compare[15]. A book which has been very influential upon me fell early into my hands, and so may stand first, though I think its influence was only sensible later on, and perhaps still keeps growing, for it is a book not easily outlived: the *Essais of Montaigne*. That temperate and genial picture of life is a great gift to place in the hands of persons of to-day; they will find in these smiling pages a magazine[16] of heroism and wisdom, all of an

益。若论对我影响至深至远的人物，现在活着的友人中很少能与哈姆雷特、罗莎琳德比肩。书中的罗莎琳德我已深爱，而戏中的罗莎琳德，我也在年轻易动情时有幸目睹，扮演者竟是演这个角色的不二人选斯科特·西登斯夫人。那种感动，那种愉悦，那种清新，我再也没有感受过，对我的影响至今犹存。在李尔王即将死去时，肯特简短的话令我震撼，在我思绪中长久低回萦绕，那话显得言者特别慷慨宽厚，感人至深，也表达得力有千钧。除莎士比亚外，我最珍爱的朋友当数《布拉热洛纳子爵》里年老的达达尼昂。我觉得没有一个人能比他更有仁心，能像他那样完美。若一个人道德迂腐之极，竟至于不能向火枪手队长学习为人之道，那我真要为他感到可怜。最后，我得提《天路历程》这本书，书中散发出既优雅又珍贵的情感。

但若论文学艺术作品，可说的并不多。这类作品影响深远，但却大作无声，恰如大自然的影响潜移默化。你接触作品，作品将你磨塑；读这类书如饮水，读者会在不知不觉中受益。只有专事道德教诲的书才能让我们条析缕陈书本对人的影响，才能将这种影响加以区别、权衡、比较。对我影响至深的一本书恰好是我早年阅读的，所以可能先被想到，但其影响却到后来才显现，可能至今仍与日俱增，这是一本能让你终生受益的书，我说的是《蒙田随笔》。那种温文和煦的生活画卷是给当代人的一件绝佳礼物，今天的人会在这些欢快的书页间感受到满溢的英雄情怀和聪颖智慧，品味出古雅的韵味。读了这随笔，人们会对体面的社会习俗和强烈的正统观

antique strain; they will have their 'linen decencies' and excited orthodoxies fluttered[17], and will (if they have any gift of reading) perceive that these have not been fluttered without some excuse and ground of reason[18]; and (again if they have any gift of reading) they will end[19] by seeing that this old gentleman was in a dozen ways a finer fellow, and held in a dozen ways a nobler view of life, than they or their contemporaries.

The next book, in order of time, to influence me, was the New Testament, and in particular the Gospel according to St. Matthew. I believe it would startle and move any one if they could make a certain effort of imagination and read it freshly like a book, not droningly and dully like a portion of the Bible[20]. Any one would then be able to see in it those truths which we are all courteously supposed to know and all modestly refrain from applying[21]. But upon this subject it is perhaps better to be silent.

I come next to Whitman's *Leaves of Grass*, a book of singular service, a book which tumbled the world upside down for me, blew into space a thousand cobwebs of genteel and ethical illusion, and, having thus shaken my tabernacle of lies, set me back again upon a strong foundation of all the original and manly virtues[22]. But it is, once more, only a book for those who have the gift of reading. I will be very frank—I believe it is so with all good books except, perhaps, fiction. The average man lives, and must live, so wholly in convention, that gun-powder charges of the truth are more apt to discompose than to invigorate his creed[23]. Either he cries out upon blasphemy and indecency, and crouches the closer round that little idol of part-truths and part-conveniences which is the contemporary deity, or he is convinced by what is new, forgets what is old, and becomes truly blasphemous and indecent himself.[24] New truth is only useful to

念产生怀疑，而且还能发现这种怀疑不无道理（当然他们得有阅读天赋），而他们最终会明白，这位老先生不管从哪方面看都是位好人，都观念高尚，当代人望尘莫及（当然这也要看读者有没有阅读天赋）。

按时间顺序算，下一本影响我的书是《新约》，特别是其中的《马太福音》。我想，如果读者能发挥些想象，用全新的目光把《新约》当书来读，而不是当经来念，那么任何人读后都会倍感惊异、深受感动。任何人都会在书中看见那些人们理应知道却又谦逊地不去实践的真理。不过讲到这个题目，可能我还是少说为妙。

下一本影响我的书是惠特曼的《草叶集》，一本作用独特的书，一本颠覆我对世界看法的书，它打破了无数道貌岸然的幻想，动摇了我谎言盘踞的圣殿，使我再次回到一个坚实的基础上，重拾本真与阳刚的美德。但阅读这本书又需要读者具有天赋。恕我坦言，我觉得除小说外，所有的好书都要求读者有阅读天赋。普通人生活在传统中，而且必须那样生活，因此井喷似的真理与其说能让芸芸众生信念倍增，还不如说会让这些人信心崩溃。他要么面对亵渎和猥亵高声挞伐，匍匐在半是真理半是为己的小偶像周围（这尊神时下拜者如云），要么他完全确信新东西，彻底忘掉旧传统，那自己也就真成了亵渎猥亵之辈了。新真理只能用来补充旧真理。粗犷的真理只是用来扩充，而非毁掉我们文明且雅致的传统。一个人若是不能在阅读中加以辨别，那么他最好还是去读小说和日报。读这些东

supplement the old; rough truth is only wanted to expand, not to destroy, our civil and often elegant conventions. He who cannot judge had better stick to fiction and the daily papers. There he will get little harm, and, in the first at least, some good[25].

Close upon the back of my discovery of Whitman, I came under the influence of Herbert Spencer. No more persuasive rabbi exists. How much of his vast structure will bear the touch of time, how much is clay and how much brass, it were too curious to inquire[26]. But his words, if dry, are always manly and honest; there dwells in his pages a spirit of highly abstract joy, plucked naked like an algebraic symbol but still joyful; and the reader will find there a caput mortuum of piety[27], with little indeed of its loveliness, but with most of its essentials; and these two qualities make him a wholesome, as his intellectual vigour makes him a bracing, writer. I should be much of a hound if I lost my gratitude to Herbert Spencer.

西，读者会少有伤害，读小说，至少还能得些好处。

紧接惠特曼后影响我的是赫伯特·斯宾塞。犹太教的拉比说教起来虽然了得，但斯宾塞也不输给他们。他硕大的理论架构中有多少经得住时间考验，多少如土会转瞬瓦解，多少是铜能长久坚实，这些都太艰深难懂，不去深究也罢。但是他的话，即便枯燥，却总是透着英气和真诚；书页中满是高度抽象却又欢乐的精神，抽象得像代数符号，却也充满欢快。在那里读者会发现虔诚只剩下抽象的框架，少有具体鲜活的一面，但虔诚的要件大都存在；而这两个特征使他成为有益健全的作家，恰如其智力的活跃，使他成为令人振奋的作家一样。若我没有对赫伯特·斯宾塞的感激之心，岂不成了忘恩负义的小人。

注 释

1. 本句翻译成"为作者设了个套"基本达意,原文中的 insidiously 一词可以不去翻译,因为该词的基本意思含有 trick 的意味,而"设套"中已包含这个意思。翻译中,不少人会保留这类词,那样当然更准确些,若译文不显得累赘别扭,也可加上去。

2. 这里的"so innocent, truly cutting so deep"显然是指 the question。在选择用什么词翻译之前最好先对这句话的意思有一了解。编辑先生到底提出了什么问题,就是这篇文章的题目,即什么书影响了你?这是个简单的问题,所谓 innocent 就是指一般普普通通的问题,用"简单"就行。但是 cutting so deep 就引出了一个隐喻形象,仿佛有一把刀伤到你了,所以 cutting 必须与伤痛联系起来,即 the question cuts deep。这要与下面的内容联系起来考虑才更清楚(见下面注释 5)。若不造成译文突兀,可直接保留原文的形象,如"尖锐锋利";若觉得那样较突兀,或可间接反映 cutting deep,如"令人伤痛"。其他译法,如"勾起你伤痛的往事""让你回忆起痛苦的过去"等,总显得文字多了些。有人翻译成"击中要害""非常深刻",都不是很符合原文的角度,比如"要害"就提示有打击的目标,但原文仅是一个问题。译成"挖得很深",确实反映了这个问题会使回答者将往事都挖掘出来(deep),但更关键的 cutting 却没有反映出来。此处显然是一个隐喻。

3. 这里的 after some reconnaissance and review 的基本意思就是 after a little thought(仔细想想后)。贴近原文的话,能保留原文的写作特征(在做了一番回顾与思考后)。但是原文的这个语言特征（reconnaissance）无大意义，保留也许能使语言更生动，反映作者的幽默，但是译文也难免有些生硬。另外，本段似乎还不算在回答问题，有点像"引子"，所以和下面几段相比，语言确实更丰富些。但似乎仍然不宜过度强调其文学性，这仅是一位作家回答编辑的文字，传达信息仍是文本的主要目的。

4. 若将 something in the nature of autobiography 仅翻译成"自传"不算最准确。something in the nature 表示接近，并非完全一样，但基本意思到位。

5. 此处的"that little, beautiful brother"以及后面的"the man we ought to have been, the man we hoped to be"其实说的是同一个人。斯蒂文森当年也有过抱负，有过理想，有过目标，他本想成为那个人，本应成为那个人，但人生的境遇并不总是如意。回首过去，斯蒂文森感慨良多，多少事与愿违的结局，多少仰天长叹的往事，于是内心的痛苦油然而生。"我"本无须受这番痛苦，可偏偏编辑先生问"我"这个问题。原本是简简单单的问题，也许有些作者写上三言两语就完事儿，可他不同，他要把为什么某本书影响至深写出来，那就不得不触及心灵深处，于是往事"都随风雨到心头"了，编辑的问题真把他伤着了（cutting so deep）。这里的 we 可以指他自己，当然也可解读成泛指。至于句中的"that little, beautiful brother"原本直译成"英俊的小兄弟"，但是汉语"小兄弟"会引申出另外的意思，后来放弃。若完全根据意思翻译，则可译成"年轻时的我"（这里就是指作者自己），但这样就从第三人称改成了第一人称，偏离了原作者的述说角度，与后面的那个第三人称的 the man 显得不很一致，不过换成"我"的优点是帮助了读者理解，免得读者去琢磨这个小年轻是谁。本译文选用了"那位英俊青年／年轻人",保留了原文第三人称的述说角度,但读者就得自己去理解这年轻人是谁了。说到读者,斯蒂文森曾说:"如果读者没有智慧,不会阅读,那么文字就会沉寂无声,对牛弹琴,作者的秘密就仍然是秘密,就像他根本没有写出来一样。"(文章结束时的一句,本文未选译)你看,译者并非每次都需要把文字嚼烂了喂给读者,有时还是让读者自己嚼一嚼更好!

6. "sometimes I am wise and say too little, and sometimes weak and say too much" 基本是在说有时他知道多说不好,所以不把话全说出来,但是有时实在想说,就说得太多了。wise 的含义比较容易解读,但是 weak 则需要从控制力的角度来解读,强就是能控制住,弱就是控制不住自己言说的欲望。

7. 这句指小说,前面半句是读者读小说不把书中的事当成自己的事,而是 "with a singular change—that monstrous, consuming ego of ours being, for the nonce, struck out",就是把自己的自我暂时从书中抽离出去了,所谓的 change 就是 that ego being struck out。注意动词 -ing 的形式。monstrous 和 consuming 解释起来有很大余地,如前者字典中就有"怪异""丑陋""强烈""巨大"等意思,但此处无非是强调自我或私心之大,"大"是这个字的核心;consuming 也一样,有"消耗""强烈"等意思,此处可选"强烈"。在这样的文本中似乎不必过度雕饰这种词,毕竟意义不大。当然在一个以语言取胜的文本中,译得更形象具体些,也许就更可取。

8. 此处的 the turn (of instruction) 应该表示 purpose,这样较容易和前面的动词搭配(serves the purpose of instruction)。另外,the turn of instruction 和后面的 the course of education 可能会有细微的差别,但是此处最好把它们理解成内容相同但语言有所变换会

更好；也就是说，是一个意思，但老重复不好，于是就换个说法。

9. 本句中的 in an impressionable hour 可能会有点难把握。我们可以至少给出两个非常接近但有细微差别的解释，如可以解释为 when he was young and easily influenced，此时这个时间段是较长的，但是也可以解释为 at a time of his life when he would be really impressed by her performance，此时 at a time of his life 就很难确定其时间段。如果解释为较长的时间段，就可以指他年轻的时候，但是也很难说就不可以指 he was in just the right mood to feel the power of that performance。参考译文选择了前者，因为第一个解释更稳妥。

10. 此处的 burthen 就是现代英语中的 burden，但可能包含两层意思，除指负担外，还可指音乐，如此处就指音乐的副歌（泛指低声部音乐），所以这里翻译成"长久低回萦绕"。

11. "so profoundly, so touchingly generous did it appear in sense, so overpowering in expression" 这里作者启用了传统的分类，即内容（sense）和形式（expression）。但此处的核心意思是 generous，其他都是起修饰作用的，也就是说，肯特的话很慷慨宽厚；至于 profoundly 和 touchingly，都是先得有 generous 才有意思，但若译文无法恢复副词修饰形容词的结构，那么转换成并列也是一个可以考虑的办法，具体见参考译文。

12. 在"for the man who is…"中的 the man 实际是以第三人称单数特指的形式，特指一类人（a specific kind of man），并非一定在说某一个人。但若译成"那个因恪守道德而近乎迂腐的人"也并不错，因为汉语也可读出泛指一类人的意思来，比如说"那个信主的人有福了"，其实就是指一类人。但是若翻译成"一个人""任何人""如果一个人"，意思似乎反而更清楚。

13. 在 a book that breathes of every beautiful and valuable emotion 中的 breathes 有些人会翻译成"书中充满了……"。但是不宜译成"充满",因为"充满"给人的是一个容器盛满了空气的图像,而 breathes 显然是一个完全不同的图像,像是在呼吸吐纳,所以这里处理成"散发"。翻译成"呼吸"也不是很好,因为书仅仅给(exhale)读者养料,这个词的使用主要是想把书看成是能呼吸的活生物。在非文学文本中,译者未必要这么谨慎,大意差不多就可以,但在有些文本的翻译中,还是需要对这类词有所拿捏,它们虽分量不重,但仍需认真对待,译者需要参照文本外因素(如翻译目的等)权衡译法。

14. 此处的 they mould by contact 仍然是指艺术作品,包括前面提到的小说,应该也包括诗歌散文之类的作品。这类书向你展现生活的画卷,你会感到正在与书中人物接触(by contact),而这种接触会潜移默化地影响你、磨塑你(mould),但却很难讲清楚道明白(little can be said)。这种接触很难在下面提到的教诲人(didactic)的书中出现。

15. 在 more specifically didactic 这类书中,有很具体的议题,如蒙田的随笔就针对很多具体生活中的议题谆谆教导,如谈恐惧,讲睡眠,论友谊,说虚荣,可谓包罗万象。所谓 follow out,字典中的意思是 to implement (an idea or action) to a conclusion,但此处是指书对我们的影响比较容易确定,这和前面的 works of art 不同,艺术作品是潜移默化的(silent)。若能把影响说清的话,当然你也就可以区别、权衡、比较(distinguish and weigh and compare)。比如你就可以将自己的行为和别人的行为比较,到底在论文中抄袭了一小段是否应该,别人抄一章,可我仅抄一段啊!但读了蒙田的随笔你还是感到一段也令你汗颜。你看，你可以实实在在地指出书对你的影响，但艺术作品的作用就不是那么直截了当，很难对号入座了。

16. 这里的 a magazine 和杂志无关。这个词原来可指装子弹的弹盒，在这里的基本意思就是 a collection of something。其实这个词当杂志解释在后，当储藏弹药的地方解释在前。
17. 这句的基本句型是 have something done（如 have the box opened）。先需要搞清楚 linen decencies 的意思。此处的 linen 似可指让人体面的遮体衣物，这个词有个旧用法指内裤；decencies 则指行为规则（见陆谷孙主编《英汉大词典》），而在韦氏词典中这个词组的定义是 "commonplace and prosperous conventionality as symbolized by fine linen"，追踪其词源，弥尔顿似最先使用（The ghost of a linen decency yet haunts us—Milton, *Areopagitica*）。就隐喻意思来看，该词组可指让人体面的社会习俗、准则、传统、禁忌（decencies），我们在生活中做的很多事都是因为不想让社会认为我们违反了这些习俗与传统。后面的 excited orthodoxies 似乎与社会普遍接受的正统观念有关，orthodoxies 一词经常指宗教观念，excited 则是表示"强烈"的意思。所以 "they will have their 'linen decencies' and excited orthodoxies fluttered" 大意就是，现代人读了蒙田的随笔，就会将这两者 fluttered。flutter 这个动词原来就是指上下摆动，如翅膀的摆动，但是这个文本距今一百多年，所以最好查旧词典，如 1828 年版韦氏词典里就有如下定义 "to disorder; to throw into confusion"。根据这个定义我们可以将 fluttered 解读为使混乱，即社会一直公认的正统观念被动摇，人们开始不那么坚信，思想混乱，受到挑战了。这里的 fluttered 就是此意，见网址：http://1828.mshaffer.com/d/search/word, flutter。

18. 这半句承接上面的解释，即这种挑战、这种怀疑并非没有道理。此处双重否定（not... without...）。ground of reason 和 excuse 近义，翻译时可以合并。

19. 这里的 end 表示 eventually 或者 in the end 的意思，就是说读书的人最终将会认识到这位老者是个好人，也可能读书那刻没有这种认识，但总有一天会意识到这点。另外 in a dozen ways 可以解释为 in many ways，dozen 没有具体的字面意义。

20. 这后半句（not droningly and dully like a portion of the Bible）当然可以翻译成"而不沉闷地把它当《圣经》的一部分读"，但是 droningly and dully 和 a portion of 果真那么重要吗？这几个词到底承载多少有意义有分量的意思，还是在这样的文本中，其意义根本不重要。看前半句再看后半句，其实就是一个对比，当书读还是当经念，翻译成"用全新的目光把《新约》当书来读，而不是当经来念"基本反映原文目的。若问原文的 droningly and dully 到哪里去了？我说"念经"这两个字里面已经包含了两个副词的意思。换作其他文本也能这么译吗？那难说，若 a portion of 在原文里有意义，就不能省掉。

21. 这里的 courteously 表示人们出于礼貌假设我们应该知道这些道理。根据上下文我们这里说的 truths 应该就是《马太福音》中的道理（真理）。当时的社会是基督教社会，任何一个人都假设你知道《圣经》中的道理（People do us the courtesy of assuming we know those truths），翻译时这个词未必要翻译出来，因为分量很轻。但是人们只是空谈而已，并没有去实践这些《圣经》中的道理，所以作者用讽刺的口吻说，人们不实践这些真理是因为他们实在太谦虚（modestly refrain from）。

22. 这是一个长句，有数处要点评。首先 a book of singular service

一开始翻译成"一本独特的书",显然忘掉了 service 的含义,后来改成"一本作用独特的书"。但这句中的亮点是隐喻连连,从 tumbled、blew into space、cobwebs,到 tabernacle、back upon foundation,表达了读《草叶集》给他带来的精神升华。他本来有一套思想体系,构成了他对世界、对社会、对人生的看法。但是惠特曼的书把他的那个世界观给彻底颠覆了(tumbled the world upside down)。不仅如此,那本书还把他心中基于传统、温文尔雅,但却道貌岸然的道德幻想都给打破了,blew cobwebs into space 就是把东西吹散了,就像你把蒲公英拿在手里,猛吹一下,蒲公英便都散开消失一样。这还没完,那本书还动摇了 my tabernacle of lies,这里的 lie 是社会一直灌输给他的已经盘踞在他头脑中的谎言。那么这是什么样的谎言呢?这个 tabernacle 是理解的关键,这不是一般的谎言,这些谎言是社会的价值观,是作者人生之所系,是神圣的,它们都盘踞在一个神圣的地方(tabernacle),所以翻译中选词就需要推敲。一开始用了"屋宇",感到差不多,反正是谎言所在的建筑物嘛!但是再一想,为什么要用这个词,难道就没有一些神圣的含义?结果最后改成"谎言盘踞的圣殿"。最后 original and manly virtues 中的 original 原词有两个意思,有创意的和原汁原味的。翻译时选词最好参考语境,这和前面的 genteel and ethical illusion 应该恰恰相反,后者是做作的、不自然的,而 original and manly 都是未经社会污染的、人的自然的反应,所以最后选用了"本真"。

23. gun-powder charges 翻译的时候也值得推敲。如果翻译成"炸药般的真理",读者仍然不很清楚你到底想说什么。所以第一个任务就是要正确解读 gun-powder charges 的含义,这个词组到底是暗指炸药很多，还是炸药有力？当然charges（an amount of something）会有很多炸药的含义，但gun-powder更多表示powerful，就是说一大堆真理迎面袭来的冲击力，所以最后选择放弃原来的隐喻，改用目前比较流行的说法"井喷似的真理"。

24. 这句必须在上下文中解读。作者刚刚在前面说过这是一本需要有阅读天赋才能阅读的书，无天赋的普通人读这类书会信心崩溃。接下来就是我们这里要讨论的这句，所以这句应该和阅读《草叶集》这类书有关，就是说无阅读天赋的人读这类书就会 either he cries out or he is convinced by，所以这两个选项都是不理想的，因为读者无阅读天赋。比如他读书后会对书大加谴责，说这书是 blasphemy and indecency，进而去迎合那种当时众人崇拜的观点，这种观点（真理）并非都不对，但是不全对，因为这是掺杂自己利益的半真理（part-truths），所谓 conveniences 就是指那种为你提供便利、好处，令你感觉良好的东西，所以这个词总是指对人有利的东西。另一类读者则可能恰恰相反，他会完全信奉了书中的内容，并完全抛弃了传统的东西（"convinced by what is new, forgets what is old"）。作者认为那样的话，读者就变成真的 blasphemous and indecent 了。斯蒂文森认为，上述两种人都是因为无阅读天赋才有偏颇的，因为这些人不会判断（cannot judge），结果走了两种相反的极端。所以他建议，若无阅读天赋，还不如去读小说或者看报纸。这话一副精英主义的腔调，但说得还真不无道理。

25. 前面一共提到两样东西，即 fiction 和 the daily papers。此处的 in the first at least 指的是两样中的前面一个或者说第一个，也就是指 fiction。

26. 其中的 clay 和 brass 典自《圣经》："Then was the iron, the clay, the brass, the silver, and the gold…"（Daniel 2: 35）。英语中也有 feet of clay 的说法，很形象地说明人站不起来，表示伟人的弱点，或泛指缺点；而《启示录》中形容耶稣基督是有"His feet were like burnished brass"（Revelation 1: 15）的说法，表示坚实，和前面的 clay 刚好相反。两种材料质地不同，硬度各异，用在本文中主要是指软弱和坚固，由于前面半句讲到经得起时间的蹂躏，所以 clay 就不如 brass 经得住时间考验。有人见了英文这两个词就自然联想到"黄钟毁弃，瓦釜雷鸣"，自己觉得和原文的两种物质对应得比较好，但是实际并不合适，因为这个中文成语比喻的是，有才德的人被弃置不用，而平庸之辈却被重用，并不是经得起时间考验的意思。但若仅仅翻译成"有多少经得住时间考验，有多少经不住考验"，则虽表达了意思，却放弃了《圣经》的典故，有些遗憾。典故未必就影响可读性，中文读者还是能理解 clay 和 brass 的含义的，何况译者还可以添加典故词的言外含义（"多少如土会转瞬瓦解，多少是铜能长久坚实"）。

27. 这里的 a caput mortuum of piety 比较费解，拉丁语原文是 head of the dead 的意思。也就是说，斯宾塞表达的虔诚很抽象，没有生活中的具体例证，就像死人的头颅一样，这里的头颅可以理解成两个意思：一个表示无细节内容，头颅（或也可以说是 skeleton）没有血肉，只有骨架；另一个意思是表示没有鲜活的表情，死人的头颅当然不能像活人的面孔有表情（见接下来那句 little indeed of its loveliness）。总之，斯宾塞是以高度抽象的方式和读者交流的，但读者还是能了解他说的大意，因为主要的东西都包括在其中了（with most of its essentials）。

> 导 读

一卷在手书香留

  这篇散文于 1887 年 5 月 13 日初次发表在《英国周刊》(*British Weekly*) 上，但没有被选入斯蒂文森的散文集中。周刊的编辑邀请当时不少有影响的作家写一写影响他们的书，这些作家包括格莱斯顿（Gladstone）、拉斯金（Ruskin）、哈默顿（Hamerton）等人。同年《英国周刊》把所有这些作家寄回来的作品都收入了一个专辑中，题目就是《那些影响了我的书》。这篇后来也收入在斯蒂文森全集中，但没有收进他的散文集。斯蒂文森写这篇文章前后，应该已是身心憔悴。自己身体不好，父亲又病重在身。这篇散文发表那天应该是他父亲的出殡日，但斯蒂文森居然因病无法参加。

  我们现在已经不怎么读书了，更不用说读纸质书，一部手机就基本吸引了我们全部的注意力。我们当然并非不阅读，只是不读书而已，或者说不读严肃的书。那种过眼烟云的消息我们其实读得真不少。但是有些人还是看出了严肃作品和快餐文字间的不同，前者促人深思，后者使人浅薄。而且媒介不同效果似乎也不一样。同一本书在网上读电子版和读纸质版也有差异。《纽约时报》有篇文章说得好："读纸质书，我会记得文字，也忘不了那本书，书的形状、封面、重量、版式、字样都有记有忆，难以忘掉。读电子书，却只记得文字。一卷在手的感觉竟完全消失了，或者说根本就没有存在过。"那种一卷在手、书香永留（books to have and to hold）的感觉在电子书那里是找不到的。不读书的后果严重吗？难道网上的各种阅读就不利于心智的成长？人们也许有不同看法，但有的人还是很担忧的:"知识的源泉随处流淌,但正在成长的一代人却在沙漠中安营扎寨,相互用手机传递故事,分享照片、音乐和文字,靠同辈间的相顾相念而欣喜若狂。同时他们的心智又拒文化和社会的传统于千里之外,而我们今日之所以是我们,却恰恰有赖于这些文化和传统。"(*The Dumbest Generation*)有老派的文化人也许是因为心里焦急,甚至出言不逊,比如耶鲁大学文学批评家哈罗德·布鲁姆就把流行文学说得一钱不值:"哈利·波特虽然出书上亿,但不出五六年,便会无人问津,只能属于垃圾堆中可以找到的读物。"他说这话已经快20年了,哈利·波特仍然大受欢迎。

我们没有必要那么极端,接触一点哈利·波特类的书没什么不可以的,但接触一些经典是很有必要的。因此斯蒂文森的这个书单就有它的价值。他至少告诉我们,有一位苏格兰人,在生命的不同阶段不停地阅读,读了本文中说的那些书,后来人家成为名作家了。他推荐的书中,至少有些我们也可以拿过来看看。比如不管怎么说,莎士比亚的作品总是可以读一读的,而且我们很幸运,汉语的莎翁全集版本不少,读者可以挑着拣着读莎士比亚。如果说提不起兴趣读《蒙田随笔》,那么《圣经》也还是值得读一读的。这无关宗教,而是涉及文化。你要真想读懂西方文化的作品,没有《圣经》的知识底蕴,总是无法彻底读懂的。斯蒂文森推荐的不少是诗作,如惠特曼、华兹华斯、歌德等。就算你不喜欢诗,也不妨找一两篇先试着读一读,诗的语言未必就一定不是你的那碗菜。总之,经典总会有经典的作用,斯蒂文森这里提到的书未必都要读,本着开卷有益的态度,挑选几本读一读还是不错的。下面来谈谈这篇文章的翻译问题。

我们在翻译较实用的文本时,特别是正规文本,会发现处理句法是个难题,但是具体词的意思、短语的意思一般问题不大,往往都有明确的词义,不用译者反复推敲权衡,且不说专业词,就是文中的非专业词大部分情况下词义也较清楚,需要借助更大语境来解释的例子不是没有,但不是很多。比如"Maritime transport is the backbone of international trade and a key engine driving globalization"这句话语义清晰明了,不需要你做过多的解释,也根本没有什么可解释的余地,翻译起来也比较简单:"海运是国际贸易的中流砥柱,是促进全球化的关键动力。"但是本篇中的一些词和句子可就不是那么清楚了。其中 in an impressionable hour 就不是个非常清楚的词组,需要结合语境才能更好地把握词义,单独一个词组会较难把握。这个 hour 是字面意义的 hour,还是隐喻意义的 hour(人生中的一段时间)?在正式的政商法律等文本中译者一般不用那么纠结,因为词义大都是"小葱拌豆腐",一清二白。再如接下来的 the burthen of my reflections for long,如果仅孤立地按字面意思看 burden,那就是"负担"的意思,但是此处却是音乐等在脑际萦绕的意思(the refrain going round and round in his mind)。再比如"The last character, ...I had the good fortune to see, I must think, in an impressionable hour, played by Mrs. Scott Siddons"中的 Mrs. Scott Siddons 这个名字,若不加任何解释翻译过来当然很准确,但对中国读者帮助不大,因为读者不知道这是什么级别的演员,而原作者觉得这个演员非同一般,不过他没有用文字表达这层意思,因为在当时这是不言而喻的。若译者到文本外去了解演员的背景知识,那就会对翻译有些帮助。原来她出身演艺世家,是19世纪著名戏剧演员,是当时演罗莎琳德的名角儿,就像马连良是演《空城计》中诸葛亮的名角儿一样。这些文本外的信息就可以帮助译者在翻译这个名字时有灵活的余地,比如翻译成"扮演者竟是演这个角色的不二人选斯科特·西登斯夫人",略有添加也未尝不可。再比如文中的 linen decencies 虽然在有些字典中有解释，但是那个解释未必能在本文中直接使用，所以更符合语境的解释就仍然需要我们对本文的主旨有所把握。换句话说，译者很难仅靠文字本身就给出一个非常合适的译法。

软文本中语言活泼、不稳定，使得读者很难确切把握。所以有些人就说少选这类文本作为翻译材料，换句话说，最好使用语言清晰明确的文本。但是语言的不确定性是语言不可避免的一部分，而且可能是比实用语言更重要的一部分。我们不妨看几段斯坦纳的观点：

> The linguistic capacity to conceal, misinform, leave ambiguous, hypothesize, invent is indispensable to equilibrium of human consciousness and to the development of man in society. Only a small portion of human discourse is nakedly informative... Thus it is inaccurate to schematize language as "information" or to identify language with "communication". Human speech conceals far more than it confides; it blurs much more than it defines; it distances more than it connects. (From *After Babel*, by George Steiner, p. 239)
>
> The 'messiness' of language, its fundamental difference from the ordered, closed systematization of mathematics or formal logic, the polysemy of individual words, are neither a defect nor a surface feature which can be cleared up by the analysis of deep structures. The fundamental 'looseness' of natural language is crucial to the creative functions of internalized and outward speech. A 'closed' syntax, a formally exhaustible semantics, would be a closed world. (From *After Babel*, by George Steiner, p. 239)

斯坦纳十分看重不整齐划一的语言，认为把语言仅说成是"信息"或"交流"是不准确的。你也许会说，这是象牙塔里的观点。在眼下国际交流盛行的环境里，我们也许确实很难接受"Only a small portion of human discourse is nakedly informative"这样的说法，但是他强调语言模糊灵性的一面似乎有很现实的意义。反观现在年轻人的语言，言语相当"单薄"，词汇非常贫乏，说法十分有限，经不起思维活跃、语言活泼的人"忽悠"，稍一使用少见的比喻，特别是有创意的说法，他们就招架不住，搞不清是什么意思，因为他们在"the ordered, closed systematization of mathematics or formal logic"的语言中生活太久了。他们不适应 the messiness of language。可是斯坦纳认为语言的不确定或不规则（messiness）并不是弊端（neither a defect），而是"正能量"，它能促人思考，激活思维。他不无揶揄地讽刺乔姆斯基早年的语言理论，认为语言不能清楚地分为"深层"和"表层"（nor a surface feature which can be cleared up by the analysis of deep structures）。

说到翻译，他也不主张把原文中的 messiness 一扫而光，也不认为译文可以天衣无缝地精准对应原文：

> Where there is difficulty, the bad translator paraphrases. Where there is elevation, he inflates. Where his author offends, he smooths. Ninety per cent of all translation since Babel is inadequate and will continue to be so. (From *After Babel*, by George Steiner, p. 417)

你看，我们在翻译时不也常常这么做吗？句子脱离语言体系了，出现作者自己的特征了，语言的表达法怪异了，这时我们就情不自禁地把那些不属于语言体系的东西，像打扫卫生一样清除掉，留下整齐划一的语言，把"不正常的"语言"正常化"。我们常用的方法不就是释义（paraphrase）吗？也许，作为一个译者，我们自有苦衷，太拗口的文字读者不爱，编辑不要，所以我们多少总有些追求语言工整清晰的倾向，但我们也应该注意语言的不确定性或模糊性。自经济大潮冲刷这个全球化的世界以来，我们一直在冷落语言的不规则性（messiness）。

因此在选择材料时，老师不应该轻视文学等软文本的翻译，在把精力放在硬文本或偏硬文本的同时，也应该把软文本和偏软文本的翻译放在一个比较适当的位置，在教学中，更加注意、充分尊重软文本语言中那些不确定、较"模糊"的语言成分，既能把不重要、无价值的 messiness 扫除掉（如使用 paraphrase 的方法），也能学会"把玩"那些有意义的 messiness。说到底，翻译学习最重要的基本功，好像主要还是在翻译软文本时练就的。

参考资料

Books which have influenced me, The Literature Network, online resources at http://www.online-literature.com/stevenson/essays-of-stevenson/8/.

Verlyn Klinkenborg, Books to Have and to Hold, *The New York Times*, Aug. 10, 2013.

Mark Bauerlein, *The Dumbest Generation*, Penguin Books, 2008.

George Steiner, *After Babel*, Oxford University Press, 1992.

Books Which Have Influenced Me (2)

Goethe's Life, by Lewes[28], had a great importance for me when it first fell into my hands—a strange instance of the partiality of man's good and man's evil[29]. I know no one whom I less admire than Goethe; he seems a very epitome of the sins of genius, breaking open the doors of private life, and wantonly wounding friends, in that crowning offence of Werther[30], and in his own character a mere pen-and-ink Napoleon[31], conscious of the rights and duties of superior talents as a Spanish inquisitor was conscious of the rights and duties of his office[32]. And yet in his fine devotion to his art, in his honest and serviceable friendship for Schiller, what lessons are contained! Biography, usually so false to its office, does here for once perform for us some of the work of fiction, reminding us, that is, of the truly mingled tissue of man's nature, and how huge faults and shining virtues cohabit and persevere in the same character[33]. History serves us well to this effect[34], but in the originals, not in the pages of the popular epitomizer, who is bound, by the very nature of his task, to make us feel the difference of epochs instead of the essential identity of man[35], and even in the originals only to those who can recognise their own human virtues and defects in strange forms, often inverted and under strange names, often interchanged[36]. Martial[37] is a poet of no good repute, and it gives a man new thoughts to read his works dispassionately[38], and find in this unseemly jester's serious passages the image of a kind, wise, and

那些影响了我的书(二)

刚拿到刘易斯的《歌德的一生》我就感到如获至宝,这书是对人善与恶割裂的奇异例子。我不欣羡的人中歌德名列榜首。他是天才与罪恶混搭的典型:若论冒犯伤害他人,少年维特可谓登峰造极,他砸开私人生活之门,鲁莽地伤害友人;而在歌德自己的性格中,他简直就是挥笔杆子的拿破仑大帝,总觉得超级天才该有他们的权利与责任,恰如西班牙宗教裁判者觉得自己的职务赋予他权利和责任。但是在他对艺术的献身中,在他对席勒的帮助和友情中,我们可学的却实在不少!传记常不能履行其职责客观地介绍一个人,但歌德传记这回却起到了某些小说的作用,提醒我们错综的人性真能交织在一起,巨大的瑕疵和发光的美德原本可以集于一身。历史在揭示人性矛盾方面对我们帮助甚大,但是这种帮助体现在原始历史文件中,而不是在畅销作家的历史概述里,这些作家天生的职责会让我们在人物中感到古今时代的宏观异同,而不是人物本身的主要特征;而即便在原始历史文件中,读者也得分辨出他们自己的德操与缺陷,是以一种奇特的形式折射在作品人物身上,而且两者往往是颠倒的,并还冠以怪异名字,也常是历史人物和读者互换。马希尔是位并无名声的诗人,这让人能客观地读他的书,并能在这些挖苦讽刺的严肃段落里看到一位仁慈、智慧、自尊的绅士,

self-respecting gentleman. It is customary, I suppose, in reading Martial, to leave out these pleasant verses; I never heard of them[39], at least, until I found them for myself; and this partiality is one among a thousand things that help to build up our distorted and hysterical conception of the great Roman Empire.

This brings us by a natural transition to a very noble book—the *Meditations* of Marcus Aurelius. The dispassionate gravity, the noble forgetfulness of self, the tenderness of others[40], that are there expressed and were practised on so great a scale in the life of its writer, make this book a book quite by itself. No one can read it and not be moved. Yet it scarcely or rarely appeals to the feelings—those very mobile, those not very trusty parts of man. Its address lies further back: its lesson comes more deeply home[41]; when you have read, you carry away with you a memory of the man himself[42]; it is as though you had touched a loyal hand, looked into brave eyes, and made a noble friend; there is another bond on you thenceforward, binding you to life and to the love of virtue.

Wordsworth[43] should perhaps come next. Every one has been influenced by Wordsworth, and it is hard to tell precisely how. A certain innocence, a rugged austerity of joy, a night of the stars, "the silence that is in the lonely hills," something of the cold thrill of dawn[44], cling to his work and give it a particular address to what is best in us[45]. I do not know that you learn a lesson; you need not—Mill did not—agree with any one of his beliefs; and yet the spell is cast[46]. Such are the best teachers: a dogma learned is only a new error—the old one was perhaps as good; but a spirit communicated is a perpetual possession. These best teachers climb beyond teaching to the plane of art; it is themselves, and what is best in themselves,

这总给人新的思想。我猜想，读马希尔时人们惯于略过那些宜人的诗行。我就从来没有听到过这些句子，至少在我发现它们前没有听到过。有成千上万的事会促使我们对罗马帝国产生歪曲与疯狂的概念，选择阅读这一偏见仅是其中之一而已。

这自然把我们带到下一本高贵的书，即马可·奥勒留的《沉思录》。厚重带着冷静，忘我尤显高尚，对他人充满柔情，这些在书中表达得淋漓尽致，也在作者的生活中得以广泛实践，这些都使本书与众不同，读后无不为之感动。但这书极少撩动人的情感，而情感这东西易变，不很靠得住。这本书关注的要比情感深多了：书所启示的也更深刻；读罢掩卷，你已把对作者的记忆放进你的行囊；你仿佛紧握着一只忠诚的手，注视着一双勇敢的眼睛，结交了一个高尚的朋友；从今往后，人生路上，你又有了一条得以维系依赖的纽带，把你与生命和美德之爱紧紧系在一起。

再数下来就应该是华兹华斯了。每个人都受华兹华斯的影响，但又很难确切地说出是怎么影响的。一点天真幼稚，些许严酷环境中的欢乐，星斗满天的夜空，"孤山中的寂静"，还有霜晨中的那点寒栗，这些都紧抱着他的作品，使作品以独特的方式打动我们心中的良知。我不知你从书中是否有所学，你其实不必同意他的任何一个信念，米尔就不同意，然而他魔法般的影响力你却无法抗拒。这些是最好的老师：学一个教条仅是增加一个新的错误（其实旧教条可能也不差），但是精神的传递却是永恒的拥有。书中这些最好的导师不低回于艺术层面的教育，他们传递的是他们自己，他们自身中最优秀的东西。

that they communicate.

I should never forgive myself if I forgot *The Egoist*[47]. It is art, if you like, but it belongs purely to didactic art, and from all the novels I have read (and I have read thousands) stands in a place by itself. Here is a Nathan for the modern David[48]; here is a book to send the blood into men's faces[49]. Satire, the angry picture of human faults, is not great art; we can all be angry with our neighbour; what we want is to be shown, not his defects, of which we are too conscious, but his merits, to which we are too blind. And *The Egoist* is a satire; so much must be allowed[50]; but it is a satire of a singular quality, which tells you nothing of that obvious mote, which is engaged from first to last with that invisible beam[51]. It is yourself that is hunted down; these are your own faults that are dragged into the day and numbered, with lingering relish, with cruel cunning and precision[52]. A young friend of Mr. Meredith's (as I have the story) came to him in an agony. "This is too bad of you," he cried. "Willoughby is me!" "No, my dear fellow," said the author; "he is all of us." I have read *The Egoist* five or six times myself, and I mean to read it again; for I am like the young friend of the anecdote—I think Willoughby an unmanly but a very serviceable exposure of myself.

I suppose, when I am done, I shall find that I have forgotten much that was most influential, as I see already I have forgotten Thoreau, and Hazlitt, whose paper "On the Spirit of Obligations" was a turning-point in my life, and Penn, whose little book of aphorisms had a brief but strong effect on me, and Mitford's *Tales of Old Japan*, wherein I learned for the first time the proper attitude of any rational man to his country's laws—a secret found, and kept, in the Asiatic islands[53]. That I should commemorate

我要是忘了提《利己主义者》就不能原谅自己。你也可以说这是艺术作品，但是纯属道德说教类的艺术作品。我读小说上千，这本与众不同。这是《圣经》中内森给大卫训诫的现代版。这是一本让人感到羞愧的书。讽刺，是一幅愤怒刻画人类错误的作品，算不上伟大的艺术。我们谁都会对邻居感到愤怒。我们需要的不是向我们展示邻居的缺陷，邻居的缺陷我们总是记得，我们要看邻居的优点，可对优点我们却是熟视无睹。姑且承认，《利己主义者》确实是一本讽刺作品；但这是一本性质奇特的讽刺作品，并不紧盯住别人眼中的木屑不放，而是从头到尾始终盯着自己看不见的梁木。正是你自己在被追踪讨伐，书中说的都是自己的过错，被一一数落，被暴露在阳光下，可作者却写得津津乐道，显得毫不留情，又能击中要害。我知道这么一个故事，梅瑞狄思先生的一个年轻朋友痛苦地和他说："你也真够损的，书中的威洛比就是我啊！"作者却回答说："不对，威洛比是我们所有人。"我读《利己主义者》已经有五六遍了，我还要再读这本书。我像上面说的那位朋友，我也认为威洛比没有英气，但是他把我自己暴露得体无完肤。

我想写毕此文，我会发现自己忘掉不少最重要的作品，这不，我已经忘掉了梭罗，还有黑兹利特，后者写的《论义务精神》是我生命的转折点；忘掉的还有威廉·佩恩，他的格言书对我影响短暂却强烈。密特福的《古日本的故事》是另一本忘掉的作品，在这本书中我第一次学到了一个理性的人对自己国家法律的正确态度，这是我在游历亚洲那个日本岛屿时获得的一个秘密，一直保留的秘密。要把所有影响我的书都拿出来巡礼非我的希望，也不是编辑的

all is more than I can hope or the Editor could ask[54]. It will be more to the point, after having said so much upon improving books, to say a word or two about the improvable reader. The gift of reading, as I have called it, is not very common, nor very generally understood. It consists, first of all, in a vast intellectual endowment—a free grace[55], I find I must call it—by which a man rises to understand[56] that he is not punctually right, nor those from whom he differs absolutely wrong. He may hold dogmas; he may hold them passionately; and he may know that others hold them but coldly, or hold them differently, or hold them not at all. Well, if he has the gift of reading, these others will be full of meat for him[57]. They will see the other side of propositions and the other side of virtues. He need not change his dogma for that, but he may change his reading of that dogma, and he must supplement and correct his deductions from it. A human truth, which is always very much a lie, hides as much of life as it displays. It is men who hold another truth, or, as it seems to us, perhaps, a dangerous lie, who can extend our restricted field of knowledge, and rouse our drowsy consciences. Something that seems quite new, or that seems insolently false or very dangerous, is the test of a reader. If he tries to see what it means, what truth excuses it[58], he has the gift, and let him read. If he is merely hurt, or offended, or exclaims upon his author's folly, he had better take to the daily papers; he will never be a reader.

And here, with the aptest illustrative force, after I have laid down my part-truth, I must step in with its opposite. For, after all, we are vessels of a very limited content[59]. Not all men can read all books; it is only in a chosen few that any man will find his appointed food[60]; and the fittest lessons are the most palatable, and make themselves welcome to the mind.

要求。说了这么多好书,也该说两句不怎么好的读者吧!我常说阅读的天赋,那其实是一种并不常见的天赋,且很少为普通人理解。首先得有足够的超常智力天赋,我称之为"天赐的免费礼物",借助这个天赋,人能在更高层次上领悟到,自己原来并不准确无误,那些与自己相左的人也不绝对错误。一个人可以笃信一种理念,而且是热烈地笃信,他可能知道其他人也信那理念,但信得不那么热烈,而且信的方法也不同,或者说完全不信。可是这都不要紧,只要你有阅读天赋,这些与己相异的其他情况都是吸取养料的地方。他人可能见到另外一种看事物的角度,另外一种美德。你不必因此而改变自己的信条,但可以改变你对教条的解释,而你必须借此补充并纠正自己的结论。人类的真理总是谎言,它既揭示生活,也掩盖生活。有些人持有一种另类的真理,或者对我们来说,那真理无异于危险的谎言,但正是那种持另类真理的人才能拓展我们被限制的知识范围,唤醒我们昏昏欲睡的意识。能否分析那个似乎是崭新、虚假或危险的东西,对读者是极大的考验。如果他设法去搞清楚这东西意味什么,到底是什么真理赋予它存在的理由,那么他就有阅读天赋,就应该让他读下去。如果他仅是感到伤痛,感到被冒犯,见了作者的愚行就大惊失色,那么他最好去读日报;他成不了一个读者。

　　说到这儿,在指出我的不全面的真理后,我必须以最恰如其分的解释能力,从相反的角度说几句。因为我们毕竟就像容器,容量是非常有限的,并不是所有的人都能读所有的书。仅仅在少数得天独厚的作品中,人才能发现适合他的食物;最合适的东西是最合胃

A writer learns this early, and it is his chief support; he goes on unafraid, laying down the law[61]; and he is sure at heart that most of what he says is demonstrably false, and much of a mingled strain, and some hurtful, and very little good for service; but he is sure besides[62] that when his words fall into the hands of any genuine reader, they will be weighed and winnowed, and only that which suits will be assimilated; and when they fall into the hands of one who cannot intelligently read, they come there quite silent and inarticulate, falling upon deaf ears[63], and his secret is kept as if he had not written.

口的，最能被读者的头脑接受。作家在很早就意识到这点，正是这点支撑着作家，于是他大胆地向前走，定下自己的原则；他心里确信，他所说的大多数话显然是假的，很多是真假参半，有些是令人痛苦的，很少有什么用；但是他也确信，如果遇见一位知音，他的文字就会被掂量推敲，仅仅那些适合读者的文字会被吸收接纳；而如果读者没有智慧，不会阅读，那么文字就会沉寂无声，如对牛弹琴，作者的秘密就仍然是秘密，就像他根本没有写出来一样。

注 释

28. *Goethe's Life* 或 *The Life of Goethe*（1864）是英国哲学家和文学批评家乔治·亨利·刘易斯写的一本有关歌德的传记,在自传体文学中颇具好评。

29. 在 partiality of man's good and man's evil 中的 partiality 在这里可以理解成为 partitioning,表示将一个东西一分为二的意思,这里指善恶割裂成两部分。

30. Werther 指歌德写的《少年维特之烦恼》(*The Sorrows of Young Werther*)。这本在 1774 年出版的书信体小说,虽然算不上自传体小说,但一般认为书中有作者自己的身影。中文有多个译本。

31. 这里的 pen-and-ink Napoleon 就是说,歌德不是真的拿破仑,而仅仅是在纸上写写的拿破仑,就是一个挥笔杆子的拿破仑。

32. 在 the rights and duties of his office 中的 office 指的就是他的职务,以及随职务而来的权利和责任。这句是说歌德也像西班牙宗教裁判者一样,自命不凡,自觉有权做他喜欢做的事。Spanish inquisitor 就是西班牙宗教裁判所的审判员,Spanish Inquisition(西班牙宗教裁判所)成立于 1478 年,是西班牙天主教建立起来的一个裁决机构,旨在保持原教旨主义教义。

33. 这一长句中有两处需要说明。首先 biography false to its office 中的 office 和前面的一样,仍然是职务的意思。就是说,在一般情况下传记不能履行其职责,起到客观地介绍人物的作用,但是这本介绍歌德的传记起到了这个作用。另外 tissue of 这个词组表示东西缠绕在一起(an interwoven series),就是说在歌德身上善与恶缠绕在一起了。至于说为什么传记不能履行其职责,那是因为一般情况下,传记总是只记叙人物的一方面,比如总说好话,不能完整呈现人物。这一点在后面的注释里有进一步说明。至于 cohabit and persevere in the same character 这部分既可"粗译",也可"细译"。所谓"粗译"就是抓住大意,放弃不影响大局的词,如翻译成"巨大的瑕疵和发光的美德原本可以在一人身上共存",反映了核心意思,但只有 cohabit,却没有 persevere 的意思。因此细译者也可以将后者补进去,如"巨大的瑕疵和发光的美德原本可以在一人身上坚持共存下去",因为 persevere 这个词总是暗示困难,所做之事必须努力坚持(continue in a course of action even in the face of difficulty)。这里选择了放弃细节的译法。

34. 短语 to this effect 大致和 in this aspect 接近,就是指前面一句中的 how huge faults and shining virtues cohabit,也就是说在揭示人性矛盾共存方面历史对我们帮助不小。

35. 承接上半句,作者马上就进一步说明,历史帮助不小,但不是所有的历史都大有帮助。此时作者将历史分成了两类,一类是 the originals(即 documents),另一类是 the pages of the popular epitomizer。前者是历史本身的实录,后者是书写历史(write about history)。作者认为,完整记录人物的是原始文件,而不是那些万人追捧的历史概述。epitomizer 一词表示的是省略细节的概述(epitome: a brief presentation or statement of something)。为什么传记不能完整描述人物呢?斯蒂文森认为,传记作者总想着要 to make us feel the difference of epochs,而不是介绍 essential identity of man。也就是说,传记作者总是带着宏观的视野,总想将人物及其所在的时代与当今时代参照对比,使我们感到时代的不同(the difference of epochs)。由于历史学家们的目的使然，宏观视野中的历史因此就被理想化了，就像我们今天看一本伟人的传记，看到的总是伟大的一面，作者经常略去不那么伟大的内容，但是实际的人物要复杂得多，历史书卷没有记录一个伟人不很光彩的私生活，但是在 the originals 中却有所记录。

36. 前面说在传记中人物描述是单方面的，但在原始历史文件中才有一个鲜活的、有血有肉的人，但是在这句中，作者又说，即便是原始文件，读者还得知道怎么判断（recognise their own human virtues and defects）。你看，他又把责任推给了读者，他不停地强调读者要有阅读的天赋。你也许会说，virtues 和 defects 有什么难于辨认的？但是当读者自己的美德与缺陷在书中的对应物以奇异的形式出现时（in strange forms, often inverted and under strange names, often interchanged），辨认就不容易，就需要读者有阅读天赋。当读者把自身的一个美德或缺陷在阅读过程中与书中的美德或缺陷对照时，过去时代的美德或缺陷会以一种对现代人来说奇怪的形式出现，有时甚至完全颠倒。比如，19世纪的一个人在婚前把一位姑娘弄怀孕了，这显然是一件坏事（defect），但在当今这似乎已经被接受，若男孩主动提出要和女孩结婚，有时甚至被认为是好事（virtue），这就是"in strange forms, often inverted"的意思；或者说读者自己的美德和缺陷在书中是以一个奇怪的名称出现，而且常是名称互换了的。所以就算是读 the originals，读者能不能穿越时空，把书中改头换面的德行与缺陷与自己时代的德行与缺陷实现内容对接，认出（recognise）改头换面的德行与缺陷，就是衡量读者会不会阅读的一个标准。

37. Marcus Valerius Martialis，英文为 Martial，古罗马诗人，出生在西班牙，约公元104年去世，主要以其警句写作出名。

38. 在 to read his works dispassionately 中的 dispassionately 表示 without prejudice。也就是说，由于马希尔并不是十分有名，所以读者可以不受他名声的影响，公正地阅读他的作品，给予公正评价。若是个名人，则书未读，名先到，阅读判断起来难免有失公正。

39. 这里的"in reading Martial, to leave out these pleasant verses"有点费解。既然是令人愉快的句子，为什么读者要把它们略过不读呢？其实有些人在选编作者的作品时一开始就没选入这些段落，读者读的时候就无从选择，或有这些文字，但故意略过，因为一般人更喜欢看作者那些辛辣讽刺的文字，反而故意忽略那些能反映作者仁慈智慧的文字，也正因此我没有听说过这些文字（I never heard of them）。但是在这些被忽略的段落里，读者能看到"一位仁慈、智慧、自尊的绅士"。

40. 这句中的 the tenderness of others，若无上下文确实可以解读成是别人的 tenderness，但是此处却是《沉思录》的作者对别人 tender。其实这句后半部分已经说明，这些品格都是作者在生活中所实践的。

41. 这里的 address 虽然是名词，但其含义仍然是这个词当动词时的意思，换句话说，可以把这句理解为"It addresses something further back"，it addresses 大约和 it talks about、it focuses、it concerns 的意思类似。而接下来的 lies further back 应该和上句联系起来看。上句在说这本书不撩拨人的情感，所以就是说这本书讲的东西 further back than feelings，要比情感更深些。而跟在冒号后面的（its lesson comes more deeply home）就是前半句的意思，只是更进一步说明而已。further back 和 more deeply 其实是类似的语言图像。

42. 有的学生将 a memory of the man 解读成那个人的记忆，显然是错误的。此处是一个明显的语言图像：你（读者）读完书后带走了你对那个人的记忆，就像你背走了一袋东西一样，用非隐喻的话说，就是你读完书就把那人记住了。后面的"touched a loyal hand, looked into brave eyes, and made a noble friend"都是以形象思维出现的那个你记住的人。

43. Wordsworth 指英国桂冠诗人威廉·华兹华斯（William Wordsworth, 1770—1850）。不少人觉得他堪称英国文学中的"第三大诗人"，紧跟在莎士比亚和弥尔顿之后。当然这第三位的候选人还有其他人，如乔叟和斯宾塞。

44. 这里指的几样都与华兹华斯的作品有关。其中 the silence that is in the lonely hills 估计是出自他的一首诗 Song at the Feast of Brougham Castle upon the Restoration of Lord Clifford，但和原诗不完全一致，原句应该是："The silence that is in the starry sky, / The sleep that is among the lonely hills."。句中的 a night of the stars 似为 a night under the stars。最费解的是 a rugged austerity of joy。显然前两个词和 joy 格格不入，但是若了解诗人的生活环境就会一下子茅塞顿开。华兹华斯谈到过他在英格兰北部的生活，那里的环境不是温馨舒适的，确实可以用 rugged austerity 来形容，而作者在这个环境里却得到了快乐。所以这句可以从此背景去解读，或可翻译成"严酷环境中获得的欢乐"。

45. 这里的 a particular address to what is best in us 比较费解。我们已在上文中遇到过 address 当名词使用，而且名词和动词意思重叠，也就是名词的意思源于动词。但同一个词在不同的语境里可能有些许变化，比如这里的 address 后面跟的是介词 to，结果这个 address 的具体含义就需要结合介词解释清楚。我们一般在下面的句子里会把 to 和 address 连起来用，如 we address an envelope to someone 或者 give an opening address to a crowd。这些语境中 to 显然是一个旨在达到的目标，而 address to 的含义就是建立起了一个交流的通道，如 address an envelope to someone 就是把信息传递给某人，give an opening address to a crowd 就是把演说内容传达给听众。因此我们这个例子便可解释为 give it a particular way of approaching us，而与我们接触交流的结果就是影响（influencing）或吸引（appealing to）我们。至于文中 to 后面的 what is best in us 则表示人最好的品格，如正义、爱心、诚实、关爱等等，换句话说，这些好的品格都被激发出来了，不过翻译时倒没有必要把这些好品格一一列举出来，用"好"字概括就行。综合上述解释，本句似乎可以翻译成"（这些）使作品以独特的方式打动我们心中的良知"。

46. 这里的 Mill 是指英国哲学家和政治经济学家穆勒（John Stuart Mill，1806—1873）。而 the spell is cast 是指读者读了他的诗后，对他作品中的观点无论同意不同意，诗人的魅力已如魔术一样施展在你的身上了，你已经无法逃避他的影响。

47. 这是英国维多利亚末期的作家乔治·梅瑞狄斯的一本小说，被称为是其小说创作的巅峰之作。有些评论家将梅瑞狄斯和汤马斯·哈代相提并论。

48. 这里说 Nathan for the modern David 是基于《圣经》中的故事（2 Samuel 12: 1-12）。先知内森指责大卫王与乌利亚的妻子通奸，然后又杀害乌利亚并夺取其妻。内森警告大卫要受到惩罚。《利己主义者》这本书就起到了训诫警告当代人的作用，因此说是"内森训诫大卫的现代版"。

49. 在没有上下文的情况下，译者会感到 to send the blood into

men's faces 含义模糊，或者会解读出不同的意思。但其实语言本身和语境还是提供给译者一些线索。有个成语叫 a rush of blood (to the head)，大意就是血液上脑使人激动甚至愤怒，结果干出蠢事。但是此处不是 blood to the head（理智），而是 into faces（颜面），所以解释成愤怒不很合理。加之，句子的逻辑是接前面的 Nathan for the modern David（见 David 后面的分号），而此训诫是在指责人做错误的事，所以做错事的人不应该愤怒，而应该"羞愧"。接下来的句子中确实有 angry 一词，但不要被这个词迷惑（接下来的句子完全是一个新句子）。

50. 这个 so much must be allowed 的解读应该靠上下文，在逻辑上必须和前面的句子连贯顺畅。其实这部分的意思是在表达让步。首先他说 *The Egoist* is a satire，接着就是这半句，也即作者承认这仅是一本讽刺之作（没错，是讽刺作品，潜台词就是"而非艺术大作"），换句话说 so much (as satire) must be allowed (admitted)。接着作者就用连接词表达转折（but it is a satire of a singular quality）。这样逻辑上就连贯了（这书是讽刺之作，这不能否认，但是这可是一本奇特的讽刺作品）。翻译时未必需要按照原文的三个部分前后串联起来，参考译文就将 so much must be allowed 移到最前面："姑且承认，《利己主义者》确实是一本讽刺作品；但这是一本性质奇特的讽刺作品"。有关 *The Egoist*，请参考"The Character of Dogs"篇注释 22。

51. 这一长句中的 mote 和 beam 典自《马太福音》(Matthew 7: 1-5)，在不同的版本中也有用其他词的，如 speck of sawdust 和 plank。有的中文《圣经》译成"你为什么看见你弟兄眼里的木屑，却不想自己眼里的梁木呢？"这句经文的意思就是说，你不应该老是看到别人的一个小缺点，却对自己的大错误视而不见。在本文中，斯蒂文森在说，《利己主义者》这本讽刺作品并不关注你眼里看来明显的（obvious）他人小错，而是关注你总是看不见的（invisible）己之大错。翻译的时候可以完全隐去《圣经》典故，如译成"并不紧盯住别人的小缺点不放，而是从头到尾始终盯着自己的大错误"。但我们书中的这个译文仍然选择保留典故（木屑与梁木）。若怕读者看不懂，还可以采取一个折中的办法，即保留典故，但附加解释，如"并不紧盯住别人眼中微尘般的小错误，而是从头到尾始终盯着自己视而不见的梁木般的大错误"。

52. 这里的 faults dragged into the day 表示把自己的错误暴露在光天化日之下，the day 是相对于 night 而言的，夜里什么都看不见，白天都看见了；而 numbered 则表示那些错误被一个一个地数落了（counted）。后半句中的 lingering 一般情况下表示不受欢迎的东西，如 lingering pain，但译者还是应该根据语境决定词义。这个 with 后面的词都是在说作者梅瑞狄斯是如何地享受写作过程，显然并非不愉快，而是相反。细查词典发现这个词也有相反的意思（Collins: to go in a slow or leisurely manner）。所以应该取这个意思（"写得津津乐道，显得毫不留情，又能击中要害"）。

53. 这句中的 Thoreau 是指 Henry David Thoreau（1817—1862），Hazlitt 则是指 William Hazlitt（1778—1830），Penn 就是指 William Penn（1644—1718），Mitford 指的是 Algernon Bertram Freeman-Mitford（1837—1916）。在密福特的《古日本的故事》中，有一系列短小的故事描写明治维新时期日本人生活的方方面面，而这里的"a secret found, and kept"说的应该就是作者在那本书中了解到的日本人对国家法律秉持的态度，而其背景可能

就是书中的《四十七士物语》。在这个故事中，四十七义士为情义而复仇杀人，但后来四十七人全部自首，束手让幕府差人拘禁，听候判决，最后幕府下令命他们集体切腹。这四十七义士（除一人外）全部剖腹而死。这里就是斯蒂文森从书中了解到的对于情义和法律的态度。为了情义他们必须报仇，但为了法律，他们又必须自首自尽，这种情法观对作者来说是一个发现的秘密。文中的 the Asiatic islands 就是指日本。

54. 这里的背景就是文章开头的那段，the Editor 就是向他约稿的编辑。

55. 这里的 a free grace 是指 a vast intellectual endowment，换句话说是一个免费的礼物。grace 一词常指上帝赠予人的爱，是白给的，不是自己挣来的。

56. rises to understand 表示人若有更高的眼界，就能看到自己并不准确无误，别人也不绝对错误。那些总认为自己对、别人错的人眼界就不高，人只能站得高才能看得远，因此才用 rises。翻译的时候如仅译成"领悟到自己原来并不准确无误……"，基本达意。若将 rises 翻译进去，则更能反映作者的视角。

57. 这里的 full of meat 指的就是对他来说有益处的东西。也就是说，观点不同等等都不要紧，只要你有阅读天赋，你就能受益。

58. 在"If he tries to see what it means, what truth excuses it"中的 it 指前句中的 something，就是那些看上去像左道旁门、危险谎言的东西。恰恰是这类东西才能打开我们的眼界，唤醒我们的意识。所以，如果一个读者有阅读天赋，会在阅读过程中设法去搞清楚这类危险东西的意义（see what it means），并去想一想，尽管这些东西看上去那么另类，那么左道旁门，它却存在了，那它存在的理由是什么（what truth excuses it）？句中 excuses 的词义就是 to provide a reason or explanation for

something bad，此处的 bad 在作者看来是带引号的，说得大众化一点就是为那另类的东西找个借口（excuse it=find an excuse for it）。作者这样说的目的就是想让我们知道，不应该将这种另类的东西不分青红皂白一棍子打死。这种态度反映了斯蒂文森观点的开明。

59. 这个 vessels of a very limited content 是隐喻的说法，其理解可以参照接下来的那句，就是"Not all men can read all books"，换句话说，limited content 就是只能读有限的书。

60. 在 his appointed food 中的 appointed 是恰当合适的意思，并不是我们一般使用时的意思。

61. 这个 laying down the law 指的是作家定下自己的原则，也就是作家自己认定的对错原则，不是别人为他定下的教导，当然就更不属于社会的法律了。

62. 这个 besides 当副词用，意思就是 in addition、as well 或者 also 的意思。其实它和介词的 besides 同源（in addition to），如"I have no other family besides my parents"。但这个词当副词还有另一个意思，如"I had no time to warn you. Besides, I wasn't sure."，此时是 moreover 的意思。

63. 这个语境中的 falling upon deaf ears 就是指读者不懂作者的意思，所以和成语"对牛弹琴"基本对应。一般情况下，有强烈汉语特色的成语不宜用在译文中，比如在译文中使用"邯郸学步"就不合适。但是有的时候，一个汉语成语虽有文化典故，但是文字的所指内容并不仅局限于中国文化，比如"牛、琴"就不仅中国有，不像"邯郸"仅在中国有；加之，这类成语已被长期使用，原文典故早被淡化，所以在译文中用一下也未尝不可。

Davos in Winter

A mountain valley has, at the best, a certain prison-like effect on the imagination, but a mountain valley, an Alpine winter, and an invalid's weakness make up among them a prison of the most effective kind[1]. The roads indeed are cleared, and at least one footpath dodging up the hill[2]; but to these the health-seeker is rigidly confined. There are for him no crosscuts over the field, no following of streams, no unguided rambles[3] in the wood. His walks are cut and dry[4]. In five or six different directions he can push as far, and no farther, than his strength permits; never deviating from the line laid down for him and beholding at each repetition the same field of wood and snow from the same corner of the road. This, of itself, would be a little trying to the patience in the course of months; but to this is added, by the heaped mantle of the snow, an almost utter absence of detail and an almost unbroken identity of colour[5]. Snow, it is true, is not merely white. The sun touches it with roseate and golden lights. Its own crushed infinity of crystals, its own richness of tiny sculpture, fills it, when regarded near at hand, with wonderful depths of coloured shadow[6], and, though wintrily transformed, it is still water, and has watery tones of blue. But, when all is said, these fields of white and blots of crude black forest are but a trite and staring substitute for the infinite variety and pleasantness of the earth's face[7]. Even a boulder, whose front is too precipitous to have retained the snow, seems, if you come upon it in your walk, a perfect

冬季达沃斯

往好了说，山谷也像牢房，禁锢人的想象，但是山谷、严冬、病弱凑在一起，就真在这氛围中营造出一个牢房，把人禁锢得寸步难行。道路确已扫清无障，至少一条路蜿蜒通向山上，但是来此求健康的人却无法离径而行，不能纵横原野，不能沿溪徜徉，不能在林中随兴漫步。行走是寻常乏味的。若体力允许，他可以向周围四五个方向前行，仅此而已，从来不能偏离为他设下的路线，每次都是从同一个角度看同一片树林雪野。几月下来，这本身已让人无法忍受，再加上层层叠叠的雪几乎毫无细节、色调单一，更难让人忍受。不错，雪不只是白色，在阳光照射下，也呈现出玫瑰金黄的色调。将雪近观细看，那挤压在一起的无限晶体，那丰富的微型雕塑，挤满雪中，也显出层层色彩。虽经过严冬而脱胎换骨，水毕竟还是水，显出深浅不一的淡蓝色。但是话虽这么说，这些白色雪野和黝黑森林的斑驳点缀，毕竟是沉闷单调的景观，无法取代世界的繁复多趣，无法令你目不暇接。散步时你巧遇岩石一块，石壁陡峭圆滑留不住雪，显露的石体似乎是一块有色彩的宝石，但即便有色彩，岩石还是不能免除你心中的不悦，促你向往其他地方，让你想

gem of colour, reminds you almost painfully of other places, and brings into your head the delights of more Arcadian days[8]—the path across the meadow, the hazel dell, the lilies on the stream, and the scents, the colours, and the whisper of the woods. And scents here are as rare as colours. Unless you get a gust of kitchen in passing some hotel, you shall smell nothing all day long but the faint and choking odour of frost[9]. Sounds, too, are absent: not a bird pipes, not a bough waves, in the dead, windless atmosphere. If a sleigh goes by, the sleigh-bells ring, and that is all; you work all winter through[10] to no other accompaniment but the crunching of your steps upon the frozen snow.

It is the curse of the Alpine valleys to be each one village from one end to the other[11]. Go where you please, houses will still be in sight, before and behind you, and to the right and left[12]. Climb as high as an invalid is able, and it is only to spy new habitations nested in the wood. Nor is that all; for about the health resort the walks are besieged[13] by single people walking rapidly with plaids about their shoulders, by sudden troops of German boys trying to learn to jödel[14], and by German couples silently and, as you venture to fancy, not quite happily, pursuing love's young dream[15]. You may perhaps be an invalid who likes to make bad verses as he walks about[16]. Alas! no muse will suffer this imminence of interruption—and at the second stampede of jödellers you find your modest inspiration fled. Or you may only have a taste for solitude; it may try your nerves to have some one always in front whom you are visibly overtaking, and some one always behind who is audibly overtaking you, to say nothing of a score or so[17] who brush past you in an opposite direction. It may annoy you to take your walks and seats in public view. Alas! there is no help for it among the

到田园生活，草地上错综的小径，榛树遍布的谷地，溪涧的百合，还有芬芳的气息和缤纷的色彩，外加风吹树林的窃窃私语。气味在这里也和色彩一样匮乏。也许走过一家旅店能闻到一阵炊事带来的气味，但一整天，除了霜雪散发出淡淡的令人窒息的气味外，就再也闻不到什么其他气味了。声音也没有，在那无风死寂的氛围里，没有禽鸟的鸣叫音，没有树枝的摇摆声。偶尔雪橇飞过你的身旁，给你带来铃声一阵，仅此而已。你在群山中熬过漫长的冬天，没有什么与你相依为伴，只有踏雪行走发出的吱吱声。

真不幸，在阿尔卑斯山，一个山谷就是一个村落。无论往哪儿走，屋宇总离不开你的视线，前后可望见房，左右能看到屋。你拖着病弱的身躯爬山，一眼望去是林中新的村落。这还不算，你若在健康疗养院附近散步，会感到不胜侵扰，没准儿遇上疾驰而过的一队花格布披肩的人，或是突然冒出来的一队学阿尔卑斯山小调的年轻人，或是一对对情侣正静静地做着初恋的美梦，你也许会发挥想象力，觉得他们没话可说并不快乐。你若是病残者，也许喜欢走来走去时哼几句歪诗，但如此烦扰，哪还有作诗的雅兴？在那第二波山歌学习者的吵闹声中，仅存的那点灵感也已离你而去。或者你只喜欢幽思独处，可是看到眼前有人你在赶超，听见身后有人在追赶你，更不用说迎面过来的十来个人跟你擦肩而过，哪还安静得下心来享受独处的乐趣。无论是坐与行，一切都在大庭广众的视野里，怎不叫你烦躁。可叹，在阿尔卑斯山谷间无法避免这些。不像戈尔

Alps. There are no recesses, as in Gorbio Valley by the oil-mill; no sacred solitude of olive gardens on the Roccabruna-road; no nook upon Saint Martin's Cape, haunted by the voice of breakers, and fragrant with the threefold sweetness of the rosemary and the sea-pines and the sea[18].

For this publicity there is no cure, and no alleviation; but the storms of which you will complain so bitterly while they endure, chequer and by their contrast brighten the sameness of the fair-weather scenes[19]. When sun and storm contend together—when the thick clouds are broken up and pierced by arrows of golden daylight—there will be startling rearrangements and transfigurations of the mountain summits. A sun-dazzling spire of alp hangs suspended in mid-sky among awful glooms and blackness; or perhaps the edge of some great mountain shoulder will be designed in living gold, and appear for the duration of a glance bright like a constellation, and alone 'in the unapparent[20].' You may think you know the figure of these hills; but when they are thus revealed, they belong no longer to the things of earth—meteors we should rather call them, appearances of sun and air that endure but for a moment and return no more. Other variations are more lasting, as when, for instance, heavy and wet snow has fallen through some windless hours, and the thin, spiry, mountain pine trees stand each stock-still and loaded with a shining burthen[21]. You may drive through a forest so disguised, the tongue-tied torrent struggling silently in the cleft of the ravine[22], and all still except the jingle of the sleigh bells, and you shall fancy yourself in some untrodden northern territory—Lapland, Labrador, or Alaska[23].

Or, possibly, you arise very early in the morning; totter down stairs in a state of somnambulism; take the simulacrum[24] of a meal by the glimmer

比奥谷的榨油作坊会停下来，这里可没有间隙；这里也没有罗卡布鲁纳路旁橄榄园神圣的幽静；也不能像在圣马丁海角处那样，倾听海浪呼啸，陶醉在迷迭香、海畔松和大海的气息中。

这种喧扰无法驱散，也无法减轻；而无时或息的暴雨也会让你叫苦连天，但是暴雨却会打破清一色的万里晴空，把你从单调无趣中振奋一下。当太阳和暴雨你争我夺时，当浓厚的云层被打碎，金色的阳光穿透云层时，你惊奇地发现，一座座山峰雄姿反复变换，旧貌呈现新颜。耀眼的山峰在阴森与黑暗的拥抱中悬挂在半空。也许山肩的边缘抹上了鲜艳的金色，一眼瞥去像星座般明亮耀眼，仿佛在依稀的空中孤芳自赏。也许你认为很熟悉这些山的姿态，但是眼前这番景色让你觉得这山已是仙境不似人间，称之为流星才对，太阳和气雾停留片刻，却再不复现。有些景观可能缠绵不去，比如又厚又湿的雪在无风的山中默默地下了几小时，瘦骨嶙峋的山松静静屹立，闪光的雪沉甸甸地挂在树上。你也许在这样隐蔽的森林中驱车而过，山沟裂缝间默默却也奋力挣扎的是冻结得不再滔滔的山涧。一切都是静的，只有雪橇上的铃声打破寂静，你会觉得自己是在仍无人迹的北极地带，比如拉普兰，拉布拉多，阿拉斯加。

也许你很早就起来了；昏沉沉蹒跚下楼；在空无一人的咖啡屋里，借孤灯在昏暗中随便吃了早餐。七点钟，披着迟迟未灭的月光，在刺骨的寒气中，你竟已站在外边。送邮件的雪橇将你捎

of one lamp in the deserted coffee-room; and find yourself by seven o'clock outside in a belated moonlight and a freezing chill. The mail sleigh takes you up and carries you on, and you reach the top of the ascent in the first hour of the day[25]. To trace the fires of the sunrise as they pass from peak to peak, to see the unlit tree-tops stand out soberly against the lighted sky, to be for twenty minutes in a wonderland of clear, fading shadows, disappearing vapours, solemn blooms of dawn, hills half glorified already with the day and still half confounded with the greyness of the western heaven—these will seem to repay you for the discomforts of that early start; but as the hour proceeds, and these enchantments vanish, you will find yourself upon the farther side in yet another Alpine valley, snow white and coal black, with such another long-drawn congeries of hamlets and such another senseless watercourse bickering along the foot. You have had your moment; but you have not changed the scene. The mountains are about you like a trap[26]; you cannot foot it up a hillside[27] and behold the sea as a great plain, but live in holes and corners[28], and can change only one for another.

上，向前奔去，在第一道曙光初照时抵达了顶端。初阳的火焰从一个山峰转到另一个山峰，你的目光也追踪着那火红的太阳；衬着明亮的天空，你看到仍未被照亮的树梢俨然挺立；长达二十分钟，你如在仙境，看清晰的阴影渐渐淡去，氤氲雾气慢慢消散，庄严的黎明在绽放，一半的山体已光辉灿烂，属于白昼，另一半山体却仍被西天的昏暗笼罩；见到这些胜境，早起带来的那点困难又算什么？然而，随着时间的推移，这些令人心旷神怡的景象便开始消失，你发现自己已在另外一个阿尔卑斯山谷了，又是雪白和煤黑，又是没完没了聚落的民宅，又是脚下喋喋不休流淌着的小溪。你刚有过那绝妙的时刻，但是其实这里的一切并没有变化。你周围的山岭如陷阱，你无法走上山腰见到平原一般的大海，只能生活在逼仄的环境里，唯一的变化就是周而复始。

注 释

1. 前面的 prison-like effect on the imagination 比较清楚，起到的效果是在想象上（on the imagination）。但是后面三个因素加起来的效果不那么清楚，因为不像前面的 prison-like，后面的是 prison of the most effective kind，前一个是明喻（prison-like），后一个是隐喻（prison）。一般来说，隐喻的力度要比明喻强大，比如我们说"Lawyers are like sharks"和"Lawyers are sharks"，一般说，后一句力度更强。我们这句中的问题是在后面的 the most effective kind 上。前面像牢房似的效果是在 imagination 上，但这里却只有强度 most effective，并没有明确说出其作用在哪里。根据常识，我们可以假设牢房的作用，其中也应该包括前面的限制想象的作用。不过根据接下来的几句话，我们似乎觉得作者这里想强调的作用主要应该是对行动的控制，就是在牢房中你无法自由走动，因为接下来的句子是说人们被 rigidly confined 了，再接下去就是怎么无法自由行走的例子，因此翻译时把 most effective 化解掉，转换到"禁锢得寸步难行"，似乎也是一种处理办法。当然如果觉得这个太自由了些，翻译成"一个最禁锢人的牢房"就有更宽广的解释空间，"禁锢得"就未必仅仅是"寸步难行"，还可以有其他方面的禁锢。但若再进一步约束译者，翻译成"最有效的牢房"，那么就开始露出原文的痕迹了，形式上更接近原文，但语言就不够灵活，因为"有效的牢房"毕竟不是最舒坦的中文。可见译者是有选择余地的。至于"但是山谷、严冬、病弱凑在一起"这部分是否可以更灵活些？如译成"若在山谷时正值严冬，又碰上一个体力衰弱的人，那就……"，这自然也是一个选择，因为意思都对，又更少原文的束缚，但我还是没有选择这更自由的译法。句中的 among them 大致是 all together 的意思。

2. 这里的 one footpath dodging up the hill 有隐喻在其中，dodging 就像人躲来躲去的样子，但这里做出躲闪动作的是山路，up the hill 是路向上的方向，你可以在头脑中形成一个图像，山路一会儿向左一会儿向右，所以可以翻译成"一条路蜿蜒通向山上"（zigzag）。在非隐喻的语境下，动词的主语一般是人，比如"He dodged through the forest"。

3. rambles 这个词一般有悠闲享受的隐含意思，而 unguided 则表示没有向导，没有事先规定的路线等意思，但是此处也可以理解成不受规定、不受拘束等意思，进而可以延伸到"随意"这个意思上。

4. 这个 cut and dry 是个习惯表达法，基本意思就是"being or done according to a plan, set procedure, or formula"，也就是说和上面的 unguided 的意思基本相似。若细分析，cut 这个词有因循守旧、少原创思想的意思，而 dry 则有 boring 的意思。但这里是一个整体，翻译时能表达大致意思的译法均可接受，这里翻译成"寻常乏味"。

5. 英语的 broken 的字面意思就是"分裂、破裂"，我们一般在形容人的性格时会把人格分裂者的性格称为 broken identity，有的甚至称 split personality。而 unbroken 则相反，表示找不到一个明确的界限把物体分裂开、区分开。所以这个词含义的基础就是没有细节。至于 unbroken identity of colour 像是绘画专业用语，斯蒂文森的亲戚朋友中有画家，他也许受到他们的影响。这个词的基本意思就是 the same color，这里译成"颜色单一",其中的 identity 就不要翻译进去了。但应注意,identity 这个词有不同的意思,在 broken identity 中表示分裂人格(the distinguishing character or personality of an individual),但在这句中的 identity 表示同一性(sameness),而不是"身份"。这句是个倒装句,正常语序应该是 an absence of detail and unbroken identity is added to this。作者没有用 are added,大概是因为最接近的名词 identity 是单数。

6. 在 fills it 中的 it 应该就是指 snow。这句中的 crushed infinity of crystals 就是在形容雪的结构,its own richness of tiny sculpture 也是在说雪的结构,说的是一回事儿,作者在描写雪的微型结构,这种结构不细看,看不出来。当然 crushed infinity of crystals 的语言结构还需要解释一下。尽管在原文中 crushed 是修饰 infinity 的,但显然合理的结构应该是 crushed crystals,也就是说一个一个的微小晶体挤在一起,至于 infinity,只说明这种晶体数量的无限。至于 depths of coloured shadow 这个词组也是绘画艺术的专业词,depths 这个词表示 shadow 的深浅不一(层层色彩)。说完细节,我们再来看看这句的总框架。这句的核心动词是 fills it,后面的 when 结构和 with wonderful depths 都是起修饰作用的。

7. 这句的理解要先看大语境,也就是说,要搞清楚作者到底想说什么。他在把达沃斯的山谷和地球上无数的欢快风景对照,他觉得达沃斯这地方是无法取代那些 pleasantness 的。在达沃斯山上的白雪和黑色的森林和地球上的 infinite variety and pleasantness 相比,前者仅是 a trite and staring substitute。trite 的意思就是"用旧了的""陈腐的",比如我们说:"Have a good one." is a trite substitute for people who realize that "Have a nice day"

is tired but don't know what else to say. 换句话说，达沃斯的景观要和 infinite variety and pleasantness 相比，那是太无趣单调了。至于 staring substitute 的意思，则最好和后面的联系起来考虑更清楚。如果我们看世界其他地方的景致，鸟语花香，满园色彩，在那样的环境中，你已目不暇接，也就是说 infinite variety 的景色给你无限选择，结果你当然也有 pleasantness 了。但是达沃斯这山谷就这么两个色调，人没有机会目不暇接，只能是景盯着你、你盯着景（staring）。作者把丰富的意思紧紧地包裹在两个词里面（staring substitute），翻译时若不解开这个包袱是不行的。所以在这类句子的翻译中，译者只需翻译出大意就行。而且这两个形容词 trite 和 staring 表达的是类似的意思，都是在说达沃斯山谷那地方单调无趣，翻译时合并起来也未尝不可。这里仍然尽量翻译出两个意思（"毕竟是沉闷单调的景观，无法取代世界的繁复多趣，无法令你目不暇接"），但是仅仅说"达沃斯单调，无法取代世界的繁复多趣"，基本上就差不多了。

8. Arcadian days 是当年希腊一个叫阿卡迪亚的地方，而 Arcadian days 就是那个时期。这个词后来已经从其特指那个特殊地区和文化演变成泛指，说明一个地方，一种生活是简单、和平、田园式的。所以后来就将 Arcadia 直接翻译成"乡村乐园"。其实你只要读一下破折号后面的文字，就是所谓 Arcadian days 的内容。翻译成泛指的"田园生活"就可以。

9. 这个 the faint and choking odour of frost 中的 choking 怎么理解？原文的词是修饰 odour 的，但有人觉得 choking 的源头是霜雪，把这解释为 choking frost，认为寒冷的天气有时会让人窒息。这类把修饰对象进行转换的情况确实有，但是却不宜经常调来调去。比如这句翻译成"除了令人窒息的霜雪有淡淡的味道外",未必算错,但译成"除了霜雪散发出淡淡的令人窒息的气味外"就更接近原文。在翻译时,特别是原文年代比较久远,作者写作时不按常理出牌,译者有时就很难完全避免一定程度的猜测。但即便是这样,译者仍然需要做足功课,把能查到的地方都查到,然后再翻译。

10. 这句中那个简单的动词 work 反而会使译者感到很麻烦。如我们换成 live all winter through,就好办多了。可偏偏是 work,我们又无法用"工作"这个词来翻译。冬天到达沃斯住的人也根本不是去工作的。词典中有一个定义较符合这个语境"to spend time trying to achieve something, especially when this involves using a great effort"。在我们的语境中住在那里的人要达到的目标就是艰难地度过严冬。从翻译角度看,处理的时候可以虚化这个词,在表达时把艰难(using a great effort)的意思糅入句中就可以了:"你在群山中熬过漫长的冬天"。另外,句子中的 through 主要强调贯穿整个冬季,这些细小的地方,译者有必要知道,但翻译时倒不必面面俱到,有些隐含的意思,若能融入句中的其他成分中就可以("熬过"的"过"字就有 through 的意思),若不重要,不去管它也可以。

11. 这里的 be each one village from one end to the other 的基本意思是指一个山谷就是一个村庄,也就是在暗示山谷中住的人很多。from one end to the other 是指山谷(from one end of a village to the other end)。

12. 这句"houses will still be in sight, before and behind you, and to the right and left"一开始翻译成"前后是房,左右是屋",但是后来发现此译法为求简洁,却忽略了 in sight 这个短语的存在。

如果说"前后是房，左右是屋"，会给你一种很拥挤的感觉，而原文却不是。原文的 in sight 暗示房子在视野内，却未必靠得那么紧，原译显得太拥挤了，因此才改成"屋宇总离不开你的视线，前后可望见房，左右能看到屋"。翻译是细活儿，有时自己觉得非常满意时，可能正是问题之所在。

13. 这个 besiege 通常有围攻（城市）的意思，比如我们说"The city was besieged"。但是在这个语境中就不是这个意思，而是干扰、骚扰的意思（annoy 或 bother 等）。英文一词多义现象很多，但多个意思之间并非完全没有联系，比方你从"围攻"可以联想到"骚扰"，所以译者可根据语境做些联想，就能想到较为合适的词。当然，为了不出差错，落笔前可以查一下词典，一般这种情况词典中都会有明确解释。

14. 这个句子中的 jödel 是指阿尔卑斯山地区的一种小调，就像我们有些地方的山歌一样，据说腔调很高，不很容易唱。另外，这里的 German boys 其实并不是从德国跨境过来的男孩子，就是指当地的年轻人。下面的 German couples 也是指当地的情侣。

15. 这里的 not quite happily 比较容易搞错。这句的语法结构是 (by) German couples silently and not quite happily pursuing love's young dream，而 as you venture to fancy 是修饰 not quite happily 的。换句话说，就是"让我斗胆想象一下"的意思，这里的 you 是作者自己（I），但他想用 you 来假设读者也会同意他的观点。之所以是"斗胆"是因为一般情侣都是愉快的，要说人家不愉快就必须有斗胆。至于说为什么会不愉快，我们很难确切地说，但恋人一起行走却不说话（silently），这一现象被作者观察到了，所以他就把这没有言语的静静的散步解读成 not happily。有人说这是"德国文化之忧郁"（German

melancholy），但我们不妨也可从天气上找找原因。刘勰《文心雕龙·物色》篇中有"春秋代序，阴阳惨舒，物色之动，心亦摇焉"的句子，说的就是天气对人心情的影响，而作者对达沃斯山谷的描述不乏令人忧郁的文字，山谷的环境会不会也影响到一对对恋人的心境，我们是否也可以这样斗胆想象一下呢？

16. 这一句中的 bad verses 应该反映出作者的谦虚。这个 an invalid 可理解成作者自己，就像汉语说"人家肚子饿死了"，虽是第三人称的形式，但也可以指代自己一样。正因如此，我们说作者自己说自己 make bad verses，就是瞎写几句诗，来几句歪诗，汉语的"歪诗"也有表达作者谦虚的意思。

17. 此处的 a score or so 是指从相反方向过来的人。至于说 to say nothing of，这个短语表示另外再添加一个例子，但这个例子的分量更重，很接近汉语的"至于……就更不用说了"。

18. 这个解释涵盖这一长句。前面列举了大量的例子说明山谷的环境令人烦扰，而且想在阿尔卑斯山谷避免这个是办不到的（no help for it＝no way to avoid it）。接下来作者说的是一系列山谷环境没有的东西，但他却马上跟上一个正面的东西与之对照，如没有间隙，但榨油作坊就有间隙，没有神圣的幽静，但罗卡布鲁纳路旁橄榄园就有，等等。最后的 breakers 一词就是指拍打海岸的大浪。而 haunted by 和 fragrant with 都是在那海角能经历的（haunted by 表示听到，fragrant with 表示闻到）。至于 threefold 这个词，主要是说后面三样东西，即 rosemary and the sea-pines and the sea，翻译的时候未必需要说进去。

19. 这句中的 chequer 就是 to diversify 的意思，也就是说，风暴使毫无变化的天气有了变化，不同了（the storms chequer

the sameness of the fair-weather scenes）。但是后面的 brighten the sameness 比较费解。首先这个用法是作者独创的，好像还没有看到类似用法。brighten 这里应该就是常规的用法，如"Will light brighten the future of the depressed patient"，就是使未来更令人愉快，也就是字典中的解释"if something brightens a situation, it becomes more pleasant, enjoyable, or favourable"，或者"if something brightens a place, they make it more colorful and attractive"。从这个定义可以看出，这个动作的结果看似作用于客观的物件，但实际是作用于人之主观心情，因为所有 pleasant, enjoyable, or favourable 的意思都得有人参与才能成立。而原文的 the sameness (of the fair-weather scenes)，表面上看是指客观的没有变化的景象，但这个词总暗指 boring。所以这里作者实际想说的就是：原来天气毫无变化，都一个样子，可暴雨一下，不仅视觉上景物有了变化，而且人也从毫无变化导致的沉闷中精神一振。这是作者的独特写法，我们会说，你为什么不写得清楚些？但译者的任务是尽可能挖掘出文句的意思，而不是问一些不会有答案的问题。当然，我并不认为这种写法是什么高明的写作特色，需要加以保留，需要在译文中翻译出来。毫无必要，把意思翻译出来就可以了。

20. 这个 in the unapparent 的短语出自雪莱的诗（P. B. Shelley, *Adonais*, l. 399. "The inheritors of unfulfilled renown / Rose from their thrones, built beyond mortal thought, / Far in the Unapparent."）。在本文中这个词组大意就是 in the sky。

21. 这里的 a shining burthen 是指压在枝头上的雪，burthen 是 burden 的旧写法，所指就是晶亮的雪。

22. 这里的 torrent 是指山间的小溪，但这个小溪似乎流得不顺畅，你看它是在 struggling，而且一般小溪流起来都会有声音，所谓小溪流水响叮咚！可是这里偏偏是 silently，这一切都说明这个小溪和一般的不同，原来它是 tongue-tied 的。这个英文词就是用来修饰不能说话的意思，在这里就是溪流不能发出声音的意思。原来这是在冬季的群山中，小溪已经被基本冻住了，也许还有那么一点水在流，但那是在 struggling。这种写法其实是依靠基本的常识，而且还是无文化障碍的常识，理解上不应该有很大的文化障碍，但需要译者富于想象。具体详见译文。

23. 这三个地方都是处于北极附近的地方，Lapland 是芬兰靠近北极的一个地方，Labrador 则是加拿大北端的地方，而 Alaska 是美国的一个州，也靠近北极。

24. 这个 simulacrum 的意思就是 something that looks like or represents something else。换句话说，指的是类似一餐早餐的食物，暗示吃得很随便，就那么垫巴垫巴吃一顿。

25. 这里我们需要注意天亮的时间。本来七点钟太阳早就升起了，可是这里说七点钟才见到早上第一道阳光。这个和地理位置有关，在有些地方，太阳确实比我们住的地方升起得晚，而且又是群山中，太阳越过山峰后的第一道阳光就会较晚，还别忘了又是冬天。

26. 这句 "The mountains are about you like a trap" 可以把 about you 换到前面（The mountains about you are like a trap），也可以将 about 换成 around。

27. 此处的 foot 当及物动词用，但 foot it 本身是一个成语，原本有两个意思，一个是 walk 的意思，另一个是 escape by running 的意思，和 beat it 同义，两个意思之间其实并不是完全无关。

这里 cannot foot it up a hillside and behold the sea 就是不能走到（爬到）山腰上见到大海。

28. 这里的 live in holes and corners 是一种形象的说法，表示生活的环境狭小，无开阔感，不像你到有些地方，一登上山腰，眼前就是开阔的景象。达沃斯山谷不行，生活在山谷里就像生活在洞里一样，无开阔感，但翻译的时候就没有必要去保留"洞"这类具体的词了，因为这些比喻（holes and corners）没有什么意义，翻译出意思就够了。

导　读

雪地冰天求健康

也许达沃斯并不像旧金山、夏威夷那样家喻户晓，但也不是个陌生之地。冬季去达沃斯滑雪，夏季到达沃斯避暑，都是很多人旅游计划中的项目，再加上世界经济领袖云集的达沃斯论坛，这个位于瑞士东部的小镇说它举世闻名并不夸张。当年的疗养去处现在已经转变成旅游胜地了。

那么我们把镜头拉回到 100 多年前，那时的达沃斯可只是个小小的村落。不过，这个冰冷的世界，却吸引着一批批特殊的人。他们来达沃斯不是为了滑雪或避暑，他们都是因病而来，且大多数是肺结核患者，有些还选在冰天雪地的冬季来到这里。19 世纪后期，欧洲流行一种说法，达沃斯冬季高山上清洁干燥的空气有益于肺部的保养，于是这个高山上的村落，就成了病人疗养的圣地。斯蒂文森正是因为这个原因在 1880 年 11 月来到了达沃斯。

斯蒂文森从小体弱。23 岁时身高已经 1.78 米，但体重仅有 107

斤。那年斯蒂文森心情非常郁闷,家乡爱丁堡对他来说如同监狱。屋漏偏遭连夜雨,他的散文"Roads"又被 *Saturday Review* 退稿了。情况显然很糟糕,朋友于是建议他去看肺科医生,因为斯蒂文森呼吸道一直也有病。克拉克医生建议他马上停止准备律师资格考试,到法国南部疗养。不过医生认为,他的主要问题不是肺疾,而是精神不稳定。斯蒂文森在法国南部住了半年,全仗着父亲的经济支柱。所以6个月后,当苏格兰春暖花开时,父亲就期待儿子回苏格兰了。可是斯蒂文森不愿意回去,精神再次崩溃。父亲不得不做出妥协。

去法国的一大收获是认识了从加州来法国的范妮·奥斯本。范妮当时仍然没有离婚,带着孩子来巴黎学习艺术。后来范妮返回加州,斯蒂文森居然随后横穿美国跟到加州。范妮在1879年离婚,次年5月与斯蒂文森正式结婚。

在如此一番折腾后,斯蒂文森的身体越来越差,朋友和医生建议他们到瑞士达沃斯去疗养一段时间。斯蒂文森和范妮携范妮的孩子便从加州东行,经纽约转伦敦,终于在1880年11月抵达瑞士东部的达沃斯。

当时的达沃斯被称为是"患者的麦加"(Mecca of the sick)。大约在19世纪60年代这个仅仅称得上是村庄的小地方开始迎来了一批批肺结核病人。一座座的疗养院建立起来了,与之配套的商店出现了,一个个教堂也应运而生。当时刚刚发现结核病菌,治疗结核病的链霉素要到半个多世纪后的1940年才问世,而其他抗结核药物要到20世纪50年代后才出现。所以当时流行的观点是,清新的空气和较为干燥的气候有助于结核病。

斯蒂文森求助的肺病专家卡尔·鲁迪(Karl Ruedi)先为他做了诊断,认为他是慢性肺炎兼带气管炎。斯蒂文森对于这位最权威也是最昂贵医生的诊断很不以为然,医生为他摘掉了肺结核的帽子,但是思想上他却没有摆脱那顶帽子。正是在达沃斯，斯蒂文森把自己看作是个"职业病人"（the professional sickest），尽管别人觉得他没那么糟糕。更麻烦的是斯蒂文森觉得达沃斯对他无大作用。他生来是个散漫的人，不喜欢管束。但是达沃斯的治疗不允许病人随性。鲁迪医生规定他晒太阳的时间，一动一静都有规范，饮食更是严加指点，得喝大量的牛奶，还要喝一种当地的酒，据说酒中含有大量单宁酸。但是抽烟是禁止的。显然斯蒂文森并没有完全忍住。对这位大烟枪来说，烟量的减少足以影响他的精神状态，难怪一整个冬天他总是萎靡不振。范妮当时体重过重，医生让她减肥，她也很难做到。结果，减肥的范妮监督戒烟的斯蒂文森，说他偷偷抽烟，斯蒂文森却反唇相讥，说范妮又在吃面包，也没有遵守医嘱。

在斯蒂文森眼里，达沃斯是个让人百无聊赖的地方，仿佛是一座雪铸的碉堡，压抑人的精神。但是在达沃斯，斯蒂文森并非茕茕孑立，另外一位文学家当时也住在那里，那就是约翰·阿丁顿·西蒙兹（John Addington Symonds）。这位诗人兼文学批评家虽然对斯蒂文森的才能略有微词，但是在达沃斯这个精神的沙漠里，两人最终还是成为了朋友。西蒙兹虽有家室，但有同性恋倾向。初到达沃斯的斯蒂文森行为举止有违常规，曾一度被人怀疑也有同性恋倾向，但是他和西蒙兹完全是一般的朋友关系。

一般认为，斯蒂文森在第一次达沃斯小住期间，写作不多，倒是热衷于在雪地上滑雪橇，甚至把自己搞得很累。不过他还是没有停止文学活动。他一直在为 *Scotland and the Union* 做准备，据说在他远离家乡苏格兰后，他开始有了浓浓的乡愁。另外，他也在为他的第一本散文集（*Virginibus Puerisque*, 1881）做最后的收集整理工作。其实，我们这里选的"Davos in Winter"也被认为是1881年的作品，另外还有三篇，分别是"Health and Mountains""Alpine Diversions"

"The Stimulation of the Alps"。这四篇以达沃斯为背景的散文应该都是在他到达后写的。但我们知道他是 1880 年 11 月 4 日才到达沃斯的。他们刚到后还得费时安顿,这中间还有个圣诞,难免有些人际往来,一共也没有几天可以留给他写作。但我们却有了这四篇扎扎实实的散文,可见写作对斯蒂文森已是件信手拈来的事儿了。四篇散文发表在伦敦的一家晚报(*Pall Mall Gazette*)上,最早一篇发表于 1881 年 2 月 17 日,最后一篇发表于 3 月 17 日。评论界一般认为,斯蒂文森在达沃斯的第一个冬天没写什么,他们大概没有把这四篇登在报纸上的文章视为文学创作吧?

鲁迪医生指示他在达沃斯待一整年,这在斯蒂文森来说是画地为牢,他那吉卜赛人的游荡性格被控制起来了。他曾在给朋友的信中说,自己就像一把小提琴被挂在了墙上,心中涌动的音乐被扼杀了。他反复和人说,他希望自己是一只小鸟。在这样的心境中,他实在写不出激情。这只要看看我们上面这四篇散文的内容就知道了。斯蒂文森最后还是没有听从医嘱,未能在达沃斯待满一年。由于范妮健康状况不佳,他们在 1881 年 4 月暂时离开了达沃斯,到巴黎等地住了一段时间,然后又去了苏格兰。在皮特洛赫里(Pitlochry)的那段时间里,斯蒂文森写作的欲望又一次燃起,他又像过去一样写作了。后来他又去了布雷马(Braemar),在那里的两个月中,他写下了大量的文字,包括后来在 1883 年出版的《金银岛》。

但是斯蒂文森毕竟是个疾病缠身的人,繁忙的写作又一次累及健康。他觉得苏格兰高原实在对他的身体不利,于是在 1881 年 10 月底又回到了达沃斯。这回他们在达沃斯山谷地处较高的地方租了一套房子。这期间,斯蒂文森写作激情高涨,写出了不少作品。但是好景不长,范妮的身体总是状况不断,胃病、心脏病、咽喉病接二连三。显然高山的寒冷干燥对斯蒂文森的健康也许有益，对范妮来说绝对是不利的。1882年4月他们带着病体，最后一次离开了达沃斯，开始了新的游荡。

看了上面长长的一个铺垫后，回头再来读我们这篇《冬季达沃斯》，就更能了解文中的种种描写了。从文章一开始，我们就知道作者对达沃斯的态度："往好了说，山谷就像牢房，禁锢人的想象，但是山谷、严冬、病弱凑在一起，就真在这氛围中营造出一个牢房，把人禁锢得寸步难行。"文章结束时，他还是没忘记要数落一下达沃斯："你周围的山岭如陷阱，你无法走上山腰见到平原一般的大海，只能生活在逼仄的环境里，唯一的变化就是周而复始。"在文中，他写达沃斯的雪，却偏重雪如何沉闷单调，无法取代世界的繁复多趣。散步时巧遇岩石一块，却拿田园里的芬芳气息和缤纷色彩来对照。他写让人叫苦连天的山雨，寒冷刺骨的山风，瘦骨嶙峋的山松，冰封不语的山涧，都是些让人却步的环境。刘勰在《文心雕龙》中说："春秋代序，阴阳惨舒，物色之动，心亦摇焉"，说的是自然界的外物对作者内心的影响。看了上面作者的身世遭逢，我们也许会觉得，达沃斯的自然环境固然影响了作者的心境，使得他郁闷低沉。但反过来看，作者的心境是否也给他描述的自然界蒙上了一层阴影？换一位内心阳光灿烂的作者，冬季的达沃斯也许会另有一番风光吧！

参考资料

Claire Harman, Myself & the Other Fellow—A Life of Robert Louis Stevenson, *Harper Perennial*, 2005.

Despised Races

Of all stupid ill-feelings, the sentiment of my fellow Caucasians towards our companions in the Chinese car was the most stupid and the worst. They seemed never to have looked at them, listened to them, or thought of them, but hated them *a priori*.[1] The Mongols[2] were their enemies in that cruel and treacherous battle-field of money. They could work better and cheaper in half a hundred industries, and hence there was no calumny too idle for the Caucasians to repeat, and even to believe.[3] They declared them hideous vermin, and affected a kind of choking in the throat when they beheld them. Now, as a matter of fact, the young Chinese man is so like a large class of European women, that[4] on raising my head and suddenly catching sight of one at a considerable distance, I have for an instant been deceived by the resemblance. I do not say it is the most attractive class of our women, but for all that[5] many a man's wife is less pleasantly favoured. Again, my emigrants[6] declared that the Chinese were dirty. I cannot say they were clean, for that was impossible upon the journey; but in their efforts after cleanliness[7] they put the rest of us to shame. We all pigged and stewed in one infamy, wet our hands and faces for half a minute daily on the platform, and were unashamed.[8] But the Chinese never lost an opportunity, and you would see them washing their feet—an act not dreamed of among ourselves—and going as far as decency permitted to wash their whole bodies. I may remark by the way that the dirtier people are in their persons the more delicate is their

被鄙视的种族

在所有愚昧的仇视心态中,我的白人同胞对华人车厢中乘客的态度,可谓愚昧恶劣之极。他们似乎对一同乘车的华人不看、不听、不顾,却又凭空憎恨。这些蒙古血统的人是他们在狡诈、残酷商场上的劲敌。人家华人在数十个行业里干起活来比你强,还更便宜,所以白人便极尽诽谤诬陷之能事,热衷于以讹传讹,甚至相信谣言。他们宣称华人阴险恶毒,见了华人就佯作恶心状。而实际上,年轻的华人男子很像某些欧洲女子,我一抬头,突然看见远处的一位华人,有那么一刻甚至以为那是欧洲女人。我不是说他们像我们的女人中最好看的那种,但就算不是最好看的,我们的妻子大多也不在其上。另外,我的移民同胞宣称华人很脏。我确实不能说他们干净,你想啊,一路风尘岂能干净,但是看了人家为洁身不遗余力,我们反倒该汗颜。车厢里谁不像圈里的猪脏得无体面可言,每天在车站的站台上只花上半分钟洗个手、擦个脸,竟浑然不觉得难为情。可人家华人却抓住任何机会把自己拾掇干净,他们还会洗脚呢,这可是我们连想都不会想到的,而且只要得体,他们还会擦洗全身。顺便说一下,身体越脏,越会感到难为情。一个干净的人在拥挤的船房脱衣露体不觉难为情,但是没洗身子的人上下床却捂

sense of modesty.[9] A clean man strips in a crowded boathouse; but he who is unwashed slinks in and out of bed without uncovering an inch of skin.[10] Lastly, these very foul and malodorous Caucasians entertained the surprising illusion that it was the Chinese waggon, and that alone, which stank. I have said already that it was the exceptions and notably the freshest of the three.[11]

These judgments are typical of the feeling in all Western America.[12] The Chinese are considered stupid, because they are imperfectly acquainted with English. They are held to be base, because their dexterity and frugality enable them to underbid the lazy, luxurious Caucasian. They are said to be thieves; I am sure they have no monopoly of that. They are called cruel; the Anglo-Saxon and the cheerful Irishman may each reflect before he bears the accusation.[13] I am told, again, that they are of the race of river pirates,[14] and belong to the most despised and dangerous class in the Celestial Empire.[15] But if this be so, what remarkable pirates have we here! and what must be the virtues, the industry, the education, and the intelligence of their superiors at home!

Awhile ago it was the Irish, now it is the Chinese that must go. Such is the cry. It seems, after all, that no country is bound to submit to immigration any more than to invasion; each is war to the knife, and resistance to either but legitimate defence.[16] Yet we may regret the free tradition of the republic, which loved to depict herself with open arms, welcoming all unfortunates. And certainly, as a man who believes that he loves freedom, I may be excused some bitterness when I find her sacred name misused in the contention.[17] It was but the other day that I heard a vulgar fellow in the Sand-lot, the popular tribune of San Francisco, roaring for arms and butchery. "At the call of Abraham Lincoln," said the orator,

得严实，生怕别人知道你是脏人一个。最后，这些又脏又臭的白人实在让人跌破眼镜，居然心生幻觉，认为臭气只来自华人车厢。我已说过，那车厢还真是个例外，显然三节车厢中唯它没有臭味。

这类成见是美国西部人们的典型心态。说华人愚蠢，因为他们说不好英文。说华人卑鄙，因为他们机巧节俭，以低价打败既懒惰又奢侈的白人对手。说华人是窃贼，我相信，偷盗这行还真不由华人垄断。还说华人残忍，但在指责别人前，盎格鲁－撒克逊和乐天的爱尔兰人更该反躬自省。有人还对我说，这些华人是江湖盗寇之流，在天朝也是极可鄙、极危险的一群。若果真如此，那我们身边的这些盗贼还真不错！至于他们故国的那些更优秀的人就定是德行、勤奋、教育、智慧的典范了！

曾几何时，是爱尔兰人必得离开，现在又嚷着要华人必得走人。也是，好像没有一个国家有义务屈服于外来移民，就像没有国家得屈服于外敌入侵一样。移民和入侵都会遭遇殊死抵抗，仿佛抵抗其中任何一个都是合理的自我捍卫。不过，那样的话，我们可能就要后悔有那共和国自由的传统了，后悔曾夸下海口，把自己的国家描绘成一个展开双臂欢迎不幸者的国家。当然，作为一个自信热爱自由的人，见到自由这神圣的名字在争辩中被践踏，我有些愤慨也该得到原谅。这不，仅仅几天前，我在旧金山的一个论坛上就听一位粗俗的家伙口吐狂言，主张武力残杀。这位演说者对听众说，你们曾响应亚伯拉罕·林肯的号召，以自由的名义，站起来解放了黑人，你们不能站起来把自己从几个肮脏的蒙古人那

"ye rose in the name of freedom to set free the negroes; can ye not rise and liberate yourselves from a few dirty Mongolians?"[18]

For my own part, I could not look but with wonder and respect on the Chinese. Their forefathers watched the stars before mine had begun to keep pigs. Gun-powder and printing, which the other day we imitated, and a school of manners which we never had the delicacy so much as to desire to imitate, were theirs in a long-past antiquity. They walk the earth with us, but it seems they must be of different clay.[19] They hear the clock strike the same hour, yet surely of a different epoch. They travel by steam conveyance, yet with such a baggage of old Asiatic thoughts and superstitions as might check the locomotive in its course.[20] Whatever is thought within the circuit of the Great Wall; what the wry-eyed, spectacled schoolmaster teaches in the hamlets round Pekin; religions so old that our language looks a halfing boy alongside;[21] philosophy so wise that our best philosophers find things therein to wonder at; all this travelled alongside of me for thousands of miles over plain and mountain. Heaven knows if we had one common thought or fancy all that way, or whether our eyes, which yet were formed upon the same design,[22] beheld the same world out of the railway windows. And when either of us turned his thoughts to home and childhood, what a strange dissimilarity must there not have been in these pictures of the mind[23] —when I beheld that old, gray, castled city, high throned above the firth, with the flag of Britain flying, and the red-coat sentry pacing over all; and the man in the next car to me would conjure up some junks and a pagoda and a fort of porcelain,[24] and call it, with the same affection, home.

Another race shared among my fellow-passengers in the disfavour of the Chinese;[25] and that, it is hardly necessary to say, was the noble red

里解放出来吗？

就我自己来说，我看华人总带着惊奇与尊重。人家的祖先观察星象时，我们的祖先还没开始圈养猪猡呢！火药和印刷术我们前不久开始从人家那里学了过来，至于人家那一整套礼仪，我们可是从来没有想学一番的雅兴，但这些早就是人家实践经年的传统。华人和我们在同一个地球上行走，但是人家想必是用不同泥土做成的。华人和我们一同听钟报时，但听到的肯定是不同时代的音讯。人家乘蒸汽机车旅行，可背负着重重的亚洲思想和神秘信仰，重得一路上会把火车压垮！万里长城内之所想，戴眼镜斜视的先生在京郊村落中之所授，令我们的语言看上去幼稚如娃的古老宗教，让我们最牛的哲学家惊叹不已的哲学智慧，所有这一切，在这数千里的行程中，越高山、过平原与我相随相伴。天知道，我们一路上是否能在某件事情上所思所幻相同，天知道，我们构造相同的眼睛从车窗望出去是否看到同一个天地。当我们各自把思绪转到家乡与童年时，我们的脑海中想必呈现出家的奇特差异：我看到的家是那座老旧、暗灰色的古堡之城，高高地屹立在海口，不列颠的旗帜高扬，穿红色衣服的哨兵四处巡逻；我们隔壁车厢里的人脑海中浮现的是帆船、宝塔、瓷器做的城堡，但他们却怀着同样的深情，将那个地方称为家乡。

另一族人也和华人一样不受我同伴乘客的待见。不必说，那就是一些作家故事中说的高尚红种人，几天来，我们在他们祖祖辈辈生活的大陆上乘火车一路前行。我没有见到野性不减、习俗依旧的

man of old story[26] — over whose own hereditary continent we had been steaming all these days.[27] I saw no wild or independent Indian;[28] indeed, I hear that such[29] avoid the neighbourhood of the train; but now and again at way stations, a husband and wife and a few children, disgracefully dressed out with the sweepings of civilisation,[30] came forth and stared upon the emigrants. The silent stoicism of their conduct, and the pathetic degradation of their appearance, would have touched any thinking creature, but my fellow-passengers danced and jested round them with a truly Cockney baseness.[31] I was ashamed for the thing we call civilisation. We should carry upon our consciences so much, at least, of our forefathers' misconduct as we continue to profit by ourselves.[32]

If oppression drives a wise man mad, what should be raging in the hearts of these poor tribes, who have been driven back and back, step after step, their promised reservations torn from them one after another as the States extended westward, until at length they are shut up into these hideous mountain deserts of the centre—and even there find themselves invaded, insulted, and hunted out by ruffianly diggers? The eviction of the Cherokees (to name but an instance), the extortion of Indian agents, the outrages of the wicked, the ill-faith of all, nay, down to the ridicule of such poor beings as were here with me upon the train,[33] make up a chapter of injustice and indignity such as a man must be in some ways base if his heart will suffer him to pardon or forget. These old, well-founded, historical hatreds have a savour of nobility for the independent. That the Jew should not love the Christian, nor the Irishman love the English, nor the Indian brave tolerate the thought of the American, is not disgraceful to the nature of man; rather, indeed, honourable, since it depends on wrongs ancient like the race, and not personal to him who cherishes the indignation.[34]

印第安人；我确实听说，这些印第安人避开了离火车近的地方；但时不时丈夫、妻子，再加上几个孩子，别扭地穿着一身文明社会弃而不用的衣物，出现在火车站旁，注视着外来的欧洲移民。他们一声不响，面无表情，一副落魄可怜相，本会勾起任何会思想者的同情，但是我的这些粗俗愚笨的同路人却围着这些印第安人跳舞逗乐。真为我们称之为文明的那套东西感到羞愧。我们至今还从父辈的可耻行为中获取利益，所以至少应该为前辈的错误行为背负些羞耻。

如果压迫驱使一个智慧的人愤怒，那么何种情绪会怒涛般地在这些可怜的印第安纳人胸中奔腾？当人家一步步把你驱赶，你只能节节后退，当国家不停西进，许诺的居住区一个个被夺走，直到最后被圈至中部环境险恶的荒山沙地，甚至在那里也还要被凶恶的淘金者侵犯、侮辱、驱赶，这样的人他胸中能不怒涛汹涌吗？对切诺基人的无端驱赶（仅举一例），印第安事务专员的巧取豪夺，令人发指的恶事、背信弃义的恶人，还有这些和我同乘一车的可怜华人，白人对他们蔑视嘲讽，这一切恰构成一本没有公正、剥夺尊严的血泪史，一个人的心要去原谅忘却这些，那人就有点是非不分了。这些历史的旧恨情有可原，而在那些独立的印第安人身上我们看到一丝高尚的情怀。犹太人不爱基督徒，爱尔兰人也不爱英格兰人，印第安的武士不能容忍美国人，这些都是人之本性，并没有什么有失风度的，相反这些心态堂堂正正，因为这种怨恨不是起于个人的私愤，而是因种族等领域百年不公而引发的不平。

注 释

1. 这个 *a priori* 源自拉丁语,常表示没有事实根据就形成观念。这个词在哲学上和康德学派有关,也就是先验论。

2. Mongols 在这里并不是表示我们现在说的内蒙古或外蒙古的人,而是指中国人。这个词广义指东亚、中亚及其附近的人,主要是基于人种,而不是文化。蒙古人种是一般人类学上说的三大人种之一,三大人种包括 Caucasoid、Negroid 和 Mongoloid 人种。

3. 在 OED 里 idle 这个词有这样一个解释:"void of any real worth, usefulness, or significance"(如 It is *idle* to propose Remedies before we are assured of the Disease)。但另一个解释是 without foundation: baseless, groundless(*Idle* hopes that lure man onward, forced back by as *idle* fears)。所以它可以和不同的词搭配生成不同的意思,在本句中理解成 baseless 似乎更合理。 此外还要注意 too… to… 结构(*too* idle for the Caucasians *to* repeat)。

4. 此处有一个表示程度的结构(so… that…),要注意到 the young Chinese man is *so* like a large class of European women, *that*…。当然,翻译时倒未必要翻译成"如此……以至于……"这样一个死板的结构。

5. 这个 for all that 表示 in spite of that 的意思。类似的句子有"This Alexander the Great for all his greatness died",或"The owl, for all his feathers, was a-cold"。有时前面会有一个 but,但这个 but 是和另外一个从句构成转折关系,并不属于 for all that 这个词组的一部分,比如"We drove like bats out of hell to get there on time, but for all that hurrying, we were still too late to board the plane"。

6. 这个 my emigrants 就是指从欧洲移民到美国的那些白人，当时他们本身就是移民。注意 emigrant 和 immigrant 这两个词的区别，它们实际就是指同一个人，当他离开原来的国家时他就是 emigrant，而当他到达一个国家时，他就是 immigrant。
7. 在 after cleanliness 中的介词 after 表示 in pursuit of 的意思，即 cleanliness 是他们追求的目标，如 in full chase after him。
8. 这句中的 pigged and stewed in one infamy 的基本意思大致可以猜出来，比如 pig 当动词用就是 to crowd (people) together like pigs 的意思，总是提示拥挤、封闭、脏乱。而 stewed 则会有好几个引申出来的意思，如 OED 就有数个解释都相关（to confine in close or ill-ventilated quarters; to bathe in perspiration; to stink, emit a stench）。翻译的时候可以将这两个词合并起来处理，抓住几个主要的特征就可以了，比如"像圈里的猪脏得要命"就基本概括了两个词的意思，无需分开两个翻译单位，也无需把流臭汗、拥挤、封闭、脏乱等等的具体内容都说进去。至于 in one infamy 主要含义就是 bad reputation，OED 的一个定义是 "evil fame or reputation; scandalous repute; public reproach, shame, or disgrace"，在本句中似乎选取 shame 或 disgrace 更合适。罗斯福在日本偷袭珍珠港后说的那句名言里就有 infamy（a date which will live in infamy），但在不同的语境中如何翻译 infamy 还需要做语境微调。最后，on the platform 可指火车上车厢连接处的那块地方（连廊），但也可指车站的站台（月台）。一般情况下多指"连廊"，但本语境中似指站台，但确实较难确定。
9. 这句中的 sense of modesty 不能翻译成"谦虚"，这个 modesty 的意思并不是我们一般意义上的谦虚。在朗文词典中有一个定义是 unwilling to show your body that may attract sexual interest，所

被鄙视的种族

以有"羞怯"（shame）的意思，但这个"羞"起源于怕自己不洁静的事实被人知晓，和性（sex）方面的羞无关。另外，形容词 delicate 也不是我们最常用的意思，如 a delicate situation 或 delicate glass。此处可以解释为"finely sensitive to what is becoming, proper, or modest, or to the feelings of others"（OED），有 remindful 的意思，这里是特别注意自己到底是否得体，就是羞耻感重。其实 the more delicate is their sense of modesty 看似费解，实际就是 the more modest they are 的意思。

10. 从 I may remark 开始到 uncovering an inch of skin，这两句都是泛指，不涉及本文中的华人和白人，但作者确实认为这节车厢中的华人是干净的，而车厢中的白人是脏的。干净的人不担心在众人面前脱光身子（strips in a crowded boathouse），但是不干净的人就把身子捂得严严实实（without uncovering an inch of skin），怕别人知道自己没洗澡身体肮脏，这个怕别人知道的心情是由动词 slinks 表达出来的（Collins: If you slink somewhere, you move there quietly because you do not want to be seen.）。这句刚好是前一句抽象观察的呼应，是前一句的具体实例。这个 boathouse 是指河边的停船棚屋，但这里应该就是指一个拥挤的公用场所，人们在这里脱衣服，至于脱衣服后干什么，文中没有说，我们也无从知晓，但可以揣测，如游泳前的换装室。

11. 根据"I have said already"，我们可以断定这里说的 the freshest of the three 是指前文中提到的三类人，即白人女性和儿童、白人男性、华人，或者更确切地说，三种人分坐的车厢。另外，文中的 exceptions 有不同版本，如 Robert Louis Stevenson, *From Scotland to Silverado* (ed. James Hart, 1966) 中就是单数 exception,

所以 it 显然是指车厢。exception 应指例外，前面说"that alone, which stank"，那些人认为华人车厢是唯一的臭气来源，唯一就是例外。斯蒂文森说，没错是个例外，但是这个例外恰恰相反，是例外的一个干净的车厢，或言最干净的。本文是斯蒂文森那本 *Across the Plains* 中的一篇，这个三类人的说法可以在描写隔离的移民火车厢的文字中见到，车上的乘客分成三类，即白人女性和儿童一个车厢，白人男性一个车厢，华人一个车厢。另外前面一句中的 waggon 是 wagon 的旧写法，这里指火车的车厢，在其他地方当然指陆地行驶的车，如马车。

12. 这里 Western America 的所指随时间不同而有变化。维基百科的定义能概括西部的概念：美国西部泛指美国西部各州。由于美国自建国以来疆域多次向西扩展，因此美国西部的定义也随着时代而变化。一般多以密西西比河作为美国东西部的分界线。如果采用广义的定义，美国西部占去了美国一半以上的土地。

13. 这个动词 bear 有不同的意思，翻译时最好根据上下文选出最合适的词义，比如此处 bear 的意思就是 bring forth 或 give birth to 的意思，和 to be born 是同源词。

14. 与海盗不同，river pirates 活动于有河流的地方，全球都有，如中国 19 世纪在长江流域就有江湖盗贼猖獗的现象。

15. Celestial Empire 指的就是中国，或叫"天朝"。

16. 先说前半句，从大结构先讲。"No country is any more than"这个结构其实是将 than 前后的两个都否定了，也就是说，移民和入侵都不屈从。类似的句子如"Flying there isn't any more expensive than getting the train"，火车飞机都不贵。另外 to be bound to 可表示不同的意思，要根据上下文而定，在 OED

中的解释是"compelled, obliged; under necessity; fated, certain"等，可见要根据语境而定，比如"We in this our miserable age are bound to admonish the world"，就更适合解释成"compelled, obliged; under necessity"，但是"Life is a waiting race, in which the best horse is bound to win"，就更适合解释成 fated、certain 的意思。在这句里，我们没有义务或责任接受移民。不过虽然作者用"我们"，但是我们不要误读作者的态度，斯蒂文森认同不能屈从侵略的态度，但是他并不认同把移民都赶回去的态度。这里的我们主要是指社会中一般民众的态度。另外，后半句的 war to the knife 是个习惯用语，表示殊死斗争的意思。but legitimate defence 中的 but 表示 only 的意思。

17. 这句中动词 excused 的用法现在不常见（I may be excused some bitterness），不过可以将 excused some bitterness 换成 pardoned for having bitterness，意思就比较清楚了。这里的 bitterness 是有些气愤的意思（OED: fig. unpalatable to the mind; unpleasant and hard to swallow or admit）。这句后半部分的 when I find her sacred name misused in the contention 就是指下面一句旧金山论坛上那位粗俗的家伙，那人就是在 misuse 自由的名字。全句大意就是，别人乱用自由，斯蒂文森有点气愤，但他觉得自己那点气愤应该得到原谅。

18. 这句没有什么理解上的问题，但是在表达后半句时会遇到一些较难拿捏的选择。他先说你们曾以自由的名义，站起来解放了黑奴，那你就不能也站起来解放自己吗？但问题是后面的 from a few dirty Mongolians 怎么融入句子。假如翻译成"将几个肮脏的蒙古人赶回去进而解放自己"，"赶回去"是不是算无端添加？很清楚说话者不喜欢这些中国人，最好不和这些人有交往，不和这些人做生意，不坐在同一班火车上，但是我们还是没有足够的信息说要把他们赶回去。所以再三思考，最后还是处理成了"你们不能站起来把自己从几个肮脏的蒙古人那里解放出来吗？"当然再离原文远一些的译法也不是没有，如"解放自己，远离蒙古人"之类的译法也可以考虑，但是总觉得准确方面欠缺些。

19. 这个 different clay 表示用不同材料做成的，但是翻译的时候翻译成"材料"会有悖这个词的文化特征。这个 clay 其实是《圣经》中常用的词，是上帝造人的材料，如 "Remember, I beseech thee, that thou hast made me as the clay; and wilt thou bring me into dust again?"（Job, 10: 9），所以为了反映这个文化背景，仍然建议保留原文的特色，采取直译。

20. 这句有好几个问题需要解释。首先 superstitions 放在这个语境中不宜翻译成很负面的词（如"迷信"），因为整段都在赞扬华人及其文化，前面又是传统的亚洲思想，斯蒂文森是在最大程度地将亚洲的文化包容进来，有正面的思想，也有一些不很理性的想法，所以译者应尽量不用很负面的词，但又不违背原文的基本语义（如"神秘信仰"）。另外一个是 check the locomotive 到底是什么意思？回答这个问题，要看这本书前面的篇章。在 *Across the Plains* 开头处有这样的描写："The rest of the afternoon was spent in making up the train. I am afraid to say how many *baggage*-waggons followed the engine, certainly a score; then came the Chinese, then we, then the families, and the rear was brought up by the conductor…"。作者用 baggage 是表示乘客大包小包的行李，一车厢一车厢的行李，多到几乎火车难以负荷。而在我们这篇文章中，作者突然把前面那段中字面意义的 baggage 转而用成隐喻（a baggage of old Asiatic thoughts and superstitions），同时也无意中把前面重负荷的含义转到这句中。如果我们把 such a baggage of old Asiatic thoughts… as might check 中的 such… as 连起来看，就能得出 such a baggage 在强调重负荷的意思，as 就是表示重负的程度，也就是重到火车都走不动（check the locomotive），这火车还能承载得下吗？当然这是隐喻，文化思想不可能有物理重量，作者是在强调一车厢的华人携带着一包一箱的行李，也带着重重的文化传统。情态动词 might 很好地说明这个动作 check 是隐喻的，不是真的火车被文化思想压垮。check 的意思不是 examine，而是 stop，就是阻止前进，如 check a horse at the edge of the cliff（悬崖勒马）。

21. 这个 halfing 就是 half 的意思，是苏格兰语，在这里表达的是没有成熟的意思。

22. 这里是在说，白种人和华人眼睛的生理构造是相同的。

23. 这句要注意，不要把双重否定看成负负得正。这句的意思根据语境应表示各自脑海中的图像不同。也就是说，不同的生长环境在他们的脑海中投射出不同的图像，但不同的图像却使他们体会到相同的温情（家）。也就是说，这两个人"殊途（不同图像）同归（同是家）"。

24. 这个 a fort of porcelain 很难百分之百地确定是什么。在19世纪的英国各种瓷器很流行，很可能是斯蒂文森看到过一个瓷器物件，上面刻画着一个城堡，但这无从确认。

25. 此处的 disfavour 一开始翻译成"受到蔑视"，就大意来说没错，根据上下文更没错，但是后来还是回到离原文文字更近的词（不待见）。虽然这是个分量不重的词，蔑视也好，不待见也罢,在大语境中意思都差不多,但是译者最好养成一个习惯,尽可能逼近原文的意思。另外,注意 share in 和 share 的细微差别。share in 一般表示几个人共同拥有并共享一个东西,比如 share in the profits、share in the success 或 share in responsibility。但是 share 则表示一个人愿意将自己拥有的东西让给别人一部分(即分享),比如说,你可以说"I share my lunch with you",但不能说"I share in my lunch with you",两个意思不一样。

26. 在斯蒂文森写作本文前,已经有些作家将美国印第安人正面描写成高尚的英雄,如詹姆斯·费尼莫尔·库柏(James Fenimore Cooper)和海伦·亨特·杰克逊(Helen Hunt Jackson)可能就是最早这样描写印第安人的。另外马克·吐温也在讽刺短文中用过 noble red man 的说法,不过马克·吐温在杂文中用讽刺的口气描写印第安人。

27. 这里的动词 steam 指火车或其他燃煤动力机车的运行,比如"The train was steaming into the station"或"Now you can rail there, unconscious as to the beauties through which you have steamed"。此处的 hereditary continent 就是指印第安人原来的大地。斯蒂文森充分意识到他们乘火车西行的大地原来都是属于印第安人的。

28. 印第安人本来远离文明社会,与自然接近,更多野性(wild),根本不受外来欧洲文明的影响(independent)。此处的 independent 应该是指独立于欧洲文化的意思。这句说明,斯蒂文森看到的印第安人已经受到欧洲文明的影响,比如穿的衣物已不再是过去部落人穿的衣物,头上也没有了羽毛,行为举止也不再是部落中的那一套,所以他才说没有见到那些独立于欧洲文明的印第安人。

29. 这个 such 是代词，一般替代前面提到的事。OED 中的定义很清楚：standing predicatively at the beginning of a sentence or clause, and referring summarily to a statement or description just made（At the end of a year he would be free to return to the cloisters, for such had been his father's bequest.）。但这里 such 指的就是前面的印第安人。

30. 动词变名词后（如动名词）会出现两种情况。一种是形式已经是个名词，但是仍然保留其动词特征，仍然指动作，比如认知语言学中有个经典例句"Cooking involves irreversible chemical changes."，这句中的 cooking 是动名词，但仍保留动词的特征，仍然指动作。有人认为这类动名词展示序列扫描（sequential scanning），像演电影一样，好像你可以看到烹调的过程。另外一种动名词，形式和实质全变成了名词，如"I like his cooking"，这时动名词强调的是过程的结果，比如这句中，你喜欢的并不是他的烹调过程，你喜欢的是他烹调的结果，是放在盘子里的菜，是一盘或两盘，是可以数的。此时就不是像演电影了，而像静止的照片，学术界也给了它一个名称叫"概括扫描"（summary scanning）。我们这个 sweepings 应该说已经完全转变成了名词，失去了原本动词的特征。OED 的一个定义符合我们的语境"that which is swept up; matter, esp. dust or refuse, that is swept together or away"，显然这个 sweepings 是物件，是可以被扫除的东西，而且是有贬义的，恰如垃圾，比如下面的例句"Sweepings of threads, formerly thrown away because the workmen could not unravel them"。这个词可以用作隐喻，一般有贬义，如垃圾之类的东西，如"The population (of Armenia) was composed largely of the

sweepings of Asia Minor, Christian tribes which had taken refuge in the mountains."。本文中指穿的衣物都是文明世界穿戴过然后丢弃的东西，sweepings 指可数的衣物。另外，介词 with 也提示后面的东西是实物。

31. Cockney 原来特指伦敦东区工人阶层，这些人思想简单、行为粗俗、大大咧咧、嘲弄别人。而 baseness 也指坏行为举止（bad character），缺乏道德准则（lack of moral principles）。这两个词加在一起就刻画出了欧洲到北美来的移民的嘴脸。翻译的时候当然可以将 with a truly Cockney baseness 用来形容动词（danced and jested），但这里译者将这个短语移植到人上，成为了名词的修饰语（这些粗俗愚笨的同路人）。在一些正规的硬文本中，这种转换要更谨慎些。

32. 此处的 carry upon our consciences 容易使人联想到班扬的《天路历程》，书中基督徒背重负，此处提示道德的重担。《天路历程》对斯蒂文森影响颇大，可参见 "Books Which Have Influenced Me" 一文。

33. the eviction of the Cherokees 指发生在 1836 到 1839 年期间驱赶切诺基人的事件。数千切诺基人被从佐治亚、南卡罗来纳、北卡罗来纳、田纳西、得克萨斯、亚拉巴马州驱赶到印第安人领地，即现在的俄克拉何马州，沿途很多人死亡，故有 Trail of Tears 之称。the extortion of Indian agents 是指美国政府负责印第安事务的专员在 19 世纪期间对印第安人的巧取豪夺。至于 "the outrages of the wicked, the ill-faith of all" 则没有具体事件相关，就是类似前面提到的巧取豪夺，outrages of the wicked 就是指恶人做出的令人发指的事件，the ill-faith of all 就是指所有背信弃义的做派。这些事件的背景就是政府强迫印第安人签署放弃土地的协议，以及后来因利益改变而撕毁协议等事件。由于后两个是泛指，所以翻译时不必太拘泥。另外，此处的 nay 并不表示否定，而是表示追加一个例子（not that only, but also）。

34. 最后一句颇费解。根据上下文，初一看仿佛作者在鼓励仇恨。但是他说这种恨是高尚的，因为下面的原因（it depends on wrongs ancient like the race, and not personal to him who cherishes the indignation）。他想说的是，这种愤恨（it）的基础是 wrongs ancient like the race，也就是说是基于历史上一直存在的错误（比如种族），而不是那种仅仅与自己相关的仇恨。作者在告诉我们，恨也有两种，一种是只考虑自己的恨，还有一种是视野更为宽广的恨，出于更多人或集体的利益，我们也会有恨，这样才能促使人去把错与罪改正过来。读者绝对不要误读斯蒂文森的意图，他不赞同泄私愤的恨（and not personal to him who cherishes the indignation），而可称为高尚的恨是那种基于种族等更为宏大视野的恨（wrongs ancient like the race）。有鉴于此，本段中的 hatreds 似不宜翻译成"恨"或"仇恨"，因为这两个词总反映出当事人心胸比较狭隘，相反，愤恨或怨恨更符合这里的语境。另外，句中的 should not（the Jew *should not* love）并非表示不应该、不必要的意思，而仅是一般否定的意思，或者说 should 有些意外的含义（竟不爱……），不过翻译时未必要表达出来。还有句中的 the Jew 和 the Irishman，有些人认为，目前这种单数名词的使用会有一丝冒犯，一般现在人们会用 Jews、Jewish people 和 the Irish。本句一开始的译文更贴近原文（因为这种心态的基础是种族那样古老的错误行径，而不是造成个人愤怒的错误行径），但总觉得此处语言结构没有特殊意思，把语义说出来就行，结果就增加了译文的解释力度："因为这种怨恨不是起于个人的私愤，而是因种族等领域百年不公而引发的不平"。

导 读

不信他族是贱人

斯蒂文森身体不好是出了名的，早期都认为他肺有病，可能是肺结核，但后来有的医生认为他并无结核病，而是气管扩张造成了咳血。但不管怎么说，他一生中病患如影随形，到底是病阻碍了他的写作还是促进了他的写作，还真说不清。耶鲁大学菲尔普斯教授（William Lyon Phelps）借用亚历山大·蒲柏（Alexander Pope）的话说，斯蒂文森的一生就是一个长长的病（a long disease）。

也正因为这病，他开始到法国南部等地寻找适合居住的地方。他外出一趟，然后再回到家乡爱丁堡，几次下来终于认识到已无法在苏格兰的湿雾中生活下去，这注定了他日后离乡背井的命运。至于说他的颠沛流离完全是寻住处的结果，还是部分由天性使然，这个就很难说清楚了。菲尔普斯教授说，斯蒂文森身上有清教徒的思想，有纵览世界的格局，也有流浪汉的天性（the vagabond）。

在法国寻找宜居地的过程中，斯蒂文森在1876年9月巧遇范妮·奥斯本，从此便结下了姻缘。后来范妮和孩子回加州与丈夫团聚，但丈夫旧习不改，他们最终婚姻破裂。斯蒂文森获悉范妮已离婚，便急忙从伦敦出发，横渡大西洋，于1879年8月17日抵达纽约，开始了他的西行历程。斯蒂文森于8月30日到达加州蒙特雷，与范妮相会。此后，斯蒂文森写下了这次历程的全过程，分成三部曲。我们这里选的《被鄙视的族群》出自这三本游记中的第二本（*Across the Plains*）。为把前因后果说清，我们这里简单地介绍一下这三本游记。

这三部游记分别是《业余移民》（*The Amateur Emigrant*），基本记录了从欧洲到纽约的航海旅程；涵盖第二段旅程的《穿越平原》（*Across the Plains*）记录了斯蒂文森乘火车从纽约到旧金山的过程；第三本是《西尔弗拉多的蜗居客》（*The Silverado Squatters*），主要写他和范妮在纳帕度蜜月的经历。《穿越平原》是三本中最长的一本，共有12篇，其中第一篇"Across the Plains"的篇名也是整本游记的书名。第一篇有7章，其中的第6章就是我们这里选的"Despised Races"。我之所以选择这篇，主要是因为他在文中详细记述了火车上的欧洲人对同车华人的态度，以及在这种态度的反衬下，斯蒂文森对华人的态度。

斯蒂文森在文章一开头就记述了车上他的白人同胞对华人的态度，并同时表明了他本人的态度："在所有愚昧的仇视心态中，我的白人同胞对华人车厢中乘客的态度，可谓愚昧恶劣之极。"接下来他又把白人和华人做了一番比较："车厢里谁不像圈里的猪脏得无体面可言，每天在车站的站台上只花上半分钟洗个手、擦个脸，竟浑然不觉得难为情。可人家华人却抓住任何机会把自己拾掇干净，他们还会洗脚呢，这可是我们连想都不会想到的，而且只要得体，他们还会擦洗全身。"在当时，从欧洲到新大陆来的人普遍认为华人肮脏，而他们洁净。斯蒂文森却觉得华人更爱干净。在当时的社会环境里，各种歧视显而易见，比如车厢就分为三类，白人妇女儿童在一节车厢里，男人在一节车厢里，另外有一节车厢是专供华人用的。大家都说车上的臭气来自华人车厢，但斯蒂文森却认为华人车厢是唯一没有臭味的车厢。

读者也许注意到这篇文章题目中的 races 是复数。这说明斯蒂文森并非只对华人"情有独钟",他所表达的观点是一种普世的是非观。他在文中也提到了其他种族的人:"另一族人也和华人一样不受我同伴乘客的待见。不必说,那就是一些作家故事中说的高尚红种人,几天来,我们在他们祖祖辈辈生活的大陆上乘火车一路前行。"这是在说印第安人。显然斯蒂文森的心胸非常宽广,不仅只为某一族裔伸张正义。他也同情同是白人的爱尔兰人:"曾几何时,是爱尔兰人必得离开,现在又嚷着要华人必得走人。"

他的这种为少数族裔伸张正义的态度源自他对正义的追求,而不仅只聚焦在族裔,任何不正义的东西他都反对。值得一提的是他旅行三部曲的第一部 *The Amateur Emigrant*。如前所述,这本游记主要记叙了他乘船从欧洲到纽约的过程。他一开始要买最底层甲板的票,在那一层里,穷苦人和船运的货物待在一起,以便体验底层人民的生活。只是在最后一刻,由于朋友的劝说,才买了最底层上面一层的票,但还是和穷人离得很近。

在他的记述中,底层船客艰难的处境,船上的铺盖,分配的食物,上等人的冷眼,不同国别的船客,都有详细描写。比如一天住上等舱的几个男女专门跑到底层客舱来猎奇。他们窃窃私语,暗地里还发出笑声。这激怒了斯蒂文森,唤起了他心中强烈的阶级意识。他如此和下层人打成一片,是有阶级认同的一面。但批评家们也认为,斯蒂文森如此表现也不无自私的考虑,他是在为他将要写的游记体验生活,甚至也不能排除省钱的因素。

但不管怎么说,斯蒂文森和社会底层人如此接近,使得主流社会的人很意外,对他描述的事件也感到很震惊。有些描写被出版商认为不适合大众阅读。甚至他父亲也觉得有些章节太过露骨,竟至于自己花钱把已经印好的书买下,不希望这书在社会上流传。所以

《业余移民》在斯蒂文森生前一直没有全部出版。这本写于 1879 到 1880 年间的游记一直要到 1895 年才正式出版，那时他已经过世一年了。

上面对他旅行三部曲的第一部分的插叙主要是想说明，斯蒂文森对人的爱不仅是聚焦在族裔上的。他在《业余移民》中描写的底层人大多是和他同一种族的人。斯蒂文森对各族裔底层人民的普遍同情说明，他不仅是个好作家，更是个好人。正如菲尔普斯所说，斯蒂文森作为一个作家堪称伟大，但作为一个人则更伟大（Great as Stevenson was as a writer, he was still greater as a Man）。

有些人在阅读斯蒂文森时会发现，他的某些言辞似乎和基督教教义并不吻合，有时甚至对教义颇有不敬，他对牧师就有不敬之语。但是抛开这些言辞的表面，我们会看到一个有浓厚宗教情怀的人。从他和一些亲朋的信件看，有的学者就认为他性格的核心仍然是宗教的（His character was essentially religious）。

上面说到斯蒂文森的爱是对人类普遍的爱。但是在我们这篇中，他主要还是在说华人。所以他对华人的同情也有理解、包容异族文化的成分。他认为我们先天的肉体是相同的，但是人的经历和他们所处的文化使他们相异。他居然能设身处地站在华人的角度看问题，这在 19 世纪的欧洲是难能可贵的："当我们各自把思绪转到家乡与童年时，我们的脑海中定呈现出家的奇特差异：我看到的家是那座老旧、暗灰色的古堡之城，高高地屹立在海口，不列颠的旗帜高扬，穿红色衣服的哨兵四处巡逻；我们隔壁车厢里的人脑海中浮现的是帆船、宝塔、瓷器做的城堡，但他们却怀着同样的深情，将那个地方称为家乡。"他甚至还能站在异族人的立场上，理解弱势族群对强势族群的激烈反应："犹太人不爱基督徒，爱尔兰人也不爱英格兰人，印第安的武士不能容忍美国人，这些都是人之本性，并没有什么有失风度的，相反这些心态堂堂正正，因为这种怨恨不是起于个人的私愤，而是因种族等领域百年不公而引发的不平。"

　　读斯蒂文森这篇专讲华人的随笔，若能超出自己族裔的眼光，从我们自己的心中流淌出更为普世的爱与同情，那才没白读这上好的文字，才对得起病中挥笔的斯蒂文森。

参考资料

William Lyon Phelps, *Essays of Robert Louis Stevenson*, New York, C. Scribner's Sons, 1906.

Claire Harman, Myself & the Other Fellow—A Life of Robert Louis Stevenson, *Harper Perennial*, 2005.

An Island Landfall

For nearly ten years my health had been declining; and for some while before I set forth upon my voyage, I believed I was come to the afterpiece of life, and had only the nurse and undertaker to expect. It was suggested that I should try the South Seas; and I was not unwilling to visit like a ghost, and be carried like a bale,[1] among scenes that had attracted me in youth and health. I chartered accordingly Dr. Merrit's schooner yacht, the Casco, seventy-four tons register; sailed from San Francisco towards the end of June 1888, visited the eastern islands, and was left early the next year at Honolulu.[2] Hence, lacking courage to return to my old life of the house and sick-room, I set forth to leeward in a trading schooner, the Equator, of a little over seventy tons, spent four months among the atolls (low coral islands) of the Gilbert group, and reached Samoa towards the close of '89.[3] By that time gratitude and habit were beginning to attach me to the islands;[4] I had gained a competency of strength; I had made friends; I had learned new interests; the time of my voyages had passed like days in fairyland; and I decided to remain. I began to prepare these pages at sea, on a third cruise, in the trading steamer Janet Nicoll.[5] If more days are granted me, they shall be passed where I have found life most pleasant and man most interesting; the axes of my black boys are already clearing the foundations of my future house; and I must learn to address readers from the uttermost parts of the sea.[6]

又见陆地

将近有十年的时间，我的健康越来越差，而且在我坐船越洋远行前有段时间，我觉得自己已到了生命的尾声，期待的只是护士和抬棺人了。大家建议我试一下南太平洋的生活；而我也并非不愿意如一件包裹那样让人携带着，像个幽灵去那里短暂造访，毕竟那些地方我在年少健康时曾何等向往！我为此包租了梅里特医生的卡斯科号帆船，吨位74。卡斯科号在1888年6月底出发，抵达了南太平洋东侧诸岛，次年初把我送达檀香山后返航。我当时实在没勇气回去再续旧宅病榻的生活，于是便乘坐另一艘70多吨位的商船赤道号顺风而行，花了4个月的时间，遍访吉尔伯特珊瑚群岛，在1889年底抵达萨摩亚群岛。岛上生活日久，我对当地的习俗日渐熟悉，与当地的土著情谊渐生，体力也恢复了。我交了不少朋友，也有了不少感兴趣的事，时光度得好不快活，仿佛生活在仙境，于是我决定留下来。我开始在海上写这本书，这回是在第三艘船上，这是一艘名为珍妮特·尼科尔的商用蒸汽船。如我寿数未尽，我就愿留在这里生活，因为这里生活更多快乐，人物更有情趣；为了建造我未来的房子，几个黑人小男孩已在刀劈斧砍清理那块宅地了；既然决定留下，我也得学会如何从天涯海角将异域风情传达给我远方的读者。

That I should thus have reversed the verdict of Lord Tennyson's hero is less eccentric than appears.[7] Few men who come to the islands leave them; they grow grey where they alighted; the palm shades and the trade-wind fans them till they die, perhaps cherishing to the last the fancy of a visit home, which is rarely made, more rarely enjoyed, and yet more rarely repeated. No part of the world exerts the same attractive power upon the visitor, and the task before me is to communicate to fireside travelers[8] some sense of its seduction, and to describe the life, at sea and ashore, of many hundred thousand persons, some of our own blood and language,[9] all our contemporaries, and yet as remote in thought and habit as Rob Roy or Barbarossa, the Apostles or the Cæsars.[10]

The first experience can never be repeated. The first love, the first sunrise, the first South Sea island, are memories apart and touched a virginity of sense.[11] On the 28th of July 1888 the moon was an hour down by four in the morning.[12] In the east a radiating centre of brightness told of the day; and beneath, on the skyline, the morning bank was already building, black as ink. We have all read of the swiftness of the day's coming and departure in low latitudes; it is a point on which the scientific and sentimental tourist are at one, and has inspired some tasteful poetry.[13] The period certainly varies with the season; but here is one case exactly noted. Although the dawn was thus preparing by four, the sun was not up till six; and it was half-past five before we could distinguish our expected islands from the clouds on the horizon. Eight degrees south,[14] and the day two hours a-coming.[15] The interval was passed on deck in the silence of expectation, the customary thrill of landfall heightened by the strangeness of the shores that we were then approaching. Slowly they took shape in the

我决定安顿下来，这与丁尼生笔下尤利西斯永不停步的英雄恰恰相反，但其实我这样也算不上异类怪诞。来这里的人很少离开海岛，他们在上岸的地方变老，在棕榈树下庇荫，在信风中沐浴，直到死去，可能到生命的最后一刻都怀揣着重回故国的幻想，但故国是极少回去的，回去了也少有欢乐，而再做回乡之旅就更为少见了。世上没有一个地方对游客有如此强的吸引力，我的任务就是要将这些地方的魅力传达给坐在火炉旁读书游世界的人，就是要描写成百上千的人在海上和岛上的生活。他们中有的与我们血脉同源语言同系，虽都是当代人，但想法迥异、习惯不同，就像苏格兰的豪杰罗布·罗伊，神圣罗马帝国的皇帝巴巴罗萨，《圣经》中的使徒或古罗马帝国的皇帝一样，与当代人大相径庭。

第一次经历是永远不可能重复的。第一次恋爱、第一次日出，第一次南太平洋岛的经历，那种记忆独一无二，触动了我处女般的感官。1888年7月28日，凌晨四点，月亮已落下一小时了。在东方，一团四射的光芒预示着白昼的来临；下面的天际线处，黑色的浓雾已经聚成一条。我们都听说过在低纬度处白昼的来去是弹指间的事。就在那一刻，擅长科学的游客会用科学去解释这瞬间的更迭，而善感的游客则会抒情感怀，他们都惊叹不已，而一些韵味十足的诗句就是在那一刻诞生的。当然这段黑夜与白昼换岗的时刻也会随季节不同而异；但下面就是一次切身体会的记录。虽然四点钟黎明已在酝酿中，但太阳要到六点才会露面；要到五点半我们才能从海平面的云雾里分辨出我们期待的岛屿。赤道以南8纬度，白昼还要两小时才会到来。这个间隙是在船的甲板上度过的，大家在沉默中

attenuating darkness. Ua-huna, piling up to a truncated summit, appeared the first upon the starboard bow; almost abeam arose our destination, Nuka-hiva, whelmed in cloud; and betwixt and to the southward, the first rays of the sun displayed the needles of Ua-pu. These pricked about the line of the horizon; like the pinnacles of some ornate and monstrous church, they stood there, in the sparkling brightness of the morning, the fit signboard of a world of wonders.[16]

Not one soul aboard the Casco had set foot upon the islands, or knew, except by accident, one word of any of the island tongues; and it was with something perhaps of the same anxious pleasure as thrilled the bosom of discoverers that we drew near these problematic shores. The land heaved up in peaks and rising vales; it fell in cliffs and buttresses; its colour ran through fifty modulations in a scale of pearl and rose and olive; and it was crowned above by opalescent clouds. The suffusion of vague hues deceived the eye; the shadows of clouds were confounded with the articulations of the mountains; and the isle and its unsubstantial canopy rose and shimmered before us like a single mass. There was no beacon, no smoke of towns to be expected, no plying pilot. Somewhere, in that pale phantasmagoria of cliff and cloud, our haven lay concealed; and somewhere to the east of it——the only sea-mark given——a certain headland, known indifferently as Cape Adam and Eve, or Cape Jack and Jane, and distinguished by two colossal figures, the gross statuary of nature. These we were to find; for these we craned and stared, focused glasses, and wrangled over charts; and the sun was overhead and the land close ahead before we found them. To a ship approaching, like the Casco, from the north, they proved indeed the least conspicuous features of a striking

期待着,海岛越来越近,奇特的海岸使久违陆地的人所惯有的激动更加强烈。黑暗慢慢淡去,海岸依稀浮现。阿胡娜岛,聚成一个平顶状的山峰,先在船的右舷弓侧隐现;接着是努卡海娃岛,我们的这个目的地几乎正对着船舷处升起,包围在云雾中;在两岛之间略偏南处,初阳照耀着瓦普岛犬牙交错的山峰。这些尖尖的山峰拔海而起,仿佛刺破了海平面。它们就像是美轮美奂大教堂的尖顶,在晨光中闪烁,恰似一则广告牌,提醒你一个奇异世界就在前方。

卡斯科船上没有一个人曾踏足岛上,除偶尔听到过几个词,对岛上的任何语言一无所知。正是怀着类似探索者常有的那种又焦虑又欢乐的心情,我们渐渐驶近将会给我们带来麻烦的海岸。陆地随着山峰和隆起的谷地渐渐升起,在绝壁和陡坡处一落千丈,但陆地色彩纷呈,珍珠、玫瑰、橄榄各种颜色应有尽有,岛的上空白云缭绕。那朦胧四溢的色彩哄骗了我们的眼睛;云影和山形混合在一起难以分辨;海岛和岛上虚无缥缈的穹顶像一个整体忽明忽现在我们眼前升起。没有灯塔,没有炊烟,也没有引航的小船。在绝壁和云雾的幻影中,隐藏着我们即将停泊的港湾;而就在港湾东侧的一处(那是地图上唯一的坐标),是一块狭长的地带,一般称之为亚当夏娃角,或也称为杰克珍妮角。那海角看上去像是两块巨大的人像,是大自然雄伟的杰作。这些是我们要找的地方;为了发现这些地方,我们引颈探望,聚焦望远镜,争相解读海图;时间已到正午时分,我们终于发现了这两个人像,陆地离我们近在咫尺了。卡斯科号从北向下驶,从这个角度看,我们寻觅的目标竟是引人注目海岸上的一个最不易发现的地方;海岸下激浪飞扬,海岸后面草木丛

coast; the surf flying high above its base; strange, austere, and feathered mountains[17] rising behind; and Jack and Jane, or Adam and Eve, impending like a pair of warts above the breakers.

Thence we bore away along shore. On our port beam we might hear the explosions of the surf; a few birds flew fishing under the prow; there was no other sound or mark of life, whether of man or beast, in all that quarter of the island. Winged by her own impetus and the dying breeze, the Casco skimmed under cliffs, opened out a cove, showed us a beach and some green trees, and flitted by again, bowing to the swell. The trees, from our distance, might have been hazel; the beach might have been in Europe; the mountain forms behind modelled in little[18] from the Alps, and the forest which clustered on their ramparts a growth no more considerable than our Scottish heath.[19] Again the cliff yawned,[20] but now with a deeper entry; and the Casco, hauling her wind, began to slide into the bay of Anaho. The cocoa-palm, that giraffe of vegetables, so graceful, so ungainly, to the European eye so foreign, was to be seen crowding on the beach, and climbing and fringing the steep sides of mountains. Rude and bare hills embraced the inlet upon either hand; it was enclosed to the landward by a bulk of shattered mountains. In every crevice of that barrier the forest harboured, roosting and nestling there like birds about a ruin; and far above, it greened and roughened the razor edges of the summit.

Under the eastern shore, our schooner, now bereft of any breeze, continued to creep in: the smart creature, when once under way, appearing motive in herself. From close aboard arose the bleating of young lambs; a bird sang in the hillside; the scent of the land and of a hundred fruits or flowers flowed forth to meet us; and, presently, a house or two appeared,

生的奇特峻岭拔地而起，杰克珍妮角，或称亚当夏娃角，就像一对格格不入的疣物悬在那里，下面是拍岸的巨浪。

于是我们沿着海岸破浪航行。我们可以听到船舷左侧巨浪拍船的爆裂声，船首处海鸟正在飞舞着捉鱼；在海岛的那一端，听不到也看不到其他生灵，无论是人还是兽，无声也无踪。借着船自身的冲力，乘着渐弱的微风，卡斯科号在悬崖下前进，驶进了宽阔的海湾，在我们面前展现的是一线海滩，一些绿树，船随浪起伏，再驶过海滩。从船上远看，树像是榛子树，海滩会让你觉得是在欧洲，海滩后的山岭有点像小一码的阿尔卑斯山，聚集在山体斜坡上的植被仿佛像是苏格兰山地上的灌丛。峭壁变得纵深开阔，卡斯科号背着风，滑行进入阿纳荷湾。可可棕榈树，那植物像是长颈鹿，既显得优雅，也看着拙笨，在欧洲人眼里实在是奇异之景。棕榈树群在海滩上成堆聚集，慢慢延伸至山岭，沿两侧陡峭的山崖边缘爬行而上。瘦骨嶙峋的山岭从两侧拥抱着那一湾狭长的水带；海湾靠陆地那一边是高高低低的山岭屏障，山与山之间的空隙处是片片树丛，像栖息在废墟上的鸟儿。高高在上的灌木把峰顶的边缘染成绿色，也使得刀刃般平整的峰缘凹凸不平了。

岛东侧的海面上，风已停歇，帆船继续缓行：这艘机灵的船一上路，似乎自有其动力。离船不远处，飘来一阵羊叫声；山边还有鸟鸣；扑面而来的是陆地的气息和无数花果的芬芳；不一会儿又见一两座房屋，高高矗立在山脚上方，其中一座四周都是花草，像是被花园环绕着。我们之前并不知道，这些显见的居所，这么一块有文明烙印的地方，是白人到过的痕迹；我们后来可能经过了上百个

standing high upon the ankles of the hills, and one of these surrounded with what seemed a garden.[21] These conspicuous habitations, that patch of culture, had we but known it, were a mark of the passage of whites; and we might have approached a hundred islands and not found their parallel[22] It was longer ere we spied the native village, standing (in the universal fashion)[23] close upon a curve of beach, close under a grove of palms; the sea in front growling and whitening on a concave arc of reef. For the cocoa-tree and the island man are both lovers and neighbours of the surf. 'The coral waxes, the palm grows, but man departs,' says the sad Tahitian proverb; but they are all three, so long as they endure, co-haunters of the beach. The mark of anchorage was a blow-hole in the rocks, near the south-easterly corner of the bay. Punctually to our use, the blow-hole spouted;[24] the schooner turned upon her heel; the anchor plunged. It was a small sound, a great event; my soul went down with these moorings whence no windlass may extract nor any diver fish it up; and I, and some part of my ship's company, were from that hour the bondslaves of the isles of Vivien.[25]

Before yet the anchor plunged a canoe was already paddling from the hamlet. It contained two men: one white, one brown and tattooed across the face with bands of blue, both in immaculate white European clothes: the resident trader, Mr. Regler, and the native chief, Taipi-Kikino. 'Captain, is it permitted to come on board?' were the first words we heard among the islands. Canoe followed canoe till the ship swarmed with stalwart, six-foot men in every stage of undress; some in a shirt, some in a loin-cloth, one in a handkerchief imperfectly adjusted;[26] some, and these the more considerable, tattooed from head to foot in awful patterns; some barbarous and knived; one, who sticks in my memory as something bestial,

岛屿，也没有发现一个有如此文化情调的地方。此后又过了好长一会儿我们才发现土著村落，和所有土著村子一样，坐落在棕榈树下弯弯的海滩上；前面的大海在流经一湾低洼暗礁时发出咆哮，激起白浪。这么靠近海是因为可可树和岛民既热爱海浪，也愿与海浪为邻。"珊瑚长大，棕榈长高，但人却要离岛"，这是大溪地当地的一则令人伤感的谚语；但是珊瑚、棕榈和人这三样只要存留下来，就会不离不弃一起环绕海滩。地图上船抛锚的标记是岩石上的一个洞，位置在海湾东南一角；凑得真巧，岩石上的锚洞正好喷出海水，帆船转了个身，锚就抛下了。抛锚声虽很小，但却开启了一个大事件；我的心灵随着这锚绳一起沉下去，牢牢地锚在这天涯海角，起锚机不能把它拽起来，潜水者也休想将它捞起；我和船上的有些人，从那一刻开始，就像被亚瑟王神话中的薇薇安施了魔法一样，与这些岛屿捆绑在一起了。

锚还没抛下时，就有一艘木舟从茅屋处摇过来。舟上有两个人，一个是白人，一个是棕色皮肤的人，后者脸上画着蓝色的条纹，都穿着白色洁净的欧洲服饰：那白人是常住岛上的商人瑞格乐先生，另一个是土著首领泰皮吉吉诺。"船长，可以上船吗？"这是我们在岛上听到的第一句话。木舟一艘接一艘摇过来，我们的帆船挤满了很多六英尺高的壮硕男人，他们遮体的衣物多寡不一，但都穿得少得可怜，有的穿衬衫，有的系腰带，还有一位用了块布遮羞但却不很成功，有的个子更大些，从头到脚都是蹩脚的刺青图案，还有的身带刀器更显野蛮，有一个人给我印象极深，一副凶神恶煞相，蹲在木舟中，口里吸吮着橘子，再把吃进的东

squatting on his hams in a canoe, sucking an orange and spitting it out again to alternate sides with ape-like vivacity—all talking, and we could not understand one word; all trying to trade with us who had no thought of trading, or offering us island curios at prices palpably absurd. There was no word of welcome; no show of civility; no hand extended save that of the chief and Mr. Regler. As we still continued to refuse the proffered articles, complaint ran high and rude; and one, the jester of the party, railed upon our meanness[27] amid jeering laughter. Amongst other angry pleasantries—'Here is a mighty fine ship,' said he, 'to have no money on board!' I own I was inspired with sensible repugnance; even with alarm. The ship was manifestly in their power; we had women on board; I knew nothing of my guests beyond the fact that they were cannibals; the Directory (my only guide) was full of timid cautions; and as for the trader, whose presence might else have reassured me, were not whites in the Pacific the usual instigators and accomplices of native outrage? When he reads this confession, our kind friend, Mr. Regler, can afford to smile.

Later in the day, as I sat writing up my journal, the cabin was filled from end to end with Marquesans:[28] three brown-skinned generations, squatted cross-legged upon the floor, and regarding me in silence with embarrassing eyes. The eyes of all Polynesians are large, luminous, and melting; they are like the eyes of animals and some Italians. A kind of despair came over me, to sit there helpless under all these staring orbs, and be thus blocked in a corner of my cabin by this speechless crowd and a kind of rage to think they were beyond the reach of articulate communication, like furred animals, or folk born deaf, or the dwellers of some alien planet.

西左右开弓吐掉，活泼机灵如猩猩。他们都在不停讲话，但我们一个字都听不懂；所有的人都想和我们做交易，而我们却不想交易，他们还想把岛上的珍奇物品用高得离谱的价格卖给我们。没有什么欢迎的话，也不来礼貌那一套，除了土著首领和瑞格乐先生，也没人和你握手。我们坚持不买他们兜售的东西，他们便开始抱怨，言语非常粗鲁；还有一位算是这群中的小丑，他觉得我们小气，便报以不怀好意的嘲笑。还有其他冷嘲热讽的话，比如他说："好大一条船，船上连钱都没有！"我承认我有些反感，甚至有些惊慌。因为这船显然任由他们掌控，而且我们船上还有女人。加之我对这些客人一无所知，只知道他们是食人者，而且引航者（也是我唯一的向导）也显得谨慎起来了；还有那位商人同样让我们担忧，他的出现若换个场合本该让我放下紧张的心，但是在太平洋岛上，白人不常唆使当地人闹事并与之合谋吗？本书出版时，我好心肠的朋友瑞格乐先生要是读到上面我对情势的误读误判，就一定忍不住会笑起来。

  那天晚些时候，我坐着写日记，小屋里前前后后挤满了棕色皮肤的马克萨斯人：老少三代人盘腿坐在地上，一声不响地看着我，让我感到好不自在。波利尼西亚人的眼睛都很大，目光深炯柔和，像是动物或某些意大利人的眼睛。我被这群一言不发的当地人挡在小屋的角落里，无助地坐在那儿，他们一双双眼睛紧盯着你，心中不免起了一丝绝望：这些人就像是一身皮毛的动物，或像是生来耳聋的人，抑或是外星人，我竟无法与他们沟通交流，想到这，不免非常恼怒。

To cross the Channel is, for a boy of twelve, to change heavens; to cross the Atlantic, for a man of twenty-four, is hardly to modify his diet. But I was now escaped out of the shadow of the Roman empire, under whose toppling monuments we were all cradled, whose laws and letters are on every hand of us, constraining and preventing. I was now to see what men might be whose fathers had never studied Virgil, had never been conquered by Cæsar, and never been ruled by the wisdom of Gaius or Papinian.[29] By the same step I had journeyed forth out of that comfortable zone of kindred languages, where the curse of Babel is so easy to be remedied; and my new fellow-creatures sat before me dumb like images. Methought, in my travels, all human relation was to be excluded; and when I returned home (for in those days I still projected my return) I should have but dipped into a picture-book without a text. Nay, and I even questioned if my travels should be much prolonged; perhaps they were destined to a speedy end; perhaps my subsequent friend, Kauanui, whom I remarked there, sitting silent with the rest, for a man of some authority, might leap from his hams with an ear-splitting signal, the ship be carried at a rush, and the ship's company butchered for the table.[30]

There could be nothing more natural than these apprehensions, nor anything more groundless. In my experience of the islands, I had never again so menacing a reception; were I to meet with such to-day, I should be more alarmed and tenfold more surprised. The majority of Polynesians are easy folk to get in touch with, frank, fond of notice, greedy of the least affection, like amiable, fawning dogs; and even with the Marquesans, so recently and so imperfectly redeemed from a blood-boltered barbarism,[31] all were to become our intimates, and one, at least, was to mourn sincerely our departure.

对于一个 12 岁的孩子来说，跨越英吉利海峡是改天换地的变化；对于一个 24 岁的人来说，横跨大西洋也就是换换饮食习惯而已。但是我现在是逃出了罗马帝国阴影的笼罩，可我们都是在帝国的残垣断壁下成长起来的，帝国的法律和文学在生活中陪伴着我们，约束限制着我们。我现在即将遇见的人会是怎样的人？他们的父辈可从来没有读过弗吉尔，没有被恺撒征服过，也没有受过盖乌斯或帕比尼安智慧的掌控啊！同时，我也游离出了同一语系间的语言舒适区，巴比塔造成的语言障碍在舒适区内是很容易克服的，但现在我眼前的这些新伙伴却像是石雕一样的哑巴，和你无法交流。当时我似乎觉得，在我接下来的旅行中，所有的人际关系都将要被切断；而我回到故土时（当时我仍然想着要回去），就像是只读了一本没有文字的画册。不仅如此，我甚至不知道我在外的游历还能延续到有回去的一天；也许命中注定这游历会戛然而止；也许后来成为朋友的卡瓦努伊，就是我刚才讲过的静静地和别人一起坐着的那位，那位有权威的人，会跳起来发出刺耳的命令：快把船给我占领了，船上的人都给我宰了吃掉。

这些吓人场景的出现可能最自然不过，但也最无根据。在我后来的海岛经历中，没有一次岛民的接待像这次那么充满恶意；如果我今天要面对如此情景，我会更加惊慌。大部分波利尼西亚人都是很容易接触的，他们很坦率，喜欢别人注意他们，拼命想求得一点感情，就像可爱乖巧的狗一样。就算是马克萨斯人，刚刚才不那么彻底地摆脱了吃人的野蛮习惯，也将会成为我们的亲密朋友，其中至少有一个，在我们离开时还会伤心之极呢！

注 释

1. 此处的 carried like a bale 应该直译成"包裹",强调斯蒂文森当时身体瘦弱,就像包裹一样由人携带着走,自己不能动。其实,在斯蒂文森登船时,他的健康状况非常糟糕,船长看到他时,觉得他随时都可能死亡,因此船长还专门买了一口棺材放在帆船上。

2. 梅里特医生(Dr. Merrit)是这艘帆船的主人,他是旧金山的医生,后来成为加州奥克兰市的第13任市长。这句中的 was left early the next year at Honolulu 需要解释一下。要注意,动词的主语是 I,也就是说 I was left at Honolulu,即这艘船把他们撂在檀香山了,主语不是船。也就是说,他包租的这艘帆船的使命在檀香山就结束了。斯蒂文森在整个南太平洋航程中,一共租用了三艘船。这艘卡斯科号(Casco)是帆船,应该是没有能源动力的,这是一艘 schooner yacht,而 yacht 是用来消遣的海上交通工具。第二艘是赤道号(the Equator),也是帆船,不同的是这艘船是从事商用的(trading schooner)。后来的第三艘船也是商用船,即珍妮特·尼科尔号(Janet Nicoll)商贸汽船(trading steamer),但是由燃煤驱动的。

3. the Gilbert group 是指吉尔伯特群岛(Gilbert Islands),由太平洋上的16个环礁岛和珊瑚岛组成,位置大约在巴布亚新几内亚和夏威夷之间。这里的 Samoa 即萨摩亚,现在正式称为萨摩亚独立国,1997年前叫西萨摩亚。萨摩亚是一个主权国家,由两个主要岛屿萨瓦伊岛和乌波卢岛和八个较小的岛屿(马诺诺岛、阿波利马岛、法努瓦塔普岛和那木瓦岛等)组成。他们有独特的萨摩亚语言和萨摩亚文化。斯蒂文森在作品中常提到上述地名。但需要注意，就在萨摩亚旁边，还有一个美属萨摩亚（American Samoa），后者是美国领地。

4. 这句话（gratitude and habit attach me to the islands）理解应该不难，大致意思就是你和那些岛屿更紧密了。换句话说，你经常接触那里的风俗习惯（habit），就慢慢接受了那些习惯；而你接触那里的人多了，他们在接触过程中对你有帮助，你也渐渐生出对这些人的感激之情（gratitude）。但是这个理解过程中引发出的意思，若都要表达出来，那么所用的语言就多了点。所以，译者要学会抓重点，放弃一些并不是非常关键的词意，特别是那些不好表达的词意，比如在这句里，gratitude 这个词就不是很容易糅到句子中去。那么是否不用这个词？因为这句主要就是对当地的风土人情渐渐地接受，甚至喜爱起来了。比如译成"岛上生活日久，我对当地的习俗日渐熟悉，与当地的土著情谊渐生"。

5. 这里说的 prepare these pages 就是后来在 1896 年发表的 *In the South Seas*。本文是该书的第一章。整本书讲述了他在南太平洋的游历生活。他是在第三艘商船珍妮特·尼科尔号上写这些文字的。

6. 这一长句基本含有三个意群：1. 若有机会我要在这里住下去（If more days are granted me, they shall be passed where I have found life most pleasant and man most interesting）；2. 那些黑人小孩已经在为我清理造房子的地基了（the axes of my black boys are already clearing the foundations of my future house）；3. 我得学习如何给远方的读者写作（I must learn to address readers from the uttermost parts of the sea）。在斯蒂文森的作品里，他大量使用

分号，有时分号之间的逻辑关系就不是很清楚，译者就得搞清楚分句间的关系，同时决定是否需要添加连接词语把分号之间的语言连贯起来。比如这里的 1 就是他对那个地方有了好感，这里的 2 是说喜欢那个地方后，决定要留下来了，而这里的 3 就是既然决定留下来，就得学习如何把这里见到的传达给远方的读者，即远在欧洲的读者。他必须学习，因为他需要熟悉了解新的环境，然后看怎么把这些见闻写成欧洲读者能懂的文字（learn to address）。我这个译文中，在第三部分前加了一个"既然决定留下"，就是考虑到连贯的因素，但是前面一个没有添加："如我寿数未尽，我就愿留在这里生活，因为这里生活更多快乐，人物更有情趣；为了建造我未来的房子，几个黑人小男孩已在刀劈斧砍地清理那块宅地了；既然决定留下，我也得学会如何从天涯海角将异域风情传达给我远方的读者。"在原文没有连接词的情况下，译者是否需要把内在的逻辑关系通过有形的词语串起来，这是一个很值得思考的问题。

7. 丁尼生笔下的英雄尤利西斯是永远不会止步的，他对所有新事物都有不尽的好奇心，他想了解不知道的东西："For my purpose holds/To sail beyond the sunset, and the baths/Of all the western stars, until I die."。但是在这里斯蒂文森不想再游历下去了，他要在南太平洋的一个岛上造房子住下来。这就显然和丁尼生笔下的尤利西斯相反了。在这个意义上说，斯蒂文森 reversed the verdict of Lord Tennyson's hero。

8. 这个 fireside travelers 是指那些坐在火炉旁，读着有关各地风光的旅游书，人虽然不到旅游点，但是思绪却在那里了。这个 fireside 在不同的场合也可能生发出其他的隐喻含义，比如我们可以说 "The English are regarded as the nation most appreciatory of

the home, the fireside",在这里 fireside 象征 home and domestic life；而这句里的 fireside 的意思又略不同于下面这句"The politician's fireside manner helped her win votes",这里表示 informal and friendly in manner 的意思。所以，译者见到这个词后还要看语境才能决定如何翻译。不过，不管是在什么语境下，词的核心意思都是很接近的。

9. 这个 some of our own blood and language 是指在那个偏僻的海岛上，已经有不少白人在生活了。

10. 罗布·罗伊（Rob Roy，1671—1734），全名罗伯特·罗伊·麦格雷戈（Robert Roy MacGregor），出生于苏格兰，被誉为苏格兰的罗宾汉。1712 年开始打家劫舍，1722 年被捕，晚年加入天主教，1734 年 12 月 28 日去世。在沃尔特·司各特的小说《罗布·罗伊》中有对其生平的描述。这里的 Barbarossa 是指神圣罗马帝国的皇帝巴巴罗萨（即腓特烈一世）。the Apostles 则是指耶稣基督的门徒。基督教称耶稣的弟子约翰、彼得等十二人为"使徒"，后泛称被耶稣派遣，奉上帝之命传教的人。the Cæsars 是指古代罗马帝国的多位皇帝，注意这是复数，是指好几个皇帝，不是特指一个皇帝。特别要注意，神圣罗马帝国（公元 962 年—1806 年）是指历史上的德意志国家，即所谓的德意志第一帝国，此后是德意志第二帝国（1871 年成立），而 1933 年成立的是德意志第三帝国（也就是希特勒的第三帝国）。神圣罗马帝国和公元前代表古罗马文明的罗马帝国是完全不同的政治实体，不可混淆。

11. 这句"The first love, the first sunrise, the first South Sea island, are memories apart"中的 apart 容易误解成上述每个经历之间互不相同。但是在这个语境中，接下来的是"and touched a virginity

of sense"，apart 所表示的区别不应该是在这几个第一次经历间的区别，而应该是在第一次和非第一次之间的区别，换句话说，这第一次非常特殊、非常震撼，而第二次第三次就没有这种感受了，所以才像 touched a virginity of sense 一样；可以翻译成"非常不同"，但结合语境翻译成"独特铭心"或"独一无二"似乎更准确。另外，这里的 virginity 在性方面的提示已相当微弱，就像汉语中的"处女"一词也已完全脱离了词的字面意思，而彻底隐喻化了。

12. 在航海中，月亮和太阳常被用来作为认定时间或地点的坐标。这里的 was an hour down by four 就是字面意思，也就是说，在凌晨四点的时候，月亮已经落下有一个小时了，即月亮在凌晨3点钟时就已经下去了。

13. 这里的 the scientific and sentimental tourist are at one 严格照语法说有点问题，因为 are 前面的名词是单数的 tourist。但是斯蒂文森应该是在这里省掉了一个 tourist，也就是说，完整的句子应该是 the scientific tourist and the sentimental tourist are at one。所谓 the scientific tourist 就是指那些有科学思维的游客，而 sentimental tourist 就是指游客中那些情感较丰富的人，比如前者在这个时候（the point）见到白昼和夜晚迅速交替的现象就会给出科学的解释（在本书的其他文章里，斯蒂文森经常使用天文学知识），而后者见到这种迅速的交替现象就会发出赞叹。至于 has inspired some tasteful poetry 的主语应该是 it，也就是 the point（it has inspired）。至于说 at one 这个短语应该是 in agreement 或 in harmony 的意思，也就是说，科学思维的游客和文艺思维的游客对那一刻的反应是一致的，但他们反应的方式不同，有科学思维的人会见这奇景生出科学解释，但有文艺思维的人则会用情感做出反应，但是他们又是一致的，他们都会对这个白昼和夜晚迅速交替的现象感到惊叹。本句较贴近原文的译法：游客中有些人擅长科学思维，有些人则以情感见长，但他们都惊叹于白昼和黑夜间迅速的交替。参考译文略有发挥，主要考虑是，上面这个较近原文的译法使原作者分出两类游客的目的不够明确，显得突兀，为什么突然说起两类游客来，和语境缺乏衔接连贯。添上两种人对迅速交替现象这个语境的不同反应就能更通顺了。

14. eight degrees south 在这里是指赤道以南 8 个纬度的地方。

15. 这里的 day two hours a-coming 是指太阳光虽然已经有了，但还要等两个钟头太阳才会升起来。

16. 这里的 signboard 是一个隐喻，也就是说，那些山峰就像是商业广告牌，告诉看到广告的人，岛上有风景请来看一看，就像商店外面的广告牌一样，告诉顾客店里面的商品如何品质优良，请来购买。作者显然是将广告的图像投射到眼前的语境上了。译者面临两个选择，一个就是把 signboard 直接翻译出来（广告牌），另一个就是把这个词的意思解释一下，如"预示前方有一个奇异的世界"。本译文采用直译的方法。句中的 fit 可解释为 suitable，就是说很好地起到了广告牌的作用，这里可翻译成"恰到好处"，但词的分量不重，翻译时忽视也未尝不可，参考译文就译成"恰似一则广告牌"。至于 a world of，虽然可以解释为 a very great deal of 的意思，如 "There's a world of difference between being alone and being lonely"，但本句中这个短语不是修饰词，而是有实质的意思（即世界）。

17. 在 feathered mountains 中的 feathered 意思随语境变化很大。我们常用的 feathered friend 就是鸟的意思，此时 feathered 就是

羽毛的意思（有羽毛的朋友）。但和不同的词搭配，意思可能完全不同，如 feathered feet 的基本意思是有羽毛覆盖的脚，至于是什么脚，那就要看语境。再比如"The Sea was feathered with a strong tide"，这里的 feathered 就是波浪（to be covered with white waves）。再比如"A craggy hill, feathered with birch"，这里 feathered 显然就和树木有关系了。在我们的语境中，较为合理的解释应该是草木（feathered mountains）大致等于 leafy mountains（草木丛生的山岭）。

18. 这个 in little 是一个习惯表达法，意思就是 on a small scale 或 in miniature，也就是说那海岛上的山脉极像阿尔卑斯山，就是小了点。换个比法，就像一辆丰田车的模型和一辆真的丰田车的关系。

19. 这句中的 the forest 就是灌木植被，不要理解成大森林。另外 their ramparts 中的 their 应该是指前面的 mountain forms，ramparts 不能理解成"城堡的围墙"，因为那是一个根本没有现代文明的海岛。所以 ramparts 这里多少有些隐喻的意味，表示屏障（barrier），也就是沿海的山坡、山崖等，因为它们像城堡的墙一样起到阻挡的作用。这里的 clustered 可解释成及物动词（the forest clustered a growth），而这个由植被构成的 a growth 和苏格兰山地上的灌木丛很像。原文的 considerable 本来表示"notably large in size, amount, or extent"的意思，但这里比较大小不是重点，就是很接近的意思（"聚集在山体斜坡上的植被仿佛是苏格兰山地上的灌丛"）。当然 no more considerable than our Scottish heath 直接说就是那些灌木植被并不比苏格兰的灌木丛大到哪里去（no considerable than = no greater than），其实二者本质上都是否定的（Neither heath nor

rampart forest are sizable），但整句强调的就是这个南太平洋岛屿山体斜坡上的植被看上去很像是苏格兰山地上的灌丛。

20. 这个 the cliff yawned 是一个隐喻表达法，其 yawned 的动作就是和打哈欠的动作一样，要把嘴张开（open out），此处张开的是 cliff，而后面的 with a deeper entry 就是更深的空间。一个是变宽，一个是变深，船就这样驶入了宽阔的海湾。但是这个隐喻没有什么意义，翻译的时候根本不用去管它，把意思说出来就可以了。

21. 这个 with what seemed a garden 有些学生翻译成花草环绕的花园，这样应该是完全可以的。但是若真从语言考虑，这样翻译和原文还是有些细微的差别，因为原文是说 seemed a garden，不是那么确定，毕竟从语言上看 what seemed a garden 和 a garden 并不完全对等。但是我们是否在所有的场合都要那么准确呢？根据皮姆提出的 good enough theory，我们其实并不是那么死板的，有时达到 90% 的准确已经符合翻译目的的要求了。所以译者应该判断自己所处的语境。在我们这个语境中，翻译得更准确些既没有什么大困难，也有这个必要（毕竟是大作家的作品），最好还是把 seemed 这个不很确定的意思也表达出来。同样的道理 the ankles of the hills 其实和 the foot of the hills 基本上差不多，但是毕竟要比山脚下略高一点，在译文里反映出来更合适（高高矗立在山脚上方）。

22. 这句中各个动词的时间点前后跳跃，容易搞混。首先我们的时间点先定在作者写文章的时候。他是先积累材料，然后才开始在船上写不久前经历的事件。所以他说 had we but known it 就是倒回去指他第一次到达这座岛时的情景，显然他们当时并不知道这些有花园的地方是西方人留下的痕迹。这个事实他们不知道，因为他们是来找土著村落的，没有想到会是白人的居所。接下来的 might have approached 和 not found 这两个动作发生在看到有花园的居所之后，因为看到有花园是他们首次和当地岛民有接触，其他看到的岛屿都只能发生在那以后，但是从写文章的时间点看，这两个动作都发生在过去，是完成的动作，所以才有了 might have approached 这个包含已完成动作的时态。遍访了上百个岛屿，却仍然没有发现可以和前面那些白人居所相媲美的居所（parallel），这里的 their 就是指是 habitations 的，而 parallel 就是指可以与前面匹敌的地方。换句话说，他想说，他们第一次见到的有花园的地方是非常独特的，后来再也没有见到与之匹敌的居所了。

23. 这句有两个问题可以讨论。首先 longer 这个词显然表示和另外一个相比更长一点。前面他们好不容易找到了那些有花园的白人居所，这回他们总算找到了土著村落，花的时间比前面发现白人居所用的时间更长（longer）；当然似乎也有可能表示比自己原来预期的更长，但前者更合理。但是这样一点细微的语言点（-er 表示的比较级）是否有必要在译文中反映出来呢？本译文选择了忽视（"此后又过了好长一会儿"），因为分量毕竟不大。译者当然可以选择保留这个比较级。这句中另外一个要解释的是 in the universal fashion。首先我们先要确定这个 standing 的主语是 village（注意是特指单数的），这样才能解释后面的 the universal fashion。看到前面白人的有花园的住所了吧？都在山脚上方，但是这个新发现的 native village 却不是高高在上，而是 standing close upon a curve of beach, close under a grove of palms, 而村落靠近海滩在棕榈树下的位置是所有土著村落所选择的位置，在这个意义上说是

in the universal fashion，这里的 universal 是在所有村落范围内的 universal，是小范围内的 universal，也就是说，在南太平洋岛屿上村落的位置是千篇一律的。

24. 这里的 punctually to our use 是针对他们抛锚而言的。前面 the mark of anchorage 应该是指海图上抛锚点的标志，punctually 是说时间凑得很巧，刚刚要想抛锚，水就喷出来了，这样就不用找到底锚在什么地方了，喷出来的水告诉了斯蒂文森抛锚的地点。

25. 这句的大意译文已经说得很清楚了。抛锚是件小事，但斯蒂文森他们把锚这么一抛就开启了大事件，因为他的南太平洋生涯就这么开始了。这里的 Vivien 需要解释一下。薇薇安是英国历史神话中亚瑟王故事里的人物，她施魔法使得魔术师梅林在一个地方待上很多年无法离开。斯蒂文森借用这个故事说明，他也将在南太平洋岛上待上很多年。

26. 这个 handkerchief imperfectly adjusted 没有理解上的问题，但是在表达上倒是颇有讲究。首先字面意思很清楚，拿了块布放在身上，注意不要理解成文明社会的手绢儿，就是一块布。如果就这么直译过来，那就是"一块布很不完美地盖在了身上"。注意 adjust 的意思在 OED 上的解释是"of a person: to arrange or neaten (one's own, or occasionally another's, clothes, item of clothing, appearance, etc.)"，很像汉语中说的"正衣冠"。而 imperfectly 则暗示这个动作的目的没有达到。其实这句就是指这个土人想用一块布遮住自己的生殖器，但是结果没有遮住。翻译时最好也像原文一样，不明说出来，因为这完全得靠语境联想，联想错的可能虽不大，但是留给读者自己去挖掘这层意思，要比译者把这层意思挑明更好。本译文采用了说一半留一半的办法，用"遮羞"一词既有生殖器的提示，但却没有把意思全说出来。

27. 这里的 meanness 是英国用法，在本语境中是小气的意思（OED: niggardly, miserly, stingy; not generous or liberal）。

28. 马克萨斯群岛（Marquesas Islands）位于太平洋中南部，法属波利尼西亚北部岛群。陆地总面积1274平方公里，人口只有8000余人。主要是波利尼西亚人。1842年沦为法国殖民地，现为法属波利尼西亚一部分。

29. 盖乌斯（Gaius Fulvius Plautianus，约150—205）是罗马富尔维乌斯氏族的一员，富尔维乌斯氏族是一个贵族家庭，自罗马共和国以来一直活跃在政治活动中。Papinian 即埃米利乌斯·帕皮尼亚努斯（约140—212），也被称为帕比尼安，是著名的罗马法学家，古罗马最受尊敬的法学家之一。

30. 这句中动词 carried 并不是我们一般用的意思，而是"to take by force, as a prisoner or captive"（OED）的意思，比如"Apprehend and carry him before a justice"。

31. 此处的 a blood-boltered barbarism 是指这些土人在不久以前还有吃人的习惯，所以翻译的时候就不必硬盯着原文的文字翻译。

导 读

海角天涯了此生

南太平洋是斯蒂文森短暂人生的最后一站，但落幕在海角天涯却并非他精心计划的结果。他怎么会在远离故乡的地方落户？这还得倒叙。

心慕远游、不怕流浪的天性当然是个原因，但南太平洋这段因缘却主要还是病。斯蒂文森自爱丁堡大学毕业后，就一直在寻找适合居住的地方，他去过法国、德国、比利时、意大利、瑞士等多个欧洲国家。有的是去旅游，有的却带着"试住"的目的，看看一城、一镇或一村是否能成为他的常居之地。在英国住了一段时间后，大约在1887年前后，已结婚的斯蒂文森又起了离乡之意，主要还是因为英国的天气不适合他的病体。

于是他决定再回纽约。出发前亲朋都来送行，其中有当时文学界的名流，比如亨利·詹姆斯（Henry James）也来为他送行，还给他带来了一箱香槟酒。当然也少不了多年来一直交往的亲朋。文学批评家西德尼·科尔文（Sidney Colvin）那晚为陪斯蒂文森，还住在同一家酒店，次日一直送他到码头。因一件小事而搞得不愉快的老友威廉·亨利和斯蒂文森的堂妹凯瑟琳也在道别之列。大家都感到有些离情别绪，反倒是斯蒂文森精神相当振奋。他因健康原因几年来困在房间里，这下子又可以与大海相处，又可以摆脱陆地上令他"腐烂"（allowed myself to rot so long on land）的日子了。

这次范妮订了Ludgate Hill号游船的票，他们一家四口（斯蒂文森、他母亲、范妮和她儿子）本想能有一段幽静的航程，却没想到过了英吉利海峡后，又有一批吵闹的新"客人"上来，扰乱了原本期待的幽静。这回上来的是一批动物，有猿猴、牛马，一艘船简直像是个动物园。但尽管如此，大海对斯蒂文森的感召仍是巨大的，他已有好多年没这么快活了。一个离别故乡的人，居然能并无眷恋却充满期待，足见他有多么不在乎家乡，又有多么向往无法预测的未来。那是1887年的8月，斯蒂文森当时虽没有下决心不再回英国，但他从此就真没有回过故乡。他的继子劳埃德·奥斯本（Lloyd Osbourne）后来写道："斯蒂文森1887年横渡大西洋到美国的旅程代表了他的生活从一个时代进入了另一个时代。"斯蒂文森从此在现代文学上更为耀眼。

确实不假,他刚到纽约,就风光无限。船一进码头,就有记者在等待他。在英国时,他根本不知道他的《化身博士》(*Dr. Jekyll and Mr. Hyde*)在商场上卖得如何。而且由于盗版,他根本没拿到几个钱。但显然这本书在美国已经火了。他到纽约后,不断有书商向他约稿,而且稿费丰厚,据说有出版商愿意出 8000 英镑买断他的《绑架》(*Kidnapped*)。人生第一次,斯蒂文森在经济上站稳了。

但是他的成名,在大西洋对面却是另一番解读。文学圈中的朋友有的认为斯蒂文森为了金钱出卖灵魂。这其中不无妒忌的成分,比如亨利就这么认为,并觉得斯蒂文森的成功有他的功劳,而斯蒂文森却忽略了他。这些随金钱名利而来的凡尘俗事当然不足为奇。

在纽约期间,他因健康原因到纽约州的萨拉纳克湖住了一段时间,时间是当年的 10 月份,次年 4 月离开。在萨拉纳克湖小住的几个月里,他保养身体,由特鲁多医生精心照顾,同时又开始了写作。海拔 1500 多米的高度,零下 20 多度的气温,家里的其他人都无法忍受,但斯蒂文森却能专心写作,活得很开心。

离开英国前,斯蒂文森和亨利发生了一次争执。原因起自范妮的一篇小说"The Nixie"(后来在 1888 年发表)。亨利认为范妮的小说抄袭了斯蒂文森堂妹凯瑟琳的作品,但斯蒂文森护妻心切,坚称没有抄袭。这场著名的纷争最终彻底破坏了他们两人的友谊,也多少影响了斯蒂文森和凯瑟琳的亲情。因出名而来的烦恼,加上这个争执,再有就是挥之不去的健康问题,使得斯蒂文森又想去寻找新的栖身之地。斯蒂文森的母亲建议乘坐游船再次出游,也许这是让斯蒂文森摆脱烦恼,增进健康的最佳方案。当时考虑的目的地其实有好几个,如印度洋地区和希腊群岛,都在考虑范围内。选中南太平洋其实纯属偶然。已经先回加州的范妮因一次偶然的机会发现豪华游艇卡斯科号（Casco）当时正在旧金山邀人租用，一趟7个月长的南太平洋之旅要价2000英镑，折合成现在的钱大约是10万英镑。斯蒂文森就算是声名鹊起、前途无限，还是觉得这是个天文数目。范妮电告斯蒂文森，说是游船10日内就可出发，让斯蒂文森速回电。此时的斯蒂文森对纽约的生活已经意兴阑珊，他急需一个生活中的转折把自己振奋起来。于是他回电范妮，让他包租卡斯科号游艇，并说10日内定赶到加州。1888年6月27日他在给朋友的信中说，这次旅行多少有点孤注一掷，若身体不能恢复，那2000英镑就无异于打水漂了。

过去他常去海拔很高的寒冷地带疗养。这回却完全相反，他要去温热的海岛生活了。卡斯科号开启了他南太平洋的游荡生涯。他们先在太平洋群岛间巡游，于1889年1月在檀香山结束卡斯科号的航程。后来他们又乘坐赤道号（Equator）从檀香山出发，到萨摩亚群岛，再后来又乘坐珍妮特·尼科尔号（Janet Nicoll）去新西兰等地。斯蒂文森之后在萨摩亚定居下来，最终埋葬在乌波卢（Upolu）岛上。自从他离开旧金山后，斯蒂文森就再也没有回到文明社会。他在那个海角天涯生活、写作、参与当地的政治活动，在短短五六年的时间里让生命大放异彩。

我们这篇短文追记了卡斯科号初到马克萨斯岛（the Marquesas Islands）的过程，是《南太平洋之旅》(*In the South Seas*) 的开篇一章。斯蒂文森初次见到海岛时心情无比激动："第一次经历是永远不可能重复的。第一次恋爱、第一次日出，第一次南太平洋岛的经历，那种记忆独一无二，触动了我处女般的感官。"他记述因语言不通和当地人相处时所产生的恐惧，有一刻他甚至感到，这些当地土人会把他们杀死吃掉。但斯蒂文森不仅记叙这些令人兴奋，使人不快,让人恐惧的时刻,也从更高的跨文化层面解读这种文化的碰撞:"对于一个 12 岁的孩子来说,跨越英吉利海峡是改天换地的变化;对于一个 24 岁的人来说,横跨大西洋也就是换换饮食习惯而已。但是我现在是逃出了罗马帝国阴影的笼罩,可我们都是在帝国的残垣断壁下成长起来的,帝国的法律和文学在生活中陪伴着我们,约束限制着我们。我现在即将遇见的人会是怎样的人?他们的父辈可从来没有读过弗吉尔,没有被恺撒征服过,也没有受过盖乌斯或帕比尼安智慧的掌控啊!"

斯蒂文森在文中表现出对不同文化的理解和包容。他并没有因为来自文明的大英帝国而对未开化的当地人居高临下,相反他认为人与人之间不应被语言文化所隔开:"就算是马克萨斯人,刚刚才不那么彻底地摆脱了吃人的野蛮习惯,也将会成为我们的亲密朋友"。实际情况也确实是那样。几年后斯蒂文森在南太平洋的一个岛上突然去世,为他抬棺的就是那些岛上的"野蛮人"。

在我们这个所谓的文明世界里,有几个文学巨匠是在远离文明社会的地方结束生命的?斯蒂文森如果不是仅有的一个,至少也是屈指可数的一个吧?

参考资料

Claire Harman, *Myself & the Other Fellow*—*A Life of Robert Louis Stevenson*, Harper Perennial, 2005.

Online website: http://robert-louis-stevenson.org/.

译后记

2020年初，一场世界级的瘟疫即将席卷全球，我生活中的暴风雨也在酝酿，这本《斯蒂文森散文翻译与赏析》就是在这样的境遇中完成的。春节过后不久，我突然患病。接下来的治疗艰难困苦，无需赘述。但新冠病毒肆虐，正常生活全被打乱，带病宅家的日子该如何度过？令我完全没有想到的是，在这几个月中，斯蒂文森竟成了我的伴侣。《倔老头和年轻人》和《圣诞说教》这最后两篇就是在这段时间完成的。

我决定在病中完成这本散文集，并不是有截止期的压力，商务印书馆没有给我任何压力。我之所以要在治疗期间继续工作，主要是它给我带来乐趣和意义。虽然我也和因疫情宅家的大多数人一样会看些电视翻些书，但这些娱乐活动都没有像翻译斯蒂文森那样给我带来真正的满足。每一句话我都在掂量权衡中品尝，在一丝不苟中玩味。新冠病毒和疾病诱发了对死亡的担忧，斯蒂文森谈生死的哲言却让担忧消释，工作已不再是负担而是良药。

何以能在这样双重的逆境里保持如此心境？70个岁月的磨炼，加上人文精神的熏陶，都是我精神家园中的养料，都起到了一定作用。一句"因病得闲殊不恶，安心是药更无方"就能抚慰我病中的焦虑和恐惧。但总觉得这些人文的寄托，多少有些小资情调。就算是"险夷原不滞胸中，何异浮云过太空"这样大气的文句，在如此强大的暴风骤雨面前，仍显得过于超然漂浮。真正让我能遇强风不倒的，还是青少年时代常记在心中的一句话：

我虽然行过死荫的幽谷，也不怕遭害，因为你与我同在，你的杖、你的竿，都安慰我。

《圣经·诗篇》23：4

2020 年 4 月 3 日